LIFE & HEALTH INSURANCE

PRINCIPLES AND PRACTICE
3rd Edition

Dearborn
R&R Newkirk
a division of Dearborn Financial Publishing, Inc.

While a great deal of care has been taken to provide accurate and current information, the ideas, suggestions, general principles and conclusions presented in this text are subject to local, state and federal laws and regulations, court cases and any revisions of same. The reader thus is urged to consult legal counsel regarding any points of law—this publication should not be used as a substitute for competent legal advice.

This text is updated periodically to reflect changes in laws and regulations. To verify that you have the most recent update, you may call Dearborn • R&R Newkirk at 1-800-423-4723.

Project Editor: Sheryl A. Lilke
Interior Design: Lucy A. Jenkins

LIFE & HEALTH INSURANCE: PRINCIPLES AND PRACTICE

© 1988, 1991, 1994 by Dearborn Financial Publishing, Inc.

Published by Dearborn • R&R Newkirk,
a division of Dearborn Financial Publishing, Inc.

All rights reserved. The text of this publication, or any part thereof, may not be reproduced in any manner whatsoever without written permission from the publisher.

Printed in the United States of America.

First printing, June 1994

Library of Congress Cataloging-in-Publication Data

Life & health insurance : principles and practice. — 3rd ed.
    p.   cm.
    Edition for 1988 entered under: Lyons, Paula.
    ISBN 0-7931-1044-0

    1. Insurance, Life—United States—Outlines, syllabi, etc.
 2. Insurance, Health—United States, Outlines, syllabi, etc.
 3. Insurance, Life—Law and legislation—United States—Outlines, syllabi, etc. 4. Insurance, Health—Law and legislation—United States—Outlines, syllabi, etc. I. Title: Life and health insurance.
HG8951.L98 1994
368.3′00973—dc20   94-4595
                                                                                    CIP

ACKNOWLEDGMENTS

The publisher would like to recognize the following individuals for their perceptive reviews, comments and suggestions:

Nicholas Boyko, CLU
The Eagle Rock Agency

Stuart M. Egrin
Dearborn Financial Institute

Andrew Homa
The Franklin Life Insurance Co.

Marsha J. Levine, LUTCF, CLU
Dearborn Financial Institute

Daniel Tromblay, FLMI, CLU
Diversified Solutions, Inc.

Introduction to the 3rd Edition

For more than five years, *Life and Health Insurance: Principles and Practice* has been used successfully to prepare candidates for state insurance licensing examinations. The 3rd edition of *Life and Health Insurance: Principles and Practice* has been revised to reflect changes in the insurance industry. For example, this book includes an extensive discussion on senior health care issues—an important subject for prospective agents and brokers in the 1990s.

As always, *Life and Health Insurance: Principles and Practice* will provide you with a solid foundation of basic life and health insurance principles. Not only will it help you prepare for your licensing examinations, but it also offers you the most complete and up-to-date information on insurance topics.

How this Book Is Organized

Notice the organization of this book; Parts I, II and III will enable you to study for the life exam only, the health exam only or both. Part I provides an introduction to the role and purpose of insurance in general and the principles that apply to both life and health insurance. It should be read by all students. Part II covers life insurance specifically, focusing on types of life policies and their provisions, underwriting practices and the many uses for life insurance. Part III is devoted to the subject of health insurance, covering types of policies and their provisions, providers of health insurance and services, underwriting standards, senior health care insurance and uses of health insurance. Each chapter concludes with a "Summary," a list of "Key Concepts" and "Questions for Review." These last three elements will prove to be helpful aids when the time comes to review the subject matter prior to the exam.

This book was carefully designed to serve the student's need for both a thorough understanding of the subject matter and a practical approach to preparing for the licensing exam. It stresses the most important aspects of life and health insurance and avoids unnecessary detail. Information that will enhance the reader's comprehension, but which may not necessarily be covered on the licensing exam, is ruled off and set aside from the rest of the content. The presentation of the subject matter within each chapter—beginning with a list of the main topics on the first page of each chapter—provides the framework for outlining. Subheads within each chapter provide an orientation to the flow and succession of the content. Key terms are italicized. Review questions stress important concepts and are written in a format similar to that which appears on the licensing exam.

(Note: This book does not contain information relative to specific state insurance laws or regulations. For that, the student should refer to his or her classroom instructor or trainer.)

Study Suggestions

- A sound study plan requires a thorough reading of each chapter. Take notes while you read; putting information in writing helps you commit it to memory.

- Once you finish reading each chapter, review the "Key Concepts" that are listed at the end of the chapter. These lists indicate topics and concepts that frequently appear on the licensing exam. Check off each concept once you feel you understand it thoroughly.

- Test your grasp of the subject matter by answering the multiple choice "Questions for Review" at the end of each chapter. Check your answers against the "Answer Key" at the back of the book. If any of your responses are incorrect, a review of the pertinent material is recommended.

- Review the sample life insurance and health insurance policies and applications in the Appendix. They will help you understand the provisions and practical applications of both life and health insurance policies. Refer to them frequently as you read the discussion of life insurance policies in Chapters 5 and 8, and on health insurance policy provisions in Chapter 20.

- Shortly before the test, re-read the "Summary" that appears at the end of each chapter. It provides a review of the major points covered in each chapter.

An Agent's Career

An insurance agent's career is one that demands professionalism in dealing with the public. This is one reason why a license is required before an individual can sell insurance. This book will provide the necessary working knowledge of basic insurance principles. Future training and educational opportunities will be offered by insurance industry organizations and associations and by your own company or agency. An individual who takes full advantage of such opportunities to enhance knowledge and performance will soon develop the professionalism necessary for a successful insurance career.

Table of Contents

PART I: PRINCIPLES OF LIFE AND HEALTH INSURANCE — 1

CHAPTER 1: PURPOSE OF LIFE AND HEALTH INSURANCE — 3

The Role of Insurance • An Industry Overview • The Nature of Insurance • The Concept of Risk • Economic Basis of Life and Health Insurance • Summary • Key Concepts • Questions for Review

CHAPTER 2: THE INSURANCE INDUSTRY — 11

Types of Insurers • How Insurance Is Sold • Regulation of the Insurance Industry • Summary • Key Concepts • Questions for Review

CHAPTER 3: LAW AND THE INSURANCE CONTRACT — 24

General Law of Contracts • Special Features of Insurance Contracts • Agents and Brokers • Other Legal Concepts • Summary • Key Concepts • Questions for Review

PART II: PRINCIPLES OF LIFE INSURANCE — 35

CHAPTER 4: LIFE INSURANCE POLICIES — 37

Categories of Life Insurance • Term Life Insurance • Whole Life Insurance • Endowment Policies • Special Use Policies • Nontraditional Life Policies • Summary • Key Concepts • Questions for Review

CHAPTER 5: LIFE INSURANCE POLICY PROVISIONS, OPTIONS AND RIDERS — 62

Rights of Policy Ownership • Standard Policy Provisions • Policy Exclusions • Nonforfeiture Values • Policy Dividends • Policy Riders • Summary • Key Concepts • Questions for Review

CHAPTER 6: LIFE INSURANCE BENEFICIARIES 81

Who Can Be a Beneficiary? • Types of Beneficiary Designations • Special Situations • Summary • Key Concepts • Questions for Review

CHAPTER 7: LIFE INSURANCE PREMIUMS AND PROCEEDS 90

Life Insurance Premiums • Primary Factors in Premium Calculations • Life Insurance Policy Proceeds • Tax Treatment of Proceeds • Summary • Key Concepts • Questions for Review

CHAPTER 8: LIFE INSURANCE UNDERWRITING AND POLICY ISSUE 107

The Purpose of Underwriting • The Underwriting Process • Field Underwriting Procedures • Policy Issue and Delivery • Summary • Key Concepts • Questions for Review

CHAPTER 9: GROUP LIFE INSURANCE 124

Principles of Group Insurance • Features of Group Insurance • Eligible Groups • Group Life Insurance • Other Forms of Group Life Coverage • Summary • Key Concepts • Questions for Review

CHAPTER 10: ANNUITIES 133

Purpose and Function of Annuities • Annuity Basics • Structure and Design of Annuities • Income Taxation of Annuity Benefits • Tax-Sheltered Annuities • Summary • Key Concepts • Questions for Review

CHAPTER 11: SOCIAL SECURITY 146

Purpose of Social Security • Who Is Covered by Social Security? • How Social Security Benefits Are Determined • Types of OASDI Benefits • Other Government Life Insurance Programs • Summary • Key Concepts • Questions for Review

CHAPTER 12: RETIREMENT PLANS 157

Qualified vs. Nonqualified Plans • Qualified Employer Retirement Plans • Qualified Plans for the Small Employer • Individual Retirement Plans • Summary • Key Concepts • Questions for Review

CHAPTER 13: USES OF LIFE INSURANCE 171

Determining Proper Insurance Amounts • Individual Uses for Life Insurance • Business Uses for Life Insurance • Summary • Key Concepts • Questions for Review

PART III: PRINCIPLES OF HEALTH INSURANCE — 187

CHAPTER 14: INTRODUCTION TO HEALTH INSURANCE — 189

Basic Forms of Health Insurance Coverage • How Health Insurance Is Purchased • Characteristics of Health Insurance • Summary • Key Concepts • Questions for Review

CHAPTER 15: HEALTH INSURANCE PROVIDERS — 195

Commercial Insurance Providers • Service Providers • Government Insurance Programs • Alternative Methods of Providing Health Insurance • Summary • Key Concepts • Questions for Review

CHAPTER 16: MEDICAL EXPENSE INSURANCE — 203

Purpose of Medical Expense Insurance • Basic Medical Expense Plans • Major Medical Expense Plans • Other Types of Medical Expense Coverage • Summary • Key Concepts • Questions for Review

CHAPTER 17: DISABILITY INCOME INSURANCE — 215

Purpose of Disability Income Insurance • Disability Income Benefits • Disability Income Policy Provisions • Disability Income Policy Riders • Summary • Key Concepts • Questions for Review

CHAPTER 18: ACCIDENTAL DEATH AND DISMEMBERMENT INSURANCE — 225

Nature of AD&D Policies • AD&D Benefits • Other Forms of AD&D • Summary • Key Concepts • Questions for Review

CHAPTER 19: SENIOR HEALTH INSURANCE PLANS — 229

Medicare • Medicare Supplement Policies • Medicaid • Long-Term Care • Summary • Key Concepts • Questions for Review

CHAPTER 20: HEALTH INSURANCE POLICY PROVISIONS — 241

NAIC Model Health Insurance Policy Provisions • Common Exclusions or Restrictions • Renewability Provisions • Summary • Key Concepts • Questions for Review

CHAPTER 21: HEALTH INSURANCE UNDERWRITING AND PREMIUMS 253

Risk Factors in Health Insurance • Health Insurance Premium Factors • Tax Treatment of Health Insurance Premiums and Benefits • Cost Containment • Summary • Key Concepts • Questions for Review

CHAPTER 22: GROUP HEALTH INSURANCE 263

Nature of Group Health Insurance • Group Health Insurance Coverages • Tax Treatment of Group Health Plans • Summary • Key Concepts • Questions for Review

CHAPTER 23: USES OF HEALTH INSURANCE 275

A Proper Health Insurance Program • Individual Needs for Health Insurance • Business Needs for Health Insurance • Summary • Key Concepts • Questions for Review

APPENDIX 283

Sample Whole Life Policy • Sample Life Insurance Application • Individual Health Policy • Major Medical Insurance Application • NALU Code of Ethics • NAHU Code of Ethics

GLOSSARY 317

QUESTIONS FOR REVIEW ANSWER KEY 337

I

Principles of
Life and
Health
Insurance

1 Purpose of Life and Health Insurance

The Role of Insurance • Industry Overview • Nature of Insurance • The Concept of Risk • Economic Basis of Insurance

The first step in the study of life and health insurance is to understand the purpose these instruments serve and the important role they play, for individuals and for society. In this chapter, we will take a look at this purpose and role, by explaining the concept of risk and showing how insurance is uniquely designed to replace the uncertainties of risk with guarantees.

The Role of Insurance

Through the centuries, people have pursued financial security for themselves and those who depend on them. We all have a compelling need for security; security is peace of mind and freedom from worry. Insecurity is doubt, fear and apprehension. Most economic actions we take are for the purpose of satisfying some need and thus attaining some degree of security.

Unfortunately, complete financial security has been elusive, in part because of certain universal problems: death, sickness, accidents and disability. These problems can strike at any time and without any warning. The emotional stress these problems bring is amplified by the financial hardships that are almost certain to follow.

Death may strike anyone prematurely. When death takes the life of a family provider, surviving family members often suffer if they are left without an adequate income or the means to provide even basic necessities. On the other hand, some people face the unpleasant prospect of outliving their income—retirement may be forced upon them before they have adequately prepared for a non-income-earning existence. Sickness and disability can also leave economic scars, often more intense than death. An accident or illness can easily result in catastrophic medical bills or the inability to work for months or even years.

Insurance evolved to produce a practical solution to such economic uncertainties and losses. *Life insurance,* which is based on actuarial or mathematical principles, guarantees a specified sum of money upon the death of the person who is insured. *Health insurance* also evolved from scientific principles to provide funds for medical expenses due to sickness or injury and to cover loss of income during a disability. *Annuities* provide a stream of income, by making a series of payments to the annuitant for a specific period of time or for his or her lifetime. *The true significance of insurance is its promise to substitute future economic certainty for uncertainty and to replace the unknown with a sense of security.*

An Industry Overview

The insurance industry plays a pivotal role in our society. Today approximately 70 percent of American adults own some form of life insurance. In the early 1990s, purchases of life insurance exceeded $1.6 trillion and benefits paid by the industry reached a record $91 billion. Most new life insurance purchased in this country is on an individual basis through a life insurance agent or broker.

The insurance industry plays an equally important role in our nation's economy. It is second only to the commercial banking industry as a source of investment funds. Why? Because insurance companies invest the billions of premium dollars they receive annually in a wide range of investments.*

The average amount of life insurance Americans own has been steadily increasing. In 1970, the average insured household had $26,000 in life insurance; and by 1990, the average amount had reached $126,800. Almost two thirds of all new policies sold were to individuals between the ages of 25 and 44, reflecting the shift in population as the postwar "baby boom" generation grows into the buying age for life insurance.

As for health insurance, more than 214 million Americans, or 86 percent of the population, are protected by one or more forms of health care coverage. More than 182 million of these individuals are covered by commercial insurers, Blue Cross and Blue Shield plans, self-funded employer plans or prepayment plans, such as health maintenance organizations (HMOs). In 1990, private health insurers paid out a record $212 billion for medical care or disability claims.

Rising health care costs continue to be one of the most difficult problems that currently face our health care system. For instance, in 1990, Americans spent more than $650 billion for medical and health care services, research and construction of medical facilities.

Truly the insurance industry is a vital one, serving the interests of individuals, businesses and society at large.

The Nature of Insurance

We are exposed to many perils. The purpose of insurance—any insurance—is to provide economic protection against losses that may be incurred due to a

---

*As we will see, one of the basic factors in life and health premiums is the interest earned by the insurance company on the premiums it receives and subsequently invests.

Ill. 1.1 Life Insurance Per Insured Household, 1970–1991

Year	Life Insurance Per Insured Household	Year	Life Insurance Per Insured Household
1970	$25,500	1981	$ 56,300
1971	27,000	1982	63,100
1972	28,300	1983	69,500
1973	30,100	1984	75,700
1974	32,500	1985	82,200
1975	34,900	1986	89,100
1976	37,100	1987	97,200
1977	40,000	1988	104,300
1978	43,200	1989	111,000
1979	48,000	1990	121,400
1980	51,100	1991	126,800

Source: *1992 Life Insurance Fact Book*

chance happening or event, such as death, illness or accident. This protection is provided through an *insurance policy,* which is simply a device for accumulating funds to meet these uncertain losses. The policy is a legally binding contract that sets forth the company's promise and obligations as follows:

> Whereby, for a set amount of money (the *premium*), one party (the *insurer*) agrees to pay the other party (the *insured* or his or her *beneficiary*) a set sum (the *benefit*) upon the occurrence of some event.

In the case of life insurance, for example, the benefit is paid when the insured dies. In the case of health or disability insurance, the benefit is paid if and when the insured incurs certain medical expenses or becomes disabled, as defined by the contract.

Basic Insurance Principles

Insurance is based on two fundamental principles: the *spreading* or *pooling of risks* (also known as "loss sharing") and the *law of large numbers*. To understand these principles, consider the following example.

Risk Pooling

Assume that 1,000 individuals in the same social club agree that if any member of their group dies, all of the members will pitch in to provide the deceased's family with $10,000. This $10,000, it was determined, would provide the family with enough funds to cover the immediate costs associated with death and to provide a cushion, for at least a few months. Because it is not known when any one individual within the group will die, the decision is made to "pre-fund" the benefit by assessing each member $10. Each individual contributes $10, thus creating the $10,000 fund. As you can see, without the agreement to help provide for each other's potential loss, each group member (and his or her family) would have to face the economic cost of death alone. But by sharing the burden and spreading the risk of death over all 1,000 group members, the most any one member pays is $10.

This is, of course, a very simplified example, but it explains the basic concept of loss sharing. By spreading a risk, or by sharing the possibility of a loss, a large group of people can substitute a small certain cost ($10) for a large unknown risk (the economic risk of dying). In other words, the risk is transferred from an individual to a group, all of whom share the losses and have the promise of a future benefit. Insurance companies pool risks among thousands and thousands of insureds, and apply certain mathematical principles to guarantee policyowners that the money will be there to pay a claim when it arises.

Law of Large Numbers

In addition to the spreading of risks, insurance relies on the principle that the larger the number of individual risks (or "exposures") that are combined into a group, the more certainty there is as to the amount of loss incurred in any given period. In other words, given a large enough pool of risks, an insurer can predict with reasonable accuracy the number of claims it will face during any given time. No one can predict when any one person will die or if any one person will become disabled. However, it is possible to predict the approximate *number* of deaths or the *likelihood* of disability that will occur among a certain group during a certain period. This principle, known as the *law of large numbers,* is based on the science of probability and the experience of mortality (death) and morbidity (sickness) statistics. The larger and more homogeneous the group, the more certain the mortality or morbidity predictions.

For example, statistics may show that among a group of 100,000 40-year-old males, 300 will die within one year. While it is not possible to predict who the 300 will be, the number will prove very accurate. On the other hand, with a small group, an accurate prediction is not possible. Among a group of 100 40-year-old males, it is not statistically feasible to predict if any in the group will die within one year. Because insurers cover thousands and thousands of lives, it is possible to predict when and to what extent deaths and disabilities will occur and, consequently, when claims will arise.

All forms of insurance—life, health, accident, property and casualty—rely on risk pooling and the law of large numbers. These principles form the foundation upon which insurance is based and allow for its successful operation.

The Concept of Risk

As we have learned, insurance replaces the uncertainty of risk with guarantees. But what exactly does the word "risk" mean? And how does insurance remove the uncertainty and minimize the adverse effects of risk?

Risk Defined

Risk can be defined as uncertainty regarding loss. Property loss, such as the destruction of a home due to fire, is an example of risk. Negligence or carelessness can give rise to a liability risk if there is potential injury to an individual or damage to property. The inability to work and earn a living due to a disability is another example of risk, as is loss of a family's income due to the death of the breadwinner. The loss that is involved with all of these risks is characterized by a lessening (or disappearance) of value.

Risks can be divided into two classes: *speculative risks* and *pure risks.*

1. ***Speculative risks.*** Speculative risks involve the chance of both loss and gain. Betting at the race track or investing in the stock market are examples of speculative risks. There is a chance for gain and a chance for loss.

2. ***Pure risks.*** Pure risks involve only the chance of loss; there is never a possibility of gain or profit. The risk associated with the chance of injury from an accident is an example of pure risk. There is no opportunity for gain if the event does not occur—only the opportunity for loss if it does occur. *Only pure risks are insurable.*

With life insurance, the risk involved is *when* death will occur. It can be tomorrow, next week, next year or well into the future. Loss can result if death is premature or comes too late. With health insurance, the risk is not when, but *if* illness or disability will strike. Losses associated with health risks include medical costs and loss of income. With annuities, the risk is living too long and outlasting one's income. Annuities cover this risk by paying a guaranteed income to the annuitant for life.

Perils and Hazards

In conjunction with risk are the concepts of "perils" and "hazards." Perils and hazards are factors that cause or give rise to risk.

A *peril* is defined as the immediate specific event causing loss and giving rise to risk. For example, when a building burns, fire is the peril. When a person dies, death is the peril. When an individual is injured in an accident, the accident is the peril. When a person becomes ill from a disease, the disease is the peril.

A *hazard* is any factor that gives rise to a peril. For purposes of life and health insurance, there are three basic types of hazards: *physical, moral* and *morale.*

1. ***Physical hazards.*** Physical hazards are individual characteristics that increase the chance of peril. For example, physical hazards may exist because of a person's physical condition, past medical history or condition at birth. Blindness and deafness are physical hazards.

2. ***Moral hazards.*** Moral hazards are tendencies that people may have that increase risk and the chance of loss. Alcoholism and drug addiction are considered moral hazards.

3. ***Morale hazards.*** Morale hazards are also individual tendencies, but they arise from an attitude or state of mind causing indifference to loss. For example, a person may have a habit of driving recklessly, with no fear of death or injury. This indifference is a morale hazard, increasing the chance of death or injury.

Treatment of Risk

How risks are treated varies greatly, depending on the situation, the degree of potential loss and the individual. Basically speaking, there are four options: *avoid the risk, reduce the risk, retain the risk* or *transfer the risk.* Let's consider each.

Risk Avoidance

One method of dealing with risk is *avoidance*—simply avoiding as many risks as possible. By choosing not to drive or own an automobile, one could avoid the risks associated with driving. By never flying, one could eliminate the risk of being in an airplane crash. By never investing in stock, one could avoid the risk of a market crash. Clearly, risk avoidance is effective, but it is not always practical. Few risks can be handled in this manner.

Risk Reduction

Risk reduction is another means of dealing with risk. Since we cannot avoid risk entirely, we often attempt to lessen the possibility of loss by taking action to reduce the risk. Installing a smoke alarm in a home will not lessen the possibility of fire, but it may reduce the risk of loss from fire.

Risk Retention

Risk retention is another method of coping with risk. This means accepting the risk and confronting it if and when it occurs. One way to handle a retained risk is *self-insurance*. Setting up a fund to offset the costs of a potential loss is regarded as self-insurance.

Risk Transference

The most effective way to handle risk is to *transfer* it so that the loss is borne by another party. Insurance is the most common method of transferring risk, from an individual or group to an insurance company. Though purchasing insurance will not eliminate the risk of death or illness, it relieves the insured individual or group of the losses these risks bring. Insurance satisfies both economic and emotional needs—it replaces the uncertainty surrounding risk with the assurance of guarantees, and it transfers the financial consequences of death, illness or disability to the insurer.

Elements of Insurable Risk

Though insurance may be one of the most effective ways to handle risks, not all risks are insurable. As noted earlier, insurers will insure only pure risks or those that involve only the chance of loss. However, not all pure risks are insurable. Certain characteristics or elements must be evident before a pure risk can be insured:

1. **The loss must be due to chance.** In order to be insurable, a risk must involve the chance of loss that is fortuitous and outside the insured's control.

2. **The loss must be definite and measurable.** An insurable risk must involve a loss that is definite as to cause, time, place and amount.

3. **The loss must be predictable.** An insurable risk must be one whose occurrence can be statistically predicted. This enables insurers to estimate the average frequency and severity of future losses and set appropriate premiums.

4. **The loss cannot be catastrophic.** Insurers typically will not insure risks that will expose them to catastrophic losses. There must be limits that insurers can be reasonably certain their losses will not exceed.

5. ***The loss exposures to be insured must be large.*** An insurer must be able to predict losses based on the law of large numbers. Consequently, there must be a sufficiently large pool to be insured and those in the pool (the "exposures") must be grouped into classes with similar risks. Individuals, for example, are grouped according to age, health, gender, occupation, etc.

6. ***The loss exposures to be insured must be randomly selected.*** In addition, the group to be insured must be randomly selected. Insurers must have a fair proportion of good risks and poor risks. A large proportion of poor risks would financially threaten the insurance company since there would be many claims without sufficient premiums to offset them. Keep in mind that there is a tendency, called *adverse selection,* for less favorable insurance risks (for instance, people in poor health) to seek or continue insurance to a greater extent than other risks.

Economic Basis of Life and Health Insurance

To fully appreciate the purpose and function of insurance, it is important to understand that its roots lie in economics and the concept of the *human life value*.

It has long been recognized that individuals have an economic value that can be measured in part by their future earning potential. This earning potential is the sum of one's net future earnings or, more precisely, the dollar value of an individual's future earning capability. The true significance of this earning potential extends beyond the individual to those who depend on him or her for their financial security. Thus, by definition, human life value is the value today of an individual's future earnings that are devoted to his or her dependents.

In the abstract, human life value is the means by which homes are purchased, college educations provided, monthly bills paid—in short, it is the essence of an individual's or family's economic existence. Yet this value is subject to loss through death, retirement, disability or poor health—any one of these perils affects earning capacity to one degree or another and, consequently, diminishes human life value. It is for this purpose—to conserve and protect human life value—that life and health insurance exist.

Summary

Life and *health insurance* evolved to provide a practical solution to the economic losses associated with death, sickness and accidents. It does so through an *insurance policy,* which is a device to accumulate funds to meet these losses. Insurance is based on "*risk pooling*" and the "*law of large numbers,*" the principles that allow insurers to spread risks among thousands of individuals and to predict losses with reasonable accuracy.

Insurance transfers *risk,* which is one of the most effective ways to deal with risk and its losses. Not all risks are insurable, however. There are certain elements every risk must contain before it can be insured: for example, it must be a pure risk; the loss it entails must be due to chance; the loss must be definite and measurable; the loss must be predictable; the loss cannot be catastrophic and the loss exposure must be part of a large group, randomly selected.

The true worth of insurance lies in its ability to protect *human life values*—the value associated with an individual's earning potential—and to provide financial security.

Key Concepts

In preparing for their licensing examinations, students should be familiar with the following concepts:

risk	methods of handling risk
risk pooling	elements of insurable risk
law of large numbers	adverse selection

Chapter 1
Questions for Review *(Answers are located at the end of the book.)*

1. "It is possible to predict the approximate number of deaths or frequency of disabilities within a certain group during a specific time."

   Which of the following insurance concepts is described in this statement?

   a. The Principle of Large Loss
   b. The Quantum Insurance Principle
   c. The Indemnity Law
   d. The Law of Large Numbers

2. The owner of a camera store is worried that her new employees may help themselves to items from inventory without paying for them. What kind of hazard is described?

   a. Physical hazard
   b. Ethical hazard
   c. Morale hazard
   d. Moral hazard

3. All of the following statements describe risk avoidance, EXCEPT:

   a. Bill won't fly in an airplane.
   b. Wendy keeps her money out of the stock market.
   c. Pat pays his insurance premium.
   d. John never drives a car.

4. Which of the following statements is correct?

   a. Only speculative risks are insurable.
   b. Only pure risks are insurable.
   c. Both pure risks and speculative risks are insurable.
   d. Neither pure risks nor speculative risks are insurable.

5. Which of the following statements does NOT describe an element of an insurable risk?

   a. The loss must not be due to chance.
   b. The loss must be definite and measurable.
   c. The loss cannot be catastrophic.
   d. The loss exposures to be insured must be large.

The Insurance Industry

Types of Insurers • How Insurance Is Sold • Industry Regulation

The insurance industry is one of the most efficiently organized and effectively operated industries in our country today. The purpose of this chapter is to provide a broad overview of the insurance industry, how it operates and how it is regulated. Please note that each state has its own laws and regulations regarding insurance and a review of your specific state laws is recommended.

Types of Insurers

There are many ways to classify organizations that provide insurance. In the broadest of terms, there are two classifications: *private* and *government.* Within these two classes are many categories of insurance providers as well as insurance plans and insurance producers.

Private Insurers

Private insurers offer many lines of insurance. Some sell primarily life insurance and annuities, some sell accident and health insurance and some sell property and casualty insurance. Companies that write more than one line of insurance are known as *multi-line insurers.*

Within this broad category of "private insurers" are specific types of insurance companies. Let's take a look at each.

Stock Insurers

A *stock insurance company* is a private organization, organized and incorporated under state laws for the purpose of making a profit for its stockholders. It is structured the same as any corporation. Stockholders may or may not be policyholders. When declared, stock dividends are paid to stockholders. In a stock company, the directors and officers are responsible to the stockholders.

Mutual Insurers

Mutual insurance companies are also organized and incorporated under state laws but they have no stockholders. Instead, the owners are the policyholders. Anyone purchasing insurance from a mutual insurer is both a customer and an owner. He or she has the right to vote for the board of director members. By issuing participating policies that pay *policy dividends,* mutual insurers allow their policyowners to share in any company earnings. Essentially, policy dividends represent a "refund" of the portion of premiums that remains after the company has set aside the necessary reserves and has made deductions for claims and expenses. Policy dividends can also include a share in the company's investment, mortality and operating profits.

Occasionally, a stock company may be converted into a mutual company through a process called "mutualization." Likewise, some mutuals are "demutualizing" by converting to stock companies. Stock and mutual companies are often referred to as *"commercial insurers."* They both can write life, health and property/casualty insurance.

Reciprocal Insurers

Similar to mutuals, *reciprocal insurers* are organized on the basis of ownership by their policyholders. However, with reciprocals it is the policyholders themselves who insure the risks of the other policyholders. Each policyholder assumes a share of the risk brought to the company by others. Reciprocals are managed by an attorney-in-fact.

Lloyd's of London

Contrary to popular opinion, *Lloyd's of London* is not an insurer, but rather an *association* of individuals and companies that individually underwrite insurance. Lloyd's can be compared to the New York Stock Exchange, which provides the arena and facilities for buying and selling public stock. Lloyd's function is to gather and disseminate underwriting information, help its associates settle claims and disputes and, through its member underwriters, provide coverages that might otherwise be unavailable in certain areas.

Reinsurers

Reinsurers are a specialized branch of the insurance industry because they insure insurers. Reinsurance is an arrangement by which an insurance company transfers a portion of a risk it has assumed to another insurer. It is a means of limiting the loss any one insurer would face should a very large claim become payable. The company transferring the risk is called the *ceding* company; the company assuming the risk is the *reinsurer.*

Assessment Mutual Insurers

Assessment mutual companies are typified by the way in which they charge premiums. A *pure assessment mutual* company operates on the basis of loss sharing by group members. No premium is payable in advance; instead, each member is assessed an individual portion of losses that actually occur. An *advance premium assessment mutual* charges a premium in advance, at the beginning of the policy period. If the original premiums exceed the operating expenses and losses, the surplus is returned to the policyholders as dividends. On the other hand, if total premiums are not enough to meet losses, additional assessments are levied against the members. Normally, the amount of assessment that may be levied is limited, either by state law or simply as a provision in the insurer's bylaws.

Fraternal Benefit Societies

Insurance is also issued by *fraternal benefit societies,* which have existed in the United States for more than a century. Fraternal societies, noted primarily for their social, charitable and benevolent activities, have memberships based on religious, national or ethnic lines. Fraternals first began offering insurance to meet the needs of their poorer members, funding the benefits on a pure assessment basis. Today few fraternals rely on an assessment system, most having adopted the same advanced funding approach other insurers use.

To be characterized as a fraternal benefit society, the organization must be nonprofit, have a lodge system that includes ritualistic work and maintain a representative form of government with elected officers. Fraternal society insurance may only be sold to members of the society. Most fraternals today issue insurance certificates and annuities with many of the same provisions found in policies issued by commercial insurers.

Service Insurers

Service insurers, or service providers, offer health insurance and health care services. The best known service providers are Blue Cross and Blue Shield. These two organizations are nonprofit and differ from other insurers in that they sell medical and hospital care *services*, not insurance. These services are packaged into various "plans" and those who purchase these plans are known as "subscribers." Blue Cross offers prepayment plans to cover hospital expenses such as room and board and miscellaneous expenses. Blue Shield covers surgical expenses and other medical services performed by physicians.

Another type of service provider is the *health maintenance organization* (HMO). HMOs offer a wide range of health care services to member subscribers. For a fixed periodic premium paid in advance of any treatment, these subscribers are entitled to the services of certain physicians and hospitals contracted to work with the HMO. Unlike commercial insurers or the Blues, HMOs are distinct because they provide financing for health care plus the health care itself. HMOs are known for stressing preventive health care and early treatment programs.

A third type of service provider is the *preferred provider organization* (PPO). Under the usual PPO arrangement, a group desiring health care services—an employer or a union, for example—will obtain price discounts or special services from certain select health care providers in exchange for referring its employees or members to them. PPOs can be organized by employers or by the health care providers themselves. The contract between the employer and the health care professional, be it a physician or a hospital, spells out the kind of services to be provided. Insurance companies can also contract with PPOs to offer services to insureds. (Service providers are discussed in detail in Chapter 15.)

Home Service Insurers

Insurance is also sold through a special branch of the industry known as *home service* or *"debit" insurers*. These companies specialize in a particular type of insurance called *industrial insurance,* which is characterized by relatively small face amounts (usually $1,000 to $2,000) with premiums paid weekly. (Industrial insurance will be discussed in Chapter 4.)

Government as Insurer

As noted at the beginning of this chapter, *federal* and *state governments* are also insurers, providing what are commonly called "social insurance programs." Ranging from crop insurance to bank and savings and loan deposit insurance, these programs have far-reaching effects because millions of people come under these plans and help support them through taxes. Social insurance programs include:

- Old-Age, Survivors and Disability Insurance (OASDI), commonly known as Social Security;

- Social Security Hospital Insurance (HI) and Supplemental Medical Insurance (SMI), commonly known as Medicare;

- Servicemembers' Group Life Insurance (SGLI);

- Veterans' Group Life Insurance (VGLI);

- Medicaid; and

- Workers' Compensation.

Each of these programs is discussed in Chapters 11 and 15. For now, understand that the government plays a vital role in providing social insurance programs. These programs pay billions of dollars in benefits every year and affect millions of people.

Self-Insurers

Though *self-insurance* can best be described as a method of dealing with risk, a discussion is appropriate here. A "self-insurer" does not transfer risk to an insurance company; instead it establishes its own reserves to cover potential losses. Self-insurance is often used by large companies for workers' compensation purposes and for funding pension plans. Many times a self-insurer will look to an insurance company to provide insurance above a certain maximum level of loss. The self-insurer will bear the amount of loss below that maximum amount.

How Insurance Is Sold

Insurance is sold by a variety of companies through a variety of methods. Most consumers purchase insurance through licensed *producers* who present insurers' products and services to the public via active sales and marketing methods. Insurance producers may be either *agents* who represent a particular company or *brokers* who are not tied to any particular company and can represent many companies' products. Brokers are agents of the buyers, representing the buyer in a sales transaction. An agent has an agent's contract; a broker must have a broker's contract. There are also *solicitors* and *special agents*. Solicitors act for agents by seeking prospects, receiving applications or collecting premiums, but they usually don't have the authority to bind coverage. Special agents, who do not actually solicit insurance business, work as field representatives, helping a company's central office and the agency force in their territory.

In any case, the agent who solicits an insurance application represents the insurer and not the insured or beneficiary in any dispute between the insured or beneficiary and the insurer. In most states, however, the agent may represent as many insurers as will appoint him or her.

Generally speaking, there are three systems that support the sale of insurance through agents and brokers. These are the *career agency system, the personal producing general agency system* and the *independent agency system*.

Career Agency System

Career agencies are branches of major stock and mutual insurance companies that are contracted to represent the particular insurer in a specific area. In career agencies, insurance agents are recruited, trained and supervised by either a manager-employee of the company or a general agent (GA) who has a vested right in any business written by his or her agents. GAs may operate strictly as managers or they may devote a portion of their time to sales.

Personal Producing General Agency System

The *personal producing general agency* (PPGA) system is similar to the career agency system. However, PPGAs do not recruit, train or supervise career agents. They primarily sell insurance although they may build a small sales force to assist them. PPGAs are generally responsible for maintaining their own offices and administrative staff. Agents hired by a PPGA are considered employees of the PPGA, not the insurance company.

Independent Agency System

The *independent agency system*, a creation of the property/casualty industry, does not tie a sales staff or agency to any one particular insurance company; rather, independent brokers represent any number of insurance companies through contractual agreements. They are compensated on a commission or a fee basis for the business they produce. This system is also known as the "American agency system."

Other Methods of Selling Insurance

While most insurance is sold through agents or brokers under the systems described above, a large volume is also marketed through *direct selling* and *mass marketing methods*.

With the *direct selling* method, the insurer deals directly with consumers—no agent or broker is involved—selling its policies through vending machines, advertisements or salaried sales representatives. Insurers that operate using this method are known as "direct writers" or "direct response insurers."

A large volume of insurance also is sold through *mass marketing* techniques, such as direct mail or newspaper, magazine, radio and television ads. Mass marketing methods provide exposure to large groups of consumers, often using direct selling methods with occasional follow-up by agents.

Regulation of the Insurance Industry

The insurance industry is regulated by a number of authorities, including some inside the industry itself. The primary purpose of this regulation is to promote the public welfare by maintaining the solvency of insurance companies. Other purposes are to provide consumer protection and ensure fair trade practices as well as fair contracts at fair prices. It is very important insurance agents understand and obey the insurance laws and regulations.

History of Regulation

A brief overview of the history of insurance regulation will show a seesaw between the authority of the states and the federal government. Though a balance between these two bodies has been reached and maintained for many years, arguments favoring control by one governing authority over another are still being waged.

1. *1868—Paul v. Virginia.* This case, which was decided by the U.S. Supreme Court, involved one state's attempt to regulate an insurance company domiciled in another state. The Supreme Court sided against the insurance company, ruling that the sale and issuance of insurance is not interstate commerce, thus upholding the right of states to regulate insurance.

2. *1905—The Armstrong Investigation.* Public outcry over abuses by insurers caused the New York state legislature to investigate life insurers in that state. It created the Armstrong Investigation. The result was the New York Insurance Code, which set a precedent and pattern for insurance regulation by other states throughout the country.

3. *1944—United States v. Southeastern Underwriters Association (SEUA).* The decision of *Paul v. Virginia* held for 75 years before the Supreme Court again addressed the issue of state vs. federal regulation of the insurance industry. In the *SEUA* case, the Court ruled that the business of insurance is subject to a series of federal laws—many of which were in conflict with existing state laws—and that insurance *is* a form of interstate commerce to be regulated by the federal government. This decision did not affect the power of states to regulate insurance, but it did nullify state laws that were in conflict with federal legislation. The result of the *SEUA* case was to shift the balance of regulatory control to the federal government.

4. *1945—The McCarran-Ferguson Act.* The turmoil created by the *SEUA* case prompted Congress to enact Public Law 15, the McCarran-Ferguson Act. This law made it clear that continued regulation of insurance by the states was in the public's best interest. However, it also made possible the application of federal anti-trust laws ". . . to the

extent that [the insurance business] is not regulated by state law." This act led each state to revise its insurance laws to conform to the federal law. Today, the insurance industry is considered to be state regulated.

5. *1958—Intervention by the FTC.* In the mid-1950s, the Federal Trade Commission (FTC) sought to control the advertising and sales literature used by the health insurance industry. In 1958, the Supreme Court held that the McCarran-Ferguson Act disallowed such supervision by the FTC, a federal agency. Additional attempts have been made by the FTC to force further federal control but none have been successful.

6. *1959—Intervention by the SEC.* In this instance, the issue was variable annuities: Are they insurance products to be regulated by the states or securities to be regulated federally by the Securities and Exchange Commission? The Supreme Court ruled that federal securities laws applied to insurers that issued variable annuities and thus required these insurers to conform to both SEC and state regulation. The SEC also regulates variable life insurance.

7. *1970—Fair Credit Reporting Act.* In an attempt to protect an individual's right to privacy, the federal government passed the Fair Credit Reporting Act, which requires fair and accurate reporting of information about consumers, including applications for insurance. Insurers must inform applicants about any investigations that are being made. If any consumer report is used to deny coverage or charge higher rates, the insurer must furnish to the applicant the name of the reporting agency conducting the investigation. Any insurance company that fails to comply with this act is liable to the consumer for actual and punitive damages. (For specific provisions of this act, refer to page 112.)

The chronology cited above reflects the roles the courts and the federal government have played in regulating the insurance industry. Let's now take a look at how individual states regulate this business and how the industry practices self-regulation.

State Regulation of the Insurance Industry

In addition to federal laws, the insurance industry is regulated at the state level by *state insurance departments, divisions* or *boards*. These in turn are headed by a *commissioner, director* or *superintendent,* depending on the state. Though specific duties will vary from state to state, the head of a state insurance department is generally responsible for

- issuing rules and regulations;

- licensing and supervising insurance companies formed within the state;

- licensing and supervising insurance agents and brokers;

- controlling the kinds of insurance contracts and policies that may be sold in the state;

- determining the amount of reserves an insurer must maintain; and

- overseeing insurance companies' marketing practices and investigating consumer complaints.

All insurance companies doing business within a given state must be *licensed* or *certified* by that state. Thus, insurance companies are referred to as "licensed" or "nonlicensed." (In some states, the terms used to designate whether or not a company is licensed are "authorized" and "nonauthorized" or "admitted" and "nonadmitted.") In addition, the following terms are frequently used to describe insurance companies and their site of incorporation:

1. ***Domestic insurers.*** A company is a domestic insurer in the state in which it is incorporated.

2. ***Foreign insurers.*** A foreign insurer is one licensed to conduct business in states other than the one in which it is incorporated.

3. ***Alien insurers.*** Alien insurers are companies incorporated in a country other than the United States, the District of Columbia or any territorial possession.

Whether companies are considered domestic, foreign or alien, they must be licensed in each state where they conduct business. State laws restrict insurance companies that are not licensed or not authorized from doing business within their borders.

Insurance Producers

Every state requires that people who sell insurance have a license from the state. However, before an insurance department will issue such a license—whether it's to a prospective agent or broker—the candidate must pass a *producer licensing exam* administered by the department. In some states, the agent's or broker's license is perpetual unless revoked; in other states, it must be renewed at stipulated intervals.

Prohibited Practices

Every state dictates acceptable marketing and sales practices for its licensed producers. While there are different standards as to what are ethical and unethical practices, certain practices have long been punishable in virtually all jurisdictions: *twisting, misrepresentation, misuse of premiums* and, in some states, *replacement* and *rebating*. These are known as "prohibited practices."

1. ***Twisting.*** Twisting is the act of persuading a policyowner to drop and replace an existing policy by misrepresenting the terms or conditions of another. Typically, the motivation for twisting is simply to induce the sale of a policy without any regard to the potential disadvantages to the policyowner. Not only is twisting illegal, it is highly unethical.

2. ***Misrepresentation.*** Misrepresentation is a false or misleading statement or representation by a producer regarding his or her own policies or those of a competitor. Agents are not allowed to misrepresent a policy's

terms or benefits or the nature of the coverage it provides. If policy dividends are payable, they cannot be represented as guaranteed.

3. *Misuse of premiums.* Misuse of premiums includes diverting premium funds for personal use. Some states require that an agent establish a separate premium account if he or she holds the money for any time prior to turning it over to the insurer. Commingling premium funds with personal funds is prohibited.

4. *Replacement.* Replacement of one policy for another means convincing a policyholder to lapse or terminate an existing policy and purchase another. While replacement is not necessarily illegal, it may not always be in the best interests of the policyowner. As we will discuss in Chapter 4, whole life insurance builds cash values over time. To interrupt one cash value insurance plan to begin another could cause serious financial problems for the policyowner.

    Where allowed, the practice of replacement is strictly regulated and requires:

    - full and fair disclosure to the policyowner of all facts regarding both the new coverage and the existing policy; and

    - notice to the existing insurer and the replacing insurer of the intended replacement.

5. *Rebating.* Rebating occurs if the buyer of an insurance policy receives any part of the agent's commission or if the agent gives the buyer anything of significant value in exchange for purchasing a policy. For example, a $25 gift certificate given in exchange for the purchase of a policy would be rebating in some jurisdictions. Most states prohibit the practice of rebating, terming it an "illegal inducement." Where rebating is allowed, strict guidelines have been imposed to control and monitor its practice.

National Association of Insurance Commissioners

All state insurance commissioners or directors are members of the *National Association of Insurance Commissioners* (NAIC). This organization has standing committees that work regularly to examine various aspects of the insurance industry and to recommend appropriate insurance laws and regulations.

Basically, the NAIC has four broad objectives:

1. to encourage uniformity in state insurance laws and regulations;

2. to assist in the administration of those laws and regulations by promoting efficiency;

3. to protect the interests of policyowners and consumers; and

4. to preserve state regulation of the insurance business.

The NAIC has been instrumental in developing guidelines and model legislation that help ensure that the insurance industry maintains a high level of public trust by conducting its business competently and fairly. This group also develops standards for policy provisions, helping ensure that policies are more uniform than disparate across the country. Notable among the NAIC's accomplishments was the creation of the *Advertising Code* and the *Unfair Trade Practices Act,* which have been adopted by virtually every state.

Advertising Code

A principal problem of states in the past was regulating misleading insurance advertising and direct mail solicitations. Many states now subscribe to the *Advertising Code* developed by the NAIC. The Code specifies certain words and phrases that are considered misleading and are not to be used in advertising of any kind. Also required under this code is full disclosure of policy renewal, cancellation and termination provisions. Other rules pertain to the use of testimonials, statistics, special offers, etc.

Unfair Trade Practices Act

Most jurisdictions have also adopted the NAIC's *Unfair Trade Practices Act.* This act, as amended in 1972, gives insurance commissioners the power to investigate insurance companies and producers, to issue cease and desist orders and to impose penalties on violators. The act also gives commissioners the authority to seek a court injunction to restrain insurers from using any methods believed to be unfair or deceptive. Included in the context of "unfair trade practices" are inequitable administration or claims settlement and unfair discrimination.

State Guaranty Associations

All states have established *guaranty funds* or *guaranty associations* to support insurers and to protect consumers if an insurer becomes insolvent. Should an insurer be financially unable to pay its claims, the state guaranty association will step in and cover the consumers' unpaid claims. These state associations are funded by insurance companies through assessments.

The NALU and NAHU

The *National Association of Life Underwriters* (NALU) and the *National Association of Health Underwriters* (NAHU) are organizations of life and health insurance agents that are dedicated to supporting both the life and health insurance industry and to advancing the quality of service provided by insurance professionals. Each organization issues a Code of Ethics that stresses the high professional duty expected of underwriters toward their clients, as well as to their companies, and emphasizes that only by observing the highest ethical balance can conflict between these two obligations be avoided. (See the Appendix for both the NALU and NAHU Code of Ethics.)

Insurance Reports

The financial strength and stability of an insurance company are two vitally important factors to potential insurance buyers and to insurance companies themselves. Guides to insurance companies' financial integrity, as well as their managerial and operational strengths, are published regularly by various *rating services,* such as A.M. Best, Inc., Standard & Poor's, Moody's and Duff and Phelps. For instance, in *Best's Insurance Reports,* companies are rated A++

III. 2.1 Insurance Company Rating Systems

A.M. BEST		S&P		MOODY'S		D&P	
Rating	Explanation	Rating	Explanation	Rating	Explanation	Rating	Explanation
A++, A+	Superior. Very strong ability to meet obligations.	AAA	Superior. Highest safety.	Aaa	Exceptional security.	AAA	Highest claims paying ability; negligible risk.
A, A−	Excellent. Strong ability to meet obligations.	AA	Excellent financial security.	Aa	Excellent security.	AA+, AA, AA−	Very high claims paying ability; moderate risk.
B++, B+	Very good. Strong ability to meet obligations.	A	Good financial security.	A	Good security.	A+, A, A−	High claims paying ability; variable risk over time.
B, B−	Good. Adequate ability to meet obligations.	BBB	Adequate financial security.	Baa	Adequate security.	BBB+, BBB, BBB−	Below average claims paying ability; considerable variability in risk over time.
C++, C+	Fair. Reasonable ability to meet obligations.	BB	Adequate financial security; ability to meet obligations may not be adequate for long-term policies.	Ba	Questionable security. Moderate ability to meet obligations.	BB+, BB, BB−	Uncertain claims paying ability.
C, C−	Marginal. Currently has ability to meet obligations.	B	Currently able to meet obligations, but highly vulnerable to adverse conditions.	B	Poor security.	CCC	Substantial claims-paying ability risk; likely to be placed under state supervision.
D	Below minimum standards	CCC	Questionable ability to meet obligations.	Caa	Very poor security; elements of danger regarding payment of obligations.		
E	Under state supervision.	CC, C	May not be meeting obligations; vulnerable to liquidation.	Ca	Extremely poor security; may be in default.		
F	In liquidation.	D	Under an order of liquidation.	C	Lowest security.		

Source: *Life Association News,* September 1992

(superior), A+ to A− (excellent), B++ to B (good), B− to C+ (adequate), C to D (below average) and E to F (poor). Experts generally recommend that insurance buyers purchase policies from companies that have a rating of A++ to A−, since these ratings indicate financial stability.

Summary

There are many types of insurance providers. *State* and *local governments* provide insurance, as do *private insurers.* Private insurers include *stock companies, mutual companies, reciprocals, assessment mutuals, fraternal societies, home service insurers* and *service providers.* Special categories of insurers include *reinsurers* and *Lloyd's of London.*

Insurance is sold through a variety of methods, the most common being through licensed *producers.* The systems that support the sale of insurance through agents and brokers are the *career agency system*, the *personal producing agency system* and the *independent agency system*.

In order to promote public welfare, the insurance industry is regulated by a number of authorities. These authorities include:

1. the states and their departments of insurance;

2. the NAIC and its model legislation; and

3. the federal government through the application of antitrust laws and the Fair Credit Reporting Act.

All states have enacted various laws and regulations that affect the business of insurance, always with consumer interest in mind. Insurance companies as well as agents and brokers are bound by these laws.

Key Concepts

In preparing for their licensing examination, students should be familiar with the following concepts:

types of insurers
organization and ownership of
    insurers
status of insurers
types of marketing/distribution
    systems
NAIC

federal regulation
Fair Credit Reporting Act
state regulation
McCarran-Ferguson Act
prohibited practices
NALU/NAHU
insurance company rating systems

Chapter 2
Questions for Review *(Answers are located at the end of the book.)*

1. In some states, an insurance salesperson who offers a $100 gourmet dinner in exchange for the purchase of a life insurance policy would be considered to have violated ethical sales practices by

    a. twisting.
    b. replacement.
    c. rebating.
    d. churning.

2. An insurance company organized and headquartered in Indiana can be described as what type of company in Indiana?

    a. Alien
    b. Home-based
    c. Foreign
    d. Domestic

3. Which of the following statements regarding types of insurers are correct?

   I. Stock insurance companies seek a profit for their shareholders.
   II. Mutual insurance companies are "owned" by their policyowners.
   III. Reinsurers work directly with individual policyowners.
   IV. Service providers generally specialize in property insurance.

   a. I and II only
   b. I and III only
   c. II and IV only
   d. III and IV only

4. Regarding landmark cases involving the regulation of insurance, all of the following statements are correct, EXCEPT:

   a. Insurers are required to disclose when an applicant's consumer/credit history is being investigated.
   b. The Securities and Exchange Commission (SEC) may regulate insurers who sell variable annuities and variable life insurance.
   c. The Federal Trade Commission (FTC) directly supervises all insurance marketing activities.
   d. The New York Insurance Code has long been a model for state insurance regulation.

5. All of the following statements regarding the National Association of Insurance Commissioners are correct, EXCEPT:

   a. The NAIC is empowered to prosecute and punish criminal violators in the insurance industry.
   b. The NAIC seeks to preserve state rather than federal regulation of the insurance industry.
   c. The NAIC promotes uniformity in state insurance laws and regulations.
   d. The NAIC seeks to promote efficient administration of insurance laws and regulations.

3 Law and the Insurance Contract

General Contract Law • Features of Insurance Contracts • Agents and Brokers • Other Legal Concepts

Life and health insurance policies are legal contracts. As such they are governed by many of the same legal principles that are applicable to the formation of any contract, plus specific principles that are pertinent to insurance only. In this chapter, we will first review the general principles of contract law, then look at insurance contracts.

General Law of Contracts

A *contract* is an agreement enforceable by law. It is the means by which one or more parties bind themselves to certain promises. With a life insurance contract, the insurer binds itself to pay a certain sum upon the death of the insured. In exchange, the policyowner pays premiums.

In order for a contract to be legally valid and binding, it must contain certain elements—*offer and acceptance; consideration; legal purpose;* and *competent parties*. Let's consider each.

Offer and Acceptance

To be legally enforceable, a contract must be made with a definite, unqualified *offer* by one party and the *acceptance* of its exact terms by the other party. In many cases, the offer of an insurance contract is made by the applicant when he or she submits the application with the initial premium. The insurance company accepts the offer when it issues the policy as applied for. In other cases, the insurance company will not issue the policy as applied for; instead, it may *counteroffer* with the issuance of another policy at different premium rates or with different terms. In these situations, the applicant has the right to accept or reject the counteroffer.

If an applicant does not submit an initial premium with the application, he or she is simply inviting the insurance company to make the contract offer. The insurer can respond by issuing a policy (the offer) that the applicant can accept by paying the premium when the policy is delivered.

Until an offer has been accepted, the person making the offer has the right to rescind it. Thus, for example, if an applicant wishes to withdraw his or her application before the insurer accepts it, the offer is terminated, even if the initial premium has been submitted. The insurer must return the premium.

Consideration

For a contract to be enforceable, the promise or promises it contains must be supported by *consideration*. Consideration can be defined as the value given in exchange for the promises sought. In an insurance contract, consideration is given by the applicant in exchange for the insurer's promise to pay benefits and it consists of the application and the initial premium. This is why the offer and acceptance of an insurance contract are not completed until the insurer receives the application and the first premium.

Legal Purpose

To be legal, a contract must have a *legal purpose*. This means that the object of the contract and the reason the parties enter into the agreement must be legal. A contract in which one party agrees to commit murder for money would be unenforceable in court because the object or purpose of the contract is not legal. In all jurisdictions, insurance is considered to possess a legal purpose.

Competent Parties

To be enforceable, a contract must be entered into by *competent parties*. With a contract of insurance, the parties to the contract are the applicant and the insurer. The insurer is considered competent if it has been licensed or authorized by the state (or states) in which it conducts business. The applicant, unless proven otherwise, is presumed to be competent, with three possible exceptions:

1. minors;

2. the mentally infirm; and

3. those under the influence of alcohol or narcotics.

Each state has its own laws governing the legality of minors and the mentally infirm entering into contracts of insurance. These laws are based on the principle that some parties are not capable of understanding the contract they agree to.

It should be noted that beneficiaries and insureds (if different from the applicant), are *not* parties to an insurance contract. As such, they do not have to have contractual capability.

Other competent parties that may enter into contracts of insurance with an insurance company include business entities, trusts and estates.

Special Features of Insurance Contracts

The elements just discussed must be contained in every contract in order for it to be enforceable by law. In addition to these, insurance contracts have their own distinguishing characteristics that set them apart from other legally binding contracts. Let's review these characteristics.

Aleatory

Insurance contracts are *aleatory* in that there is an element of chance for both of the contracting parties and the dollar values exchanged may not be equal. Simply stated, the benefits provided by an insurance policy may or may not exceed the premiums paid. For example, an individual who has a disability insurance policy will collect benefits *if* he or she becomes disabled; if no disability strikes, no benefits are paid.

The opposite of an aleatory contract is a *commutative* contract, where there is no element of chance and the parties exchange goods of equal value. A real estate transaction is a commutative contract—the seller agrees to sell property for a certain sum and the buyer agrees to buy the property for the same sum.

Adhesion

Insurance contracts are contracts of *adhesion*. This means that the contract has been prepared by one party (the insurer); it is not the result of negotiation between the parties. In effect, the applicant "adheres" to the terms of the contract when he or she accepts it.

Unilateral

Insurance contracts are *unilateral* in that only one party—the insurer—makes any kind of enforceable promise. Insurers promise to pay benefits upon the happening of a certain event, such as death or disability. The applicant makes no such promise—he or she does not even promise to pay premiums, and the insurer cannot require that they be paid. Of course, the insurer has the right and will cancel the contract if premiums are not paid.

A unilateral contract can be contrasted to a *bilateral* contract, in which each contracting party makes enforceable promises.

Conditional

An insurance contract is *conditional* in that the insurer's promise to pay benefits is dependent on (or a condition of) the occurrence of the risk insured against. If the risk does not materialize, no benefits are paid. Furthermore, an insurance contract is also dependent on certain acts by the policyowner, such as the payment of premiums, supplying proof of death or disability, etc.

Valued, Indemnity or Reimbursement

A *valued contract* pays a stated amount in the event of a loss. In this case, an insurer agrees to pay a specified amount of money, regardless of the extent of the loss, to the insured. A life insurance contract that will pay $50,000 to a beneficiary upon the insured's death is a valued contract. On the other hand, an *indemnity contract* pays an amount (or repairs or replaces the loss) to offset all or part of an insured loss. A hospital expense policy that pays the insured a flat $100 a day for each day of hospitalization is an indemnity contract.

With a *reimbursement contract,* the insured is receiving a payment from the insurer for a covered expense or loss. A reimbursement contract compensates the insured for the actual amount of the loss incurred; however, there are usually limitations on the amount of the reimbursement. For example, a medical expense insurance plan might reimburse the insured for up to 80 percent of actual medical expenses incurred.

Utmost Good Faith

Insurance is a contract of *utmost good faith.* Both the policyowner and the insurer must know all material facts and relevant information. There can be no attempt by either party to conceal, disguise or deceive. An insurer issues a policy based primarily on what the applicant reveals in the application; a consumer purchases a policy based largely on what the insurer and its agent claim are its features, benefits and advantages. Associated with this are the concepts of *warranties, representations* and *concealment.*

Warranty

A *warranty* in insurance is a statement made by the applicant that is *guaranteed* to be true. It becomes part of the contract and, if found to be untrue, can be grounds for revoking the contract. Warranties are presumed to be material because they affect the insurer's decision to accept or reject an applicant.

Representation

A *representation* is a statement made by the applicant that he or she *believes* to be true. It is used by the insurer to evaluate whether or not to issue a policy. Unlike warranties, representations are not a part of the contract and need be true only to the extent that they are material and related to the risk. Most states require that life insurance policies contain a provision that all statements made in the application be deemed representations, not warranties. If an insurance company rejects a claim on the basis of a representation, the company bears the burden of proving materiality.

Concealment

The issue of *concealment* is also important to insurance contracts. Concealment is defined as the failure by the applicant to disclose a known material fact when applying for insurance. If the purpose for concealing information is to defraud the insurer (i.e., to obtain a policy that might not otherwise be issued if the information were revealed), the insurer may have grounds for voiding the policy.* Again, the insurer must prove concealment and materiality.

---

*In most instances, life insurers have only a limited period of time to uncover false warranties, misrepresentations or concealment. After that time period passes, usually two years from policy issue, the contract cannot be voided or revoked for these reasons. (See "Incontestable Clause," Chapter 5.) Health insurance contracts follow slightly different rules. (See "Time Limit on Certain Defenses," Chapter 20.)

Ill. 3.1 Elements of an Insurance Contract

Elements Associated With All Legal Contracts
- Offer and Acceptance
- Consideration
- Legal Purpose
- Competent Parties

+

Elements Unique To Insurance Contracts
- Valued, Indemnity or Reimbursement
- Utmost Good Faith
- Insurable Interest
- Aleatory
- Adhesion
- Unilateral
- Conditional

Insurable Interest

Another element of a valid insurance contract is *insurable interest*. This means that the person acquiring the contract (the applicant) must be subject to loss upon the death, illness or disability of the person being insured. A policy obtained by a person not having an insurable interest in the insured is not valid and cannot be enforced.

Thus, insurable interest must exist between the applicant and the individual being insured. When the applicant is the same as the person to be insured, there is no question that insurable interest exists—individuals are presumed to have insurable interest in themselves. Questions tend to arise when the applicant is *not* the person to be insured. As a general rule, the consent of the person to be insured is required before a policy is issued, even if the applicant has an insurable interest. Insurers have a legal responsibility to verify insurable interest and obtain the insured's consent. (See also "Does Insurable Interest Exist?" Chapter 8.)

One important point to note about insurable interest with life and health contracts is that the interest must exist at the *inception* of the policy. It does not have to continue throughout the duration of the policy nor does it have to exist at the time of claim. This is in contrast to property/casualty insurance policies where insurable interest must exist at the time of claim.

Agents and Brokers

Because contracts of insurance are binding and enforceable, certain legal concepts extend to those who bring together the contract parties—the applicant and the insurer. In most cases, bringing the parties together is done by an agent or a broker. In Chapter 2 we discussed some of the more important regulations that states impose on those who solicit and sell insurance; here we will focus on legal aspects of negotiating and placing contracts of insurance.

The Concept of Agency

As noted earlier, an agent is an individual who has been authorized by an insurer to be its representative to the public and to offer for sale its goods and services. Specifically, this role entails:

- describing the company's insurance policies to prospective buyers and explaining the conditions under which the policies may be obtained;

- soliciting applications for insurance;

- in some cases, collecting premiums from policyowners; and

- rendering service to prospects and to those who have purchased policies from the company.

The authority of an agent to undertake these functions is clearly defined in a "contract of agency" (or agency agreement) between the agent and the company. Within the authority granted, the agent is considered identical with the company. The relationship between an agent and the company he or she represents is governed by *agency law*.

Principles of Agency Law

By legal definition, an agent is a person who acts for another person or entity (known as the "*principal*") with regard to contractual arrangements with third parties. Implicit in this definition is the concept of *power*—an authorized agent has the power to bind the principal to contracts (and to the rights and responsibilities of those contracts). With this in mind, we can review the main principles of agency law:

- The acts of the agent (within the scope of his or her authority) are the acts of the principal.

- A contract completed by an agent on behalf of the principal is a contract of the principal.

- Payments made to an agent on behalf of the principal are payments to the principal.

- Knowledge of the agent regarding business of the principal is presumed to be knowledge of the principal.

Agent Authority

Note above the parenthetical explanation "within the scope of his or her authority." *Authority*—that which an agent is authorized to do on behalf of his or her company—is another important concept in agency law. Technically, only those actions for which an agent is actually authorized can bind a principal. In reality, however, an agent's authority can be quite broad. In essence, there are three types of agent authority: *express, implied* and *apparent*. Let's take a look at each.

1. ***Express authority.*** Express authority is the authority a principal intends to—and actually does, in fact—give to its agent. Express authority is granted by means of the agent's contract, which is the principal's appointment of the agent to act on its behalf. For example, an agent has the express authority to solicit applications for insurance on behalf of the company.

2. ***Implied authority.*** Implied authority is authority that is not expressly granted, but which the agent is assumed to have in order to transact the business of the principal. Implied authority is incidental to express authority since not every single detail of an agent's authority can be spelled out. For example, an agent's contract may not specifically state that he or she can print business cards that contain the company's name, but the authority to do so is implied.

3. ***Apparent authority.*** Apparent authority is the appearance of, or the assumption of, authority based on the actions, words or deeds of the principal or because of circumstances the principal created. For example, by providing an individual with a rate book, application forms and sales literature, a company creates the impression that an agency relationship exists between itself and the individual. The company will not later be allowed to deny that such a relationship existed.

The significance of authority—whether express, implied or apparent—is that it ties the company to the acts and deeds of its agent. The law will view the agent and the company as one and the same when the agent acts within the scope of his or her authority.

Agent as a Fiduciary

Another legal concept that governs the activity of an agent is that of *fiduciary*. A fiduciary is a person who holds a position of special trust and confidence. Agents act in a fiduciary capacity when they accept premiums on behalf of the insurer or offer advice that affects people's financial security. Agents have fiduciary responsibilities to both their clients and the insurance companies they represent. Acting as a fiduciary requires that an agent:

- be fit and proper;

- be honest and trustworthy;

- have a good business reputation;

- be qualified to perform insurance functions;

- have knowledge of, and abide by, state laws and regulations; and

- act in good faith.

Brokers vs. Agents

As noted earlier, brokers, unlike agents, legally represent the insureds and do not have the legal authority to bind the insurer. Brokers solicit and accept applications for insurance and then place the coverage with an insurer. The business is not in force and the insurance company is not bound until it accepts the application. Technically speaking, brokers represent themselves in the solicitation of insurance policies; once prospects or clients request coverage, brokers represent their buyers.

In practice, the legal distinction between brokers and agents is not significant. Both brokers and agents are licensed as insurance *producers* and both are subject to insurance laws and regulations.

Professional Liability Insurance

Just as doctors should have malpractice insurance to protect against legal liability arising from their professional services, insurance agents need *errors and omissions* (E&O) professional liability insurance. Under this insurance, the insurer agrees to pay sums that the agent legally is obligated to pay for injuries resulting from professional services that he or she rendered or failed to render. Under E&O policies, the insurer will defend any suits covered by the policy, even if the suits are groundless, false or fraudulent. Any claim arising from injuries, real or alleged, comes within the scope of this coverage.

Other Legal Concepts

In addition to the principles of contract law and agency law, there are other legal concepts that are applicable to insurance and the power of agents. These are *waiver, estoppel,* the *parol evidence rule, void vs. voidable contracts* and *fraud.*

Waiver

A *waiver* is the voluntary giving up of a legal, given right. If an insurer voluntarily waives a legal right it has under a contract, it cannot later deny a claim based on a violation of that right. For example, assume a life insurance contract specifies that premium payments are to be made by the policyowner directly to the company at the home office address. John, one of the company's insureds, has instead made his payments over the years to his agent and the company has accepted this arrangement. In so doing, the company has effectively "waived" the direct payment provision and cannot later deny payment of claim on John's policy on the grounds that premiums were not remitted directly to the company.

Estoppel

The concepts of waiver and *estoppel* are closely related. Estoppel is the legal impediment to one party denying the consequences of its own actions or deeds if such actions or deeds result in another party acting in a specific manner or if certain conclusions are drawn. In other words, using the example above, if the insurer has waived its right to have premiums remitted to it directly, it will be *estopped* from denying John's claim because he gave his premium payments to his agent. Another example of estoppel is if a company severs its agency relationship with an agent, but later accepts an application from this individual—thereby reasserting the agency relationship—the company will be estopped from claiming an agency relationship did not exist at the time it entered into the contract with the insured.

Parol Evidence Rule

Parol evidence is oral or verbal evidence, or that which is given verbally in a court of law. The *parol evidence rule* states that when parties put their agreement in writing, all previous verbal statements come together in that writing, and a written contract cannot be changed or modified by parol (oral) evidence.

Void vs. Voidable Contracts

The terms "void" and "voidable" are often incorrectly used interchangeably. A *void contract* is simply an agreement without legal effect. In essence, it is not a contract at all, for it lacks one of the elements specified by law for a valid contract. A void contract cannot be enforced by either party. For example, a contract having an illegal object is void, and neither party to the contract can enforce it.

A *voidable contract,* on the other hand, is an agreement which, for a reason satisfactory to the court, may be set aside by one of the parties to the contract. It is binding unless the party with the right to reject it wishes to do so. Say that a situation develops under which the insured has failed to comply with a condition of the contract: he or she ceased paying the premium. The contract is then voidable and the insurance company has the right to void the contract and revoke the coverage.

Fraud

In the event of *fraud,* insurance contracts are unique in that they run counter to a basic rule of contract law. Under most contracts, fraud can be a reason to void a contract. With life insurance contracts, an insurer has only a limited period of time (usually two years from date of issue) to challenge the validity of a contract. After that period, the insurer cannot contest the policy or deny benefits based on material misrepresentations, concealment or fraud. (This is explained in more detail in "Incontestable Clause," Chapter 5 and "Time Limit on Certain Defenses," Chapter 20.)

Summary

An insurance policy is a legally binding *contract* between the applicant/owner and the insurance company. As such, it must contain *offer* and *acceptance, consideration, legal purpose* and *competent parties*—elements required of all enforceable contracts. In addition, contracts of insurance are distinguished by other features unique to the purpose and scope of insurance. Among these special features is the element of *insurable interest.*

Agents and brokers—and the companies they conduct business with—operate under the concept of "agency" and the principles of *agency law.* One of the most important aspects of agency law is that it gives the agent the power to act on behalf of the principal-insurer and to bind it to contracts. Agents are empowered by three types of authority: *express, implied* and *apparent.*

Finally, there are additional legal concepts that have direct application to insurance and insurance contracts. These include *waiver, estoppel,* the *parol evidence rule, void* vs. *voidable contracts* and *fraud.*

Key Concepts

In preparing for their licensing examination, students should be familiar with the following concepts:

offer and acceptance	representations
consideration	concealment
legal purpose	waiver
competent parties	estoppel
aleatory	parol evidence rule
adhesion	fraud
unilateral	void vs. voidable contract
conditional	express authority
valued vs. reimbursement	implied authority
insurable interest	apparent authority
warranties	

Chapter 3
Questions for Review *(Answers are located at the end of the book.)*

1. The authority that an insurer gives to its agents by means of the agent's contract is known as

    a. implied authority.
    b. express authority.
    c. fiduciary responsibility.
    d. general authority.

2. "An insurance contract is prepared by one party, the insurer, rather than by negotiation between the two contract parties."

    Which of the following statements explains this feature of insurance contracts?

    a. The insurance contract is an aleatory contract.
    b. The insurance contract is a contract of acceptance.
    c. The insurance contract is a contract of adhesion.
    d. The insurance contract names only the insurer as the competent party.

3. All of the following statements regarding insurable interest are correct, EXCEPT:

    a. A party has an insurable interest in a life insurance contract when he or she is subject to a loss upon the death of the insured.
    b. Only immediate family members can have insurable interest in each others' lives.
    c. Persons are presumed to have an insurable interest in themselves.
    d. Generally, the person to be insured must give his or her consent before a policy is issued, even if the applicant has an insurable interest.

4. Which of the following statements are correct?

   I. Express authority is granted by means of the agent's contract.
   II. Express authority is expressed orally.
   III. Implied authority is not overtly extended in the agent's contract, but does permit many of the agent's operations.
   IV. Apparent authority permits an insurer to disavow the acts of an agent.

   a. I and II only
   b. I and III only
   c. II and III only
   d. II and IV only

5. Which of the following statements regarding utmost good faith in insurance contracts is correct?

   a. The concept of utmost good faith—that there is no attempt to conceal, disguise or deceive—applies only to the insurer.
   b. Although a warranty is a statement, technically it is not part of the contract.
   c. A representation is a statement that the applicant guarantees to be true.
   d. Most states consider statements made in an application for an insurance policy to be representations, not warranties.

II Principles of Life Insurance

Life Insurance Policies

*Categories of Life Insurance • Term • Whole Life
• Endowment • Special Use Policies • Nontraditional Policies*

There are many types of life insurance policies, all of which are designed to serve different needs. This chapter will introduce you to these various policies. We will begin by defining the general categories of life insurance coverage and then move to the basic kinds of life insurance plans today's insurers provide. From there, we will focus on special types of policies as well as some of the newer, nontraditional policies.

Categories of Life Insurance

Life insurers issue three basic kinds of coverage: *ordinary insurance, industrial insurance* and *group insurance.* Many companies offer all; some companies specialize in one or another. These coverages are distinguished by types of customers, amounts of insurance written, underwriting standards and marketing practices.

Ordinary Insurance

Ordinary life insurance includes many types of temporary and permanent insurance protection plans with premiums paid monthly, quarterly, semiannually or annually. Most ordinary insurance is marketed and sold by insurance agents and brokers.

Industrial Insurance

Industrial life insurance is characterized by comparatively small issue amounts, such as $1,000, with premiums collected on a weekly basis by the agent at the policyowner's home. Industrial insurance, or "debit insurance," offers a way for individuals who cannot afford larger policies to obtain some measure of insurance coverage. Quite often it is marketed and purchased as burial insurance. As mentioned in Chapter 2, industrial insurance is sold by "home service" companies.

37

Group Insurance

Group life insurance is written for employer-employee groups, associations, unions and creditors to provide coverage for a number of individuals under one contract. Underwriting is based on the group, not the individuals who are insured. Group insurance, which has grown tremendously over the past few decades, will be discussed in detail in Chapter 9.

Keep in mind that the coverages described above are general categories of insurance. Let's turn our attention now to the various life insurance plans: *term, whole life* (or *permanent*) and *endowment*.

Term Life Insurance

Term life insurance is the simplest type of life insurance plan. It provides insurance protection for a specified period (or term) and pays a benefit only if the insured dies during that period. For example, assume Harry purchases a 5-year $50,000 level term policy on his life, naming his sister, Joan, the beneficiary. If Harry dies at any time within the policy's five-year period, Joan will receive the $50,000 death benefit. If Harry lives beyond that period, nothing is payable. The policy's term has expired. If Harry cancels or lapses the policy during the 5-year term, nothing is payable; there are no cash values in term policies.

Term life is also called "temporary" life insurance since it provides protection for a temporary period of time.

The period for which these policies are issued can be defined in terms of *years* (1-year term, 5-year term or 20-year term, for example) or in terms of *age* (term to age 45, term to age 55, term to age 70, for example). Term policies issued for a specified number of years provide coverage from their issue date until the end of the years so specified. Term policies issued until a certain age provide coverage from their date of issue until the insured reaches the specified age.

Basic Forms of Term Life

There are a number of forms of term life insurance that insurers offer. These forms, distinguished primarily by the amount of benefit payable, are known generally as *level term, decreasing term* and *increasing term*.

Ill. 4.1 Level Term Insurance

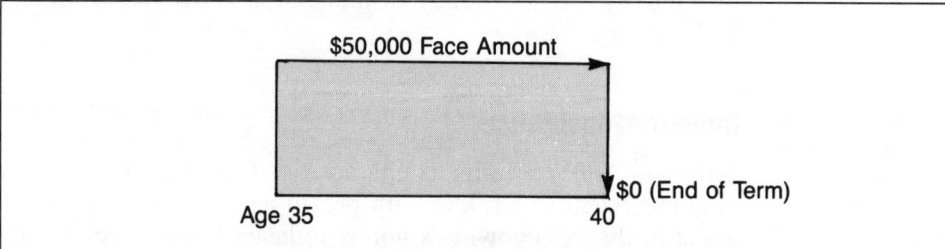

The term insurance plan illustrated is a $50,000 5-year level term policy. The insured has a level $50,000 worth of coverage for a period of five years, after which the policy—and its benefits—expire.

Level Term Insurance

Level term insurance provides a level amount of protection for a specified period, after which the policy expires. A $100,000 10-year level term policy, for example, provides a straight, level $100,000 of coverage for a period of ten years. A $250,000 term to age 65 policy provides a straight $250,000 of coverage until the insured reaches age 65. If the insured under the $100,000 policy dies at any time within those ten years, or if the insured under the $250,000 policy dies prior to age 65, their beneficiaries will receive the policies' face amount benefits. If the insureds live beyond the ten-year period or past age 65, the policies expire and no benefits are payable.

Decreasing Term Insurance

Decreasing term policies are characterized by benefit amounts that decrease gradually over the term of protection. A 20-year $50,000 decreasing term policy, for instance, will pay a death benefit of $50,000 at the beginning of the policy term; that amount gradually declines over the 20-year term and reaches $0 at the end of the term.

Decreasing term insurance is best used when the need for protection declines from year to year. For example, a family breadwinner who has a $100,000 30-year mortgage could purchase decreasing term mortgage insurance that would retire the mortgage balance should he or she die during the 30-year mortgage paying period. Credit life insurance, sold to cover the outstanding balance on a loan, is also based on decreasing term.

Increasing Term Insurance

Increasing term insurance is term insurance that provides a death benefit that increases at periodic intervals over the policy's term. The amount of increase

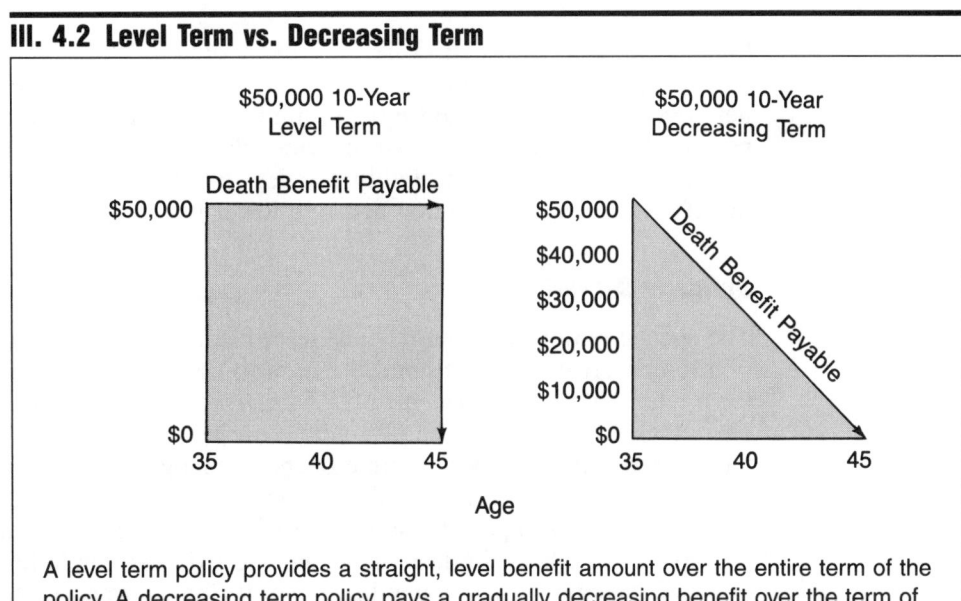

Ill. 4.2 Level Term vs. Decreasing Term

A level term policy provides a straight, level benefit amount over the entire term of the policy. A decreasing term policy pays a gradually decreasing benefit over the term of the policy.

is usually stated as specific amounts or as a percentage of the original amount. Or it may be tied to a cost of living index, such as the Consumer Price Index. Increasing term insurance may be sold as a separate policy; however, it is usually purchased as a *cost of living rider* to a policy. (See "Cost of Living Rider," Chapter 5.)

Features of Term Life

Though term policies are issued for a specified period, defined in terms of years or age, most contain two options that can extend the coverage period, if the policyowner desires. These are the *option to renew* and the *option to convert* the policy.

Option to Renew

The *option to renew* allows the policyowner to renew the term policy before its termination date, *without having to provide evidence of insurability* (i.e., without having to prove good health). For example, a 5-year renewable term policy permits the policyowner to renew the same coverage for another five years at the end of the first five-year term. The premiums for the renewal period will be higher than the initial period, reflecting the insurer's increased risk (see "Term Life Premiums," below). Renewal options with most term policies typically provide for several renewal periods or for renewals until a specified age. The advantage of the renewal option is that it allows the insured to continue insurance protection, even if he or she has become uninsurable.

A common type of renewable term insurance is *annually renewable term* (ART) (also called *yearly renewable term,* or YRT). Essentially, this type of policy represents the most basic form of life insurance. It provides coverage for one year and allows the policyowner to renew his or her coverage each year, without evidence of insurability. Again, most insurers limit the number of times such a policy can be renewed or specify an age limit. However, it is not uncommon for ART policies to be renewable to age 65 or beyond.

Some renewable term plans offer a *re-entry option.* With re-entry term policies, the policyowner is guaranteed, at the end of the term, to be able to renew his or her coverage without evidence of insurability, at a premium rate specified in the policy. However, this policy also provides that, at periodic intervals, the insured may submit evidence of insurability and, if found acceptable by the insurer, qualify for renewed protection at a rate lower than what the contract states.

Option to Convert

The second option common to most term plans is the *option to convert.* The option to convert gives the insured the right to convert or exchange the term policy for a whole life (or permanent) plan *without evidence of insurability.* This exchange involves the issuance of a whole life policy at a premium rate reflecting the insured's age at either the time of the exchange (the *"attained age method"*) or at the time when the original term policy was taken out (the *"original age method"*). For example, if Sharon were 35 years old when she converted her term policy to whole life insurance, and she paid the whole life premium for age 35, she converted at her attained age. But if Sharon were 30 years old when her term policy was issued and, at age 35 she converted to whole life insurance at the age-30 premium rate, she made the conversion on the basis of her original age.

If a conversion is made on the original age basis, the premium for the new policy will naturally be lower. However, the policyowner may have to pay an additional amount to make up the difference between the term and permanent insurance from the date of the term policy's original issue to the time of conversion. By paying the difference, the policyowner enjoys a lower premium and builds cash values more rapidly in the new policy than if conversion had been at the attained age.

The option to convert generally specifies a time limit for converting, such as three or five years before the policy expires.

The option to convert and the option to renew can be (and typically are) combined into a single term policy. For instance, a 10-year convertible renewable policy could provide for renewals until age 65 and be convertible any time prior to age 55.

Term Life Premiums

Though a detailed discussion of premiums appears in Chapter 7, a simplified introduction is appropriate here. To begin, understand that the amount of premium any insurance plan entails reflects, in part, the degree of risk the insurer accepts when it issues a policy. With life insurance, age is a significant risk factor: the higher the age, the more likely is death. Consider two males, one age 25, the other age 55. Both make an application to purchase a 10-year $50,000 term policy. Statistically speaking, it's more likely that the 55-year-old man will die within the ten-year period than the 25-year-old; consequently, it's more likely that the insurance company will pay benefits on the older man's policy than the younger man's. Due to this increased risk (and assuming all other factors are equal), the 55-year-old will pay a higher premium for his protection than will the 25-year-old.

Because the probability of death increases with age, so too do premiums increase gradually with age. At older ages, this increase becomes quite sharp, reflecting the higher death rates at advanced ages. Few people could afford the premium rates that would be charged at higher ages; therefore, insurance companies offer term insurance plans on a *level-premium* basis—premiums are calculated and charged so that they remain level throughout the policy's term period. If the policy is renewed, the premium is adjusted upward, reflecting a higher rate for the increased age and will remain level at that amount for the duration of the renewed term. The phrase used to describe this method of premium payments is *"step-rate."* If you picture a staircase, the first step represents the premium amount payable for the initial term; at the end of the term, the premium "steps up" to a higher amount for the second term and remains at that level until the second term expires, and so on.*
(See Ill. 4.3.)

---

*An exception to the level premium approach is *deposit term insurance*. This type of term policy requires a premium payment in the first year that is much higher than the level premiums required in the second and subsequent years. At the end of the policy's term, the policyowner receives some of the premium back; the amount returned is typically a multiple of the difference between the higher first-year premium and the lower second-year premium. Deposit term insurance accounts for a very small percentage of term insurance sold today.

Ill. 4.3 Level Term Premium vs. Renewable Term Premium

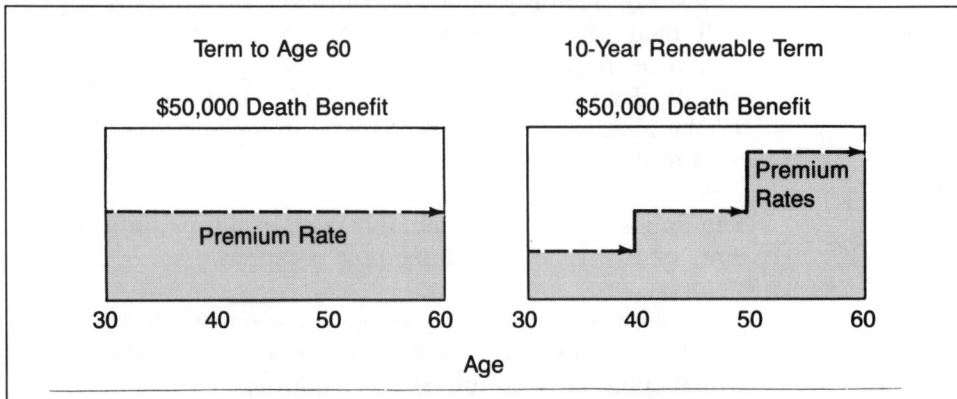

A term to age 60 policy, issued at the insured's age 30, has premiums that are fixed and level over the 30-year term period. A 10-year renewable policy, issued at the insured's age 30, will have premium increases at each of the renewal periods.

Term policies that include the option to renew, the option to convert, or both, will carry a higher premium than those policies that do not have these features.

Whole Life Insurance

A second type of life insurance plan is *whole life insurance* (also known as "permanent" or "cash value" insurance). Whole life insurance is so called because it provides permanent protection for the "whole of life"—from the date of issue to the date of the insured's death, provided premiums are paid. The benefit payable is the face amount of the policy, which remains constant throughout the policy's life. Premiums are set at the time of policy issue and they too remain level for the policy's life.

Features of Whole Life

In addition to its permanence, there are certain other features of whole life insurance that distinguish it from term insurance: *cash values* and *maturity at age 100*. These two features combine to produce "*living benefits*" to the policyowner.

Cash Values

Unlike term insurance, which provides only death protection, whole life insurance combines insurance protection with a savings or accumulation element. This accumulation, commonly referred to as the policy's *cash value*, builds over the life of the policy, increasing each year the policy is kept in force. Though it is an important part of funding the policy, it is often regarded as a "savings element" because it represents the amount of money the policyowner will receive if the policy is ever cancelled. It is often called the *cash surrender value*. This value is a result of the way premiums are calculated and paid on whole life insurance and the policy reserves that build under this premium-paying system.

The amount of a policy's cash value depends on a variety of factors, including

1. the face amount of the policy;

2. the duration and amount of the premium payments; and

3. how long the policy has been in force.

Generally speaking, the larger the face amount of the policy, the larger the cash values; the shorter the premium-payment period, the quicker the cash values grow; and the longer the policy has been in force, the greater the build up in cash values. The reason for these things can be clarified with an understanding of the maturity of a whole life policy.

Maturity at Age 100

Whole life insurance is designed to *mature* at age 100. The significance of age 100 is that, as an actuarial assumption, every insured is presumed to be dead by then. (While some people live beyond age 100, the number who do is not a statistically significant portion of the population.) Consequently, the premium rate for whole life insurance is based on the assumption that the insured will be paying premiums for the whole of life, to age 100. At age 100, the cash value of the policy has accumulated to the point that it equals the face amount of the policy, as it was actuarially designed to do. At that point, the policy has completely matured or endowed. No more premiums are owed; the policy is completely paid up.

For those lucky insureds who live to age 100, the insurance company will issue checks for the full value of their policies. At that point, the policy expires; the contract has been completed. Thus, when whole life is defined as a policy that provides a death benefit "whenever death occurs," some qualification is required. Whole life insurance provides a death benefit if death occurs *before age 100*; if the insured has not died by age 100, the full maturity value of the policy is paid out to the insured as a living benefit and the policy terminates. In either event, age 100 defines the point at which the cash value of the policy equals the face amount (or death benefit amount) of the policy. (See Ill. 4.4.)

Practically speaking, very few people live to age 100. It's far more likely that a whole life policy will be cashed in for its surrender value or that its face amount will be paid out as a death benefit prior to maturity.

Living Benefits

Another unique feature of whole life insurance is the "*living benefits*" it can provide. Through the cash value accumulation build up in the policy, a policyowner has a ready source of funds that may be borrowed at reasonable rates of interest. These funds may be used for a personal or business emergency, to help pay for a child's education or to pay off a mortgage. It is not a requirement of the policy that the loan be repaid. However, if a loan is out-

Ill. 4.4 Whole Life Insurance

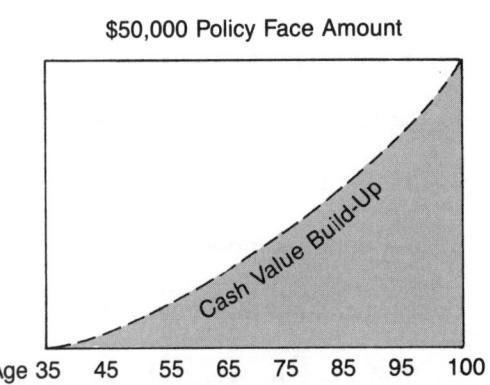

At the insured's age 100, the cash value of a whole life policy equals the face amount and will be paid to the insured as a "living benefit," if he or she is still living.

standing at the time the insured dies, the amount of the loan plus any interest due will be subtracted from the death benefit before it is paid. Indeed, policy loans are more "benefit advances" than loans.

In addition, because life insurance is considered property with a quantifiable cash value, it may be used as collateral or security for loans. Also, the policyowner may draw on the cash value to supplement retirement income.

Cash values belong to the policyowner. The insurance company cannot lay claim to these values. This concept is discussed in more detail in Chapter 5, under "Nonforfeiture Value."

Whole Life Premiums

As noted, whole life is actually designed as if the insured will live to age 100. Accordingly, the amount of premium for a whole life policy is calculated, in part, on the basis of the number of years between the insured's age at issue and age 100. This time span represents the full premium-paying period, with the amount of the premium spread equally over that period. This is known as the *level premium* approach. As is the case with level premium term insurance, this approach allows whole life insurance premiums to remain level rather than increase each year with the insured's age. To put it simply, the premium amount is calculated so that in the early years it is more than necessary to meet anticipated claims and expenses and is less than adequate in the later years when the claims will likely be paid. The balanced result is a level amount payable over the entire period.

Basic Forms of Whole Life

Just because whole life premiums are calculated as if they were payable to age 100, they do not necessarily have to be paid this way. Whole life is flexible and a number of policy types have been developed to accommodate different premium-paying periods. Three notable forms of whole life plans are *straight whole life, limited pay whole life* and *single-premium whole life*.

Straight Whole Life

Straight whole life is whole life insurance, providing permanent level protection, with level premiums, from the time the policy is issued until the insured's death (or age 100).

Limited Pay Whole Life

Limited pay whole life policies have level premiums that are limited to a certain period (less than life). This period can be of any duration. For example, a "20-pay life policy" is one in which premiums are payable for 20 years from the policy's inception, after which no more premiums are owed. A "life paid-up at 65" policy is one in which the premiums are payable to the insured's age 65, after which no more premiums are owed.

The names of the policies denote *how long* the premiums are payable. For example, a 30-year-old applicant who purchases a "life paid-up at 65" policy will pay premiums for 35 years and then have a paid-up policy. If the same applicant buys a "20-pay life" policy, he or she will pay premiums for 20 years and have a paid-up policy at age 50.

Keep in mind that even though the premium payments are limited to a certain period, the insurance protection extends until the insured's death, whenever that may be, or to age 100.

Single-Premium Whole Life

The most extreme form of limited pay policies is a single-premium policy. A *single-premium whole life* policy involves a large one-time-only premium payment at the beginning of the policy period. From that point, the policy is completely paid for.

Premium Periods

The shorter the premium-paying period, the higher the premium. It's the same principle that applies when a person purchases an item on a credit installment plan—the shorter the payment period, the higher each payment will be. As Ill. 4.5 shows, the premium rates at age 35 for a 20-pay life policy are over one and a half times those for a straight life policy, per $1,000 of insurance coverage. This is because the 20-pay life policy has a premium-paying period of 20 years, while the straight life policy assumes a premium-paying period of 65 years, or until age 100.

The length of the premium-paying period also affects the growth of the policy's cash values. The shorter the premium-paying period (and conse-

---

Ill. 4.5 Premium Rates Per $1,000 of Insurance

Issue Age	1-Year Term	Straight Whole Life	Life Paid-Up at 65	20-Pay Life
35	$ 1.35	$16.29	$21.07	$26.00
45	3.10	23.17	32.16	32.16
55	12.68	36.44	70.01	50.12

Ill. 4.6 How Cash Values Grow

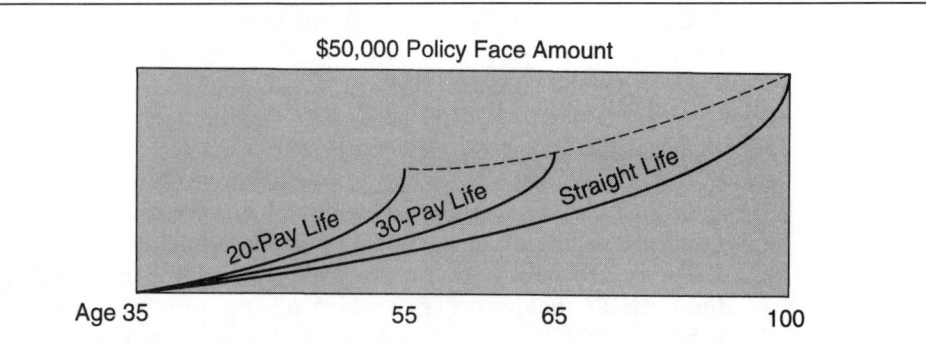

The diagonal lines represent increasing cash values. These are shown as solid lines during the premium-paying period and as a dotted line thereafter.

quently, the higher the premium), the quicker the cash values grow. This is because a greater percentage of each payment is credited to the policy's cash values. By the same token, the longer the premium-paying period, the slower the cash values grow. Illustration 4.6 shows how the cash values grow in a 20-pay, a 30-pay and a straight whole life policy. As this illustration also shows, the cash values build up in the limited pay policies faster during the premium-paying years than during the non-premium-paying years. After the premium-paying period, the cash values continue to grow, but more slowly, until the policy matures and the cash value equals the face amount, again, at age 100.

It should be noted that life insurance policies must now meet certain statutory definitions and tests, which are primarily aimed at limited pay policies and single-premium policies.

Other Forms of Whole Life

There are many other forms of whole life insurance, most of which are characterized by some variation in the way the premium is paid. Let's review these policies next.

Modified Whole Life

Modified whole life policies are distinguished by premiums that are lower than typical whole life premiums during the first few years (usually five) and then higher than typical thereafter. During the initial period, the premium rate is only slightly higher than that of term insurance. Afterwards, the premium is higher than the typical whole life rate at age of issue.

The purpose of modified whole life policies is to make the initial purchase of permanent insurance easier and more attractive, especially for individuals who have limited financial resources, but the promise of an improved financial position in the future. Actuarially, the premiums are equivalent to standard whole life policies.

Graded Premium Whole Life

Similar to modified whole life, *graded premium policies* also redistribute the premiums. Premiums are lower than typical whole life rates during the preliminary period following issue (usually five to ten years) and increase *each year* until leveling off after the preliminary period. Again, the premium rates are actuarially equivalent to standard whole life.

Minimum Deposit Whole Life

Minimum deposit insurance begins building cash values immediately upon payment of the first premium. From that point, the policyowner systematically borrows from the cash value to pay some or all of the premium.

Indeterminate Premium Whole Life

Indeterminate premium whole life policies are those in which the premium rate can be adjusted based on the insurance company's *anticipated future experience*. The maximum premium that the insurer can charge is stated in the contract, though the premium payable at issue is much lower and is fixed at the lower rate for a specified initial period (typically two to three years). After the initial period, and based on the company's expected mortality, expense and investment projections, the premium may be raised, kept the same or lowered.

Enhanced ("Economatic") Whole Life

"*Economatic" whole life policies* are offered by some mutual insurers. Though the precise makeup of these plans differs from company to company, the process in all cases is similar: Use the participating policy's dividends to provide extra death benefits to reduce future premiums.

Indexed Whole Life

The face amount of *indexed whole life* insurance automatically increases as the Consumer Price Index (CPI) increases. Two basic pricing methods are used with this type of policy: (1) The policyowner assumes the risk of future increases and thus must pay additional premium with each face amount increase, or (2) The insurer assumes the risk and thus the policyowner does not pay a higher premium with face amount increases.

Regardless of the method used, the policyowner is not required to furnish evidence of insurability to obtain the face amount increase.

Endowment Policies

Besides term and whole life insurance, life insurers also issue *endowment policies*. An endowment policy is characterized by cash values that grow at a rapid pace so that the policy matures or endows at a specified date (i.e., before age 100). An endowment policy provides benefits in one of two ways:

1. as a death benefit to a beneficiary if the insured dies within the specified policy period (known as the *endowment period*); or

Ill. 4.7 Types of Endowment Policies

Description	Type of Policy
These policies will all endow for the face amount at the end of the premium-paying period. That is, premiums are paid to the time of endowment.	• 10-Year Endowment • 20-Year Endowment • 25-Year Endowment • 30-Year Endowment • Endowment at Age 55 • Endowment at Age 60 • Endowment at Age 65
In these policies, the premium payments are completed before the time of endowment. After premiums stop, the cash value increases from interest earnings and equals the face amount at the time of endowment. Insurance protection extends to the time of endowment.	• 20-Pay Endowment at Age 60 • 20-Pay Endowment at Age 65 • Single Premium Endowment

   2. as a living benefit to the policyowner if the insured is alive at the end of the endowment period, at which time the policy has fully matured.

Because an endowment policy pays a death benefit if the insured dies during a certain period, it can be compared to level term insurance. The new concept presented here is that of *pure endowment*. Pure endowment insurance is a contract that guarantees a specified sum payable *only if the insured is living* at the end of a stated time period—nothing is payable in the case of prior death. These two elements—level term insurance and endowment—together provide the guarantees endowment contracts offer.

Endowment policies can be compared to whole life policies with accelerated maturity dates; age 65 is a common maturity age. At the maturity age, the cash value has grown to match the face amount, just as what occurs at age 100 with a whole life policy.

Illustration 4.7 shows some of the more common endowment policies that insurers offer. The name of each policy establishes how long premiums are payable, how long the insurance lasts and when the policy endows. A 20-year endowment policy, for example, calls for premiums to be paid for 20 years. During this period, the insured will have insurance protection. If he or she lives for 20 years and the policy remains in force, the policy will endow and the company will pay the policyowner the full face amount.

Because they are designed to build cash values quickly, endowment policies are typically purchased to provide a living benefit for a specified future time—for retirement, for example, or to fund a child's college education.

Endowment Premiums

Due to their rapid cash value buildups to provide early policy maturity, endowment policies have comparatively high premiums. Remember that the shorter the policy term, the higher the premiums. Illustration 4.8 shows some typical

Ill. 4.8 Premium Rates Per $1,000 of Endowment Insurance

Issue Age	Endowment at Age 65	20-Year Endowment
20	$15.30	$43.59
30	$22.35	$44.03
40	$36.14	$45.74

premium costs for a 20-year endowment and an endowment at age 65, issued at various ages. Compare these premium costs to those shown for term and whole life policies in Ill. 4.5.

It should be noted that the purchase of endowment policies has been on the decline for several years. This is because they no longer meet the income tax definition of "life insurance" and consequently, no longer qualify for the favorable tax treatment life insurance is given. Essentially, the Tax Code specifies that life insurance products cannot endow before age 95. Because one objective of endowment policies is to provide a living benefit by building an endowment fund for a definite future objective (presumably before the insured reaches age 95), they generally do not qualify as life insurance. Though a number of endowment policies are still in force today, very few new policies are being sold.

Modified Endowment Contracts

In 1988, Congress enacted the Technical and Miscellaneous Revenue Act, commonly referred to as TAMRA. Among other things, this Act revised the tax law definition of a "life insurance contract," primarily to discourage the sale and purchase of life insurance for investment purposes or as a tax shelter. By redefining life insurance, Congress effectively created a new *class* of insurance, known as *modified endowment contracts,* or MECs.

For the producer who sells life insurance and for the consumer who purchases life insurance, the significance of this is the way a life policy, if it is deemed a MEC, will be taxed. Historically, life insurance has been granted very favorable tax treatment. For example:

- Cash value accumulations are not taxed to the policyowner as they build inside a policy.

- Policy withdrawals are not taxed to the policyowner until the amount withdrawn exceeds the total amount the policyowner paid into the contract. Policy loans are not considered distributions and are not taxed to the policyowner unless or until a full policy surrender takes place, and then, only to the extent that the distribution exceeds what was paid into the policy.

However, for those policies that do *not* meet the specific test (described below) and consequently are considered MECs, the tax treatment is different—and it is the policyowners who pay.

If a policy is deemed a MEC and the policyowner receives any amount from it in the form of a loan or withdrawal, that amount will be taxed *first* as ordinary income and second as return of premium, if there is any gain in the contract over premiums paid. There is also a 10 percent penalty tax imposed on these amounts if they are received before the policyowner's age 59½.

How does a life insurance policy become a MEC? More importantly, how does a policy *avoid* being classified as a MEC? It must meet what is known as the "*7-pay test.*" This test states that if the total amount a policyowner pays into a life contract during its first years *exceeds* the sum of the net level premiums that would have been payable to provide paid-up future benefits in seven years, the policy is a MEC. And once a policy is classified as a MEC—which it can be at any time during the first seven years—it will remain so throughout its duration.

Let's look at a very simple example. Suppose a policyowner purchased a $100,000 7-year limited pay whole life policy. The scheduled premiums are $7,500 a year, payable for seven years. At the end of that period, the policy will be completely paid up. The first year, the policyowner pays $7,500. The second year, the policyowner pays $8,000. At that point, the policy would become a MEC because the policyowner paid more into the policy than the net level premiums required to provide paid-up benefits in seven years. From that point on, any withdrawals or loans the policyowner takes from that policy will be taxed as income, to the extent there is gain in the policy.

Now let's assume that this policyowner paid $7,500 in the first year and $7,000 in the second year. In the third year, he or she can make an $8,000 payment and not run afoul of the 7-pay test—he or she is still within the guidelines of the *sum* of the net level premiums payable. However, if that sum total limit is ever exceeded in those first seven years, the policy will become a MEC.

Making sure that policies meet the definition of life insurance and comply with the 7-pay test is the responsibility of insurers and their actuaries. Agents do not have the time or resources; consumers do not have the knowledge or understanding. However, because the potential for misuse—or even abuse—exists with single-pay, limited pay and universal life policies, and because consumers may be lured into purchasing insurance for its tax benefits instead of its protection guarantees, producers must be alert to this law and its implications.

Special Use Policies

In addition to the basic types of life insurance policies—term, whole life and endowment—there are a number of "*special use*" *policies* insurers offer. Many of these are a combination or "packaging" of different policy types, designed to serve a variety of needs.

Family Income Policies

A *family income policy* is a combination of whole life and decreasing term covering a select period of years. If the insured dies within a specified period, this policy provides a certain monthly income from the date of death until the end of the specified period. This period is known as the "income period" and the monthly payments are accomplished by the term insurance. At the end of the specified income period, the face amount of the whole life policy is payable to the beneficiary. If the insured lives beyond the specified income period, only the face amount of the whole life policy is payable.

Family income insurance usually is sold in monthly *income units,* each valued at $10 or more (per $1,000 of the base whole life policy's face amount). In other words, one unit will include enough insurance to provide $10 or more per month to the family during the income period. Five, 10, 15 and 20 years are commonly used term periods.

The specified income term period starts *when the policy is issued.* If the insured dies during the term period, monthly income to the family begins at the time of death and continues to the end of the term period, at which time the face amount of the whole life policy is payable.

Family Maintenance Policies

Family maintenance policies are similar to family income policies, but use level term insurance rather than decreasing term insurance to provide the monthly income payments. At the insured's death, the family maintenance plan provides for payment of monthly income for a selected period of years, beginning *from the date of death.* (The face amount of the whole life insurance is usually paid at the beginning of the fixed period, though some plans pay it at the end of the period.) Note that this differs from the family income plan whereby the fixed income period begins from the date of issue.

A family income policy plan and a family maintenance policy plan are compared in Ill. 4.9.

Ill. 4.9 Family Income vs. Family Maintenance Plans

The family income and family maintenance plans are both designed to provide a period of monthly income following the death of the insured, if death occurs during the specified period. The distinction between the two plans is when the income period begins.

The diagrams above show a family income plan and a family maintenance plan that provide for monthly benefits should the insureds die at any time during the first 20 years. Under the family income plan, the income period begins when the policy is *issued* and ends 20 years later, at the insured's age 50. Thus, if the insured died at age 40, the family income plan would pay monthly benefits for ten years, at which time the base policy's face amount is paid. Under the family maintenance plan, the income period begins when the insured *dies* and continues for the full specified period. Thus, if the insured under the maintenance plan died at age 40, monthly income benefits would be paid for 20 years.

Family Plan Policies

The *family plan policy* is designed to insure all family members under one policy. Coverage is sold in units. A typical plan would insure the family breadwinner for, say, $10,000 or $15,000, the spouse for $3,000 and each child for $1,000. Usually the insurance covering the family head is permanent insurance; that covering the spouse and children is level or decreasing term. These plans generally cover all children presently in the family within certain age limits—for example, older than 14 days and younger than 21. Children who are born later are covered automatically at no extra premium. The children's coverage is usually convertible without evidence of insurability.

Multiple Protection Policies

A *multiple protection policy* pays a benefit of double or triple the face amount if death occurs during a specified period. If death occurs after the period has expired, only the policy face amount is paid. The period may be for a specified number of years—10, 15, or 20, for example—or to a specified age, such as 65. These policies are combinations of permanent insurance and, for the multiple protection period, level term insurance.

Joint Life Policies

A *joint life policy* is one policy that covers two people. Using some type of permanent insurance (as opposed to term), it pays the death benefit when the first insured dies. The survivor then has the option of purchasing a single individual policy without evidence of insurability. The premium for a joint life policy is less than the premium for two separate policies. The ages of the two insureds are "averaged" and a single premium is charged for both lives.

A variation of the joint life policy is the *last survivor policy,* also known as a "second-to-die" policy. This plan also covers two lives, but the benefit is paid upon the death of the second insured.

Juvenile Insurance

Insurance written on the lives of children (ordinarily age one day to age 14 or 15 years) is called *juvenile insurance.* Application for insurance and ownership of the policy rest with an adult such as a parent or guardian. The adult applicant is usually the premium-payor as well, until the child comes of age and is able to take over the payments. A *payor provision* is typically attached to juvenile policies. It provides that, in the event of death or disability of the adult premium-payor, the premiums will be waived until the insured child reaches a specified age (such as 25) or until the maturity date of the contract, whichever comes first. (See "Payor Rider," Chapter 5.)

A special form of juvenile insurance is the *"jumping juvenile"* or *"junior estate builder"* policy. These policies are typically written on children ages 1 to 15 in units of $1,000, which automatically increase to $5,000—or five times the face amount—at age 21. Although the face amount increases automatically, the premium remains the same and no evidence of insurability is required.

It should be noted that some states limit the amount of life insurance that can be written on a child at the early ages. They do so by specifying a maximum that can be in force on a child's life during his or her early years, such as up to age five, age ten or age 15.

Credit Life Insurance

Credit life insurance is designed to cover the life of a debtor and pay the amount due on a loan if the debtor dies before the loan is repaid. The type of insurance used is decreasing term, with the term matched to the length of the loan period (though usually limited to ten years or less) and the decreasing insurance amount matched to the declining loan balance.

Credit life is sometimes issued to individuals as single policies, but most often it is sold to a bank or other lending institution as group insurance that covers all of the institution's borrowers. (See "Group Life Insurance," Chapter 9.)

Nontraditional Life Policies

In the 1980s, insurance companies introduced a number of new policy forms, most of which are more flexible in design and provisions than their traditional counterparts. The most notable of these are *interest-sensitive whole life, adjustable life, universal life, variable life* and *variable universal life*.

Interest-Sensitive Whole Life

Also known as *current-assumption whole life,* this policy is characterized by premiums that vary to reflect the insurer's changing assumptions with regard to its death, investment and expense factors. In this respect, it is similar to indeterminate premium whole life. However, interest-sensitive products also provide that the cash values may be greater than the guaranteed levels, if the company's underlying death, investment and expense assumptions are more favorable than expected. In this way, policyowners have two options: lower premiums or higher cash values.

If underlying assumptions turn out to be less favorable than anticipated, which otherwise would call for a higher premium than that at policy issue, the policyowner may either pay the higher premium or choose to reduce the policy's face amount and continue to pay the same premium.

Adjustable Life

Adjustable life policies are distinguished by their flexibility that comes from combining term and permanent insurance into a single plan. The policyowner determines how much face amount protection he or she needs and how much premium he or she wants to pay. The insurer then selects the appropriate plan to meet those needs. Or the policyowner may specify a desired plan and face amount, and the insurer will calculate the appropriate premium. As financial needs and objectives change, the policyowner can make adjustments to his or her coverage, such as

- increasing or decreasing the premium and/or the premium-paying period or

- increasing or decreasing the face amount and/or the period of protection.

Consequently, depending on the desired changes, the policy can be converted from term to whole life or from whole life to term; from a high premium contract to a lower premium or limited pay contract.

Most adjustable life policies contain limits that restrict the changes in face amounts or premium payments to specified minimums and maximums. Typically, increases in the face amounts on these policies require evidence of insurability. Moreover, due to its design and flexibility, adjustable life is usually more expensive than conventional term or whole life policies.

Universal Life

Universal life is a variation of whole life insurance, characterized by considerable flexibility. Unlike whole life, with its fixed premiums, fixed face amounts and fixed cash value accumulations, universal life allows its policyowners to determine the amount and frequency of premium payments and to adjust the policy face amount up or down to reflect changes in needs. Consequently, no new policy need be issued when changes are desired.

Universal life provides this flexibility by "unbundling" or separating the basic components of a life insurance policy—the insurance (protection) element; the savings (accumulation) element and the expense (loading) element. As with any other life policy, the policyowner pays a premium. Each month, a mortality charge is deducted from the policy's cash value account for the cost of the insurance protection. This mortality charge may also include an expense, or loading, charge.

Like term insurance premiums, the universal life mortality charge steadily increases with age. Actually, universal life is technically defined as term insurance with a policy value fund. Even though the policyowner may pay a level premium, an increasing share of that premium goes to pay the mortality charge as the insured ages.

As premiums are paid and as cash values accumulate, interest is credited to the policy's cash value. This interest may be either the *current interest rate,* declared by the company (and dependent on current market conditions) or the *guaranteed minimum rate,* specified in the contract. As long as the cash value account is sufficient to pay the monthly mortality and expense costs, the policy will continue in force, whether or not the policyowner pays the premium. Of course, premium payments must be large enough and frequent enough to generate sufficient cash values. If the cash value account is not large enough to support the monthly deductions, the policy terminates.

At stated intervals (and usually upon providing evidence of insurability), the policyowner can increase the face amount of the policy. Or a decrease in face amount can be requested. A corresponding increase (or decrease) in premium payment is not required, again as long as the cash values can cover the mortality and expense costs. By the same token, the policyowner can elect to pay more into the policy, thus adding to the cash value account, subject to certain guidelines that control the relationship between the cash values and the policy's face amount.

Another factor that distinguishes universal life from whole life is the fact that *partial withdrawals* can be made from the policy's cash value account. (Whole life insurance allows a policyowner to tap cash values only through a policy loan or a complete cash surrender of the policy's cash values, in which case the policy terminates.) Also, the policyowner may surrender the universal life policy for its entire cash value at any time. However, the company probably will assess a surrender charge unless the policy has been in force for a certain number of years.

UL Death Benefit Options

Universal life insurance offers two death benefit options. Under *Option One,* the policyowner may designate a specified amount of insurance. The death benefit equals the cash values plus the remaining pure insurance (decreasing term plus increasing cash values). If the cash values approach the face amount before the policy matures, an additional amount of insurance called the "corridor," is maintained in addition to the cash values. (Illustration 4.10 illustrates Option One.)

Under *Option Two,* the death benefit equals the face amount (pure insurance) plus the cash values (level term plus increasing cash values). To comply with the Tax Code's definition of "life insurance," the cash values cannot be disproportionately larger than the term insurance portion. (Illustration 4.10 illustrates Option Two.)

Variable Life Insurance

Variable life insurance is permanent life insurance with many of the characteristics of traditional whole life insurance. The main difference is in the *reserves.* In traditional whole life insurance, the reserves are invested by the insurance company in typically conservative investments, such as bonds, real estate, mortgage loans, etc. Because of the high safety factor involved with such investments, the company can guarantee the policy's cash value and the nonforfeiture options that are based on the cash values. Traditional life insurance reserves are held in the company's *general accounts.*

With variable life insurance, the policyowner chooses how the cash values will be invested (for example, in common stocks, bonds, money market accounts or

Ill. 4.10 Universal Life Death Benefit Options

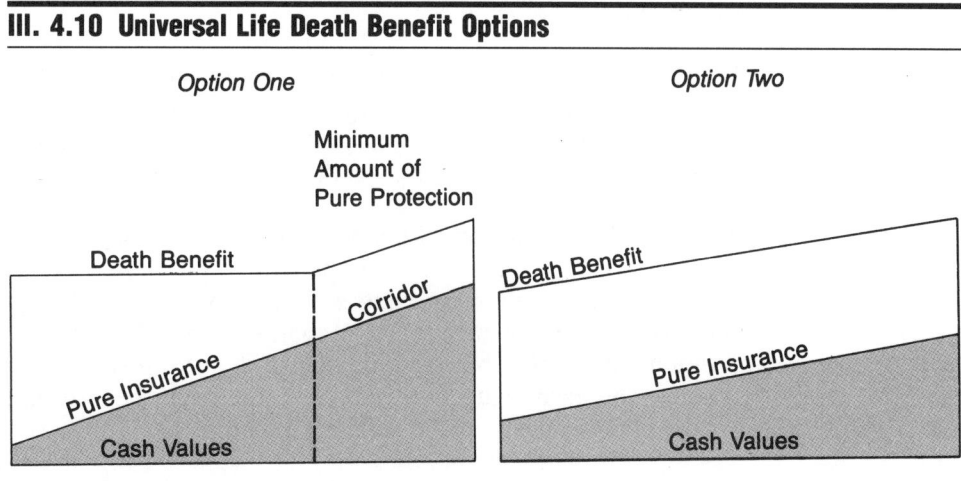

other equity-type securities). Consequently, the cash values—which will fluctuate in relation to the investment performance of the equities selected by the policyowner—are not guaranteed. Variable life insurance reserves are held in special *separate accounts* of the insurer that can be invested in riskier (though potentially higher yielding) investments than are general account reserves.

As with traditional permanent life insurance, the cash values of a variable life policy become part of the policy's death benefit. Depending upon investment results, of course, the variable life death benefit will increase or decrease; however, a minimum death benefit equal to the face amount of the policy is guaranteed.

Although variable life insurance is a life insurance product, the federal government has declared that it is a "security," because there is investment risk to the policyowner. Thus, it is regulated by both state insurance departments and the Securities and Exchange Commission (SEC). In order to sell variable life insurance, an individual must hold a life insurance producer's license and a National Association of Securities Dealers (NASD) registered representative's license. Also, state insurance departments may require a special variable life insurance license or special addendum to the regular life insurance license.

Since variable life insurance is a security, there must be full and fair disclosure provided to the prospective policyowner under the Securities Act of 1933. Therefore, a variable life insurance sales interview cannot be conducted unless it is preceded or accompanied by a *prospectus,* prepared and furnished by the insurance company and reviewed by the SEC. A prospectus contains information about the nature and purpose of the insurance plan, the separate account and the risk involved. It is a major source of information for the prospect. Also, all other materials used in selling and promoting variable life insurance (such as direct mail letters, brochures, advertising, etc.) must have prior approval of the SEC.

Variable Universal Life

Variable universal life (VUL) is a flexible premium variable life product. Sometimes referred to as universal variable life, VUL combines certain characteristics of variable life policies—such as a death benefit and cash value that vary according to performance of a separate account—and characteristics of universal life—principally, premium payments and death benefits that may be adjusted by the policyowner.

Under a VUL policy, the policyowner can purchase a single insurance contract and thereafter adjust premium payments and the death benefit according to his or her changing needs. The policyowner also can steer investments underlying one or more separate accounts funding the VUL product.

The policyholder, subject to underwriting limitations, may adjust benefits by changing the face amount and the pattern of premium payments. He or she also elects the premium-payment schedule. As long as the cash value of the policy is sufficient to meet current charges, the policyholder is free to adjust premium payments. That is, policy lapse is not linked to cash value of the contract. The cash value and, indirectly, the death benefit, is linked to the investment performance of the separate account.

Like variable life, VUL policies are subject to state and federal regulation.

Summary

Today's life insurers offer a vast array of life insurance plans, which are designed to serve various functions and meet different needs. *Term insurance,* the simplest type of plan, provides pure protection only, for a specified temporary period or term. At the end of the term, the protection expires. If a policyowner desires, he or she can extend the coverage through two options: the *option to renew* the term policy for another term and/or the *option to convert* the term policy to a whole life, or permanent, plan.

Whole life insurance provides protection for the whole of life and pays a death benefit if the insured dies at any time prior to age 100. Whole life insurance is characterized by *cash values* that accumulate over time, eventually reaching a level equal to the policy's face amount at the insured's age 100. At that point, the policy has *matured* or *endowed.* Premiums for whole life insurance are level throughout the policy's period and are calculated as though the insured were to pay them until age 100. A large percentage of whole life policies, known as *straight life* policies, are purchased on this basis. However, if a policyowner desires, the premium-paying period can be limited to a certain age or for a specified number of years; these policies are known as *limited pay life* policies. The most extreme example of limited pay life is *single-premium whole life.* Other types of whole life plans—such as modified whole life, graded premium whole life, minimum deposit whole life and indeterminate premium whole life—also provide permanent protection, but vary the way in which premiums are paid.

Endowment insurance combines the principles of term insurance and pure endowment. If the insured dies at any time within the endowment period, the policy pays a death benefit. If the insured lives to the end of the endowment period, the policy matures and is paid off as a completely endowed policy.

Various *special use plans,* which combine features of term and whole life into single policies, are available to fit different needs. These include *"family" policies, multiple protection policies, joint life policies, juvenile insurance* and *credit life insurance.*

Finally, there are a number of newer, nontraditional life policies that have been introduced over the past decade or so. These policies are characterized in part by increased flexibility and current market returns. Most notable of these new policy forms are *interest-sensitive whole life, adjustable life, universal life, variable life* and *variable universal life.*

Key Concepts

In preparing for their licensing examination, students should be familiar with the following concepts:

ordinary insurance	increasing term
industrial insurance	whole life
group insurance	graded premium whole life
level term	modified whole life
decreasing term	single-premium whole life

enhanced whole life
indexed whole life
limited pay whole life
endowment policies
modified endowment contracts
family income policy
family maintenance policy
joint and last survivor policy
minimum deposit

credit life
juvenile insurance
multiple protection plan
adjustable life
interest-sensitive whole life
universal life
variable life
variable universal life

Chapter 4
Questions for Review *(Answers are located at the end of the book.)*

1. Life insurance that is characterized by low issue amounts and weekly at-home premium collection is known as

   a. mini-life.
   b. direct life.
   c. ordinary life.
   d. industrial life.

2. "A life insurance policy provides a straight $100,000 of coverage for a period of five years."

   Which of the following terms correctly apply to this policy?

   I. Permanent
   II. Term
   III. Level
   IV. Variable

   a. I and III only
   b. I and IV only
   c. II and III only
   d. II and IV only

3. All of the following statements are correct, EXCEPT:

   a. A three-year renewable policy allows a term policyowner to renew the same coverage for another three years.
   b. A three-year renewable policy allows a term policyowner to increase coverage for the next three years.
   c. An option to convert provides that a term life insurance policy can be exchanged for a permanent one.
   d. Both the option to renew and the option to convert relieve the policyowner from furnishing evidence of insurability on the life of the insured.

4. When level premium insurance is renewed, the premium amount rises to reflect the increased mortality risk of the insured's older age.

   What phrase best describes this approach to increasing premiums?

   a. Variable rate
   b. Targeted rate
   c. Step rate
   d. Seniority rate

5. Which of the following statements describing whole life insurance are correct?

   I. The face amount of the policy stays the same as long as the policy remains in force.
   II. The shorter a premium period is, the slower the cash value will grow.
   III. The policy's cash value decreases each year the policy is in force.
   IV. Whole life insurance is designed to mature at age 100.

   a. I and II only
   b. I and III only
   c. I and IV only
   d. II and IV only

6. The _____ is the party to whom the life insurance policy cash values belong.

   a. policyowner
   b. insured
   c. insurer
   d. beneficiary

7. All of the following statements regarding basic forms of whole life insurance are correct, EXCEPT:

   a. Generally, straight life premiums are payable, at least annually, for the duration of the insured's life.
   b. The owner of a 30-pay life policy will owe no more premiums after the 30th year the policy is in force.
   c. Limited payment life provides protection only for the years during which premiums are paid.
   d. A single-premium life policy is purchased with a large one-time only premium.

8. Which of the following statements regarding modified endowment contracts (MECs) is/are correct?

   I. A 1988 revenue act, commonly known as TAMRA, greatly increased the popularity of modified endowment contracts.
   II. Congress has granted the modified endowment contract the most favorable tax status among all life insurance policies.
   III. To avoid being classified as a modified endowment contract, a life insurance policy must satisfy the "7-pay test."
   IV. According to the "7-pay test," if the total amount a policyowner pays into a life contract during its first seven years is less than the sum of the net level premiums that would have been payable to provide paid-up future benefits in seven years, the policy is a modified endowment.

   a. I and II only
   b. II and III only
   c. III only
   d. III and IV only

9. Which of the following whole life insurance policies attempts to make insurance premiums more manageable by offering lower premiums during the first few years following issue?

   I. Graded premium whole life
   II. Modified whole life

   a. I only
   b. II only
   c. Both I and II
   d. Neither I nor II

10. All of the following statements regarding special use policies are correct, EXCEPT:

   a. A family income policy combines whole life and decreasing term insurance into one policy package.
   b. A family maintenance policy combines whole life and level term insurance into one policy package.
   c. A joint life policy is available using term insurance only.
   d. A multiple protection policy pays double or triple death proceeds if the insured dies during a specified period.

11. What type of policy would be the best choice to insure the declining balance on a home mortgage?

   a. Level term
   b. Decreasing term
   c. Whole life
   d. Universal life

12. Which of the following statements regarding universal life insurance is NOT correct?

   a. Although premiums and cash value allocations are flexible in a universal life policy, the amount of death protection always remains the same.
   b. A mortality charge is deducted from the policy's cash value monthly.
   c. Interest may be available at either the contract's guaranteed minimum rate or at the current interest rate as declared by the company.
   d. To avoid tax problems, premium allocations to a universal life insurance policy's cash account must fall within guidelines.

13. Which of the following statements regarding universal life insurance is correct?

   a. Unlike whole life insurance, a universal life insurance policy permits partial withdrawals.
   b. Universal life insurance offers one death benefit option incorporating increasing term plus increasing cash values.
   c. An adjustable life insurance policy is somewhat more flexible than a universal life policy.
   d. The owner of a universal life insurance policy should take advantage of the opportunity to make unlimited allocations to the policy's cash value account.

14. Before purchasing any variable life insurance policy, the policyowner should examine a/an _____ that discloses the risks involved with the investment selected.

   a. S&P report
   b. investment advisory letter
   c. prospectus
   d. commissioner's statement

15. Which of the following characteristics correctly applies to a variable universal life insurance policy?
    a. The policyowner must select only one investment for the cash value at any given time.
    b. Because of the fluctuating nature of the investments selected, the insurance company must dictate the premium-payment schedule.
    c. A variable universal life policy combines unscheduled premium payments with death benefits that are limited to the investment performance of the separate account.
    d. Variable universal life policies cannot tap the cash values to satisfy the protection element because the cash values fluctuate constantly.

5 Life Insurance Policy Provisions, Options and Riders

Rights of Policy Ownership • Standard Policy Provisions • Policy Exclusions • Nonforfeiture Values • Policy Dividends • Policy Riders

It is easy to think of a life insurance policy as little more than a piece of paper. Unfortunately, this attitude diminishes the true value of a life insurance contract. Life insurance is property, and policyowners have important rights, as well as responsibilities, inherent in this special type of property. The policy provisions spell out the owner's rights, responsibilities and limitations. In addition, life insurance, like many other forms of property, can be customized to meet the specific needs of the owner through policy riders and options. This chapter will look at policy rights, provisions, riders and options that give the life insurance contract its form and flexibility.

Rights of Policy Ownership

Before we discuss specific policy provisions, it is important to mention the *rights of ownership* that policyowners have. Although there are no provisions in a life insurance policy specifically titled "Rights of Ownership," the fact is, owning a life insurance policy does entail important rights. These rights are woven throughout the policy in various clauses and provisions. The most significant rights of ownership include the following:

- The right to designate and change the beneficiary of the policy proceeds

- The right to select how the death proceeds will be paid to the beneficiary

- The right to cancel the policy and select a nonforfeiture option

- The right to take out a policy loan, assuming the policy is a whole life or other permanent plan, and a cash value exists

- The right to receive policy dividends and select a dividend payment option, if it is a participating policy

- The right to assign ownership of the policy to someone else

The clauses and provisions that set forth these rights will be examined in this and later chapters.

Standard Policy Provisions

Despite efforts by insurance companies to offer products distinct from their competitors, insurance policies are more notable for their many similarities than differences. This high degree of uniformity is rooted in the state-level regulation of the industry and the adoption of NAIC guidelines.

As discussed in Chapter 2, regulators in each state protect consumers by establishing strict guidelines as to what must, and must not, be included in an insurance policy. Furthermore, in an effort to promote state-by-state uniformity of insurance industry regulation, most states have adopted, to one degree or another, the standard wording of NAIC Model Regulations. Accordingly, policy language is strikingly similar among the many different life insurance contracts available to consumers.

We will begin this section with a discussion of the *standard provisions* that appear in most life insurance contracts, then take a look at some of the common *exclusions*. It should be noted that while the provision names used here are commonly accepted terms, individual contracts may use different wording. For example, the "Entire Contract" clause falls under the heading "The Contract" in one company's policy, "Entire Contract" in another's and "General" in a third. (It may be helpful to review the sample policy in the Appendix as you read this section.)

Entire Contract Provision

The *entire contract* provision, found at the beginning of the policy, states that the policy document, the application (which is attached to the policy) and any attached riders constitute the entire contract. Nothing may be "incorporated by reference," meaning that the policy cannot refer to any outside documents as being part of the contract. For example, a company could not claim that a special rider, not attached to the policy but on file in the home office, is part of the policy.

The entire contract clause has another important function—it prohibits the insurer from making any changes to the policy, either through policy revisions or changes in the company's bylaws, after the policy has been issued.

This clause does not prevent a mutually agreeable change from being made to the policy if the policy specifically provides a means for modifying the contract after it has been issued (for example, changing the face amount of an adjustable life policy).

Insuring Clause

The *insuring clause* or provision sets forth the company's basic promise to pay benefits upon the insured's death. Generally, this clause is not actually titled as such, but appears on the cover of the policy.

One company's insuring clause reads:

> "The Insurance Company agrees, in accordance with the provisions of this policy, to pay to the beneficiary the death proceeds upon receipt at the Principal Office of due proof of the insured's death prior to the maturity date.
>
> "Further, the Company agrees to pay the surrender value to the owner if the insured is alive on the maturity date."

The insuring clause is typically undersigned by the president and secretary of the insurance company.

Free-Look Provision

The *free-look* provision, required by most states, gives policyowners the right to return the policy for a full premium refund within a specified period of time, if they decide not to purchase the insurance. Most policies provide for a ten-day free look.

It is important to note that the free-look period begins when the policy document is actually *received* by the policyowner, not when the application is signed nor when the policy is issued by the insurance company.

Consideration Clause

As we learned in Chapter 3, "consideration" is the value given in exchange for a contractual promise. The *consideration clause* or provision in a life insurance policy specifies the amount and frequency of premium payments that the policyowners must make to keep the insurance in force. Often, the amount and frequency of required premiums are listed on the "Schedule" or "Specifications" page. A separate page will provide details on the manner in which premiums must be paid (as well as the consequences of not making a premium payment).

Grace Period Provision

The *grace period* provision undoubtedly has saved many life insurance policies from lapsing. If policyowners forget or neglect to pay their premiums by the date they are due, the grace period allows an extra 30 days or one month (possibly less for some industrial policies) during which premiums may be paid to keep policies in force.

If an insured dies during the grace period and the premium has not been paid, the policy benefit is payable. However, the premium amount due is deducted from the benefits paid to the beneficiary.

Reinstatement Provision

It is always possible that, due to nonpayment of premiums, a policy may lapse, either deliberately or unintentionally. In cases where a policyowner wishes to reinstate a lapsed policy, the *reinstatement provision* allows him or her to do so, with some limitations. With reinstatement, a policy is restored to its *original* status and its values are brought up to date.

Most insurers require the following in order to reinstate a lapsed policy:

1. all back premiums must be paid;

2. interest on past-due premiums may be required to be paid;

3. any outstanding loans on the lapsed policy may be required to be paid; and

4. the policyowner may be asked to prove insurability.

In addition, there is a limited period of time in which policies may be reinstated after lapse. This period is usually three years, but may be as long as seven years, in some cases. A new contestable period usually goes into effect with a reinstated policy, but there is no new suicide exclusion period. (See "Incontestable Clause," below and "Suicide Provision," page 67.)

Policy Loan Provision

State insurance laws require that cash value life insurance policies include a *policy loan* provision. This means that, within prescribed limits, policyowners may borrow money from the cash values of their policies if they wish to do so.

Actually, a policy loan is more an advance on proceeds than a true loan. As such, these "loans" may not be "called" by the company and can be repaid at any time by the policyowners. If not repaid by the time the insured dies, the loan balance and any interest accrued are deducted from the policy proceeds at the time of claim. If the policy is surrendered for cash, the cash value available to the policyowner is reduced by the amount of any outstanding loan plus interest.

Interest rates on policy loans vary, but most states stipulate a maximum allowable rate. Some newer policies are issued with a variable interest rate tied to current market rates; older policies still in force stipulate a flat rate of interest, such as 5 to 8 percent.

Loan values and cash surrender values are shown as identical amounts in a policy and are often listed under the single column heading of "Cash or Loan Value." (See Ill. 5.1.)

Incontestable Clause

The *incontestable clause* or provision provides that after a specified period of time (usually two years from the issue date and while the insured is living), the insurer no longer has the right to contest the validity of the life insurance policy so long as the contract continues in force. This means that after the policy has been in force for the specified term, the company cannot contest a death claim or refuse payment of the proceeds *even on the basis of a material misstatement, concealment or fraud.* Even if the insurer learns that an error was deliberately made on the application, it must pay the death benefit at the insured's death if the policy has passed the contestable period.

Although the incontestable clause applies to death benefits, it generally does *not* apply to accidental death benefits or disability provisions if they are part of the policy. Because conditions relating to accidents vary and are often uncertain, the right to investigate them usually is reserved by the company.

The incontestable clause applies to the policy face amount, plus any additional death benefit added by rider that is payable in the case of normal death.

It should be noted that there are three situations to which the incontestable clause does *not* apply. A policy issued under any of these circumstances would not be considered a valid contract, which gives the insurer the right to contest and possibly void the policy at any time:

1. *Impersonation.* When application for insurance is made by one person but another person signs the application or takes the medical exam, the insurer can contest the policy and its claim.

2. *No insurable interest.* If no insurable interest existed between the applicant and the insured at the inception of the policy, the contract is not valid to begin with; as such, the insurer can contest the policy at any time.

3. *Intent to murder.* If it is subsequently proven that the applicant applied for the policy with the intent of murdering the insured for the proceeds, the insurance company can contest the policy and its claim.

Assignment Provision

People who purchase life insurance policies are commonly referred to as "policy*owners*" rather than "policy*holders*" because they actually own their policies and may do with them as they wish. They can even give them away, just as they can give away any other kind of property they own. This transfer of ownership is known as "*assignment.*"

The assignment provision in a life insurance contract sets forth the procedure necessary for ownership transfer. This procedure usually requires that the policyowner notify the company in writing of the assignment. The company will then accept the validity of the transfer without question. A policyowner does not need the insurer's permission to assign a policy.

The new owner is known as the *assignee.* If, for example, an individual gave a policy to his church as a donation, the church would be the assignee. An insurable interest does *not* have to exist between the insured and the assignee.

As the owner of the policy, the assignee is granted all the rights of policyownership, including the right to name a beneficiary. If the assignee does not change the beneficiary designation, the proceeds will be paid to the beneficiary named by the original owner. Note, however, the assignee does have the right to change the beneficiary designation.* If a policyowner names an *irrevocable beneficiary* (meaning the beneficiary cannot be changed), he or she must get the beneficiary's agreement to any assignment. (See Chapter 6.)

---

*Most jurisdictions, however, will not allow an assignee to change the beneficiary designation if it was originally designated irrevocable. (See "Changing a Beneficiary," Chapter 6.)

There are two types of assignments: *absolute* and *collateral*.

1. **Absolute assignment.** Under an *absolute assignment,* the transfer is complete and irrevocable, and the assignee receives full control over the policy and full rights to its benefits.

2. **Collateral assignment.** A *collateral assignment* is one in which the policy is assigned to a creditor as security, or collateral, for a debt. If the insured dies, the creditor is entitled to be reimbursed out of the benefit proceeds for the amount owed. The insured's beneficiary is then entitled to any excess of policy proceeds over the amount due the creditor. Once the debt is repaid, the policyowner is entitled to the return of the rights assigned.

Suicide Provision

The *suicide provision,* found in most life policies, protects the company and its policyowners against the possibility that a person might buy an insurance policy and deliberately commit suicide to provide a sum of money for the beneficiary. With this provision, a life insurance policy discourages suicide by stipulating a period of time (usually one or two years from the date of policy issue) during which the death benefit will *not* be paid if the insured commits suicide. If that happens, however, the premiums paid for the policy will be refunded.

Of course, if an insured takes his or her own life after the policy has been in force for the period specified in the suicide clause, the company will pay the entire proceeds, just as if death were from a natural cause.

Because of the instinct for self-preservation, most courts will assume a death was unintentional unless there is strong evidence to the contrary. So even if death occurs during the suicide exclusion period and suicide is suspected, the company must prove it beyond a reasonable doubt; otherwise, the policy proceeds generally must be paid to the beneficiary.

Misstatement of Age or Sex Provision

The *misstatement of age or sex provision* is important because the age and sex of the applicant are critical factors in establishing the premium rate for a life insurance policy. To guard against a misunderstanding about the applicant's age, the company reserves the right to make an adjustment at any time. Likewise, an adjustment is made if an applicant's sex is incorrectly indicated in a policy because, age for age, premium rates for females generally are lower than for males. Normally, such adjustments are made either in the premium charged or in the amount of insurance.

Assume an error in age is discovered after the death of an insured. If the insured was younger than the policy showed, the amount of proceeds would be increased to a sum the premium paid would have bought at the correct age. On the other hand, if the insured was older than the policy indicated, the amount of proceeds would be decreased to whatever the premium paid would have purchased at the correct age.

If an error is discovered while the insured is living, the premium will be adjusted downward if the insured is younger than the policy shows and a refund of the premium overpayments will be made. By the same token, if the insured is older than the policy indicates, the company will either adjust the premium upward and require the difference in premium or it will reduce the amount of insurance to what it should be for the amount of premium being paid.

Automatic Premium Loan Provision

A provision that is now commonly added to most cash value policies is the *automatic premium loan.* This provision authorizes the insurer to withdraw from the policy's cash value the amount of premium due if the premium has not been paid by the end of the grace period. The amount withdrawn becomes a loan against the cash value, bearing the rate of interest specified in the contract.

Depending on the insurer, this provision may be standard to the contract or added as a rider, with no additional charge to the policyowner.

Other Policy Provisions

There are two additional provisions that appear in all policies: the *beneficiary designation,* whereby the policyowner indicates who is to receive the proceeds, and *settlement options,* whereby the ways in which the proceeds can be paid out, or "settled," are explained. Beneficiaries are discussed in Chapter 6; settlement options are discussed in Chapter 7.

Policy Exclusions

Most life insurance policies contain restrictions that exclude from coverage certain types of risks. If there were no *exclusions,* premium rates would be much higher. Exclusions can be stated in the policy itself or attached as riders. The most common types of exclusions include:

1. *War.* This exclusion provides that the death benefit will not be paid if the insured dies as a result of war.

2. *Aviation.* This exclusion is commonly found in older policies; very few policies issued today exclude death as a result of commercial aviation. However, some insurers will exclude aviation deaths for other than fare-paying passengers.

3. *Hazardous occupations or hobbies.* Individuals who have hazardous occupations, such as stunt people, or who engage in hazardous hobbies, such as auto racing, may find that their life insurance policies exclude death as a result of their occupation or hobby. Or, these risks may be covered, but an increased (or "rated") premium will be charged.

4. *Commission of a felony.* Some contracts will exclude death when it results from the insured committing a felony.

5. *Suicide.* As previously noted, almost all policies exclude payment of the benefit if the insured commits suicide during the specified time period. After that period passes, death by suicide is covered.

Because these exclusions are allowed by state regulators to be included in policies at the discretion of the insurance company, they are also called "optional provisions." Note, however, the term "exclusions" more precisely defines their purpose.

Nonforfeiture Values

In Chapter 4 we learned that an important feature of whole life insurance is its cash value, which is created in part by the level premium funding method. As a policy matures, cash values grow until, when the policy endows, the cash value equals the face amount of the policy. Ownership of a policy's cash value rests solely with the policyowner. Even though the cash value is an important part of the underlying funding of the policy, the policyowner is entitled to receive the accrued cash value at any time. When a policy is active, the owner can *borrow* from the cash value. If a policy is lapsed or surrendered, the owner is entitled to the *cash surrender value*.

Until the beginning of the 20th century, it was common for insurers to keep part or all of the cash value in a surrendered policy. The idea that it was the policyowner, not the insurer, who was entitled to a policy's cash value did not gain universal acceptance until the 1905 Armstrong Investigation looked at a number of insurer abuses, including the practice of keeping policy cash values upon policy surrender.

Ill. 5.1 Table of Guaranteed Values

Face Amount: $100,000   Annual Premium: $2,000

End of Policy Year	Cash or Loan Value	Reduced Paid-Up	Extended Term Years	Extended Term Days
1	$ 0	$ 0	0	0
2	50	210	0	66
3	960	3,600	2	290
4	2,150	7,250	6	09
5	4,000	12,000	8	111
6	5,975	16,110	10	147
7	7,210	19,880	12	22
8	9,340	23,800	14	18
9	11,415	27,620	15	312
10	13,005	30,990	16	362
11	14,770	34,010	17	202
12	16,785	37,880	18	116
13	19,430	40,940	18	01
14	23,000	43,985	17	144
15	26,990	47,010	16	302
16	30,215	50,600	15	347
17	34,600	53,815	15	88
18	38,910	56,910	14	117
19	43,020	60,010	13	361
20	47,910	63,715	13	47
Age 65	56,770	78,700	11	36

This table is an example of how the guaranteed ("nonforfeitable") values are presented in a life insurance policy. These figures reflect the values available to the policyowner at different points in the policy's life for purposes of surrendering the policy for cash, taking out a loan against the policy, purchasing a reduced paid-up policy or purchasing an extended term policy. (See also the sample policy in the Appendix.)

Today every state has legislated laws, modeled after the NAIC "Standard Nonforfeiture Law," assuring policyowners that they are fully entitled to the accrued cash values of their policies. The term *"nonforfeiture value"* refers to the fact that a policy's cash value is not forfeitable. *Nonforfeiture options* are the ways in which cash values can be paid out to or used by policyowners, if they choose to lapse or surrender their policies.

Nonforfeiture Options

There are three nonforfeiture options from which policyowners can select: *cash surrender, reduced paid-up insurance* and *extended term insurance.*

Cash Surrender Option

If they desire, policyowners may request an immediate *cash payment* of their cash values when their policies are surrendered. A table of cash surrender values is included in every permanent life insurance policy, as illustrated in Ill. 5.1, under the heading "Cash or Loan Value." The amount of cash value the policyowner receives is reduced by any outstanding policy indebtedness.

Insurers are required to make cash surrender values available for ordinary whole life insurance after the first three policy years and, for industrial insurance, after five years. In practice, however, most policies begin to generate cash values in as little as one year.

Most states permit insurers to postpone payment of cash surrender values for up to six months after policyowners request payment. This *"delayed payment provision"* is a protective measure for companies should an economic crisis arise, but such delays are rarely invoked.

Reduced Paid-Up Option

A second nonforfeiture option is to take a *paid-up policy for a reduced face amount of insurance.* By doing this, the policyowner does not pay any more premiums but still retains some amount of life insurance. In essence, the cash

Ill. 5.2 Reduced Paid-Up Option

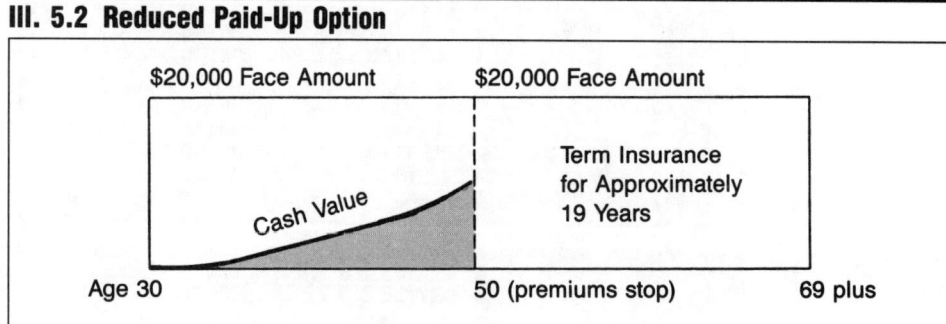

Using the above diagram as an example, assume Lyman purchased a $20,000 whole life policy at age 30 and now, at age 50, decides to discontinue premium payments and use the accumulated cash value to make a single payment to purchase a reduced amount ($12,500) of permanent paid-up insurance. Lyman has exercised the "reduced paid-up" nonforfeiture option. (Amounts shown are illustrative only.)

Ill. 5.3 Extended Term Option

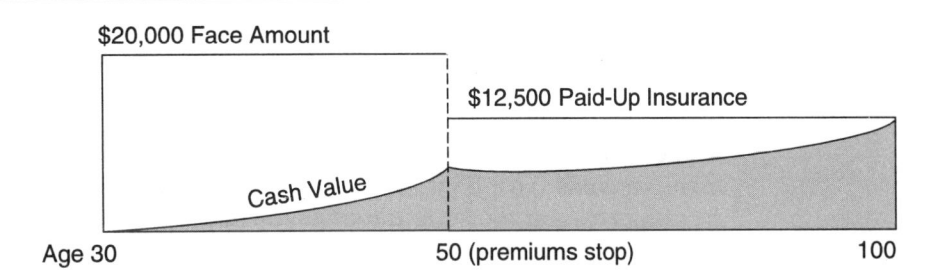

Using the above diagram as an example, assume Lyman purchased a $20,000 life policy at age 30 and now, at age 50, decides to discontinue premium payments and use the accumulated cash value to purchase a $20,000 term policy. The cash value will provide $20,000 of protection for approximately 19 years, until Lyman is about 69. Lyman has exercised the "extended term" nonforfeiture option. (Extended term shown is illustrative only.)

value is used as the premium for a single-premium whole life policy, at a lesser face amount than the original policy.

When this option is exercised, the paid-up policy is the same kind as the original, but for a lesser amount of coverage. For example, if the original policy was a participating whole life policy, the paid-up policy also will be a participating whole life policy. The paid-up policy is computed as a single-premium policy at the attained-age rate. Any term insurance rider and disability or accidental death benefits from the original policy are excluded when the amount of paid-up life insurance is calculated.

Once the paid-up policy has been issued, the new face value remains the same for the life of the policy, which also builds cash values. (See Ill. 5.2.)

Extended Term Option

The third nonforfeiture option is to use the policy's cash value to *purchase a term insurance policy* in an amount equal to the original policy's face value, for as long a period as the cash value will purchase. When the term insurance expires, there is no more protection. Moreover, all supplemental benefits included with the original policy, such as a term rider or accidental death or disability benefits, are dropped. (See Ill. 5.3.)

In the case of endowment insurance, the extended term insurance will not be provided beyond the maturity date of the original endowment policy. The cash value of an endowment policy will eventually exceed the amount needed to buy extended term insurance so, in that case, the excess cash value is used to purchase a pure endowment policy with the same maturity date as the original policy.

Policy Dividends

As noted previously, life insurance policies may be either participating or nonparticipating, and it is important to distinguish between the two in order to understand the source of *policy dividends*. At any given age, people who buy participating (par) policies normally pay premiums that are slightly higher than premiums paid by those who purchase nonparticipating (nonpar) policies. This is because an extra charge to cover unexpected contingencies is built into premiums for par policies.

At the end of each year, the insurance company analyzes its operations. If fewer insureds have died than was estimated, a "divisible surplus" results and the company can return to the policyowners a part of the premiums paid for participating policies. A company also can issue returns stemming from positive operating or investment income. These payments are called "dividends," but should not be confused with the dividends paid on stocks. Policy dividends are really a "return of part of the premiums paid." As such, policy dividends are not taxable income, unlike corporate dividends, which are reportable for income tax purposes.

The payment of policy dividends hinges on several "ifs" (unexpected contingencies, as noted). And because all of those conditions will affect the amount of the dividend, policy dividends normally will vary from year to year and *cannot* be guaranteed.

Thus, when an insurance company gives a policy illustration that includes dividends, it is purely an estimate or approximation of what future dividends might be. To protect life insurance buyers against the misuse of dividend illustrations, most states require life insurance proposals containing a dividend illustration to state clearly that future dividends are not guaranteed.

Dividends usually become payable at the end of the first or second policy year. A provision in each participating policy states when the policyowner can expect to begin receiving any dividends.

Dividend Options

Policyowners are generally permitted by insurers to utilize their dividends through one of five options:

1. *Take dividends in cash.* When dividends become payable, they usually are paid on policy anniversary dates. Policyowners who elect to take their dividends in cash automatically receive their dividend check after the company approves a dividend.

2. *Apply dividends against premium payments.* Dividends can also be applied directly to the policyowner's premium payments, lowering the owner's out-of-pocket expense.

3. *Allow dividends to accumulate at interest.* A third option is to leave the dividends with the company to accumulate with interest, for withdrawal at any time. Note that while policy dividends are not taxable, any interest paid on them is taxable income in the year the interest is credited to the policy, whether or not it is actually received by the policyowner.

4. *Use dividends to buy paid-up additions.* Dividends can also be used to purchase paid-up additions of life insurance, of the same kind as the

Ill. 5.4

> **Paid-Up Additions: A Popular Option**
>
> The *paid-up additions* dividend option is popular with many policyowners. A close look at the benefits of this option will explain why.
>
> When a dividend is declared, it is used in effect as the premium for a single-payment whole life policy of the same type as the base policy under which the dividend is declared. The face amount of this "paid-up addition" is generally small, but over time the sum of these additions can be substantial.
>
> The paid-up addition enjoys all the advantages of any whole life policy. It will accrue a cash value. It possesses all the tax advantages of whole life insurance. Most significantly, it is issued to the policyowner without any additional premium requirement beyond the premium being paid for the base policy.
>
> Consider the example of a policyowner with a $100,000 par policy who is paying a level premium of $1,300 annually. As each year passes, a paid-up addition is added. In time, the total face amount of the policy will grow as more paid-up additions are added; perhaps after ten years the total face amount may be $115,000. The cash value of this policy will increase at an ever-faster rate as the paid-up additions' cash values are added to the base policy's cash value. And all of this will occur with the same $1,300 annual outlay as was required when the policy was first purchased.

original or base policy. The premium rate is based on the attained age of the insured at the time the paid-up additions are purchased.

5. *Use dividends to purchase one-year term insurance.* A fifth option, though not utilized as frequently as the others, is to use dividends to purchase as much one-year term insurance as possible or to purchase one-year term insurance equal to the base policy's cash value. This is done through specific application for and issue of a separate rider. Sometimes called the "fifth dividend option," this provision allows for any excess dividend portions to be applied under any of the other regular options.

Policy Riders

The flexibility of life insurance policies is well demonstrated by the ability policyowners have to customize a policy to meet their specific needs. Imagine buying a new car without being able to purchase optional features, such as air conditioning or a tape deck. Chances are good you might not even buy that car. Insurers offer their applicants the privilege of adding options—in the form of *policy riders*—to their policies to meet their unique needs. Like new car options, policy riders are available at an extra cost (through increased premiums), but are justified because of the increased value the riders give to the base policy.

Most of the optional riders described below must be selected at the time the policy is applied for. The automatic premium loan rider (if it is an option and not a standard policy feature) is the only optional rider available at no cost to the policyowner. It can sometimes be added after the policy is in force.

Guaranteed Insurability Rider

For an extra premium, the *guaranteed insurability* rider may be attached to a permanent life insurance policy at the time of purchase. It permits the insured, at specified intervals in the future, to buy specified amounts of additional insurance *without evidence of insurability.*

Typically, this option allows the insured to purchase additional life insurance at stated policy intervals or at stated ages. The amount of insurance that can be purchased at each option date is subject to minimums and maximums specified in the rider, but the insurance is available at *standard premium rates,* whether or not the insured is still insurable.

These riders generally allow the insured to buy additional life insurance at three-year intervals, beginning with the policy anniversary date nearest his or her age 25 and terminating at the anniversary date nearest age 40. (Guaranteed insurability options usually do not extend past age 40.) Thus, the option dates listed in the rider are for the insured's ages 25, 28, 31, 34, 37 and 40. The insured normally has 90 days in which to exercise an option to purchase. If no purchase is made within that time, the option for that particular age expires automatically. The expiration of one option will not affect the exercise of future options.

Company practice varies, but if a waiver of premium or accidental death benefit (both are explained below) is included with the original policy, most companies allow these benefits to be added to the additional life insurance purchased under the guaranteed insurability option, if the policyowner wants to pay the additional premium.

Waiver of Premium Rider

The *waiver of premium* rider provides valuable added security for policyowners. It can prevent a policy from lapsing for nonpayment of premiums while the insured is disabled and unable to work.

Under the waiver of premium, if the company determines that the insured is totally disabled, the policyowner is relieved of paying premiums as long as the disability continues. Some companies include the waiver of premium as part of the contract, with the cost built into the overall premium. In other companies, the waiver may be added to a policy by rider or endorsement for a small, additional premium.

Some policies specify that an insured must be totally and permanently disabled for the waiver to take effect. It does not apply to short-term illnesses or injuries. In fact, an insured generally must be seriously disabled for a certain length of time, called the "waiting period" (usually 90 days or six months). The policyowner continues paying premiums during the waiting period. If the insured is still disabled at the end of this period, the company will refund all of the premiums paid by the policyowner from the start of the disability.

The company then continues to pay all premiums that become due while the insured's disability continues. If the insured recovers and can start back to work, premium payments then must be resumed by the policyowner. No premiums paid by the company, however, have to be repaid by the policyowner.

For the waiver to become operative, the insured must meet the policy's definition of "totally disabled." "Totally disabled" may be defined as the insured's inability to engage in *any* work for which he or she is reasonably fitted by education, training or experience. Or, as with some policies, the definition is worded in terms of the insured's inability to work at his or her *own* occupation for a stated period (e.g., 24 months) and at any occupation thereafter.

A waiver of premium rider generally remains in effect until the insured reaches a specified age, such as 60 or 65. When the provision expires, the policy premium is reduced accordingly. If an insured becomes disabled prior to the specified age, *all* premiums usually are waived while the disability continues—even those premiums falling due after the insured passes the stipulated age.

Although premiums are waived for a disabled insured, the death benefit remains the same, cash values increase at their normal rate and dividends for a participating policy are paid as usual. In fact, cash values continue to be available to the policyowner at all times while the insured's disability continues.

Automatic Premium Loan Rider

The *automatic premium loan* feature, first discussed on page 68, is a standard feature in some life insurance policies; in others, its provisions are added to the policy by rider. In either case, it is available to the policyowner at no additional charge. As previously noted, it allows the insurer to pay premiums from the policy's cash value if premiums have not been paid by the end of the grace period. These deductions from cash values are treated as "loans" and are charged interest; in time, if the loan is not repaid, the interest will also be deducted from the cash value. Should the insured die, the loan plus interest will be deducted from the benefits payable.

Automatic premium loans provide that, as long as premiums are not paid, the loan procedure will be repeated until the cash value of the policy is exhausted. When the cash value is depleted, the policy lapses.

An automatic premium loan option can be elected at the time of application or, with some insurers, added after the policy is issued.

Payor Rider

As noted earlier in the discussion of juvenile insurance, a *payor provision* is usually available with such policies, providing for waiver of premiums if the adult premium-payor should die or, with some policies, become totally disabled.

Typically, this payor provision, also known as a "death and disability payor benefit," extends until the insured child reaches a specified age, such as 21 or 25. It is available for a small extra premium but, before it is issued, the adult who is to pay the premium usually must show evidence of insurability.

Accidental Death Benefit Rider

The *accidental death benefit* rider (sometimes called a "double indemnity" provision) provides an additional amount of insurance, usually equal to the face amount of the base policy, if death occurs under stated conditions. Con-

> **Ill. 5.5**
>
> ### Which Rider to Purchase?
>
> Riders can work in tandem. Consider the insured policyowner who has both a *guaranteed insurability* and *waiver of premium* rider on her policy. At age 29, she becomes totally and permanently disabled. Because she meets the definition of total disability in her policy, her premiums will be waived and in two years, when she is 31, she can increase the face amount of her policy to the maximum permitted under the guaranteed insurability rider—all without having to pay any premiums.

sequently, if the insured died as a result of the stated circumstances, and he or she had a double indemnity rider, the total benefit paid would be double the policy's face—the benefit payable under the policy plus the same amount payable under the rider. A "triple indemnity" provision would provide a total death benefit of three times the face amount. Any policy loans are subtracted from the policy's face amount, and not from the accidental death riders.

"Accidental death" is strictly defined. It does *not* include accidents resulting, directly or indirectly, from an ailment or physical disability relating to the insured. The additional proceeds are paid only if the insured dies as a result of bodily injury from some external, violent and purely accidental cause. Also, death must occur within a specified time (usually 90 days) following the accident. Deaths that might be considered accidental, such as those resulting from self-inflicted injury, war or private aviation activities, are excluded.

Many companies do not offer the accidental death benefit to anyone older than age 55 or 60, and the extra protection generally expires after the insured reaches age 60 or 65. While in effect, the additional insurance does *not* build any cash value.

The extra premium for this benefit is not payable beyond the date when the additional benefit expires. Nor does the benefit apply to any paid-up additions that may be purchased with policy dividends. The benefit also drops off in the event the policyowner surrenders the policy and selects one of the nonforfeiture options.

Cost of Living Rider

Some companies offer their applicants the ability to guard against the eroding effects of inflation. A *cost of living* (COL) or *cost of living adjustment* (COLA) rider can provide increases in the amount of insurance protection *without requiring the insured to provide evidence of insurability.* The amount of increase is tied to an increase in an inflation index, most commonly the Consumer Price Index (CPI). Depending on the type of base policy, these riders can take several different forms.

For standard whole life policies, a COL rider is usually offered as an *increasing term insurance* rider that is attached to the base policy. The COL rider provides for automatic increases in the policy death benefit in proportion to increases in the CPI. Generally there is a maximum percentage increase, such as 5 percent, allowed in any one year. When the increase becomes effective, the policyowner is billed for the additional coverage. It is important to note that declines in the CPI are not matched by a decline in the amount of coverage; instead, future increases are held off until the CPI again exceeds its prior high point.

Adjustable life insurance, which is characterized in part by giving the policyowner limited freedom to increase and decrease the policy's face amount, frequently includes a COL agreement. The COL agreement waives the need for evidence of insurability for limited face amount increases that are intended to match increases in the CPI. The face amount increase is accompanied by an increase in premium, although the agreement itself is usually offered at no charge to the policyowner.

The COL agreement can also be used, with certain restrictions, with term and whole life policies. They are not practical with universal life policies, however, because of the high degree of flexibility already present in UL policies.

Other Insureds Rider

A rider that is useful in providing insurance for more than one family member is the *other insureds* rider. Usually this rider is offered as a term rider, covering a family member other than the insured, and is attached to the base policy covering the insured. Sometimes this is called a *children's rider* if it covers only the children; otherwise, it is often referred to as a *family rider.* This type of rider is used in "family plan" policies, discussed in Chapter 4.

Accelerated Benefits Rider

Up until quite recently, traditional whole life insurance policies provided cash benefit payments in the event of the insured's death (or in the rare case of an insured living to a contract's maturity date). The only way the insured could access the policy's cash value while he or she was living was through a policy loan or policy surrender. In the event the insured was faced with a life-threatening medical condition, the life insurance policy, by design, could provide no immediate financial relief.

Today, many insurers offer an *accelerated benefits* rider to their life insurance policies. This rider allows the early payment of some portion of the policy face amount should the insured suffer from a terminal illness or injury. The death benefit, less the accelerated payment, is still payable. For example, a $250,000 policy that provides for a 75 percent accelerated benefit would pay up to $187,500 to the terminally-ill insured, with the remaining $62,500 payable as a death benefit to the beneficiary when the insured dies.

More and more insurers are beginning to offer accelerated benefits, either as policy riders or as provisions in the life policies themselves. Accelerated payments can be made in a lump sum or in monthly installments over a specified period, such as one year.

Summary

All life insurance policies are characterized by standardized *policy provisions* that identify the rights and obligations of the policyowner and the insurance company. There are many standard provisions that are required by state insurance regulators to be included in policies. Other provisions, dealing with *exclusions* and *restrictions* of coverage, are optional and can be included at the discretion of the insurer.

Whole life policies generate cash values to which policyowners are entitled. Policyowners may borrow from a policy's cash value or, upon lapse or surrender of the policy, may select one of three possible *nonforfeiture options*.

Participating policies share in the divisible surplus of company operations by returning part of the premium to the owner as a policy dividend. There are five *dividend options* available to policyowners in deciding how to use their policy dividends.

Policyowners can customize their policy to meet their specific insurance needs by including, generally at a cost, one or more *policy riders*.

Key Concepts

In preparing for their licensing examination, students should be familiar with the following concepts:

owner's rights	policy exclusions (optional
entire contract provision	provisions)
insuring clause	nonforfeiture options
free look	policy dividends and options
consideration clause	guaranteed insurability rider
grace period	waiver of premium
reinstatement	automatic premium loan
policy loans	payor benefit
incontestable clause	accidental death benefit
assignment provision	cost of living adjustments
suicide provision	other insureds rider
misstatement of age or sex clause	accelerated benefits rider

Chapter 5
Questions for Review *(Answers are located at the end of the book.)*

1. All of the following are situations in which an incontestable clause does NOT apply, EXCEPT:

    a. impersonation of the applicant by another.
    b. no insurable interest.
    c. intent to murder.
    d. concealment of smoking.

2. An error in age is discovered after the death of an insured, but before any policy death proceeds are distributed. The insured was older than previously assumed. How would an insurance company handle such a situation?

   a. No adjustment would be made because the contestable period had passed.
   b. The amount of death proceeds would be reduced to reflect the statistically diminished mortality risk.
   c. The amount of death proceeds would be reduced to reflect whatever benefit the premium paid would have purchased at the correct age.
   d. The beneficiary would be required to pay all underpaid back premiums before the death benefit is received.

3. The _____ allows an extra 30 days or one month (possibly less for some industrial policies) during which premiums may be paid to keep policies in force.

   a. grace period
   b. reinstatement clause
   c. incontestable clause
   d. waiting period

4. Which of the following statements regarding the assignment of a life insurance policy is NOT correct?

   a. Absolute assignment involves a complete transfer, giving the assignee full control over the policy.
   b. Under a collateral assignment, a creditor is entitled to be reimbursed out of the policy's proceeds only for the amount of the outstanding credit balance.
   c. Under a collateral assignment, policy proceeds in excess of the collateral amount pass to the insured's beneficiary.
   d. All beneficiaries must expressly approve any assignments of life insurance policies.

5. Which of the following is/are common life insurance policy exclusions?

   I. War
   II. Death by accidental means

   a. I only
   b. II only
   c. Both I and II
   d. Neither I nor II

6. All of the following phrases describe life insurance policy nonforfeiture options, EXCEPT:

   a. cash surrender option.
   b. one-year term insurance option.
   c. extended term insurance option.
   d. reduced paid-up (permanent) insurance option.

7. Which of the following statements best describes the role of policy dividends?

   a. Policy dividends represent earnings to shareowners who hold stock in insurance companies.
   b. Policy dividends impact the costs of virtually all insurance policies issued today.
   c. Policy dividends are an intentional return of a portion of the premiums paid.
   d. Policy dividends provide policyowners with a level, known annual cash inflow.

8. The most common guaranteed insurability riders allow additional life insurance to be purchased on the insured within a range of ages. The common age range in which guaranteed insurability is available is

   a. from age 16 to age 65.
   b. from age 21 to age 59½.
   c. from age 25 to age 40.
   d. from age 30 to age 70½.

9. Which life insurance provision allows the policyholder to inspect and, if dissatisfied, to return the policy for a full refund?

   a. Waiver of premium
   b. Facility of payments
   c. Probationary period
   d. Free look

10. Which of the following statements regarding a cost of living (COL) rider on a life insurance policy are correct?

    I. A cost of living rider seeks to protect against inflation's erosion of life insurance policy values.
    II. To purchase additional amounts of life insurance under a cost of living rider, evidence of insurability will be required.
    III. An inflation index, usually the Consumer Price Index, determines the amount of inflation adjustment that must be made to the policy up to a maximum percentage increase.
    IV. Declines in the CPI cause corresponding declines in the amount of insurance coverage.

    a. I and II only
    b. I and III only
    c. II and III only
    d. II and IV only

11. "If an insurance company determines that the insured is totally disabled, the policyowner is relieved of paying the policy premiums as long as the disability continues." This above statement describes

    a. the premium suspension clause.
    b. the waiting period exemption.
    c. the disability income rider.
    d. the waiver of premium rider.

12. To what period would a ten-day free-look provision apply?

    a. The first ten days after the application has been signed by the applicant.
    b. The first ten days after the application has been received by the insurer.
    c. The first ten days after the policy has been issued by the insurer.
    d. The first ten days after the issued policy has been received by the insured.

6 LIFE INSURANCE BENEFICIARIES

Who Can Be a Beneficiary? • Types of Beneficiary Designations
• Special Situations

In chapter 5 we noted that a right involved with owning a life insurance policy is the right to name a beneficiary. The beneficiary is the party designated to receive the policy's proceeds upon the insured's death. Determining the proper beneficiary is a matter of utmost importance. In order to counsel their clients competently, life insurance agents must fully understand the laws and the practices involved with naming policy beneficiaries.

Who Can Be a Beneficiary?

Life insurance companies place very few restrictions on who may be named the *beneficiary* of a life insurance policy. The decision rests solely with the owner of the policy. However, in some cases, the insurer must consider the issue of *insurable interest*.

As we have learned, insurable interest is not a concern when the applicant for a policy is also the insured. In those cases, a person can apply for as much life insurance as the company will issue and can name anyone as beneficiary, whether or not insurable interest exists between the applicant-insured and the beneficiary. This is because, by law, individuals are presumed to have an unlimited insurable interest in their own lives.

The situation is different when the policy applicant is not the insured (i.e., a "*third-party applicant*"). When a third-party applicant names himself or herself as beneficiary, insurable interest must exist between the applicant and insured. When a third-party applicant names yet another as beneficiary, most states require that insurable interest must exist between that beneficiary and the insured. For example, if Bill were to apply for life insurance coverage on Sue and name himself as beneficiary, insurable interest would have to exist between Bill and Sue. If Bill were to apply for life insurance coverage on Sue but name Jason as beneficiary, insurable interest would probably have to exist between Jason and Sue.

With this in mind, let's take a look at what kinds of entities are commonly designated beneficiaries.

Individuals as Beneficiaries

In most cases, an individual is selected to be the sole or proportional beneficiary of a life insurance policy. There may be one named individual or more than one. For example, a policyowner could designate his wife as the sole beneficiary or designate that she receive half the proceeds of his policy, with the remainder to be split equally between his two children.

Businesses as Beneficiaries

There is no question that insurable interest exists in business relationships. For example, professional sports clubs have an insurable interest in the lives of their best players. Partnerships have an insurable interest in the lives of their partners. Small corporations have an insurable interest in the lives of their key employees. Creditors have an insurable interest in the lives of people who owe them money. Life insurance policies may designate businesses as beneficiaries.

Trusts as Beneficiaries

A trust is a legal arrangement for the ownership of property by one party for the benefit of another. Designating a trust as the beneficiary of a life insurance policy means that the proceeds will be paid to the trust for the ultimate benefit and use by another. Trusts are managed by trustees, who have the fiduciary responsibility to oversee and handle the trust and its funds for its beneficiaries.

Estates as Beneficiaries

Policyowners may designate their estates as beneficiaries, so that, upon death, the proceeds can be used to meet federal estate taxes, debts and other administrative costs, leaving other assets intact to pass on to heirs. The primary drawback to leaving proceeds to an estate is that the value of the policy will be included in the insured's gross estate for estate tax purposes.

Charities as Beneficiaries

Naming a charity as the beneficiary of a life insurance policy is another commonly accepted practice. Life insurance is one of the most attractive and flexible ways to make a contribution to a church, educational institution, hospital, public welfare agency or similar nonprofit organization. One of the benefits of making a contribution of life insurance proceeds—in contrast to leaving a bequest in a will—is that the gift cannot be contested by disgruntled heirs. This is because life insurance proceeds are not part of the insured-donor's probate estate.

Minors as Beneficiaries

Naming minors as life insurance beneficiaries can present some legal and logistical complications. For instance, the minor may not have the legal capacity to give the insurance company a signed release for receipt of the policy proceeds. (Some states have adopted special laws that only allow minors of specified ages, such as 15, to sign a valid receipt.) If an insurer were to pay out the proceeds and not receive a receipt, the minor could legally demand payment a second time, once he or she has reached the age of majority. Furthermore, the minor may simply lack the judgment or expertise to properly manage the proceeds.

Nonetheless, insurers recognize that policyowners may want minors to benefit from an insurance policy. In those cases, and in accordance with the laws of the particular state, insurers may:

- make limited payments to an adult guardian for the benefit of the minor beneficiary;

- retain the policy proceeds at interest and pay them out when the child reaches majority or when an adult guardian is appointed; or

- place the proceeds in a trust for the present or future benefit of the minor, as determined by the trustee.

"Classes" as Beneficiaries

There is also a beneficiary designation known as a *"class designation."* This means that rather than specifying one or more beneficiaries by name, the policyowner designates a class or group of beneficiaries. For example, "Children of the insured" and "My children" are class designations.

Types of Beneficiary Designations

There are a number of ways to classify beneficiary designations: by the order of succession (or preference); by the number named; by line of descent; or by whether or not the designation(s) can be changed. A discussion of these various types of designations follows. In any event, it is important to select and arrange beneficiary designations carefully, because once they are in effect, the insurance company must follow them to the letter.

Order of Succession

It is always possible that a beneficiary to a life insurance policy may predecease the insured. To meet this contingency, policyowners are encouraged to designate *primary, secondary* and occasionally, *tertiary* beneficiaries.

Primary Beneficiaries

A *primary beneficiary* is the party designated to receive the proceeds of a life insurance policy when they become payable. There may be more than one primary beneficiary, and how the proceeds are to be split is up to the policyowner.

Secondary (Contingent) Beneficiaries

A *secondary beneficiary* may also be named and stands second in line to receive the proceeds of a life insurance policy *if* the primary beneficiary dies before the insured. Secondary beneficiaries are entitled to policy proceeds only if no primary beneficiaries are living. Secondary beneficiaries are also known as "contingent" or "successor" beneficiaries.

Tertiary (Contingent) Beneficiaries

A *tertiary beneficiary* stands third in line to receive the proceeds of a life insurance policy, in cases where all primary and secondary beneficiaries predecease the insured.

Example of Beneficiary Succession

For example, assume that Deborah takes out a $150,000 life policy on her life and establishes the beneficiary designations as follows: her husband, Rob, is to receive the full benefit; if he predeceases her, her two children are to share equally in the benefit; if her husband and both her children predecease her, the benefit is payable to Homestate College, her alma mater. In this situation, Rob is the primary beneficiary; the children are contingent secondary beneficiaries; Homestate College is the contingent tertiary beneficiary.

If no beneficiary is named, or if all primary and contingent beneficiaries are deceased at the time of the insured's death, the proceeds are paid to the policyowner or to his or her estate, if the policyowner is deceased.

More than One Beneficiary Per Category

Policyowners may name more than one beneficiary in any category, whether the category is primary, secondary or tertiary. When they do so, however, they should specify the percentage or dollar amount of the proceeds that each is to receive. Most companies recommend that each beneficiary's share be indicated as a fraction. For instance, assume Harry specifies that the proceeds of his $50,000 life insurance policy are to be paid out as follows: $25,000 to his wife, Louise, and the remaining $25,000 to his son, Jack. When Harry dies, there is a $20,000 loan against the policy. Consequently, in accordance with the way Harry designated his beneficiaries, Louise will receive $25,000 and Jack will receive $5,000. Had Harry specified that his wife and his son were to share equally (50 percent) in the proceeds, the remaining death benefit would have been distributed more equitably—$15,000 to each—which probably was Harry's intent.

Following is an example of a beneficiary designation that properly takes the proportioning of the proceeds into account:

> "One-half to my wife, Shirley Dawn Brown; one-fourth to my son, Curtis Rodney Brown; one-fourth to my daughter, Mary Lee Brown. In the event of the death of any beneficiary, their share shall be divided equally between the survivors or all shall go to the sole survivor."

Distribution by Descent

When life insurance policy proceeds are to be distributed to a person's descendents, a *per stirpes* or a *per capita* approach is generally used.

Per Stirpes

The term *"per stirpes"* means "by way of" or "by branches." A per stirpes distribution means that a beneficiary's share of a policy's proceeds will be passed on down to his or her living child or children in equal shares should he or she (the named beneficiary) predeceases the insured.

Per Capita

The term "*per capita*" means "per person" or "by head." A per capita distribution means that a policy's proceeds are paid only to the beneficiaries who are living and have been named in the policy.

Example of Per Stirpes vs. Per Capita

To illustrate the difference between per stirpes and per capita distributions, assume that Arthur names his wife as primary beneficiary and his two married children, Sam and Linda, as secondary beneficiaries to share equally "per stirpes." If Arthur's wife died before her husband, Sam and Linda would share equally in the proceeds, if they were living. But if Sam also were to predecease his father, leaving three children of his own, his share of the proceeds would be divided equally among his three children. Linda's share would remain the same.

Had Arthur used a per capita designation, naming Sam and Linda secondary beneficiaries, the full proceeds would be paid to Linda—her mother, the primary beneficiary, had already died and the only other named beneficiary, Sam, had also died. Sam's children would not be entitled to his share of the proceeds under a per capita distribution.

In short, the per capita beneficiary claims in his or her own right, while the per stirpes beneficiary receives the proceeds through the rights of another. Today, the per stirpes method of distribution is by far the more common approach.

Changing a Beneficiary

Beneficiary designations are also typified according to whether or not they may be changed after the policy is issued. Recall that the right to change beneficiary designations is a right of ownership, and it is one that policyowners may retain or give up at their discretion. The terms used to indicate this are *revocable beneficiary* and *irrevocable beneficiary*.

Revocable Beneficiary

When beneficiaries are designated "*revocable*," the policyowner can change them anytime he or she wants. A revocable beneficiary has no vested claim on the policy or its proceeds as long as the insured (or the policyowner, if different) is living.

Irrevocable Beneficiary

When beneficiaries are designated "*irrevocable*," the policyowner gives up the right to change them. Irrevocable beneficiaries have a vested right in the policy and the policyowner cannot exercise his or her rights of ownership without the beneficiary's consent. For example, a policyowner cannot borrow from the policy or assign it without written consent from the beneficiary.

If irrevocable beneficiaries agree in writing, control of the policy may be regained by the policyowners. Moreover, if irrevocable beneficiaries die before the insureds, control automatically reverts to the policyowners.

Special Situations

There are a few special situations that insurers must occasionally address with regard to the payment of policy proceeds. These include the simultaneous deaths of the insured and the beneficiary, how to prevent the proceeds paid to a beneficiary from being attached by creditors and situations in which insurers can pay proceeds to nondesignated beneficiaries.

Simultaneous Death

When an insured dies and the death benefit is payable to a named beneficiary, usually there is nothing to complicate the transaction. But what if the insured and the primary beneficiary die in the same accident and there is no evidence to show which one died first? How and to whom does the insurer pay the proceeds?

To address this problem, the *Uniform Simultaneous Death Act* has been enacted in most states. This law stipulates that if the insured and the primary beneficiary are killed in the same accident and there is not sufficient evidence to show who died first, the policy proceeds are to be distributed as if the *insured died last*. This law allows the insurance company to pay the proceeds to a secondary or other contingent beneficiary. If no contingent beneficiary has been named, the insured's estate will receive the proceeds.

The Uniform Simultaneous Death Act is only a partial solution to the problem, however. There are situations in which the primary beneficiary clearly outlives the insured, but only for the briefest time—minutes, hours or a few days. In these cases where the beneficiary obviously outlived the insured, if the provisions of the insurance contract were strictly followed, the insurer would pay the proceeds to the estate of the recently deceased primary beneficiary. Chances are, this would be contrary to the policyowner's wishes. The policyowner likely would have preferred that the proceeds be paid to a secondary beneficiary or to his or her own estate.

The problems resulting from the proximate but not (proven) simultaneous death of both the insured and the primary beneficiary prompted insurance companies to develop and offer a *common disaster provision* that gives policyowners greater control over payment of the policy proceeds. This provision, which may be part of the policy itself or incorporated into the beneficiary designation, activates only when the insured and the primary beneficiary die as a result of the same accident. It provides that:

1. If the insured and primary beneficiary die in the same accident, it is presumed that the insured died last. (This coincides with the Uniform Simultaneous Death Act.)

2. In addition, the primary beneficiary must outlive the insured by a definite period of time, as stipulated by the policyowner—14 days or 30 days are typical choices—or it is still assumed that the insured died last.

Thus, with a common disaster provision operating, a policyowner can be sure that if both the insured and the primary beneficiary die within a short period of time, the death benefits will be paid to the secondary beneficiary (if there is one) or to the insured's estate. Let's look at an example.

Burt and Carol, his wife by a second marriage and primary beneficiary of his $100,000 life insurance policy, are both killed in a single auto accident. Carol survives Burt by only 24 hours. Without a common disaster clause, the proceeds of Burt's policy would be paid to Carol's estate and possibly go to her children by her first marriage. Burt's children by his first marriage could be left out entirely. But because a common disaster provision was in effect in Burt's policy, the proceeds were instead paid to his estate, and distribution of the estate's assets made according to his wishes by virtue of his will.

Spendthrift Trust Clause

The *spendthrift trust clause* is another commonly used clause in life insurance policies. Its purpose is to help protect beneficiaries from the claims of their creditors. More precisely, it shelters life insurance proceeds that have not yet been paid to a named beneficiary from the claims of either the beneficiary's or policyowner's creditors.

The spendthrift clause does *not* apply to proceeds paid in one lump sum. As we will learn in the next chapter, proceeds may be held in trust by the insurer and paid to the beneficiary in installments over a period of time. The spendthrift clause pertains to these installment payment arrangements. Generally, the clause states that policy distributions payable to the beneficiary after the insured dies are not assignable or transferable and may not be attached in any way.

For example, assume Al is receiving monthly installment income payments from the proceeds of his late wife's life insurance policy. He buys an expensive sports car and later finds out that he cannot meet the payments on the car. If the finance company is awarded a judgment when it sues Al, his unpaid life insurance proceeds are protected against the claim. Of course, the finance company can still go after Al's other assets.

The spendthrift trust clause does not operate to protect proceeds that belong to the policyowner and are payable as income to the policyowner. It applies only to money held in trust by the insurance company that is earmarked to be paid to the named beneficiary at some future time. Spendthrift trust clauses are valid in the majority of states and are found in many life insurance policies.

Facility-of-Payment Provision

There are a few limited situations in which an insurer must pay proceeds to someone not designated as a beneficiary. A *facility-of-payment provision,* most typically found in industrial policies, permits an insurer to pay all or a portion of the proceeds to someone who, though not named in the policy, has a valid right. These situations include cases in which

- the named beneficiary is a minor;
- the named beneficiary is deceased;
- no claim is submitted within a specified period of time; or
- costs were incurred by another party for the deceased insured's final medical expenses or funeral expenses.

Summary

Designating an individual or entity as the *beneficiary* of a life insurance policy is one of the policyowner's most important rights. Insurance companies place very few conditions on this right, but care must be taken because the insurer is bound to follow the designation once it is established.

There are many ways to classify beneficiary designations: by *order of succession*—primary, secondary or tertiary; by the *number named* within each order; and *by descent*—per stirpes or per capita. Whether or not a beneficiary designation can be *changed* is also a consideration.

There are a few special situations insurers must address regarding the payment of life insurance proceeds. Should the insured and the primary beneficiary die simultaneously or within a short time of each other, the appropriate and fair disbursement of proceeds could be compromised. The *Uniform Simultaneous Death Act* and the *common disaster provision* help assure that the proceeds will be paid in line with the insured's wishes, as far as possible. The *spendthrift trust clause* protects unpaid insurance proceeds from claims by the beneficiary's creditors. Finally, the *facility-of-payment provision* allows an insurer to pay proceeds to someone not named in the policy, but who due to special circumstances, has a right to them.

Key Concepts

In preparing for their licensing examination, students should be familiar with the following concepts:

beneficiary designation options	irrevocable beneficiary
classifications of beneficiaries	Uniform Simultaneous Death Act
per stirpes	common disaster provision
per capita	spendthrift trust clause
revocable beneficiary	facility-of-payment provision

Chapter 6
Questions for Review *(Answers are located at the end of the book.)*

1. Sandra has a life insurance policy that states her husband, Gerald, is to receive the full death benefit. If he predeceases her, their three children are to share the benefit equally. If her husband and all three children predecease her, the benefit is payable to the First Community Church.

   All of the following statements are correct, EXCEPT:

   a. Gerald is the primary beneficiary.
   b. The three children are all secondary beneficiaries.
   c. The First Community Church is the tertiary beneficiary.
   d. The designation of the First Community Church can be contested by any of Sandra's relatives who survive the children.

2. The beneficiary on Walter's life insurance policy reads, "Children of the Insured."

   Which of the following phrases best describes this type of beneficiary designation?

   a. Juvenile beneficiaries
   b. Class beneficiaries
   c. Generational beneficiaries
   d. Attractive nuisance beneficiaries

3. Which of the following statements is/are correct?

   I. A "per capita" distribution specifies that a policy's proceeds are paid only to those beneficiaries who are living and have been named in the policy.
   II. A "per stirpes" distribution means that a beneficiary's share of a policy's proceeds will be passed down to his or her living child or children if the named beneficiary predeceases the insured.

   a. I only
   b. II only
   c. Both I and II
   d. Neither I nor II

4. If an irrevocable beneficiary dies before the insured, the _____ gains control of a life insurance policy.

   a. insured
   b. irrevocable beneficiary's children
   c. policyowner
   d. insurer

5. Christine's policy has a clause that reads as follows: "Should the primary beneficiary and the insured die in the same accident and the primary beneficiary fails to survive the insured by 14 days, it will be assumed that the beneficiary predeceased the insured."

   Which of the following phrases best describes this clause?

   a. Secondary beneficiary provision
   b. Facility-of-payment provision
   c. Uniform Simultaneous Death Act
   d. Common disaster provision

Life Insurance Premiums and Proceeds

Life Insurance Premiums • Premium Factors
• Life Insurance Policy Proceeds • Tax Treatment of Proceeds

People buy life insurance for the same basic reason they buy any product—it satisfies a need. In the case of life insurance, the need is financial security. Policyowners pay for this product through premiums. Upon the insured's death, policy proceeds (the "death benefit") are payable to the beneficiary in any one of a variety of ways, depending on the unique situation and needs of the beneficiary. This chapter examines these two important aspects of life insurance—premiums and proceeds. It also reviews the tax treatment of life insurance premiums and proceeds.

Life Insurance Premiums

The task of determining an insurance company's *premium* rates rests with the company's *actuaries*. Actuaries are mathematicians by education who are responsible for bringing together the financial and statistical data that have an influence on life (and health) insurance premium rates. Establishing realistic premium rates is a critical function in any life insurance company. Rates must be high enough to cover the costs of paying claims and doing business, yet low enough so that they are competitive with other insurers' rates.

Life insurance premium rates are generally expressed as an *annual cost per $1,000 of face amount.* For example, one company's rate for a male, age 35, is $13.73. What exactly does this mean? It means that for the particular policy in question (say, a $50,000 participating straight whole life policy), the policyowner, a male who was 35 when he purchased the policy, pays an annual premium of $13.73 for every $1,000 of face amount he purchased, or $686.50 ($13.73 × 50). Because it is a straight whole life policy, this policyowner will pay $686.50 per year for his life (or to age 100, if he is fortunate to live that long).

Primary Factors in Premium Calculations

Three primary factors are considered when computing the basic premium for life insurance: *mortality, interest* and *expense*. Of these, the mortality factor

Ill. 7.1 How the Life Insurance Premium Dollar Is Used

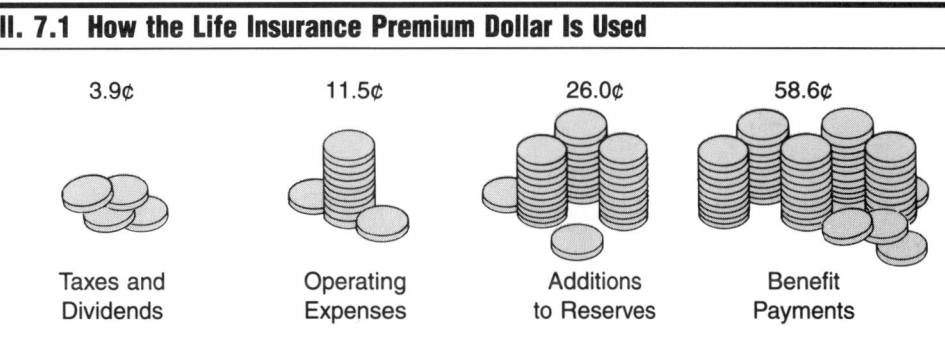

3.9¢	11.5¢	26.0¢	58.6¢
Taxes and Dividends	Operating Expenses	Additions to Reserves	Benefit Payments

Source: *1992 Life Insurance Fact Book*

has the greatest effect on premium calculations (commonly termed "*rate-making*"). That is, while an insurer's interest and expense factors are generally the same for all of its policyholders, the mortality factor can vary greatly, depending on personal characteristics of individual insureds.

Mortality Factor

A basic principle of life insurance is that it must be based on an accurate prediction of *mortality,* i.e., the average number of deaths that will occur each year in each age group. Throughout the years, statistics have been compiled, showing how many and at what ages people can generally be expected to die. Compiled, these statistics become *mortality tables,* which reflect death rates at each age.

In order for a mortality table to be accurate, it must be based on two things: *a large cross section of people* and *a large cross section of time.*

Illustration 7.2 is a sample mortality predictions table, taken from the 1980 Commissioner's Standard Ordinary, or CSO, Mortality Table. For easier reading, the starting group has been reduced to 100,000. (The complete CSO table reflects 10,000,000 lives.) Also, only ten-year age intervals are shown and the ages in between (except age 99) are not included.

The significance of mortality predictions to an insurance company is that they provide a basis to estimate how long its insureds will live, how long they will be paying premiums and at what future dates the company will have to pay out benefits. Consequently, the portion of the premium associated with mortality reflects the pure cost of providing death protection. Actuaries use mortality tables and mortality data as the first step in establishing premium rates.

Interest Factor

When policyowners pay premiums to a life insurance company, the funds do not sit idle in the insurer's vaults. They are combined with other funds and invested to earn *interest.* Among other things, this interest earned helps hold down the cost of life insurance premiums.

An insurer makes two assumptions with regard to interest. First, it assumes that a *specific net rate of interest will be earned* on all its investments. Actu-

Ill. 7.2 1980 CSO Mortality Table

Age	Number Living at Start of Year	Deaths Within Year
0	100,000	418
10	98,783	72
20	97,542	185
30	95,800	166
40	93,772	283
50	89,666	602
60	80,842	1,300
70	62,742	2,479
80	32,745	3,237
90	6,458	1,432
99	108	108
100	0	0

The figures above are a sampling from the 1980 CSO Mortality Table, showing, out of a starting group of 100,000 individuals, how many are expected to die within certain years. For example, out of 100,000 people, 93,772 are expected to be living at the age of 40; during that 40th year, 283 are expected to die.

Notice the mortality patterns this table reveals. The first year of life is one of relatively high mortality. The mortality rate of 418 deaths during the year out of the original group of 100,000 is not matched again until age 45 (not shown in this illustration).

At age 1 (not illustrated), the number dying is 107, and the rate continues to decline until age 10 (with 72 deaths, it is the lowest in the table). Then begins the climb up. Older teens and young adults face an increased risk of death. But from a rate of 185 deaths at age 20, the mortality actually decreases as this population matures through its 20s. The rate at age 29 is 164, the lowest it will be for the remainder of this population's average life expectancy.

From a high of 3,300 at age 78 (the highest rate in the table), the rate once again begins to decline—a sign that if one can make it this long, the odds of making it to 100 actually improve.

Actuaries know that many people live longer than the average life expectancy. Nonetheless, it is an indisputable fact that everyone dies eventually, so actuaries have set age 100 as the somewhat arbitrary age at which the last person in the original population of 100,000 dies. It is at age 100, therefore, that whole life policies mature or endow.

---

ally, some investments will earn more than the assumed rate and some will earn less, so the company selects an average rate for its assumption. The assumed interest rate may seem low (generally, 3½ percent to 4½ percent), but it directly affects the premium levels that are guaranteed to policyowners for years into the future. Thus, the assumed rates must be reasonably conservative.

The second assumption made by the company is that one full year's interest will be earned by each premium policyowners pay. Therefore, it must be assumed that *all premiums are paid at the beginning of the year.*

Because there is no reliable basis for predicting future interest rates or trends, a company must remain conservative in its interest assumptions, because it is committed to the interest rate guaranteed in its life insurance policies for as long as those policies remain in force. Interest earnings on invested premiums is the second consideration in premium rate calculations; the higher the assumed rate of interest, the lower the premium rate charged to policyowners.

Expense Factor

The third factor affecting premium rates is *expenses*. As does any business, an insurance company has various operating expenses. Personnel must be hired and paid; sales forces must be recruited, trained and compensated; supplies must be purchased; rent must be paid; and buildings must be maintained. Too, local, state and federal taxes must be paid. Each premium must carry its small proportionate share of these normal operating costs.

Thus, an expense factor is computed and included in the premium rates for life insurance. Sometimes the expense factor is called the "loading charge."

Net vs. Gross Premiums

The factors basic to premium calculations—mortality, interest and expense—are only a portion of the equation. Actuaries use the assumptions underlying these factors and translate them into *net single premium, net level premiums* and *gross premiums*.

The *net single premium* can be defined as the single amount needed today to fund the future benefit. Basically, it is the amount of premium, when combined with interest, that will be sufficient to pay the future death benefit. However, only rarely do people purchase life insurance with a single premium because of the large cash outlay required. Most pay premiums over a number of years. Thus, the net single premium is converted into *net annual level premiums,* with some adjustments due to a lesser amount of interest these smaller premiums will earn. Finally, the *gross premium* is determined, which reflects the addition of the expense factor. The gross premium is what the policyowners are required to pay.

In very general terms, actuaries deduct the assumed interest earnings from the mortality cost. The mortality cost less the assumed interest earnings equals the net premium. The expense factor then is added to the net premium to arrive at the gross premium.

The two key formulas to keep in mind are:

1. Net single premium = mortality cost − interest

2. Gross premium = net single premium + expense

Other Premium Factors

The preceding discussion focused on the three primary factors underlying all life insurance premiums. When evaluating *individual* applications for life insurance, other premium factors come into play, all of which influence mortality, to one degree or another.

1. *Age.* As we have seen, the age of an individual has a direct bearing on mortality, and mortality is figured directly into premium calculations. The older the insured, the greater the mortality risk.

2. ***Sex.*** The sex of the applicant also has a bearing on mortality. Experience has shown that, on the average, women live five or six years longer than men. Statistically, then, they are considered better life insurance risks than men and their premium rates have usually been lower than those for men.*

3. ***Health.*** Another factor influencing mortality is the health of the applicant. Obviously, those in poorer health represent a higher risk than those in good health.

4. ***Occupation or avocation.*** An applicant's occupation or avocation can also affect mortality. Those employed in hazardous occupations pose a greater risk to an insurer, as do those who engage in dangerous hobbies.

5. ***Habits.*** An individual's personal habits may also influence the premium rate he or she will be assessed. Habits such as smoking or overeating adversely affect health and may increase the risk of death.

Factors such as these are considered carefully by insurance company underwriters, whose job it is to evaluate and select risks. In those cases where an individual applicant represents a higher-than-normal risk to the insurer, due to one or more of these personal characteristics, he or she is known as a "*substandard risk.*" Of course, insurers can reject a substandard risk, and some applicants are denied. However, another way to treat a substandard case is to adjust the premium to reflect the increased risk. This approach is known as "*rating.*"

Methods of Rating Substandard Risks

There are a number of approaches insurance companies use to set or adjust premiums for substandard cases. These methods include *extra percentage tables, permanent flat extra premiums, temporary flat extra premiums, rate-up in age* and *liens*. Let's briefly review each.

Extra Percentage Tables

Although the *extra percentage tables* rating system varies somewhat from company to company, it is the one used most extensively today. This method involves a numerical system for rating substandard cases, so the premium charged, for example, may be from 125 percent to 500 percent of standard. A number of premium rates usually are established for each age and type of policy. The system assumes there are a certain number of extra deaths per thousand that will increase with age for all kinds of cases.

Permanent Flat Extra Premiums

The *permanent flat extra premiums* rating system adds a fixed charge of so many dollars per $1,000 of insurance for substandard cases. This additional

---

*It should be noted that many insurance companies have adopted "unisex" rating tables, which effectively disregard the difference in mortality rates and charges between men and women of the same age.

charge is assessed for the extra risk, which is measured in extra deaths per thousand. The flat extra premiums do not increase the policy's cash or nonforfeiture values. Any extra premium may be removed when the insured's condition is believed to have changed to a point where the risk is reduced.

Temporary Flat Extra Premiums

The *temporary flat extra premiums* rating system is identical to the permanent flat extra premium system, except that the fixed additional premium is charged for a specified number of years. With either permanent or temporary flat extra premiums, the amount of the additional charge generally will vary with the type of policy. A temporary extra premium may be charged when most of the extra risk is anticipated during the early years the policy is in force (e.g., perhaps the first few years following surgery).

Rate-Up in Age

Though the *rate-up in age* system of rating substandard cases is no longer widely used, it warrants mention. Under this method, the proposed insured is assumed to be a number of years older than he or she really is and the policy is issued with a correspondingly higher premium.

Lien System

Under the *lien system,* a policy is issued at standard rates on a substandard applicant, but with a lien against the policy. This lien reduces the amount of insurance automatically in the event the insured dies from a cause cited in the policy (and which resulted in the rating). Generally, this system is used now only with some money-purchase pension plans where premiums are uniform. However, this system has had major drawbacks, primarily because insureds have not understood that they are getting less protection than is shown as the face amount of their policies.

Level Premium Funding

As mentioned earlier, the age of an insured has direct influence on the mortality charge—the higher the age, the higher the mortality charge. Since the mortality charge has a direct impact on the amount of premium, it stands to reason that as a person ages, the premium rate for that person should increase.

In Chapter 4, it was pointed out that term insurance is characterized, in part, by steadily increasing premiums. The most dramatic example of this is annually renewable term insurance. With ART policies, policyowners are paying for pure insurance protection only, meaning that they will pay, in any given year, the cost of insurance for that year. The older an insured becomes, the higher the mortality charge becomes and, thus, the higher the premium becomes.

In Chapter 4, the concept of *level premiums* was also introduced. As we discussed, life insurance is issued with premiums calculated and payable on a level basis for the policy's life. If the policy is a term policy, the premiums are level for the duration of the term; if the policy is a whole life policy, the premiums are level for life or, in the case of a limited pay policy, for the duration of the premium-paying period.

How is this possible? If the mortality rate (and consequently the mortality charge) for an insured increases each year, how can any type of life insurance permit its premiums to remain level for the life of the policy? The answer lies in the funding method underlying the policy.

All forms of permanent insurance (and those types of term whose periods extend beyond one year) are based on the *level premium funding method*. A full explanation of this complex actuarial concept is beyond the scope of this book; however, it is possible to simplify the explanation. Under the level premium funding method, the insured pays *more* than the insurance protection requires in the policy's early years; in the policy's later years, when the increasing mortality charge would normally increase the premium to a very high level, the excess paid in the early years is used to help fund the additional cost now required.

Interest plays an important role in this process. The "excess" funds paid in the early years will earn interest, thus making it possible to keep the actual premium level lower than if interest were not considered. In essence, *the level premiums collected under a permanent policy are actuarially (i.e., mathematically) equivalent to the sum of the increasing annual renewable term rates for the same insured risk and for the same period of time*. Because of the "time value of money," (that is, the influence of interest) the actual sum of out-of-pocket premiums paid under a permanent policy (or a term policy that extends for a number of years) will be significantly less than those paid under an ART policy, all other factors (e.g., age and policy face amount) being equal.

Reserves vs. Cash Values

What happens to those "excess funds" that are paid in the early years of a permanent policy? Because they are not actually required to cover the insurance risk at that time, they are set aside for the future time when they will be required. As one might guess, the unused funds belong to the policyowner; they constitute the policy's *cash value*. It is easy to see how important these funds are to the overall funding of the policy, especially in the policy's later years. This also explains why any loan against the cash value must be offset by a reduction in the proceeds paid out of the policy, unless the policyowner returns the borrowed funds, with interest.

People sometimes confuse the term *policy cash value* with *policy reserve*. While the two are similar in concept, there are some important differences. Basically, the cash value is a tangible amount that represents the additional funds paid in the early years of a whole life policy. It is, quite literally, the "savings element" of a whole life policy. The policy reserve is more intangible; it is a fund required by each state's insurance laws to be set aside to assure that money will be available to pay future claims.

Literally, the policy reserve is the amount which, when added to the present value of future *net* premiums, will equal the present value of future claims. A very simple example will better illustrate this. Note that the term "present value" simply means the value *today* of a sum which will be larger in the future, after it accrues interest.

Assume the policyholder is 38 years old, owns a $50,000 permanent policy and is actuarially expected to live to age 78. The annual net premium is $450, and the company is using an assumed interest rate of 4 percent.

1. Present value of the future claim: $10,400
2. Present value of the future premiums: −8,900
3. Reserve liability (1−2): $1,500

This example shows that, with a 4 percent interest rate assumption, the present value of the $50,000 death benefit is $10,400. In other words, if $10,400 were invested at 4 percent interest for the next 40 years, it would grow to $50,000. The present value of future premiums is $8,900. If this amount were set aside to earn 4 percent interest, it would accumulate to an amount actuarially equivalent to the $450 premium the owner is paying each year. The difference, $1,500, is the required policy reserve.

Reserves are treated as a liability, meaning that companies must keep the reserve amount as a liability, not an asset, on their books. It is money that must be set aside to assure policyowners (and state regulators) that sufficient funds will be available when a claim arises.

Modes of Premium Payment

Policyowners ordinarily may pay their premiums under one of four modes: annually, semi-annually, quarterly or monthly. On any policy anniversary date (or at other times, if company rules permit) a policyowner may change from one payment mode to another, provided the payment is not less than a minimum specified by the company. There is a slight extra charge when premiums are not paid annually, as all gross premiums are calculated on an annual basis. The extra charge is to cover the additional paperwork and to make up for interest lost by the company because it does not have the full annual premium in advance to invest.

All premiums are payable in advance. The first premium is due on the day the policy is issued. Subsequent premiums become payable at the end of the period for which the preceding premium was paid. The first premium usually is paid to the agent at the time of application. If not paid then, it must be paid at the time of policy delivery. Premiums have to be paid to keep a policy in force, although policyowners have the right to stop paying premiums at any time.

Tax Treatment of Premiums

As a general rule, premiums paid for personal life insurance policies by individual policyowners are considered to be personal expenses and, therefore, are not deductible from gross income. Also, premiums paid for business life insurance usually are not deductible. For example, if the ABC Corporation purchased a key-person life insurance policy on the life of its president, the premiums are not deductible by the corporation.

But there are a few exceptions to this rule:

- Premiums paid for life insurance owned by a qualified charitable organization *are* deductible.

- Premiums paid for life insurance by an ex-spouse as part of an alimony decree *are* deductible (as alimony).

> **Ill. 7.3**
>
> ### The Claims Process
>
> It is the duty of the insurance company's *claims department* to make sure that a death claim is handled promptly and properly. At the very least, the claims examiner will require a certified death certificate, which states in part the cause of the insured's death. The examiner will review the policy to determine if there is a reason to contest the claim. For example, if the cause of death was suicide, the claims examiner will want to know if the policy is still within the suicide exclusion period. If the insured was murdered, the laws of most states prevent life insurance proceeds from being paid to the beneficiary if the beneficiary was an accomplice to the murder.
>
> Even if death resulted from natural causes, the examiner will review the policy carefully, especially if it is within the contestable period, to determine if the insured's application contained any misrepresentations that could void the contract. At the very least, the claims examiner will make sure that the actual age and sex of the insured agree with company records. Assuming that there is no reason to contest the claim (which is true in the majority of cases), the examiner will authorize payment of the death benefit to the policy beneficiary.
>
> The next question the examiner will seek to answer is, did the policyowner wish the proceeds to be paid in any particular manner or can the beneficiary select the manner of proceeds distribution (more properly called the *settlement option*). If the policyowner did not specify a particular option, and if the beneficiary does not wish to select any settlement option, the claim will be paid as a lump sum. Oftentimes, though, either the policyowner or the beneficiary will select a settlement option.

- Premiums paid by a business creditor for life insurance purchased as collateral security for a debt *are* deductible.

- Premiums paid by an employer for employee group life insurance *are* deductible as an employee benefit business expense, as long as certain conditions are met.

Tax Treatment of Cash Values

The yearly increase in the cash value of a whole life insurance policy is not taxed during the period it accumulates inside the policy. If the cash value is taken out while the insured is still living—for example, as retirement income—a substantial portion of each retirement income payment is received tax free, because it represents a return of principal. Let's look at this in more detail.

With regard to the taxation of surrendered cash values, a policyowner is allowed to receive tax free an amount equal to what he or she paid into the policy over the years in the form of premiums. The sum of the premiums paid is known as the policyowner's *cost basis*. However, when the accumulated cash value exceeds the premiums paid—when the cash value is greater than the policyowner's cost basis—the difference is taxable. For example, assume that at the age of 65, Mel decides to surrender his whole life policy and take the $28,000 accumulated cash value in a lump sum. He paid a total of $19,000 in premiums over the years. The difference between his cost basis and the accumulated value ($28,000 − $19,000 = $9,000) will be treated as taxable income in the year Mel actually receives it.

As long as a policy is not surrendered, the cash value continues to accumulate tax free. There is never a tax imposed on the policyowner, even if the cash value exceeds the cost basis, as long as the cash value remains in the policy.

Life Insurance Policy Proceeds

One thing that distinguishes life insurance from other forms of insurance is that a life insurance policy kept in force long enough is inevitably going to pay a benefit. When this benefit is payable due to the death of the insured, it is known as the policy's *death proceeds*.

The proceeds of a life insurance policy can be paid out in a variety of ways. The choice is up to the policyowner, as a right of ownership, or he or she may leave the decision to the beneficiary. These payment options are known as *settlement options*.

Types of Proceeds Settlement Options

The selection of the appropriate settlement option should be based on the wishes of the insured and the needs of the beneficiary. The variety of options insurers offer makes the selection fairly easy, since the decision usually rests on whether the beneficiary will need the entire amount at once or as income, payable over time. There are five settlement options available.

Lump-Sum Cash Option

Many years ago, all life insurance policy proceeds were paid out in single *lump-sum cash* settlements. Today, this option is still available, though not used to the extent of some of the others.

Interest-Only Option

Under the *interest-only option,* the insurance company holds the proceeds for a specified period of time and, at regular intervals, pays the beneficiary a

Ill. 7.4 Interest-Only Option

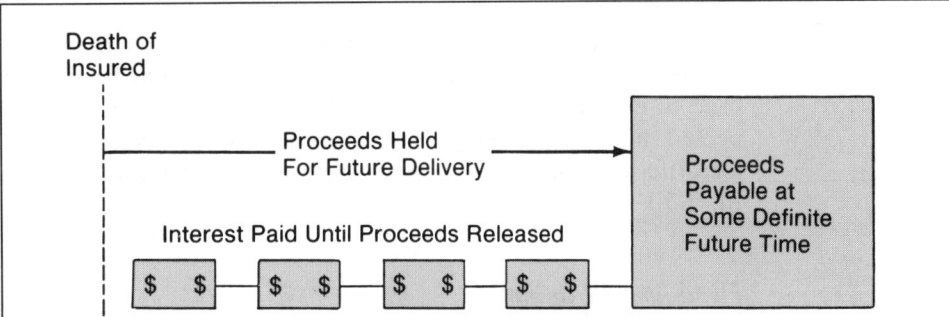

The interest-only option provides that the insurance company hold the death proceeds in trust for a specified time, during which the interest earned on the proceeds is paid to the beneficiary at stated intervals. For example, a policyowner may direct that upon his death, the beneficiary is to receive interest payments until age 60, and then the proceeds should be paid out as monthly income from then on, under a life income plan.

Ill. 7.5 Fixed-Period Option

A fixed-period settlement option provides for equal payments of an amount that will exhaust the principal and interest by the end of the fixed period.

guaranteed rate of interest on the proceeds. The proceeds themselves are then paid out at the end of the specified period, either in cash or under one of the other settlement options.

Because the interest is paid out rather than accumulated, the proceeds of the policy remain the same and intact. Interest payments to the beneficiary may be made monthly, quarterly, semi-annually or annually. The interest rate will never be lower than the guaranteed rate specified in the policy, but it can be higher. If the company has sufficiently high earnings, it might pay additional interest over and above the guaranteed minimum. (See Ill. 7.4.)

Fixed-Period Option

Under the *fixed-period* (or fixed-time) *option,* the company pays the beneficiary equal amounts of money at regular intervals over a *specified period of years.* This option pays out both principal (proceeds) and the interest earned. The amount of each installment payment is determined by the *length of the desired period of income.* Thus, the longer the period of income, the smaller each payment will be. Conversely, the shorter the period, the larger each payment amount.

If company earnings are large enough to permit paying excess interest, the excess interest will be used to make each payment larger. It will *not* be used to extend the payment period. If company earnings are lower than expected, the guaranteed payments to the beneficiary cannot be reduced. Guaranteed life insurance payments may always be more, but may never be less. (See Ill. 7.5.)

Fixed-Amount Option

Under a *fixed-amount option,* the policy proceeds plus interest are used to pay out a *specified amount of income* at regular intervals for as long as the proceeds last. The policyowner or beneficiary requests the size of payment desired. The amount of each income payment is fixed, and the duration of the payment period varies according to the payment amount. If excess interest is credited, it will be used to extend the payment period; the amount of each payment remains the same. (See Ill. 7.6.)

Ill. 7.6 Fixed-Amount Option

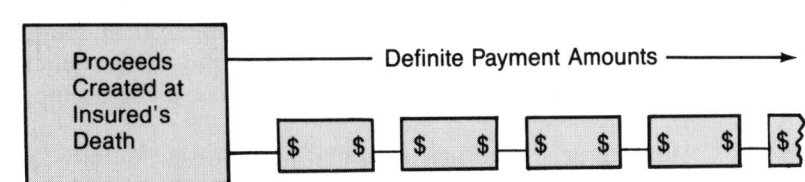

The fixed-amount option involves the payment of equal installments of a stated amount, payable until the principal and interest are exhausted. For example, if the proceeds of a $25,000 policy are paid out under this option at a guaranteed 3 percent rate and the monthly income amount selected was $200, the duration of the payment period would be longer than if the monthly payments were $300.

Life Income Options

Under a *life income option,* of which there are many, the beneficiary receives a *guaranteed income for life*—no matter how long he or she lives. This unique concept is successful because the principal and interest of life insurance proceeds are paid out together, with the amount of payment actuarially calculated and guaranteed to last a lifetime. Even if the principal is depleted, income payments will continue, so long as the primary beneficiary lives. Essentially, the insurance company uses the death benefit to purchase a *single payment immediate annuity* for the beneficiary. As you will learn in Chapter 10, the purpose of annuities is to provide an income stream for the *duration of an individual's life.*

Because the life income settlement options are the same as annuity income options, a detailed discussion is reserved for Chapter 10. For now, note that these options are:

- Straight life income option
- Cash refund option
- Installment refund option
- Life with period certain option
- Joint and survivor option
- Period certain option

Tax Treatment of Proceeds

To understand the taxation of life insurance proceeds, remember one basic principle—*death benefits* paid under a life insurance policy to a named beneficiary are free of federal income taxation. However, *interest* paid by an insurance company on death benefit proceeds left with the company is taxable income, just as interest payments made by any financial institution are taxable. The same principle applies in the case of life insurance policy dividends; the *dividends* themselves are free of income taxation, but *interest* under a dividend option is taxable in the year the interest is paid.

Proceeds Paid at the Insured's Death

When an insured dies, proceeds of a life insurance policy paid as a lump-sum death benefit to a beneficiary are exempt from federal income tax. The amount paid under a double indemnity provision and the benefits from any paid-up additions to a life insurance policy also are tax exempt.

When proceeds to an individual are paid out on any kind of installment basis—as would be the case with the fixed-amount, fixed-period or life income options—a portion of each payment consists of principal and a portion consists of interest. The portion of the proceeds attributed to interest is taxable; the remaining portion of the proceeds is received tax free. This method of taxing life insurance proceeds is consistent with what is known as the *annuity rule*.

Under the annuity rule, a fixed, unchanging fraction of each payment is considered a return of principal and so is excluded from gross income for tax purposes. Thus, that portion of the proceeds representing principal is received tax free. The balance of each payment representing interest income is taxable as ordinary income. The percentage of each payment to be exempted is determined by dividing the insured's investment in the contract by the expected return. The expected return is based on the insured's life expectancy.

On the other hand, when the death proceeds of a policy are held by the insurance company under the *interest-only option* (the company holds the proceeds for a specified period of time and, at regular intervals, pays the beneficiary a guaranteed rate of interest on the proceeds), the interest payments are taxable as ordinary income to the beneficiary. The principal amount, when it is finally paid out, still represents tax-free income.

Accumulated *dividends,* which are not properly classed as life insurance proceeds, also are exempt from federal income tax. The interest element in installment payments, as explained above, is taxable income.

Transfer for Value Rule

Another tax provision applies in certain cases. This is called the *"transfer for value"* rule. If a policy is transferred by assignment or otherwise for "valuable consideration" (i.e., the policy is sold to another party) and the insured dies, the person who then owns the policy will be taxed on the excess of the proceeds over the consideration paid, including any premiums paid by the transferee. However, the rule does *not* apply to certain transfers, including transfers for value to the insured, to a partner (or partnership) of the insured or to a corporation in which the insured is a shareholder or an officer.

Proceeds Paid During the Insured's Lifetime

As noted on page 98, the taxation of accumulated values received when a policyowner surrenders a policy is determined by his or her cost basis. Only the excess of such proceeds over the cost of the policy is taxable. (The policyowner's cost basis is figured as total premiums paid, less policy dividends received, less any policy loan and less extra premiums paid for supplementary benefits, such as waiver of premium or accidental death benefits.)

Endowment policy proceeds, even though left with the company at maturity under an interest-only option, will be partially taxable under the rule of *constructive receipt*. The taxable amount will be the excess of the proceeds over the premiums paid, the rationale being that the insured has the right to withdraw the endowed proceeds and so has them in "constructive receipt."

The policyowner has 60 days, after the policy maturity date, to exercise an annuity option before the rule of constructive receipt takes effect.

1035 Policy Exchanges

Another provision of the Internal Revenue Code pertains to life insurance policies that are exchanged or transferred for another "like-kind" policy. Typically, when an individual realizes a gain on a financial transaction, that gain is taxed. For example, as we just learned, if a policyowner surrenders a life insurance policy and receives the cash value, he or she will realize a gain to the extent that the cash value exceeds the amount of premiums paid. That gain is considered ordinary income and is fully taxable. However, if a policy is exchanged for another, Section 1035 of the Tax Code stipulates that no gain (or loss) will be recognized. Consequently, the transaction is not subject to any tax. The following kinds of exchanges are allowed under this provision:

- a life insurance policy for another life insurance policy, endowment policy or annuity contract;

- an endowment policy for an annuity contract; and

- an annuity contract for another annuity contract.

Life Insurance and the Insured's Estate

When an insured dies, the value of any life insurance policy he or she owned is included in his or her gross estate for federal *estate tax* purposes. State death taxes also may be payable. The proceeds payable at death to a beneficiary, as explained previously, are not subject to federal income tax.

Any accumulated policy dividends, although exempt from income tax, are also included in the insured's gross estate for federal estate tax purposes.

Summary

There are three primary factors in a life insurance premium. The *mortality charge* has the greatest influence in making one insured's premium different from another insured's, assuming the two people represent different risks to the insurance company. The mortality charge is reduced by expected *interest earnings,* which is the second premium factor; these two factors constitute the *net premium*. The insurer's cost of doing business is partly recouped through an *expense charge,* the third premium factor which, when added to the net premium, equals the *gross premium*.

Generally, life insurance premiums are not tax deductible unless the premiums qualify as some other form of expense that is tax deductible (e.g., alimony payments or charitable contributions).

Life insurance proceeds can be paid out in a variety of ways. The standard means of paying a death benefit is in a lump sum. However, either the policyowner or the beneficiary can select another *settlement option,* as an alternate method of paying a policy's proceeds.

Life insurance death benefits are paid with no income tax consequence, with one exception. If the *transfer for value* rule applies, the recipient of the proceeds will be taxed on a portion of the proceeds that exceeds the amount paid for the policy.

Federal income taxes are payable on interest earnings credited to a policy on either death benefit proceeds or policy dividends that have been left with the company.

Key Concepts

In preparing for their licensing examination, students should be familiar with the following concepts:

premium factors
cash value
settlement options

tax treatment of premiums and proceeds

Chapter 7
Questions for Review *(Answers are located at the end of the book.)*

1. A mortality table reveals which of the following?

   a. There is no death rate for persons age 99.
   b. Who will die in any given year
   c. The average number of deaths that will occur each year in any age group
   d. The death rate normally is higher in the lower age groups.

2. All of the following are primary premium factors, EXCEPT:

   a. expense.
   b. interest.
   c. dividends.
   d. mortality.

3. Which of the following statements pertaining to life insurance premiums is/are correct?

   a. Lucy, who is substantially overweight, has applied for a life insurance policy. Her weight may affect her insurability, but not the amount of premium on her policy.
   b. Harold and Billy, both age 25, each buy a whole life policy from the same company. However, Harold has a participating policy, while Billy's policy is nonparticipating. Harold will pay a higher premium.
   c. The most significant factor in premium rate calculation is interest.
   d. All of the above

4. Which of the following statements pertaining to life insurance premiums is correct?

   a. The premiums for a policy that insures a spouse are tax deductible.
   b. A company may purchase key-person life insurance and deduct the premiums as a business expense.
   c. Premiums for group term insurance covering employees are tax deductible, assuming certain requirements are met.
   d. Premiums for policies in which the insured is someone other than the policyowner are tax deductible.

5. Art, the owner and insured under a $75,000 life policy, is killed in an accident. He had paid total premiums of $26,000. How much of the death benefit will be included in his gross estate for estate tax purposes?

   a. $26,000
   b. $49,000
   c. $0
   d. $75,000

6. With regard to the situation described in Question 5, how much of the $75,000 death benefit that was paid to Art's wife in a lump sum is taxable income to her?

   a. $0
   b. $26,000
   c. $49,000
   d. $75,000

7. All of the following statements pertaining to life insurance policy settlement options are correct, EXCEPT:

   a. By using the interest-only option, two or more settlement options can be combined for added flexibility.
   b. Payments under the interest-only option may be made at a rate higher than the guaranteed minimum.
   c. Diane and Rhonda each are receiving monthly income from their deceased husbands' identical life insurance policies under the fixed-period option. Diane's payments are to be made for 15 years and Rhonda's for 20 years. Diane receives the larger monthly payments.
   d. Under the fixed-period option, the payment of excess interest will lengthen the payment period.

8. Assume the following persons buy identical life insurance policies from the same company. Generally speaking, who will pay the lowest premium, if all have standard ratings?

   a. Linda, age 28
   b. Thomas, age 28
   c. Louise, age 40
   d. Joe, age 45

9. Sarah, age 65, the owner of a $150,000 whole life policy, decides to surrender the policy and take the $90,000 cash value in a lump sum. Over the years, she has paid a total of $54,000 in premiums. How much, if any, of the payment will be taxed?

   a. $0
   b. $36,000
   c. $54,000
   d. $90,000

10. Beth, age 50, the beneficiary of her late husband's life insurance policy, has elected to receive the proceeds in monthly installments over the next five years. Due to the insurer's interest earnings, Beth notices that the amount of the payments is often more than what she was guaranteed. What kind of settlement option did Beth select?

   a. Life income option
   b. Fixed-amount option
   c. Cash value option
   d. Fixed-period option

11. Under the _____ option, the insurer holds the death proceeds for a specified period of time and, at regular intervals, pays the beneficiary a guaranteed rate of interest on the proceeds.

   a. fixed-period
   b. interest-only
   c. fixed-amount
   d. life-income

8

LIFE INSURANCE UNDERWRITING AND POLICY ISSUE

Purpose of Underwriting • The Underwriting Process
• Field Underwriting Procedures • Policy Issue and Delivery

Who is qualified to purchase life insurance and who is not? The process of answering this question is called *risk selection,* a function that is performed by insurance company underwriters. Sales representatives are sometimes called field underwriters, indicating the important role they also play in helping the company decide if an applicant is an insurable or uninsurable risk. This chapter looks at the overall underwriting process, as well as the important processes of policy issue and policy delivery.

The Purpose of Underwriting

Insurance companies would like nothing more than to be able to sell their policies to anyone wishing to buy them. However, they must exercise caution in deciding who is qualified to purchase insurance. Issuing a policy to someone who is uninsurable is an unwise business decision that can easily mean a financial loss for the company.

Each insurer sets its own standards as to what constitutes an insurable risk versus an uninsurable risk, just as each insurer determines the premium rates it will charge its policyowners. Every applicant for insurance is individually reviewed by a company underwriter, to determine if he or she meets the standards established by the company to qualify for its life insurance coverage.

Underwriting, another term for risk selection, is the process of reviewing the many characteristics that make up the risk profile of an applicant to determine if the applicant is insurable and, if so, at standard or substandard rates. There are two basic questions underwriters seek to answer about an applicant:

1. Is the applicant *insurable?*

2. If the applicant and insured are two different people, *does an insurable interest exist* between the two of them?

Ill. 8.1

What Constitutes Insurable Interest?

Though laws differ slightly from state to state, in general the following types of relationships automatically carry insurable interest:

- An individual has an insurable interest in his or her life.
- A husband or wife has an insurable interest in a spouse.
- A parent has an insurable interest in his or her child.
- A child has an insurable interest in a parent or grandparent.
- A business has an insurable interest in the lives of its officers, directors and key employees.
- Business partners have an insurable interest in each other.
- A creditor has an insurable interest in the life of a debtor (but only to the extent of the debt).

Does Insurable Interest Exist?

As discussed in Chapter 3 and Chapter 6, *insurable interest* is extremely important in life insurance. Without this requirement, people could purchase life insurance and the policy would be nothing more than a wagering contract. As we have established, an insurable interest exists when the death of the insured would have a clear financial impact on the policyowner. Individuals are presumed to have an insurable interest in themselves; therefore, when the applicant and proposed insured are the same person, there is no question that insurable interest exists. Questions are raised, however, with "third-party" contracts—those in which the applicant is not the insured. Some relationships are automatically presumed to qualify as an insurable interest—spouses, parents, children and certain business relationships. (See Ill. 8.1.) In most other cases, the burden is upon the applicant to show that an insurable interest exists.

It bears repeating that with life insurance, an insurable interest must exist only at the policy inception; it does not necessarily have to exist when the policy proceeds are actually paid. Thus, for example, a policyowner could assign a life policy to someone who has no insurable interest in the insured, and the assignment would nonetheless be valid.

Is the Applicant Insurable?

Once the underwriter determines that insurable interest exists, the next question is, "Is the applicant insurable?" The answer lies in the underwriting process.

The Underwriting Process

The underwriting process is accomplished by reviewing and evaluating information about an applicant and applying what is known of the individual against the insurer's standards and guidelines for insurability and premium rates.

Underwriters have several sources of underwriting information available to help them develop a risk profile of an applicant. The number of sources checked usually depends on several factors, most notably the size of the requested policy and the risk profile developed after an initial review of the application. The larger the policy, the more comprehensive and diligent the underwriting research. Regardless of the policy size, if the application raises questions in the underwriter's mind about the applicant, that, too, can trigger a review of other sources of information.

The most common sources of underwriting information include the *application*, the *medical report*, an *attending physician's statement*, the *Medical Information Bureau, special questionnaires, inspection reports* and *credit reports*.

The Application

The *application* for insurance is the basic source of insurability information. Regardless of what other sources of information the underwriter may draw from, the application—the first source of information to be reviewed—will be evaluated thoroughly. Thus, it is the agent's responsibility to see that an applicant's answers to questions on the application are recorded fully and accurately. (A sample application appears in the Appendix.)

There are three basic parts to a typical life insurance application: *Part I—General, Part II—Medical* and *Part III—Agent's Report.*

Part I—General

Part I of the application asks general questions about the proposed insured, including name, age, address, birth date, sex, income, marital status and occupation. Also to be indicated here are details about the requested insurance coverage:

- type of policy;

- amount of insurance;

- name and relationship of the beneficiary;

- other insurance the proposed insured owns; and

- additional insurance applications he or she has pending.

Other information sought may indicate possible exposure to a hazardous hobby, foreign travel, aviation activity or military service. Whether or not the proposed insured smokes is also indicated in Part I.

Part II—Medical

Part II focuses on the proposed insured's health and asks a number of questions about the health history, not only of the proposed insured, but of his or her family, too. This medical section must be completed in its entirety for every application. Depending on the proposed policy face amount, this section may or may not be all that is required in the way of medical information. The individual to be insured may be required to take a medical exam.

Part III—Agent's Report

Part III of the application is often called the "agent's report." This is where the agent reports his or her personal observations about the proposed insured. Because the agent represents the interests of the insurance company, he or she is expected to complete this part of the application fully and truthfully.

In this important section, the agent provides first-hand knowledge about the applicant's financial condition and character, the background and purpose of the sale and how long the agent has known the applicant.

The agent's report also usually asks if the proposed insurance will replace an existing policy. If the answer is "yes," most states demand that certain procedures be followed to protect the rights of consumers when policy replacement is involved.

The Medical Report

Quite often a policy is issued on the basis of the information provided in the application alone. Most companies have set nonmedical limits, meaning that applications for policies below a certain face amount (perhaps $50,000 or even $100,000) will not require any additional medical information other than what is provided by the application. However, for larger policies (or smaller policies when the applicant is older than a certain age) a *medical report* may be required to provide further underwriting information. If the application's medical section raises questions specific to a particular medical condition, the underwriter may also request an *"attending physician's statement"* (APS) from the physician who has treated the applicant. The statement will provide details about the medical condition in question.

Medical reports must be completed by a qualified person, but that person does not necessarily have to be a physician. Many companies accept reports that are completed by a paramedic or a registered nurse. Usually the applicant can select the physician or paramedic facility to perform the exam; insurers are also prepared to recommend paramedic facilities where the exam can be given. In almost all cases, the expense for the exam is borne by the insurance company.

When completed, the medical report is forwarded to the insurance company, where it is reviewed by the company's medical director or a designated associate.

The Medical Information Bureau

Another source of underwriting information that specifically focuses on an applicant's medical history is the *Medical Information Bureau* (MIB). The MIB is a nonprofit central information agency that was established years ago by a number of insurance companies to aid in the underwriting process. The bureau is supported by more than 700 member insurance companies.

Its purpose is to serve as a reliable source of medical information concerning applicants and to help disclose cases where an applicant either forgets or conceals pertinent underwriting information, or submits erroneous or misleading medical information with fraudulent intent. The MIB operations help to hold down the cost of life insurance for all policyowners through the prevention of misrepresentation and fraud.

This is how the system works: If a company finds that one of its applicants has a physical ailment or impairment listed by the MIB, the company is pledged to report the information to the MIB in the form of a code number. By having this information, home office underwriters will know that a past problem existed should the same applicant later apply for life insurance with another member company. The information is available to member companies only and may be used only for underwriting and claims purposes.

Each member company and its medical director sign a pledge to follow the rules and principles of the MIB. The basic requirements are:

- Applicants for life insurance must be notified in writing that the insurance company may make a brief report on their health to the MIB.

- Applicants must be advised that, should they apply to another MIB company for coverage or if a claim is submitted to such a company, the MIB will supply any requested information in its files to the company.

- Applicants must sign authorization forms for information from the MIB files to be given to a member company.

- The MIB will arrange the disclosure of any information it has concerning an applicant upon request by the applicant. Medical information, however, will be disclosed only to the individual's physician, who then can interpret best the facts for the applicant (patient).

Special Questionnaires

When necessary, *special questionnaires* may be required for underwriting purposes to provide more detailed information related to aviation or avocation, foreign residence, finances, military service or occupation. For example, if an applicant has a hobby of skydiving, the insurance company needs detailed information about the extent of his or her participation to determine whether or not the insurance risk is acceptable. The most common of these special questionnaires is the *aviation questionnaire* required of any applicant who spends a significant amount of time flying, such as an airline pilot.

Inspection Reports

Inspection reports usually are obtained by insurance companies on applicants who apply for large amounts of life insurance. These reports contain information about prospective insureds, which is reviewed to determine their insurability. Insurance companies normally obtain inspection reports from national investigative agencies or firms.

The purpose of these reports is to provide a picture of an applicant's general character and reputation, mode of living, finances, and any exposure to abnormal hazards. Investigators or inspectors may interview employees, neighbors and associates of the applicant as well as the applicant.

Inspection reports ordinarily are not requested on applicants who apply for smaller policies, although company rules vary as to the sizes of policies that require a report by an outside agency.

Credit Reports

Some applicants may prove to be poor credit risks, based on information obtained before a policy is issued. Thus, *credit reports* obtained from retail merchants' associations or other sources are a valuable underwriting tool in many cases.

Applicants who have questionable credit ratings can cause an insurance company to lose money. Applicants with poor credit standings are likely to allow their policies to lapse within a short time, perhaps even before a second premium is paid. An insurance company can lose money on a policy that is quickly lapsed, because the insurer's expenses to acquire the policy cannot be recovered in a short period of time. It is possible, then, that home office underwriters will refuse to insure persons who have failed to pay their bills or who appear to be applying for more life insurance than they reasonably can afford.

The Fair Credit Reporting Act of 1970

To protect the rights of consumers for whom an inspection report or credit (or consumer) report has been requested, Congress in 1970 enacted the *Fair Credit Reporting Act*. As previously mentioned, this federal law applies to financial institutions that request these types of consumer reports, including insurance companies.

The Fair Credit Reporting Act, or FCRA, established procedures for the collection and disclosure of information obtained on consumers through investigation and credit reports; it seeks to ensure fairness with regard to confidentiality, accuracy and disclosure. The FCRA is quite extensive. Included in it are the following important requirements pertaining to insurers:

- Applicants must be notified (usually within three days) that the report has been requested. The insurer must also notify the applicant that he or she can request disclosure of the nature and scope of the investigation. If the applicant requests such disclosure, the insurer must provide a summary within five days of the request.

- The consumer must be provided with the names of all people contacted during the preceding six months for purposes of the report. People contacted who are associated with the consumer's place of employment must be identified as far back as two years.

- If, based on an inspection or consumer report, the insurer rejects an application, the company must provide the applicant with the name and address of the consumer reporting agency that supplied the report.

- If requested by the applicant (more formally, the "consumer"), the consumer reporting agency—not the insurance company—must disclose the nature and substance of all information (except medical) contained in the consumer's file. Note that the file may be more extensive than the actual report that was provided to the insurer. The Fair Credit Reporting Act does not give consumers the right to see the actual report, although most reporting agencies do routinely provide copies of the report, if requested.

- If the applicant/consumer disagrees with information in his or her file, he or she can file a statement giving his or her opinion on the issue.

Classification of Applicants

Once all the information about a given applicant has been reviewed and evaluated, the underwriter seeks to classify the risk that the applicant poses to the insurer. In a few cases, an applicant represents a risk so great that he or she is considered uninsurable and his or her application will be rejected. However, the vast majority of insurance applicants fall within an insurer's underwriting guidelines and accordingly will be classified as a *standard risk, substandard risk* or *preferred risk.*

Standard Risk

Standard risk is the term used for individuals who fit the insurer's guidelines for policy issue without special restrictions or additional rating. These individuals meet the same conditions as the tabular risks on which the insurer's premium rates are based.

Substandard Risk

A *substandard risk* is one below the insurer's standard or average risk guidelines. An individual can be rated as substandard for any number of reasons: poor health, a dangerous occupation or attributes or habits that could be hazardous. Some substandard applicants are rejected outright; others will be accepted for coverage but with an increase in their policy premium.

Preferred Risk

Many insurers today reward exceptionally good risks by assigning them to a *preferred risk* classification. Preferred risk premium rates are generally lower than standard risk rates. Personal characteristics that contribute to a preferred risk rating include not smoking, weight within an ideal range and favorable cholesterol levels.

Field Underwriting Procedures

As noted earlier, an agent plays an important role in underwriting. As a *field underwriter,* he or she initiates the process and is responsible for many important tasks: proper solicitation, completing the application thoroughly and accurately, obtaining appropriate signatures, collecting the initial premium and issuing a receipt. Each of these tasks is vitally important to the underwriting process and policy issue.

Proper Solicitation

As a representative of the insurer, an agent has the duty and responsibility to solicit "good business." This means that an agent's solicitation and prospecting efforts should focus on cases that fall within the insurer's underwriting guidelines and represent profitable business to the insurer. At the same time, the agent has a responsibility to the insurance-buying public to observe the highest professional standards when conducting insurance business. All sales solicitations should be open and aboveboard, with the agent clearly identifying the insurer he or she represents and the reason for the call. In addition, good sales practices avoid "high pressure tactics" and are aimed at helping applicants select the most appropriate policies to meet their needs.

In many states, an agent is required to deliver to the applicant a *"Life Insurance Buyer's Guide"* and a *"Policy Summary."* These documents are usually delivered before the agent accepts the applicant's initial premium. Typically, the "Buyer's Guide" is a generic publication that explains life insurance in a way that average consumers can understand. It speaks of the concept in general, and does not address the specific product or policy being considered.

The "Policy Summary" addresses the specific product. It identifies the agent, the insurer, the policy and each rider. It includes information about premiums, dividends, benefit amounts, cash surrender values, policy loan interest rates and life insurance cost indexes of the specific policy being considered.

Completing the Application

As mentioned earlier, the application is one of the most important sources of underwriting information and it is the agent's responsibility to see that it is completed fully and accurately. As part of the process, several signatures are required and to overlook a needed signature will cause delay in issuing a policy. Note that in some jurisdictions, a child must be a minimum age (e.g., 15 or 18) to sign a life insurance application; otherwise, an adult, such as a parent, must sign.

Each application requires the signatures of the *proposed insured,* the *policyowner* (if different from the insured) and the *agent* who solicits the application. If the policyowner is to be a firm or corporation, one or more partners or officers, other than the proposed insured generally must sign the application.

If additional questionnaires regarding an applicant's aviation or avocation activities are required for underwriting purposes, they also need the signatures of the applicant and the agent.

Where required by state law, the agent also must sign a form attesting that a disclosure statement has been given to the applicant. Moreover, a form authorizing the insurance company to obtain investigative consumer reports or medical information from investigative agencies, physicians, hospitals or other sources generally must be signed by the proposed insured and the agent as witness.

When premiums are to be paid according to an automatic check plan, forms for that purpose also must be signed by the applicant.

Initial Premium and Receipts

It is generally in the best interests of both the proposed insured and the agent to have the initial premium (or a portion of it) paid with the application. For the agent, this will usually help solidify the sale and may accelerate the payment of commissions on the sale. The proposed insured benefits by having the insurance protection become effective immediately, with some important restrictions.

On the other hand, if a premium deposit is not paid with the application, the policy will not become valid until the initial premium is collected. Recall from the discussion in Chapter 3 that one of the requirements for a valid contract is *consideration*. In the case of an insurance contract, the consideration is the first premium payment plus the application. An insurer will not allow an applicant to possess a policy without receipt of the initial premium. There is one exception to this rule. The applicant may be allowed to sign an *inspection receipt* and obtain the policy for inspection purposes. However, the ten-day free-look policy provision makes this generally unnecessary today.

Applicants who pay a premium deposit with the application are entitled to a *premium receipt*. It is the type of receipt given that determines exactly when and under what conditions an applicant's coverage begins. The two major types of receipts are *conditional receipts* and *binding receipts* (sometimes called *temporary insurance agreements*).

Conditional Receipts

The most common type of premium receipt is the *conditional receipt*. A conditional receipt indicates that certain conditions must be met in order for the insurance coverage to go into effect. There are two types of conditional

---

Ill. 8.2

Conditional Receipts

When a conditional receipt is given, the applicant and the company form what might be called a *"conditional contract"*—contingent upon conditions that exist at the time the application is signed (or when the medical exam is completed, if required). In providing early coverage, the insurer conditionally assumes the risk and will provide coverage from the specified date, on the condition that the applicant is approved for policy issue.

For example, assume an agent sells a $50,000 nonmedical life insurance policy to Matthew, who hands the agent his signed application with a check for the first premium. In turn, Matthew receives from the agent a conditional receipt for the premium. Two days later, Matthew becomes seriously ill and enters the hospital. So long as the company finds that Matthew qualifies for the policy as applied for, the company will issue the policy, regardless of his condition in the hospital. In fact, if Matthew died before the policy was issued, but was qualified at the time of application, his beneficiary still would receive the $50,000 death benefit.

However, in this example, if the company's underwriter determined that Matthew was uninsurable, and thus rejected the application, then there is no coverage, even during the period when the receipt was effective.

receipts: the *insurability type* and the *approval type*. Both specify what conditions are required for coverage; the primary distinction between the two is when the coverage goes into effect.

1. **Insurability Receipt.** The insurability type of receipt provides that when the applicant pays the initial premium, coverage is effective—on the condition that the applicant proves to be insurable—either on the date the application was signed or the date of the medical exam, if one is required. For instance, with this type of receipt, if the applicant dies between the date of application or of the medical exam and the date the insurer actually approves the application, the coverage is retroactively effective, as long as the applicant proved to be insurable on the specified date.

    On the other hand, with the insurability type of receipt, if the applicant proves to be uninsurable as of the date of application or of the medical exam, no coverage takes effect and the premium is refunded.

2. **Approval Receipt.** The approval type of receipt is more restrictive than the insurability type. In general, with the approval type, coverage is effective only after the application has been approved by the insurer (and before the policy is actually delivered to the policyowner). Because they offer only a short period of special protection and are usually frowned upon by the courts, approval types of receipts are rarely used today.

With conditional receipts, if the applicant is found to be insurable, but only on a substandard or rated basis, no retroactive protection is provided. This is because the applicant did not qualify for the policy he or she applied for (and to which the receipt pertains); instead, the insurer will counter with an offer of another policy at a different rate. Consequently, if an applicant who has a conditional receipt is found to be substandard, and dies prior to accepting the rated policy counteroffered by the insurer, there would be no coverage.

Companies usually impose a limit on the amount of coverage provided under a conditional receipt (generally $100,000 or less). Therefore, even if the applicant is applying for a policy with a much higher face amount, the insurer will usually restrict the conditional coverage to a specified limit.

Binding Receipts

Under the *binding receipt* (or temporary insurance agreement), coverage is guaranteed, even if the proposed insured is found to be uninsurable, until the insurer formally rejects the application. Since the underwriting process can often take several weeks or longer, this can place the company at considerable risk; accordingly, binding receipts are often reserved only for a company's most experienced agents.

Like the conditional receipt, a binding receipt typically stipulates a maximum amount that would be payable during the special protection period.

The provisions a binding receipt contains can vary slightly from company to company. Generally, however, upon payment of the initial premium at time of application, the receipt provides the following:

- The applicant is covered at the time of application (or on the date a later medical examination is completed, if required) for the amount of insur-

III. 8.3 Life Insurance Policy Cost Comparison Methods

> Insurance producers sometimes encounter a competitive situation in which a prospect is considering two or more policies. In a situation like this, producers who can accurately compare the true costs of each policy may have an advantage.
>
> Rarely are two policies so closely alike that a true "apples to apples" comparison can be made (one company may provide a "free" waiver of premium provision, for example). Fortunately, however, there are some established methods of comparing policy costs. While it is beyond the scope of this book to provide an in-depth review of each, producers should be familiar with the two primary methods: *traditional net cost* and *interest adjusted net cost*.
>
> #### Traditional Net Cost Method
>
> Under the *traditional net cost method*, projected premiums for a certain time period (say, 20 years) are totalled. Projected policy dividends (if any) and the cash value at the end of that period are subtracted from the total. The resulting number, divided by the number of years in the comparison, yields the net cost per thousand per year.
>
> This method is no longer permitted in many states because of one significant flaw—it ignores the time value of money. Money placed in an investment vehicle (like insurance) earns interest. Different companies apply different interest rates to their policies. By ignoring this fact, traditional net cost comparison falls short in projecting the real cost of a policy.
>
> #### Interest Adjusted Net Cost Method
>
> The *interest adjusted net cost method* is widely used today to compare policy costs. It is calculated in much the same way as the traditional net cost method, except that it adds the extra component of *interest* to the formula. The interest factor used is based on each company's projected interest rate. In this way, the cost estimates more accurately reflect the actual cost of a policy.

ance applied for—but usually not to exceed a maximum of $100,000 under all outstanding receipts. The temporary coverage continues until the policy is issued as requested, until the company offers a different policy or until the company rejects the application—but in no event for more than 60 days from the date the agreement was signed.

- If a medical examination is required, the temporary insurance coverage does not begin until the examination has been completed. But, if death *accidentally* occurs within 30 days from the date of the agreement, the death benefit is paid even though the medical examination was not taken.

- The applicant must pay in advance at least one month's premium for the policy being applied for. Furthermore, there must be no material misrepresentations in the application, and the death must not result from suicide.

Policy Effective Date

An important question that must be addressed in any life insurance sale is, when does the policy become effective? The effective date is important for two reasons: not only does it identify when the coverage is effective, it establishes the date by which future annual premiums must be paid, as well.

If a receipt (either conditional or binding) was issued in exchange for the payment of an initial premium deposit, the date of the receipt will generally be noted as the policy effective date in the contract.

If a premium deposit is *not* given with the application, the policy effective date is usually left to the discretion of the insurer. Often, it will be the date the policy is issued by the insurance company. However, the policy will not be truly effective until it is delivered to the applicant, the first premium is paid and a "Statement of Continued Good Health" is obtained.

Back Dating

As we have learned, the premiums required to support a life insurance policy are determined, in part, by the insured's age. If an applicant can be treated by the insurance company as being a year younger, the result can be a lifetime of slightly lower premiums. Thus, it is understandable that applicants might want to *"back date"* a policy, making it effective at an earlier date than the present, in order to "save age."

As surprising as it may seem, many insurers are willing to let an applicant back date a policy. As one might guess, though, there are some important conditions that must be met before this step can be taken.

First of all, the insurer must allow back dating. Second, the company will usually impose a time limit on how far back a policy can be back dated (typically six months, the limit imposed by most states' laws). More important, the policyowner is required to pay all back-due premiums and the next premium is due at the back-dated anniversary date (which can be as close as six months in the future).

Preliminary Term for Interim Coverage

Some applicants for life insurance desire immediate protection but, for one reason or another, want to defer the issue dates of their policies for several months or to some specific date in the future. This usually can be accomplished by using *preliminary* (or interim) *term insurance.*

Companies ordinarily allow preliminary term to be used to defer the effective date of the original policy from 1 to 11 months. Premiums for preliminary term are based on the age of the insured at the time of application. The premium for the principal policy involved is based on the age of the insured at the end of the interim period.

By using preliminary term, the applicant can be insured without delay and still postpone payment of premium on the principal policy for one or more months.

Policy Issue and Delivery

After the underwriting is complete and the company has decided to issue the policy, other departments in the company assume the responsibility for issuing the policy. Once issued, the policy document is sent to the sales agent for delivery to the new policyowner. The policy usually is not sent directly to the policyowner, since as an important legal document it should be explained, by the sales agent, to the policyowner.

Constructive Delivery

From a legal standpoint, policy delivery may be accomplished without physically delivering the policy into the policyowner's possession. *"Constructive delivery,"* which satisfies the legal interpretation, is accomplished technically if the insurance company intentionally relinquishes all control over the policy and turns it over to someone acting for the policyowner, including the company's own agent. Mailing the policy to the agent for unconditional delivery to the policyowner also constitutes constructive delivery—even if the agent never personally delivers the policy. However, if the company instructs the agent not to deliver the policy unless the applicant is in good health, there is no constructive delivery.

Mere possession of a policy by the client does not actually establish delivery if all conditions have not been met. For example, a policy may be left with an applicant for inspection and an inspection receipt obtained to indicate that the policy is neither in force during the inspection period nor will it be in force until the initial premium has been paid.

Explaining the Policy and Ratings to Clients

Most applicants will not remember everything they should about their policies after they have signed the application. This is another reason agents should deliver policies in person. Only by personally delivering a policy does the agent have a timely opportunity to review the contract, its provisions, exclusions and riders. In fact, some states (and most insurers) insist that policies be delivered in person for this very reason. The agent's review is especially important, for it helps to reinforce the sale. It can also lead to future sales by building the client's trust and confidence in the agent's abilities and desire to be of genuine service.

Explaining the policy and how it meets the policyowner's specific objectives helps avert misunderstandings, policy returns and potential lapses. Agents sometimes may have a chance to prepare applicants in advance when it appears that policies may be rated as substandard. And sometimes both agent and policyowner may be surprised when the policy is issued as a rated contract. In either case, the agent usually can stress reasons why the insured has an even greater need for insurance protection because of the physical impairment or condition. Indeed, it may be the policyowner's "last chance" to purchase such coverage, because a worsening of the condition responsible for the rating could render the person completely uninsurable.

Obtaining a Statement of Insured's Good Health

In some instances, the initial premium will not be paid until the agent delivers the policy. In such cases, common company practice requires that, before leaving the policy, the agent must collect the premium and obtain from the insured *a signed statement attesting to his or her continued good health.*

The agent then is to submit the premium with the signed statement to the insurance company. Because there can be no contract until the premium is paid,

Ill. 8.4 From Application to Policy Delivery

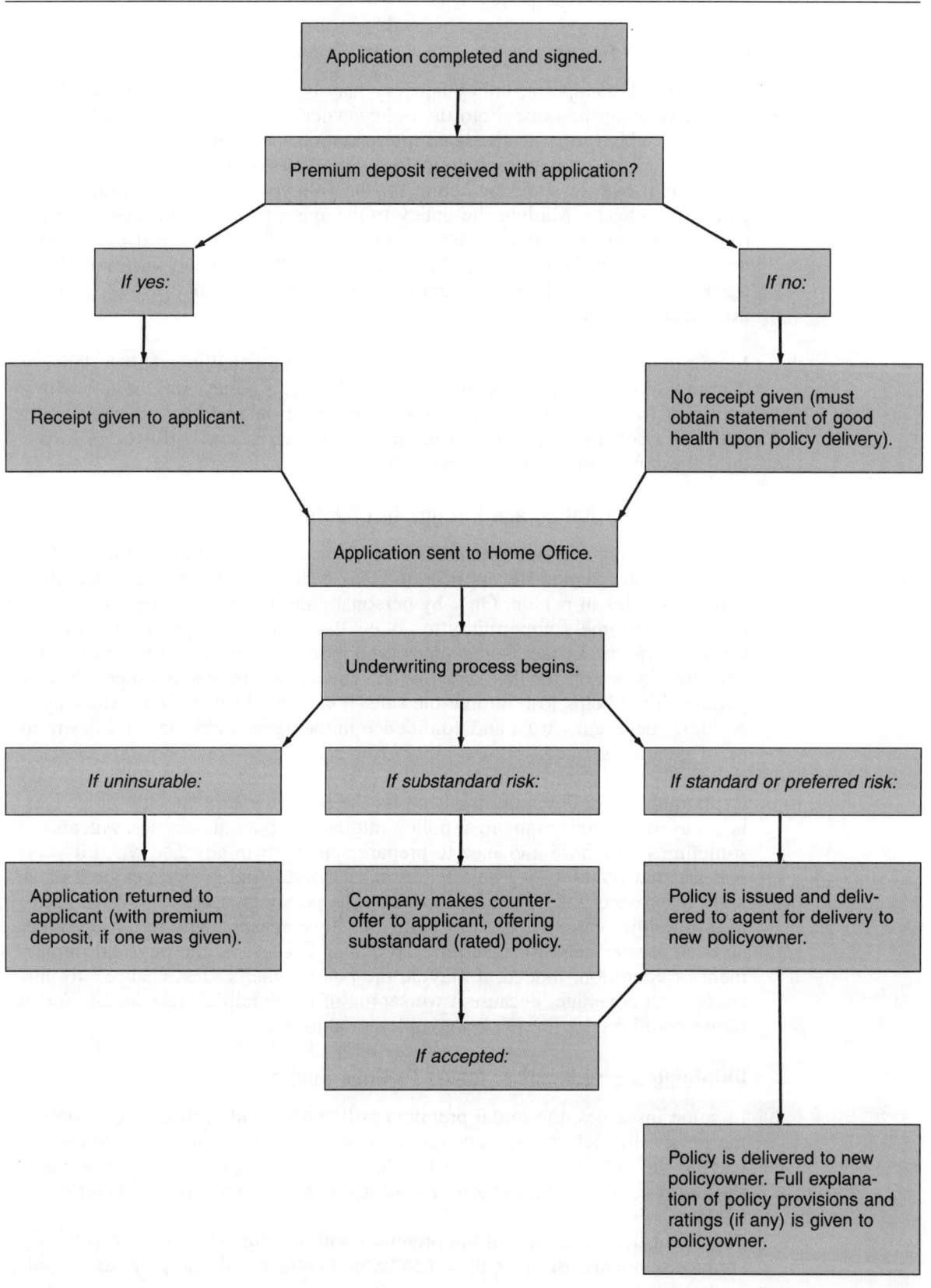

the company has a right to know that the policyowner has remained in reasonably good health from the time he or she signed the application until receiving the policy. In other words, the company has the right to know if the policyowner represents the same risk to the company as when the application was first signed.

Summary

It is during the *underwriting process* that an insurance company decides if it is going to issue a policy to an applicant. The underwriter seeks to determine if the proposed insured is *insurable,* and if so, at *standard, substandard* or *preferred* rates. Underwriters *assign* rates to proposed insureds, based on the risks the applicants represent to the insurers.

The effective date of the policy depends on whether or not an initial premium deposit was paid with the application (thus requiring the agent to issue either a *conditional* or *binding receipt*) as well as the date requested by the applicant (policies can be *back dated* in some situations).

Policy delivery is an important responsibility of the sales agent.

Key Concepts

In preparing for their licensing examination, students should be familiar with the following concepts:

- the underwriting process
- standard vs. substandard ("rated") policies
- insurable interest
- Medical Information Bureau
- consumer and investigative reports
- Fair Credit Reporting Act
- the application
- standard risk
- substandard risk
- preferred risk
- required signatures
- initial premium deposits
- conditional receipts
- binding receipts
- policy delivery
- effective date of coverage
- statement of good health
- explaining the policy to the client
- proper solicitation
- traditional net cost method
- interest adjusted net cost method

Chapter 8
Questions for Review *(Answers are located at the end of the book.)*

1. Underwriting is a process of
   a. selection and issue of policies.
   b. evaluation and classification of risks.
   c. selection, reporting and rejection of risks.
   d. selection, classification and rating of risks.

2. Which of the following statements pertaining to a life insurance policy application is correct?

   a. The names of both the insured and the beneficiary are indicated on the application.
   b. If an applicant's age is shown erroneously on a life insurance application as 28 instead of 29, the result may be a premium quote that is higher than it should be.
   c. The size of the policy being applied for does not affect the underwriting process.
   d. The agent's report in the application must be signed by the agent and the applicant.

3. If a medical report is required on an applicant, it is completed by

   a. a home office underwriter.
   b. a paramedic or examining physician.
   c. the agent.
   d. the home office medical director.

4. Which of the following statements pertaining to the Medical Information Bureau (MIB) is correct?

   a. The MIB is operated by a national network of hospitals.
   b. Information obtained by the MIB is available to all physicians.
   c. The MIB provides assistance in the underwriting of life insurance.
   d. Applicants may request that MIB reports be attached to their policies.

5. Which of the following statements regarding the Fair Credit Reporting Act (FCRA) is correct?

   a. Applicants must be notified within a short period of time that their credit report has been requested.
   b. If an applicant for insurance is rejected based on a consumer report, the name of the reporting agency must be kept confidential.
   c. If requested to do so, the insurance company must provide the actual consumer report to the applicant.
   d. Consumer reports are final in nature and cannot be disputed by an applicant.

6. All of the following statements about the classification of applicants are correct, EXCEPT:

   a. A substandard applicant can never be rejected outright by the insurer.
   b. Applicants who are preferred risks have premium rates that are generally lower than standard rate risks.
   c. An individual can be rated as a substandard risk because of a dangerous occupation.
   d. A standard applicant fits the insurer's guidelines for policy issue without special restrictions.

7. The Fair Credit Reporting Act

    a. prohibits insurance companies from obtaining reports on applicants from outside investigative agencies.
    b. provides that consumers have the right to question reports made about them by investigative agencies.
    c. applies to reports about applicants that are made by insurance agents to their companies.
    d. All of the above

8. Elaine signs an application for a $50,000 nonmedical life policy, pays the first premium and receives a conditional insurability receipt. If Elaine were killed in an auto accident two days later

    a. the company could reject the application on the basis that death was accidental.
    b. her beneficiary would receive $50,000, if Elaine qualified for the policy as applied for.
    c. the premium would be returned to Elaine's family because the policy had not been issued.
    d. the company could reject the death claim because the underwriting process was never completed.

9. Generally, the party who delivers an insurance policy to the new policyowner is

    a. the insurance company's home office.
    b. the sales agent.
    c. the state insurance commissioner's office.
    d. the underwriter.

10. The primary distinction between the insurability and approval types of conditional receipts is when the

    a. applicant pays the initial premium.
    b. coverage goes into effect.
    c. medical exam is given.
    d. applicant proves insurable.

Group Life Insurance

Principles of Group Insurance • Features of Group Insurance
• Eligible Groups • Group Life Insurance
• Other Forms of Group Life Coverage

Up to this point, the focus of our discussion has been individual life insurance plans, policies and underwriting. However, as noted in Chapter 4, one of the general categories of insurance is group insurance. Group insurance is a way to provide life insurance and/or health insurance coverage for a number of people under one contract. Typically, group insurance is provided by an employer for its employees; however, it is available to other kinds of groups, as we will see. In this chapter, we will take a look at the principles of group insurance in general, focusing specifically on group life insurance plans. Group health and disability plans are also available and will be discussed in detail in Chapter 22.

Principles of Group Insurance

The basic principle of *group insurance* is that it provides insurance coverage for a number of people under a single *master contract* or *master policy*. Because a group policy insures a group of people, it is the group—not each individual—that must meet the underwriting requirements of the insuring company.

Group insurance is most typically provided by an employer for its employees as a *benefit*. In these cases, the employer is the applicant and contract policyholder; the employees, as group members, are not parties to the contract—in fact, they are not even named in the contract. Instead, each employee who is eligible to participate in the plan fills out an enrollment card and is given a *certificate of insurance,* which summarizes the coverage terms and explains the employee's rights under the group contract. A list of individual employees covered under the contract is maintained by the insurer.

In most cases, it is the policyholder—the employer—that selects the type of insurance coverage the group will have and determines the amount of coverage the contract will provide for covered group members. In addition, it is typical for the employer to pay all or a portion of the premium. When an employer pays all of the premium, the plan is a *noncontributory plan* since the employees are not required to contribute to premium payments. If a group plan requires its members to pay a portion of the premium, it is a *contributory plan.*

Features of Group Insurance

To individual members covered by a group life or group health insurance plan, the function the insurance serves is identical to an individual plan. In the case of group life, should the covered member die, his or her beneficiary will receive a stated amount in death proceeds. In the case of group health, should the covered member become ill or disabled, the plan will provide a stated benefit amount to help cover the corresponding medical costs or replace income lost due to the disability. Thus, the purpose of group life and health plans is the same as individual life and health plans. However, there are a number of features of group plans that set them apart from individual plans.

Master Contract

As noted, the foremost distinction of a group plan is that it insures a number of people under *one contact.* Because of this, individual underwriting and individual evidence of insurability are generally not required. When it comes to underwriting, the insurer looks at the group as a whole, not at the health or habits or characteristics of individual members. Group insurance involves *experience rating,* which is a method of establishing a premium for the group based on the group's previous claims experience. The larger and more homogeneous the group, the closer it comes to reflecting standard mortality and morbidity rates.

Low Cost

Another characteristic of group insurance is that, per unit of benefits, it is available at *lower rates* than individual insurance, due primarily to the lower administrative, operational and selling expenses associated with group contracts. And because most employers pay all or part of the group premium, individual insureds are able to have insurance coverage for far less than what they would normally pay for an individual or personal plan.

Flow of Insureds

Finally, group insurance is distinguished by a *flow of insureds,* entering and exiting under the policy as they join and leave the group. In fact, in order for it to operate effectively, group insurance requires a constant influx of new members into the group, to replace those who leave and to keep the age and health of the group stable.

Eligible Groups

What kinds of groups are eligible for group insurance coverage? Generally, almost any kind of "natural group"—those formed for a purpose *other* than to obtain insurance—will be considered by an insurer. Insurable groups most typically fall into one of the following categories:

- Single-employer groups
- Labor unions
- Trade associations
- Creditor/debtor groups
- Fraternal organizations

In years past, only groups of a certain size, such as 50 or more, were eligible for group insurance. Today, in accordance with NAIC guidelines that do not set a minimum size limit, insurers often issue coverage to groups with as few as ten (or fewer) members.* It is important to note, however, that once a group policy is issued, insurers usually require that a certain number or percentage of eligible members must participate in order to keep the coverage in force.

Eligibility of Group Members

By its very nature, group insurance provides for participation by virtually all members of a given insured group. Whether or not an individual member chooses to participate usually depends on the amount of premium he or she must pay, if the plan is contributory. If the plan is noncontributory and the employer pays the entire premium, full participation is the general rule.

On the other hand, employers and insurers are allowed some latitude in setting minimum *eligibility requirements* for employee participants. For example, employees must be full-time workers and actively at work to be eligible to participate in a group plan. If the plan is contributory, the employee must authorize payroll deductions for his or her share of premium payments. In addition, a *probationary period* may be required for new employees, which means they must wait a certain period of time (usually one to six months) before they can enroll in the plan. The probationary period is designed to minimize the administrative expense involved with those who remain with the employer only a short time. The probationary period is followed by the *enrollment period,* the time during which new employees can sign up for the group coverage. If an employee does not enroll in the plan during the enrollment period (typically 31 days), he or she may be required to provide evidence of insurability if later he or she does want to enroll. This is to protect the insurer against adverse selection.

With these basics in mind, let's turn our attention to group life insurance plans. As noted, group health plans are discussed in Chapter 22.

---

*It should be noted that most states impose their own regulations on group insurance and often stipulate a minimum number of participants, usually ten, that constitute an eligible group.

Group Life Insurance

Today, approximately 40 percent of life insurance in force in the United States is group life insurance and billions of dollars more are purchased every year. In fact, as far as coverage amounts go, group life is the fastest growing life insurance line. At the end of 1991, group life insurance in force in the United States totaled more than $4 trillion. This represents an 8.1 percent increase in one year and is over two times the amount in force at the end of 1981. More and more, employees look to their group coverage to provide the foundation for their life insurance programs.

Types of Group Life Plans

There are many types of group life plans that insurers offer employers. The appropriate choice depends on the employer's objectives, needs and resources. Group life can be either term or permanent.

Group Term Life

Most group life plans are term plans, which use *annual renewable term (ART) insurance* as the underlying policy. This gives the insurer the right to increase the premium each year (based on the group's experience rating), and it gives the policyholder the right to renew coverage each year. As is characteristic of ART policies, coverage can be renewed without evidence of insurability. The prevalent use of ART insurance is another reason why the cost of group insurance is fairly low.

Group Permanent Life

Some group life plans are permanent plans, using some form of permanent or whole life insurance as the underlying policy. The most common types of permanent group plans are *group ordinary, group paid-up* and *group universal life*.

Group ordinary insurance is any type of group life plan—and there are many variations—that uses cash value life insurance in the plan. In some cases, the employees are allowed to own the cash value portion of the policy if they contribute to the plan. In other instances, an employee's termination results in the forfeiture of the cash value, which is then used to help fund the plan for the remaining employees.

With *group paid-up* plans, a combination of term and whole life insurance is used. Usually the employer pays for the term portion of the plan and employee contributions are used to purchase units of single-premium whole life. The sum of the employees' paid-up insurance and the employer-paid term insurance (usually decreasing term, to offset the annually increasing amount of paid-up insurance) equals the amount of life insurance the employees are entitled to under the plan. At retirement or termination, employees possess their paid-up policies.

A growing number of group life plans are using *universal life* insurance policies due to the flexibility these policies provide. The underlying policy contains the same features as individual universal life, but the policy is admin-

> **Ill. 9.1**
>
> ### Taxation of Group Life Premiums and Proceeds
>
> To encourage employers to provide employee benefits—such as a group life insurance plan—the federal government has granted these plans favorable tax treatment. To begin with, an employer may deduct the group plan premiums as a business expense. Secondly, the employee does not have to report the employer-paid premiums as income, as long as the insurance coverage is $50,000 or less. (Employees who are provided with more than $50,000 of coverage must declare as taxable income the premiums paid by the employer for the excess coverage.)
>
> Proceeds paid under a group life plan to a deceased employee's beneficiary are exempt from income taxation if they are paid in a lump sum. If the proceeds are paid in installments, consisting of principal and interest, the interest portion is taxed.
>
> In order for a group life insurance plan to receive favorable tax treatment, the government imposes some requirements to ensure that rank-and-file employees are not discriminated against in favor of select key employees. Basically, these requirements apply to eligibility and the type and amount of benefits provided. Regarding eligibility, the requirements are that:
>
> 1. the plan must benefit at least 70 percent of all employees; or
>
> 2. at least 85 percent of all participating employees must not be key employees.
>
> Regarding benefits, the requirements state that, again, the plan cannot discriminate in favor of key employees. For example, the amount of life insurance provided to all employees must bear a uniform relationship to their level of compensation or position.
>
> If a group life plan fails to meet these nondiscrimination requirements, the cost of the first $50,000 of coverage—normally excluded from gross income—will be included in a key employee's gross income for tax purposes. Rank-and-file employees are not so penalized.

istered in much the same way as any group ordinary policy. Characteristic of group universal life plans is that the employees pay most of the premium; however, they are given certain rights to policy ownership that are not found in ordinary group life plans.

How Benefits Are Determined

The type and amount of benefits provided to each insured member under a group life plan are typically predetermined by the employer as policyholder. Most employers will establish benefit schedules according to *earnings, employment position* or as a *flat benefit*. A set schedule, such as one of these, helps protect the insurer against adverse selection, since the employees do not have the option to insure themselves for any more or any less than the schedule allows.

1. *Earnings.* Under an earnings schedule, the amount of life insurance provided to individual employees is based on their salary or earnings. It can be a flat amount per earnings level or a percentage of earnings. For instance, an earnings schedule could provide each employee with life insurance coverage equal to 1½ times their salary.

2. *Employment position.* An employment position schedule sets the amount of life insurance according to an employee's position with the company. For example, general staff employees may be provided with $30,000 of life insurance, managers with $50,000, account supervisors with $75,000 and vice presidents with $100,000.

3. *Flat benefit.* A flat benefit schedule provides the same amount of life insurance to all employees, regardless of their earnings or position. Flat benefit schedules are most frequently used when the employer wants to provide only a small amount of insurance to its employees.

Conversion to Individual Plan

Once coverage becomes effective for an individual under a group life plan, it remains effective until he or she leaves the employer group (or the plan is terminated). Most group life policies contain a *conversion provision* that allows individual insured members to convert to an individual plan without evidence of insurability, if their employment is terminated. Usually, the employee has a limited period of time following termination (typically 31 days) in which to exercise the conversion privilege. This means that the group coverage will continue in force for the terminated employee for the duration of the conversion period, even if no conversion takes place. Thus, if a group-insured ex-employee were to die within 31 days after termination of employment, the group insurance death benefit would be payable to his or her beneficiary.

Most group conversion provisions require the individual to convert to a whole life policy, as opposed to term. The premium for the new policy is based on the individual's attained age at the time of conversion.

Other Forms of Group Life Coverage

There are a number of other kinds of group life insurance plans, three of which should be noted—*franchise life insurance plans, credit life insurance plans,* and *blanket life insurance plans.* In addition, as alternatives to traditional insured plans, *multiple employer trusts* and *multiple employer welfare arrangements* are becoming popular options.

Franchise Life Insurance

Franchise life insurance, sometimes called *wholesale insurance,* is a form of group insurance in that those covered are employees of a common employer or are members of a common association or society. However, franchise insurance deviates from the typical group insurance arrangement in that the employer or association is not the master policyholder; rather, it simply serves as the "sponsor" of the plan and collects premiums from its employees or members and remits them to the insurance company. (A franchise plan may provide for employer contributions.) Each individual insured under a franchise arrangement is given an individual policy. As long as he or she maintains a valid relationship with the employer or association and continues to pay the premiums, the insurance policy will remain in force. Under a franchise plan, the type and amount of insurance available to individual members is determined by the sponsoring association.

Franchise life plans are commonly used for small groups whose numbers are less than the minimum required by state law for group insurance coverage.

Group Credit Life Insurance

Group credit life insurance is another form of group insurance. A type of decreasing term insurance, it is issued by insurance companies to creditors to cover the lives of debtors in the amounts of their respective loans. Typically, it is provided through commercial banks, savings and loan associations, finance companies, credit unions and retailers.

If an insured dies before his or her loan is repaid, the policy proceeds are paid to the creditor to settle the remaining loan balance. Unlike regular group life insurance, premiums for group credit life may be paid wholly by the individual insureds. State laws, which vary, generally set a maximum amount of group credit life insurance per individual creditor (generally the creditor must have a minimum of 100 debtors per year) and limit the amount of insurance per borrower, which may not exceed the amount of indebtedness. Debtors cannot be forced to take the coverage from any particular insurance company. They have the right to choose their insurers.

Blanket Life Insurance

Blanket life insurance covers a group of people exposed to a common hazard. Individuals do not need to apply for blanket coverage and insurers do not need to provide each person with a certificate of coverage. Insureds are not specifically named in the policy because coverage is temporary. In fact, individuals may be covered for only a few hours at a time. Members of the group are automatically covered, but only while participating in the specific hazards named in the policy. For example, a blanket policy can be issued to the owner of an airline to cover its passengers. A person is covered by the blanket policy only while a passenger on that airline.

State insurance laws generally allow a number of groups to hold blanket life insurance policies. Some common policyholders include the following:

- A college, school or its principal, covering students, teachers or employees

- A religious, recreational or civic organization, covering its members while participating in specific hazards as part of an activity sponsored by the organization

- An employer, covering any group of employees who participate in specified hazards of employment

- A sports team, covering members while they are participating on the team

- A volunteer fire department, covering its firefighters while participating in specific hazards related to membership (such as fighting fires)

- A newspaper, covering its carriers

Multiple Employer Trusts (METs) and Multiple Employer Welfare Arrangements (MEWAs)

Some small businesses do not have enough employees to form a group large enough to qualify for group insurance. Insurance companies often permit small organizations of a similar nature to join together for insurance coverage, thereby forming a group of acceptable size. These groups are called *multiple employer trusts* (METs).

A *multiple employer welfare arrangement* (MEWA) is similar to a MET except that in a MEWA, a number of employers pool their risks and self-insure, rather than obtaining coverage from an insurance company.

Summary

Group insurance is a way to provide insurance coverage for a number of individuals under one *master policy*. It is generally purchased by an employer as a benefit for employees. Usually the employer pays all or a portion of the premium on behalf of its employees. Employer-pay-all plans are known as *noncontributory plans;* plans that require partial premium contributions from employees are *contributory plans*.

When a group plan is initially installed, all employees who meet the *eligibility requirements* are eligible for coverage. Individual underwriting is usually not done; instead, the insurer looks at the characteristics of the group as a whole. New employees who are hired after the plan is in effect are usually subject to a *probationary period* before they are allowed to enroll.

Most group life insurance plans are term plans that use *annually renewable term insurance* as the underlying policy. Permanent group life plans include *group ordinary, group paid-up* and *group universal life*. The amount of life insurance coverage individual employees receive is determined by the employer, based on earnings, employment position or flat benefit schedule.

Other types of group plans are *franchise life, group credit life, blanket life, multiple employer trusts* and *multiple employer welfare arrangements*.

Key Concepts

In preparing for their licensing examination, students should be familiar with the following concepts:

- master policy
- certificate of insurance
- experience rating
- probationary period
- enrollment period
- annually renewable term
- group ordinary
- group paid-up
- group universal life
- franchise life insurance
- group credit life insurance
- blanket life insurance
- multiple employer trusts
- multiple employer welfare arrangements

Chapter 9
Questions for Review *(Answers are located at the end of the book.)*

1. With regard to group insurance plans, which of the following statements is/are true?

   a. Group insurance plans are a means for employers to provide a benefit for their key employees, without having to include all employees.
   b. The sponsoring employer of a group insurance plan is given a master certificate of insurance that lists the names of all employees covered by the plan.
   c. Per unit of benefits, group insurance is generally available at rates lower than those for individual plans.
   d. All of the above

2. Group insurance plans that require employees to pay a portion of the premium are called

   a. underwritten.
   b. contributory.
   c. participatory.
   d. shared.

3. All of the following statements pertaining to the conversion privilege of group term life insurance are correct, EXCEPT:

   a. An insured employee typically has 31 days following termination of employment in which to convert the group insurance.
   b. An insured employee must convert to the same type of coverage as was provided under the group plan (i.e., term).
   c. Insureds who convert their coverage to individual plans pay a premium rate according to their attained age.
   d. An insured employee may exercise the conversion privilege regardless of his or her insurability.

4. Jackie has just signed up to participate in her employer's franchise life insurance program. She will receive

   I. a certificate of insurance.
   II. an individual policy.

   a. I only
   b. II only
   c. Both I and II
   d. Neither I nor II

5. The type of insurance most frequently used in group life plans is

   a. annually renewable term.
   b. ten-year renewable term.
   c. limited pay whole life.
   d. single-premium whole life.

10 ANNUITIES

Purpose and Function of Annuities • Classification of Annuities • Income Taxation of Annuities • Tax-Sheltered Annuities

As noted in Chapter 7, there are several options available when it comes to deciding how the proceeds of a life insurance policy are to be paid out or "settled." One such option is the life income option. This option (which actually consists of about half a dozen choices) gives beneficiaries an important guarantee: *they can never outlive the income provided under the contract.*

When individuals select a life income option, they are actually using the proceeds to purchase an *annuity* and selecting an *annuity payout option.* Annuities are a means of providing a stream of income for a guaranteed period of time, a period which is most typically defined in terms of the recipient's life. The value of this concept should be apparent to anyone in the business of providing financial advice.

Purpose and Function of Annuities

An *annuity* is a mathematical concept that is quite simple in its most basic definition. Start with a lump sum of money, pay it out in equal installments over a period of time until the original fund is exhausted, and you have an annuity. An annuity is simply a vehicle for liquidating a sum of money. Of course, in practice the concept is more complex. An important factor not mentioned above is interest. The sum of money that has not yet been paid out is earning interest, and that interest is also passed on to the income recipient (the "annuitant").

Anyone can provide an annuity. By knowing the *original sum of money* (the *principal*), the *length of the payout period* and an assumed *rate of interest,* it is a fairly simple process to calculate the payment amount. Actuaries have constructed tables of annuity factors that make this process even easier.

For example, the "present value interest factor for a $1 annuity" (a formal name for one of the aforementioned tables; see Ill. 10.1) shows that the factor

> **Ill. 10.1**
>
> ## Present Value of $1 Payable
>
> The following is a present value annuity table that shows the amount which, if deposited today at 7 percent interest, would produce an annual income of $1 for the specified number of years. In other words, this table reflects the value today of a series of payments tomorrow. For example, the present value of $1 payable for 25 years, at 7 percent interest, is $11.65. This means that $11.65 deposited today at 7 percent interest would generate a payment of $1 for 25 years.
>
> | Years | Present Value (@ 7 percent) | Years | Present Value (@ 7 percent) |
> |---|---|---|---|
> | 5 | 4.10 | 30 | 12.40 |
> | 10 | 7.02 | 35 | 12.94 |
> | 15 | 9.10 | 40 | 13.33 |
> | 20 | 10.59 | 45 | 13.60 |
> | 25 | 11.65 | 50 | 13.80 |
>
> In more practical terms, suppose you wanted to know how much money you should have on hand at age 65 that would generate $5,000 a year in income for ten years, assuming you could earn 7 percent interest while the fund was being paid out. The present value of $1 payable for ten years is 7.02; therefore, the present value of $5,000 payable for ten years is $35,100 ($5,000 × 7.02).

for a 20-year annual payment of $1, based on a 7 percent interest factor, is 10.59. This means that if a person set aside $10.59, and could earn 7 percent interest while the fund was being depleted, an annual income of $1 could be paid for 20 years. The income recipient would receive a total of $20 for the original $10.59 invested in the annuity.

There are other tables similar to this that solve for related problems (for example, how long can income be paid for any given amount of principal). The basic underlying principle, however, is the same in every case—the amount of an annuity payment is dependent upon three factors: *starting principal, interest* and *income period.*

There is one important element absent from this simple definition of an annuity, and it is the one distinguishing factor that separates life insurance companies from all other financial institutions. While anyone can set up an annuity and pay income for a stated period of time, only life insurance companies can do so and *guarantee income for the life of the annuitant.*

Because of their experience with mortality tables, life insurance companies are uniquely qualified to combine an extra factor into the standard annuity calculation. Called a *survivorship factor,* it is, in concept, very similar to the mortality factor in a life insurance premium calculation. Thus, it provides insurers with the means to guarantee annuity payments for life, regardless of how long that life lasts.

Annuities vs. Life Insurance

It is important to realize that annuities are *not* life insurance contracts. In fact, it can be said that an annuity is a mirror image of a life insurance contract—they look alike but are actually exact opposites. Whereas the principal function of a life insurance contract is to *create an estate* (an "estate" being a sum of money) by the periodic payment of money into the contract, an annuity's principal function is to *liquidate an estate* by the periodic payment of money out of the contract. Life insurance is concerned with how soon one will die; life annuities are concerned with how long one will live.

It is easy to see the value of annuities in fulfilling some important financial protection needs. Their role in retirement planning should be obvious; guaranteeing that an annuitant cannot outlive the payments from a life annuity has brought peace of mind to countless numbers of people over the years. Annuities can play a vital role in any situation where a stream of income is needed for only a few years or for a lifetime.

Annuity Basics

An annuity is a cash contract with an insurance company. Unlike life insurance products where policy issue and pricing are based largely on mortality risk, annuities are primarily investment products. Individuals purchase or fund annuities with a single sum amount or through a series of periodic payments; the insurer credits the annuity fund with a certain rate of interest, which is not currently taxable to the annuitant. In this way, the annuity grows. The ultimate amount that will be available for payout is, in part, a reflection of these factors. Most annuities guarantee a death benefit payable in the event the annuitant dies before payout begins; however, it is usually limited to the amount paid into the contract plus interest credited.

With any annuity, there are two distinct time periods involved: the *accumulation period* and the *payout* or *annuity period.* The accumulation period is that time during which funds are being paid into the annuity, in the form of payments by the contractholder and interest earnings credited by the insurer. The payout or annuity period refers to the point at which the annuity ceases to be an accumulation vehicle and begins to generate benefit payments on a regular basis. Typically, benefits are paid out monthly, though a quarterly, semi-annual or annual payment arrangement can be structured.

Structure and Design of Annuities

Annuities are flexible in that there are a number of options available to the purchaser that will enable him or her to structure and design the product to best suit his or her needs.

- *Funding method.* Single lump-sum payment or periodic payments over time

- *Date annuity benefit payments begin.* Immediately or deferred until a future date

- *Investment configuration.* A fixed (guaranteed) rate of return or a variable (nonguaranteed) rate of return

- *Payout method.* A specified term of years or for life, or a combination of both.

Let's take a closer look at each of these options. (They are illustrated in graphic form in Ill. 10.2.)

Funding Method

An annuity begins with a sum of money, called the *principal.* Annuity principal is created (or funded) in one of two ways: immediately with a *single payment* or over time with a series of *periodic payments.*

Single Payment

Annuities can be funded with a *single, lump-sum payment,* in which case the principal is created immediately. For example, an individual nearing retirement whose financial priority is retirement income, could surrender his or her whole life policy and use the cash value as a lump-sum payment to fund an annuity.

Periodic Payments

Annuities can also be funded through a series of *periodic payments* that, over time, will create the annuity principal fund. At one time, it was common for insurers to require that periodic annuity payments be fixed and level, much like insurance premiums. Today, it is more common to allow annuitants flexibility as to when and how much they pay into their contracts.

Ill. 10.2 Annuities Classification Chart

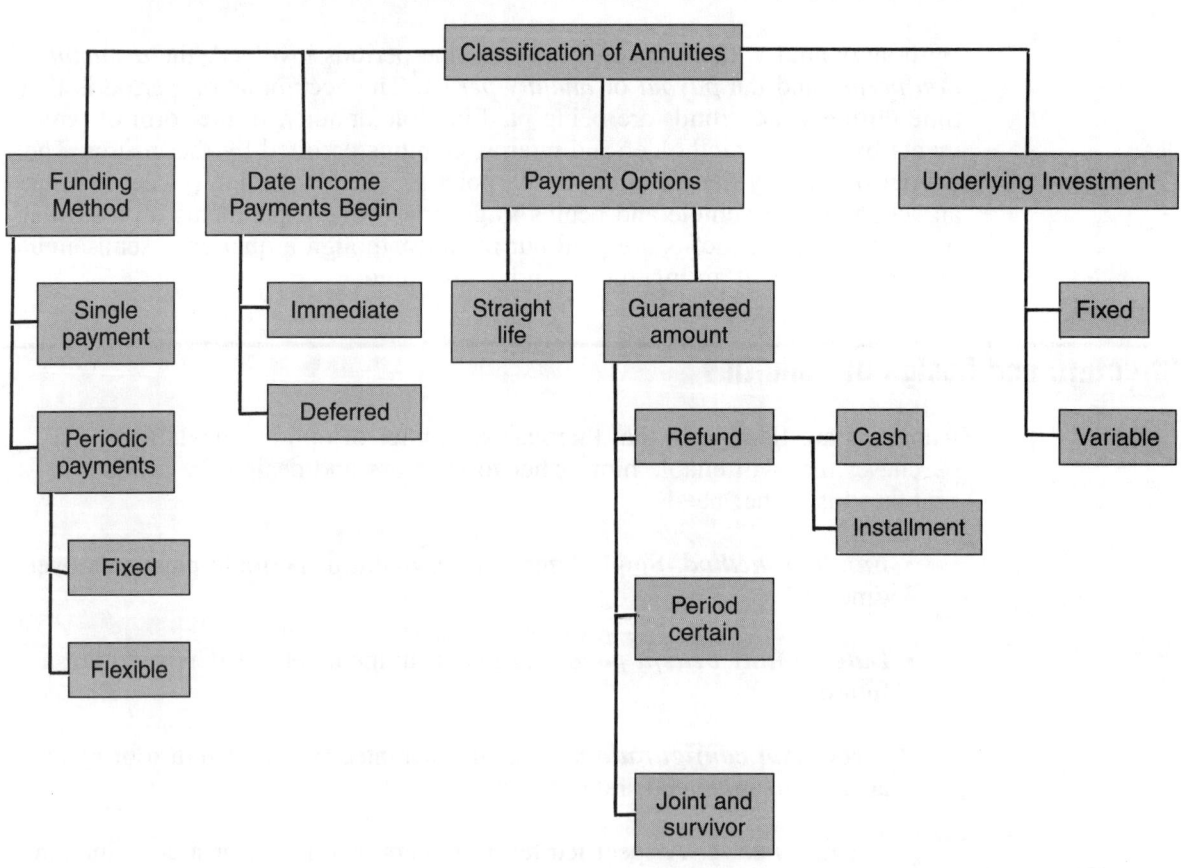

Date Annuity Income Payments Begin

Annuities can be classified by the date the income payments to the annuitant begin. Depending on the contract, annuity payments can begin *immediately* or they can be *deferred* to a future date.

Immediate Annuities

An *immediate annuity* is designed to make its first benefit payment to the annuitant at one payment interval from the date of purchase. Since most annuities make monthly payments, an immediate annuity would typically pay its first payment one month from the purchase date. Thus, an immediate annuity has a relatively short accumulation period.

As you might guess, immediate annuities can only be funded with a single payment, and are often called *single-payment immediate annuities* or SPIAs. An annuity cannot simultaneously accept periodic funding payments by the annuitant and pay out income to the annuitant.

Deferred Annuities

Deferred annuities are those that provide income payments at some specified *future* date. Unlike immediate annuities, deferred annuities can be funded with periodic payments over time. Periodic payment annuities are commonly called *flexible premium deferred annuities,* or FPDAs. Deferred annuities can also be funded with single payments, in which case they're called *single-payment deferred annuities.*

Insurance companies impose restrictions on how far into the future income benefit payments may be deferred. Typically, deferred annuities must be *annuitized* (that is, converted from the deferred annuity to an income-paying annuity) before the annuity owner reaches a maximum age, such as 75.

Annuity Payout Options

Just as life insurance beneficiaries have various settlement options for the disposition of policy proceeds, so too do annuitants have various *income payout options* to specify the way in which an annuity fund is to be paid out. In fact, as noted in Chapter 7, selecting any of the life income options as a life insurance settlement (see page 101) is the same as using the policy proceeds to purchase a single-payment immediate annuity and selecting an annuity income option.

There are a number of annuity income options available: *straight life income, cash refund, installment refund, life with period certain, joint and survivor* and *period certain.*

Straight Life Income Option

A *straight life income* annuity option (often called a *life annuity* or a *straight life annuity*) pays the annuitant a guaranteed income for his or her lifetime. When the annuitant dies, no further payments are made to anyone. If the annuitant dies before the annuity fund (i.e., the principal) is depleted, the balance, in effect, is "forfeited" to the insurer. It is used to provide payments to

Ill. 10.3 Life Income Option

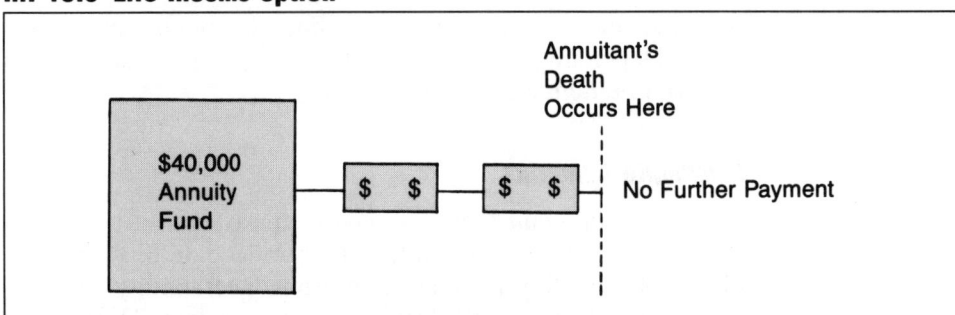

A straight life annuity income option provides for annuity payments to the annuitant for as long as he or she lives. Upon the annuitant's death, no further payments are made.

other annuitants who live beyond the point where the income they receive equals their annuity principal. (See Ill. 10.3.)

Cash Refund Option

A *cash refund* option provides a guaranteed income to the annuitant for life and, if the annuitant dies before the annuity fund (i.e., the principal) is depleted, a lump-sum cash payment of the remainder is made to the annuitant's beneficiary. Thus, the beneficiary receives an amount equal to the beginning annuity fund *less* the amount of income already paid to the deceased annuitant. (See Ill. 10.4.)

Installment Refund Option

Like the cash refund, the *installment refund* option guarantees that the total annuity fund will be paid to the annuitant or to his or her beneficiary. The difference is that under the installment option, the fund remaining at the annuitant's death is paid to the beneficiary in the form of continued annuity payments, not as a single lump sum. (See Ill. 10.5.)

Ill. 10.4 Cash Refund Option

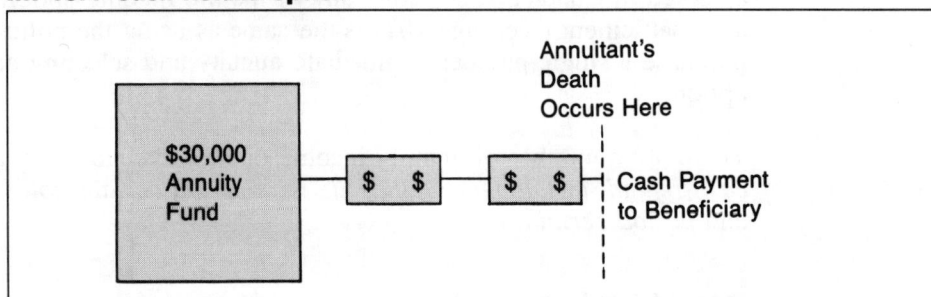

A cash refund option provides for payments to the annuitant for his or her life and, if the annuitant dies before the principal fund is depleted, the remainder is to be paid in a single cash payment to the annuitant's beneficiary. Thus, the total annuity fund is guaranteed to be paid out.

Ill. 10.5 Installment Refund Option

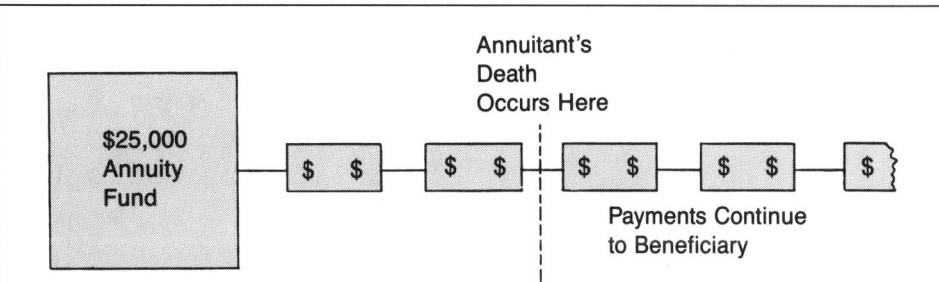

The installment refund option guarantees payments to the annuitant for his or her life and, if the annuitant dies before the principal fund is depleted, the same annuity payments will continue to the beneficiary until the fund is paid out.

Life with Period Certain Option

Also known as the "life income with term certain" option, this payout approach is designed to pay the annuitant an income for life, but guarantees a definite minimum period of payments. For example, if an individual has a ten-year period certain annuity, and receives monthly payments for six years before dying, his or her beneficiary will receive the same payments for four more years. Of course, if the annuitant died after receiving monthly annuity payments for ten or more years, his or her beneficiary would receive nothing from the annuity. (See Ill. 10.6.)

Joint and Full Survivor Option

The *joint and full survivor* option provides for payment of the annuity to two people. If either person dies, the same income payments continue to the survivor for life. When the surviving annuitant dies, no further payments are made to anyone. (See Ill. 10.7.)

Ill. 10.6 Life with Period Certain Option

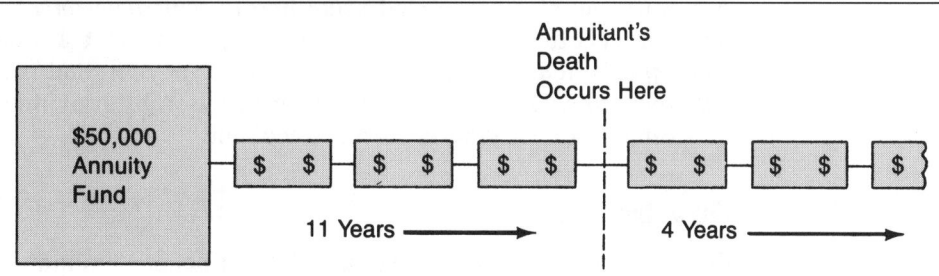

The life with period certain annuity option provides income to the annuitant for life but guarantees a minimum period of payments. Thus, if the annuitant dies during the specified period, benefit payments continue to the beneficiary for the remainder of the period. For example, if an individual has a 15-year life with period certain annuity, receives monthly benefit payments for 11 years and then dies, his or her beneficiary will receive the same payments for the remainder of the period certain, or four years.

Ill. 10.7 Joint and Survivor Options

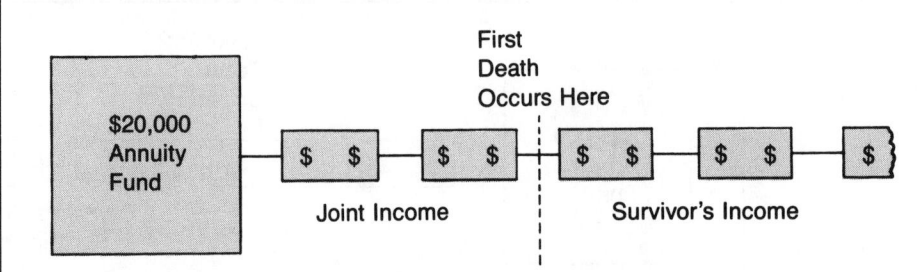

A joint and survivor annuity option provides for benefit payments to two people. If either dies, benefit payments continue to the survivor for the remainder of his or her life. A *full* survivor option pays the same benefit amount to the survivor; a *two-thirds* survivor option pays two-thirds of the original joint benefit; a *one-half* survivor option pays one-half of the original joint benefit.

There are other joint arrangements offered by many companies:

1. *Joint and Two-Thirds Survivor.* This is the same as the above arrangement, except that the survivor's income is reduced to two-thirds of the original joint income.

2. *Joint and One-Half Survivor.* This is the same as the above arrangement, except that the survivor's income is reduced to one-half of the original joint income.

Period Certain Option

The *period certain option* is not based on life contingency; instead, it guarantees benefit payments for a certain period of time, such as 10, 15 or 20 years, whether or not the annuitant is living. At the end of the specified term, payments cease.

Investment Configuration

Annuities can also be defined according to their *investment configuration,* which affects the income benefits they pay. The two classifications are *fixed annuities,* which provide a fixed, guaranteed payout, and their alternative, *variable annuities,* which attempt to offset inflation by providing a benefit linked to a variable underlying investment account.

Fixed Annuities

Fixed annuities provide a guaranteed fixed benefit amount to the annuitant, stated in terms of dollars per benefit payment period (i.e., "$500 a month"). During the period in which the annuitant is making payments to fund the annuity (the "accumulation period"), the insurer invests these payments in fixed securities and earns a certain, known return. An established rate of interest is credited to the annuity on a regular basis.

Because they provide a specified benefit amount, guaranteed payable for the life of the annuitant (or any other period the annuitant desires), fixed annuities can offer security and financial peace of mind. On the other hand, since the benefit amount is fixed, annuitants may see the purchasing power of their payments decline over the years due to inflation.

Variable Annuities

In the early 1950s, a group of people representing a teacher's association reviewed the annuity principle that was the foundation of their pension plan. The question of protection against inflation arose; it was noted that someone who retired with a given amount of income (say, $200 per month) would find that after a decade or so of inflation, the real purchasing power of that income would diminish. Attention then turned to solving the problem, and the solution was the birth of the *variable annuity*.

Chapter 4 discussed variable life insurance. The same underlying principles of variable life insurance apply to variable annuities. As is true with variable life, variable annuities shift the investment risk from the insurer to the contract owner. If the investments supporting the contract perform well (as in a "bull market"), the owner will probably realize investment growth that exceeds what is possible in a fixed annuity. However, the lack of investment guarantees means that the variable annuity owner can see the value of his or her annuity decrease in a depressed market or in an economic recession.

Variable annuities invest deferred annuity payments in an insurer's *separate accounts,* as opposed to an insurer's *general accounts* (which allow the insurer to guarantee interest in a fixed annuity). Because variable annuities are based on non-guaranteed equity investments, such as common stock, a sales representative who wants to sell such contracts must be registered with the National Association of Securities Dealers, or NASD, as well as hold a state insurance license.

Not only can the value of a variable annuity fluctuate in response to movements in the market, so too will the amount of annuity income fluctuate, even after the contract has annuitized. It was for that reason the product was developed in the first place. In spite of inevitable dips in the amount of benefit income, the theory is that the general trend will be an increasing amount of income over time as inflation pushes up the price of stocks—a theory that has generally held true.

In order to accommodate the variable concept, a new means of accounting for both annuity payments and annuity income was required. The result is the *accumulation unit* (which pertains to the accumulation period) and the *annuity unit* (which pertains to the income payout period).

Accumulation Units

In a variable annuity, during the accumulation period, contributions made by the annuitant, less a deduction for expenses, are converted to *accumulation units* and credited to the individual's account. The value of each accumulation unit varies, depending on the value of the underlying stock investment.

For example, assume that the accumulation unit is initially valued at $10, and the holder of a variable annuity makes a payment of $200. This means she has purchased 20 accumulation units. Six months later, she makes another payment of $200, but during that time, the underlying stocks have declined and the value of the accumulation unit is $8. This means that the $200 payment will now purchase 25 accumulation units.

The value of one accumulation unit is found by dividing the total value of the company's separate account by the total number of accumulation units outstanding. Thus, if a company had $20 million in its separate account, and a total of 4 million accumulation units outstanding, the value of one accumulation unit would be $5. As the value of the account rises and falls, the value of each accumulation unit rises and falls.

Annuity Units

At the time the variable annuity benefits are to be paid out to the annuitant, the accumulation units in the participant's individual account are converted into *annuity units*. At the time of initial payout, the annuity unit calculation is made and, from then on, the *number* of annuity units remains the same for that annuitant. The *value* of one annuity unit, however, can and does vary from month to month, depending on investment results.

For instance, let's say that our annuitant has 1,000 accumulation units in her account by the time she is ready to retire and these units have been converted into ten annuity units. She will always be credited with ten annuity units—that number does not change. What does change is the *value* of the annuity units, in accordance with the underlying stock. Assume when she retired, each annuity unit was valued at $40. That means her initial benefit payment is $400 (10 × $40). As long as the value of the annuity unit is $40, her monthly payments will be $400. But what if the value of the stock goes up and her annuity unit value becomes $45? Her next monthly payment will be $450 (10 × $45).

The theory has been that the payout from a variable annuity over a period of years will keep pace with the cost of living and thus maintain the annuitant's purchasing power at or above a constant level. As with fixed annuities, the variable annuity owner has various payout options from which to choose. These options usually include the life annuity, life annuity with period certain, unit refund annuity (similar to a cash refund annuity) and a joint and survivor annuity.

Retirement Income Annuities

While all annuities are well suited to provide retirement income, there is one type of annuity that is especially designed for retirement planning uses. Called the *retirement income annuity,* this plan is basically a deferred annuity policy to which a decreasing term life insurance rider is added.

If the policyowner reaches retirement age (usually age 65), the term insurance expires and the deferred annuity is used to provide retirement income under standard annuity principles. The unique feature of this plan is the death protection it provides. If the insured dies before retirement, the combination of the deferred annuity values and the term insurance benefits are paid to the beneficiary. The beneficiary may use the combined benefits to select any settlement option.

Income Taxation of Annuity Benefits

Annuity benefit payments are a combination of principal and interest. Accordingly, they are taxed in a manner consistent with other types of income: the portion of the benefit payments that represents a return of principal (i.e., the contributions made by the annuitant) are not taxed; the portion representing interest earned on the declining principal is taxed. The result, over the benefit payment period, is a tax-free return of the annuitant's investment and the taxing of the balance.

Though a detailed discussion of how to compute the taxable portion of an annuity payment is beyond the scope of this text, the basics are not difficult to understand. An "exclusion ratio" is applied to each benefit payment the annuitant receives:

$$\frac{\text{Investment in the contract}}{\text{Expected return}} = \text{Exclusion ratio}$$

The "investment in the contract" is the amount of money paid into the annuity; the "expected return" is the annual guaranteed benefit the annuitant receives, multiplied by the number of years of his or her life expectancy. The resulting ratio is applied to the benefit payments, allowing the annuitant to exclude from income a like percentage.

Deferred annuities accumulate interest earnings on a tax-deferred basis. While no taxes are imposed on the annuity during the accumulation phase, taxes are imposed when the contract begins to pay its benefits (in accordance with the "exclusion ratio" just described). To discourage the use of deferred annuities as short-term investments, the Internal Revenue Code imposes taxes on early withdrawals (and loans) from annuities. Partial withdrawals are treated first as earnings income (and are thus taxable as ordinary income); only after all earnings have been taxed are withdrawals considered a return of principal. Furthermore, a 10 percent penalty tax is imposed on withdrawals from a deferred annuity before age 59½; withdrawals after age 59½ are not subject to the 10 percent penalty tax, but are still taxable as ordinary income.

1035 Contract Exchanges

As discussed in Chapter 7, Section 1035 of the Internal Revenue Code provides for tax-free exchanges of certain kinds of financial products, including annuity contracts. Recall that no gain will be recognized (meaning no gain will be taxed) if an annuity contract is exchanged for another annuity contract or if a life insurance or endowment policy is exchanged for an annuity contract.

Tax-Sheltered Annuities

There is a special type of annuity plan reserved for nonprofit organizations and their employees. It is a *tax-sheltered annuity,* also known as a TSA, *"403(b) plan"* or a *"501(c)(3) plan,"* since it was made possible by those sections of the Tax Code. For many years, the federal government, through its tax laws, has encouraged specified nonprofit charitable, educational and religious organizations to set aside funds for their employees' retirement. Plans that are available to teachers employed by public school systems fall into this category. Regardless of whether the money is actually set aside by the employers for the employees of such organizations, or the funds are contributed by the employees through a reduction in salary, such funds may be placed in tax-sheltered annuities and are excludable from the employee's current taxable income.

Upon retirement, payments received by employees from the accumulated savings in tax-sheltered annuities are treated as reportable income. However, as the total annual income of the employees is likely to be less after retirement, the tax to be paid by such retirees is likely to be less than while they were working. Furthermore, the benefits can be spread out over a specified period of time or over the remaining lifetime of the employee so that the amount of tax owed on the benefits in any one year generally will be small.

Summary

Annuities are ideally suited for providing peace of mind to anyone who is concerned about receiving income for life. The exact opposite of the life insurance concept, annuities start with a large fund and reduce it through a series of payments. Life insurance companies are the only financial institutions that can guarantee annuity payments will be made to the annuitant for life. Like beneficiaries of life insurance policies, annuitants have a variety of *payout options* as to how they can receive their annuity benefit payments.

While many annuitants find comfort in the guarantees of a traditional *fixed annuity,* many others prefer the potential investment gains possible with *variable annuities.* Because variable annuities are recognized by the Securities and Exchange Commission as an investment, sales people who want to sell them must be licensed by and registered with the NASD. All states also require salespeople to hold a valid life insurance license to sell any type of annuity.

Key Concepts

In preparing for their licensing examination, students should be familiar with the following concepts:

single-premium annuities
periodic payment annuities
immediate and deferred annuities
fixed and variable annuities

annuity payout options
taxation of annuities
tax-sheltered annuities

Chapter 10
Questions for Review *(Answers are located at the end of the book.)*

1. All of the following statements regarding annuities are true, EXCEPT:

    a. Generally, annuity contracts issued today require fixed, level funding payments.
    b. Annuities are sold by life insurance agents.
    c. An annuity is a periodic payment.
    d. The annuitant can pay the annuity premium in a lump sum.

2. What annuity payout option provides for lifetime payments to the annuitant but guarantees a certain minimum term of payments, whether or not the annuitant is living?

   a. Installment refund option
   b. Life with period certain
   c. Period certain
   d. Straight life income

3. Which of the following statements regarding annuity payout options is NOT correct?

   a. Under a straight life annuity option, all annuity payments stop when the annuitant dies.
   b. In a cash refund annuity, the annuitant's beneficiary always receives an amount equal to the beginning annuity fund plus all interest.
   c. A period certain annuity guarantees a definite number of payments.
   d. Joint and survivor annuities guarantee payments for the duration of two lives.

4. James died after receiving $180 monthly for six years from a $25,000 installment refund annuity. His wife Lucy, as beneficiary, now will receive the same monthly income until her payments total

   a. $2,160.
   b. $12,040.
   c. $12,960.
   d. $25,000.

5. "Annuity payments are taxable to the extent that they represent interest earned rather than capital returned."

   What method is used to determine the taxable portion of each payment?

   a. The exclusion ratio
   b. The marginal tax formula
   c. The surtax ratio
   d. The annuitization ratio

6. Before he died, Gary received a total of $9,200 in monthly income payments from his $15,000 straight life annuity. He also was the insured under a $25,000 life insurance policy that named his wife, Darlene, as primary beneficiary. Considering the two contracts, Darlene would receive death benefits totaling

   a. $15,000.
   b. $25,000.
   c. $30,800.
   d. $40,000.

7. When a cash value life insurance policy is converted into an annuity in a nontaxable transaction, that event is generally known as a

   a. rollover.
   b. 1035 exchange.
   c. modified endowment.
   d. pension enhancement.

11 SOCIAL SECURITY

Purpose • Who Is Covered • Determination of Benefits
• Types of Benefits • Other Government Programs

How does one judge the justness of a society? One test is its willingness to provide its citizens with a floor of protection against the financial loss that often accompanies death, disability or old age—events beyond people's control. The Social Security program—more formally known as OASDI—offers Americans just such a foundation of protection. This chapter reviews this important government-sponsored program.

Purpose of Social Security

There is much confusion and misunderstanding surrounding the *Social Security* program and the role it serves in our society. This misunderstanding has led to unrealistic expectations of Social Security benefits and what they mean to an individual's overall financial plan. Life insurance producers have the important duty to make sure their clients understand the true function of Social Security and recognize the purpose for which it was designed.

The Social Security system was enacted in 1935—in the throes of the Great Depression—for one purpose: to provide a basic floor of protection to all working Americans against the financial problems brought on by death, disability and aging. That remains the primary objective of Social Security. Its purpose has always been to augment—not replace—a sound personal insurance plan. Unfortunately, too many Americans have come to expect Social Security to fulfill all their financial needs. The consequence of this misunderstanding has been disillusionment by many Americans who found, often too late, they were inadequately covered when they needed life insurance, disability income or retirement income.

The Social Security program, administered at the federal level by the Social Security Administration, is more formally called OASDI. This acronym aptly identifies the types of protection provided under the program: "Old Age" (i.e., retirement), "Survivors" (i.e., death benefits) and "Disability

Insurance."* Social Security is an entitlement program, not a welfare program; Americans are entitled to participate in the program's benefits, provided they meet basic eligibility requirements. With few exceptions, most gainfully employed people are covered by Social Security today and are, or will be, eligible for the program's benefits. It is estimated that over 43 million Americans are currently receiving benefits under the system and another 137 million Americans can expect to receive benefits in the future.

Who Is Covered by Social Security?

With only a few exceptions, Social Security extends coverage to virtually every American who is employed or self-employed. Those *not* covered include:

- Most federal employees hired before 1984 who are covered by Civil Service Retirement or another similar pension plan;

- Approximately 20 percent of state and local government employees who are covered by a state pension program and who have elected not to participate under the Social Security program (each state and local government unit decides for itself whether or not to participate); and

- Railroad workers who are covered under a separate federal program, the Railroad Retirement System.

It is easy to see that Social Security is quite broad in its reach, excluding only a small fraction of the working population. In addition to covering workers, Social Security provides for spouses, dependent children and, in some cases, dependent parents of covered workers. It is important to note that a basic condition for coverage is that a person must *work;* OASDI is funded by a payroll tax (called the FICA tax) and eligibility is contingent upon a person contributing to the system during his or her working years.

Coverage vs. Eligibility

There is a significant difference between being covered by Social Security and being eligible for Social Security benefits. Being *covered* means that a worker is actively participating in the program through FICA tax contributions, but he or she may or may not be eligible for benefits. *Eligibility* for benefits is based on a person's insured status, which can be described as either fully insured or currently insured. Being *fully insured* entitles a worker and his or her family to full retirement and survivor (i.e., death) benefits. A *currently insured* status qualifies a worker for a limited range of survivor benefits.

Quarters of Coverage

One's insured status—currently or fully—is based on his or her accrued *quarters of coverage.* A quarter of coverage is earned for each $620 of annual earnings on which FICA taxes are paid. (This $620 was the amount in 1994;

---

*Social Security also provides health insurance (HI) through its Medicare program.

it is adjusted frequently and will almost certainly increase.) Only four quarters of coverage can be earned in any one year. A worker who earned $1,860 in 1994, for example, was credited with three quarters of coverage; someone who earned $2,480 or more was credited with the maximum of four quarters.

Fully Insured vs. Currently Insured

A worker is *fully insured* if he or she has either 40 quarters of coverage (representing approximately ten years of work) *or* at least one quarter of coverage for each year since turning age 21 (a minimum of six quarters of coverage must be earned). Again, fully insured status provides eligibility for full retirement and survivor benefits.

To be considered *currently insured* and thus eligible for limited survivor (i.e., death) benefits, a worker must have earned six quarters of coverage during the 13-quarter period ending with the quarter in which the worker died.

How Social Security Benefits Are Determined

The amount of benefits to which a worker is entitled under Social Security is based on his or her earnings over the years. There is a direct relationship between the amount of FICA taxes paid and the level of benefits earned. Workers who pay the maximum FICA tax over their lifetimes will receive higher benefits than those who pay less than the maximum. However, the FICA tax is not necessarily applied to all of a worker's earnings; the FICA tax is assessed only up to a maximum amount of earnings (known as the *maximum taxable wage base,* discussed later). Accordingly, Social Security benefits actually bear an inverse relationship to earnings: the more the person makes over his or her lifetime in excess of the maximum taxable wage base, the less Social Security provides in benefits *as a proportion to earnings.* Conversely, a person who earned relatively little will receive a higher level of benefits *in proportion to his or her earnings.*

Critics of Social Security sometimes complain of the apparent unfairness of a system in which the rich do not have to pay taxes above the maximum taxable wage base. These critics fail to point out, however, that those same wealthy people will receive benefits no greater than a worker who earned only the amount of the maximum taxable wage base.

Social Security Taxes

To understand Social Security, one must understand the basis upon which it is funded. Social Security is a "pay-as-you-go" system; the taxes paid by workers today are used to provide benefits today. Excess contributions are placed in a fund for future benefits, but are not earmarked for individual contributors. As noted, OASDI is supported by a payroll tax, paid by employees, employers and self-employed individuals.

This payroll or FICA tax, is applied to employees' incomes up to a certain limit, called the *taxable wage base.* A portion of the FICA tax funds OASDI benefits; the other portion funds Medicare benefits. Employers pay an equal amount on behalf of each employee. Self-employed workers pay a higher rate (roughly equal to the sum of an employee's plus an employer's rate), but on

III. 11.1 Calculating FICA Taxes

Let's look at some examples of how FICA taxes are levied on workers. In 1994, Bill earned $26,000, Janice earned $60,600 and Sam earned $140,000. All are covered by Social Security. All of Bill's earnings were subject to the full FICA tax, so in 1994 he paid:

$$\$26{,}000 \times .0620 = \$1{,}612 \text{ toward OASDI}$$
$$\$26{,}000 \times .0145 = \underline{\$377} \text{ toward Medicare}$$
$$\text{Total} = \$1{,}989$$

All of Janice's earnings were subject to the full FICA tax, so in 1994 she paid:

$$\$60{,}600 \times .0620 = \$3{,}757.20 \text{ toward OASDI}$$
$$\$60{,}600 \times .0145 = \underline{\$878.70} \text{ toward Medicare}$$
$$\text{Total} = \$4{,}635.90$$

Now as to Sam, only the first $60,600 of his earnings were subject to the OASDI portion of the FICA tax. There is no longer a limit on the earnings on which you pay the Medicare tax (in 1993, only the first $135,000 in earnings were subject to the Medicare portion of the FICA tax). In 1994, Sam paid:

$$\$60{,}600 \times .0620 = \$3{,}757.20 \text{ toward OASDI}$$
$$\$140{,}000 \times .0145 = \underline{\$2{,}030} \text{ toward Medicare}$$
$$\text{Total} = \$5{,}787.20$$

annual income up to the same taxable wage base. When a worker's salary exceeds the taxable wage base in a calendar year, no more FICA tax is deducted from his or her salary for the remainder of that year.

The maximum taxable wage base was, until 1971, quite stable. However, since 1972, the wage base has increased every year, meaning that more and more of a worker's earning are subject to FICA taxes. Up until 1991, the same wage base was used to calculate FICA taxes for both OASDI and Medicare; now, however, the wage base to which the Medicare portion of the tax applies has been greatly extended. In 1994, the taxable wage base for OASDI was $60,600. This means that in 1994, the first $60,600 of an employee's earnings was subject to the full FICA tax—OASDI and Medicare. However, with the passage of the Revenue Reconciliation Act of 1993, the cap on earnings for the Medicare portion of the FICA tax has been repealed. Beginning in 1994, *all* wages and self-employment income are subject to the full Medicare payroll tax.

The FICA tax rate is also subject to increases, though not as frequently as the wage base. In 1994, the rate for employees and employers alike was 7.65 percent, of which 6.20 applied to OASDI and 1.45 applied to Medicare. The tax rate for self-employed persons in 1994 was 15.3 percent.

Calculating Benefits

Social Security benefits were computed on a worker's *average monthly wage* (AMW) if the person became eligible for benefits prior to 1979. For people becoming eligible in 1979 or later, the calculation is based on the worker's *average indexed monthly earnings* (AIME). The AIME, like its predecessor the AMW, is an average of the worker's lifetime earnings that were subject to the FICA tax. The AIME adds the additional, and critical, step of "weighting" a worker's past earnings to take inflation into account and to bring them up to current economic standards; failure to do so would result in exceptionally small benefits.

Consider, for example, the worker now retiring who earned any more than the taxable wage base in, say, 1970. At the time, the taxable wage base was $7,800. If the worker's retirement benefit today were directly based on earnings of $7,800 in 1970 (and so on) it is easy to see how painfully small his or her level of retirement income would be by today's economic standards. Through weighting, the AIME "increases" past earnings to equal what they would be worth by current economic standards.

The averaged monthly earnings figure derived by the AIME is next applied to a formula to yield the *primary insurance amount* (PIA). The PIA is actually the amount equal to the worker's full retirement benefit at age 65 (benefits are reduced for early retirement) or benefits to a disabled worker. Benefits payable to workers and their spouses and dependents are usually expressed as a percentage of the worker's PIA. For example, a person who elects to retire at age 62 with Social Security retirement benefits will receive benefits equal to 80 percent of his or her PIA. It should be noted that this reduced amount does not increase to 100 percent of the PIA when the worker reaches age 65; the reduction stays in effect for the remainder of the worker's life.

Types of OASDI Benefits

Now that you have a basic understanding of how Social Security benefits are determined, let's take a closer look at the benefits themselves. Specifically, we will review the *death, retirement* and *disability* benefits provided under Social Security. (Medicare benefits will be discussed in Chapter 19.)

Death Benefits

Upon the death of an eligible worker, Social Security provides *death benefits* to a surviving spouse, dependent children and dependent parents. These death benefits are more commonly called "*survivor benefits.*"

Lump-Sum Death Benefit

Social Security provides a one-time lump-sum death benefit to a deceased worker's surviving spouse or children. The amount of this benefit is equal to three times the worker's PIA, up to a maximum of $255. This benefit is designed to help defray funeral expenses. Only surviving spouses or eligible children may receive this benefit.

Surviving Spouse's Benefit

The eligible surviving spouse of a fully insured deceased worker is entitled, at age 65, to a monthly life income equal to the worker's PIA at death. Or, if he or she wishes to receive these benefits early, the surviving spouse can elect reduced benefits, starting as early as age 60.

If the surviving spouse has a child under age 16 (or age 22, if disabled) and the child was a dependent of the deceased worker, an additional benefit of 75 percent of the worker's PIA is payable, regardless of the spouse's age, until the child reaches age 16. Disabled children will entitle the surviving spouse to this benefit indefinitely, as long as the child remains disabled and under the care of the surviving spouse.

Child's Benefit

A child who is under age 18 (or disabled before age 22) whose parent is a deceased worker, may receive a benefit equal to 75 percent of the worker's PIA until he or she turns 18 (19 if still in high school). If the child marries prior to age 18, the benefit terminates.

Parents' Benefits

Beginning at age 62, each parent of a deceased fully insured worker is eligible to receive a monthly benefit *if* the parent was at least one-half supported by the worker at the time of death. When two parents are eligible, each receives 75 percent of the worker's PIA; if only one parent is eligible, he or she receives 82½ percent of the worker's PIA.

Maximum Survivor Benefits

It should be noted that Social Security has placed limits on the total amount of survivor benefits that any one family may receive. This limit is known as the *maximum family benefit,* and it varies according to the PIA. If the sum of the individual benefits paid to members of one family exceeds this maximum limit, they will be reduced proportionately to bring the total within the limit.

Retirement Benefits

Social Security also provides "*old age*" or *retirement* benefits to qualified (fully insured) workers and their families. These benefits are paid monthly.

Worker's Retirement Benefit

Fully insured workers are eligible for full retirement income benefits (i.e., 100 percent of the PIA) at age 65. Permanently reduced benefits are available from age 62 for those who elect to retire early and draw benefits; slightly greater benefits are available for those who delay retirement beyond age 65.

Spouse's Benefit

The spouse of any worker eligible for retirement benefits is entitled to an "old age" income at his or her age 65, or a reduced benefit at age 62. At age 65, the spouse's benefit is 50 percent of the retired worker's PIA; at age 62, the spousal benefit is 37½ percent of the PIA.

If there is a dependent child under age 16 (or disabled prior to age 22), the spouse is eligible to receive the 50 percent spousal benefit, regardless of his or her age.

Child's Benefit

An unmarried child of a worker on retirement income is generally eligible to receive a monthly benefit of 50 percent of the worker's PIA, until he or she turns 18. If the child is disabled prior to age 22, his or her benefit will continue indefinitely.

Maximum Retirement Benefits

As is the case with survivor benefits, a maximum family benefit amount also applies to Social Security retirement benefits. In addition, retired workers are subject to an *earnings test.* Anyone under age 70 who is drawing Social Security retirement benefits and continues to work is allowed to earn only so much each year without having his or her benefits reduced. For example, in 1994, the maximum amount an individual age 65 to 69 could earn—before losing $1 in benefits for each $3 earned—was $11,160. For those under age 65, the maximum amount that could be earned before losing $1 for every $2 earned over the maximum was $8,040. (These amounts are expected to increase regularly, to reflect increases in the cost of living.) Currently, there is no earnings limitation for Social Security recipients age 70 or older who continue to work.

Disability Benefits

A fully insured worker who becomes disabled is entitled to *disability benefits* under Social Security, as are his or her spouse and dependent children.

Disabled Worker's Benefit

A disabled worker is entitled to a monthly benefit equal to his or her PIA at the time the disability occurred. There is no reduction in benefits if they begin prior to age 65; however, if the worker becomes disabled after age 63 and had been receiving a reduced retirement benefit, his or her disability benefits will be reduced to take into account the retirement benefits already received.

Spouse's Benefit

The spouse of a qualified disabled worker may also receive benefits from Social Security, depending on his or her age. If the spouse is 65, the benefit is equal to 50 percent of the worker's PIA. A spouse who is 62 can elect reduced benefits equal to 37½ percent of the worker's PIA.

If there is a dependent child under age 16 (or who is disabled, regardless of age), the spouse can receive the 50 percent spousal benefit, regardless of his or her age.

Child's Benefit

An unmarried dependent child of a disabled worker who is under 18 (or a child who was disabled prior to age 22) is eligible for monthly benefits equal to 50 percent of the worker's PIA.

Maximum Disability Benefits

Again, a maximum family benefit applies, limiting the amount of disability benefits one family can receive on the worker's earning record. The earnings test is also applicable and pertains individually to each family member.

It should be noted that qualification for Social Security disability benefits is subject to rigid requirements. To begin with, the worker must meet Social Security's definition of disability, which is the inability to engage in "any substantial gainful work that exists in the national economy," taking into consideration the worker's age, education and work experience. The disability must be the result of a medically determinable physical or mental impairment that can be expected to last at least 12 months or to result in an earlier death.

Disability benefits begin after the worker has satisfied a waiting period of five consecutive months, during which he or she must be disabled. The benefits may be paid retroactively for as long as 12 months (excluding the waiting period) preceding the date an application for benefits is filed.

Taxation of Social Security Benefits

Until 1984, all Social Security benefits were exempt from federal income taxes. Beginning that year, however, up to one-half of Social Security benefits are now treated as taxable income for recipients whose income exceeds certain base amounts. Currently, the threshold amounts are $25,000 for single taxpayers, $32,000 for married taxpayers filing jointly and $0 for married taxpayers filing separately. Only a few states impose state income taxes on Social Security benefits.

Other Government Life Insurance Programs

The federal government also has established life insurance programs to benefit active members of the armed services and veterans. Three of the most notable programs are *Servicemembers' Group Life, Veterans' Group Life* and *National Service Life*.

Servicemembers' Group Life Insurance

Servicemembers' Group Life Insurance (SGLI) was established in 1965 to provide armed services personnel on active duty with group insurance. Coverage is offered by a consortium of commercial life insurance companies.

Servicemembers are automatically eligible for $100,000 of coverage when they enter active duty, with the option to elect additional coverage (for a larger premium) in increments of $10,000, up to the maximum coverage of $200,000. Servicemembers do not need to provide a certificate of health if they elect to increase coverage later.

The service personnel pay the share of the premium required to cover peacetime mortality costs and expenses. The federal government pays the additional mortality costs associated with military conflict. The insurance remains effective for 120 days following discharge from the service.

Veterans' Group Life Insurance

Following military discharge, an insured may elect to convert his or her SGLI coverage to a five-year, nonrenewable term policy known as *Veterans' Group Life Insurance* (VGLI).

VGLI is paid for entirely by the insured owner and must be for the same amount of protection as was available under the SGLI coverage. At the end of the five-year term period, the VGLI policy may be converted to an individual whole life policy with any of the companies participating in the program.

National Service Life Insurance

Many *National Service Life Insurance* (NSLI) policies, which were issued by the federal government to members of the Armed Forces during World War II, are still in force. No new NSLI coverage has been issued since 1951. Basically, NSLI was group term insurance (issued in maximum amounts of $10,000 per individual) that could be renewed indefinitely or converted all, or in part, to permanent insurance at any time without evidence of insurability.

Summary

The federally managed *Social Security program,* more formally called OASDI ("Old Age, Survivors, and Disability Insurance"), is the government's attempt to provide a basic floor of financial protection to all working Americans. It is a pay-as-you-go system funded by a mandatory *FICA payroll tax* on almost all workers. While Social Security benefits do provide an important source of income for retirees and the surviving spouses and children of covered workers, these benefits alone are not sufficient to maintain a meaningful standard of living. Social Security benefits augment, but do not replace, a well-founded personal insurance program.

Key Concepts

In preparing for their licensing examination, students should be familiar with the following concepts:

OASDI benefits	PIA
currently insured status	earnings test
fully insured status	taxation of Social Security benefits
quarters of coverage	SGLI
taxable wage base	VGLI
AIME	NSLI

Chapter 11
Questions for Review *(Answers are located at the end of the book.)*

1. Ellen works part time to supplement her family's income. In 1994, she earned $2,000 and worked at least part of every month. With how many quarters of coverage will she be credited for 1994?

   a. One
   b. Two
   c. Three
   d. Four

2. Anne earned $63,000 in 1994. Assuming 1994 Social Security rates, how much did her employer deduct from her salary for FICA taxes that year?

   a. $3,450
   b. $4,670
   c. $4,820
   d. $5,123

3. All of the following statements regarding Social Security survivor benefits are correct, EXCEPT:

   a. A surviving widow, age 66, will be entitled to a life income equal to her husband's PIA.
   b. A healthy dependent child of a deceased worker will be entitled to an income benefit until age 18, or to age 22, if he or she attends college.
   c. A surviving widower, age 47, has a 13-year-old child who was also a dependent of the deceased worker. The widower is entitled to monthly income until the child reaches age 16, at which time benefits will cease to the widower until the widower reaches at least age 60.
   d. A deceased covered worker was providing one-half of the support for a 62-year-old parent who is confined to a nursing home. The parent is entitled to a survivor's benefit.

4. Which of the following examples pertaining to Social Security benefits is correct?

   a. Simon has a Social Security PIA of $700 at the time of his death. His surviving spouse will receive a lump-sum death benefit of $2,250.
   b. Lola, age 30, has a daughter, age 10. Her husband, who is covered under Social Security, died unexpectedly last month following surgery. Both Lola and her daughter are entitled to receive monthly survivor benefits until her daughter reaches age 18.
   c. Mason, who is married with one son, age 16, is a fully insured retired worker receiving Social Security benefits. In addition, his spouse is eligible for benefits at age 62 and his son, normally, is eligible for benefits until he is 18 years old.
   d. Arlene, the 20-year-old daughter of a fully insured retired worker, becomes totally and permanently disabled from injuries received in a car accident. Because her disability occurred after age 16, Arlene is not eligible for her father's Social Security benefits.

5. In determining Social Security retirement benefits, which of the following statements is/are correct?

   I. Average indexed monthly earnings (AIME) are adjusted for inflation.
   II. Average monthly wages (AMW) are adjusted for inflation.
   III. The primary insurance amount (PIA) is a determination of the amount equal to the worker's full retirement benefit at age 65.
   IV. Workers retiring past age 59½ can receive 100 percent of their primary insurance amounts (PIA).

   a. I only
   b. I and II only
   c. I and III only
   d. III and IV only

6. Ruddy is eligible for full death, retirement and disability benefits under Social Security. His worker status is

   a. completely insured.
   b. currently insured.
   c. fully insured.
   d. partially insured.

7. Which of the following statements pertaining to servicemembers' and veterans' life insurance is correct?

   a. Wayne is a member of his state's National Guard. He is eligible for Servicemembers' Group Life Insurance (SGLI) when participating in the Guard's training exercises.
   b. Juanita, who is insured with Servicemembers' Group Life Insurance (SGLI), has just been discharged from the U.S. Navy. She has 90 days following her release in which to convert her SGLI to National Service Life Insurance (NSLI).
   c. National Service Life Insurance (NSLI) is issued to U.S. military personnel as permanent life insurance.
   d. Arnold, a pilot in the U.S. Air Force, has $50,000 of coverage under SGLI when he is released from active duty. Arnold may convert his SGLI to Veterans' Group Life Insurance (VGLI), which is issued and paid for by the federal government.

12 RETIREMENT PLANS

Qualified vs. Nonqualified Plans • Employer-Sponsored Plans
• Small Employer Plans • Individual Plans

As stated in the last chapter, Social Security benefits should be regarded as a basic floor of financial protection and not as a source that alone can provide a meaningful standard of living. Individuals must take the initiative if they want full security in meeting financial challenges. This means maintaining adequate life insurance to meet the costs of death, health insurance to cover the expenses of becoming ill and a well-planned retirement program to maintain a desired standard of living when employment income ceases. In this chapter, we will discuss the broad topic of retirement plans. Although this subject is complex and can be covered only superficially here, life insurance professionals should recognize this as an important part of the overall insurance concept and should be prepared to learn more about retirement planning as they progress through their careers.

Qualified vs. Nonqualified Plans

The field of retirement planning has grown tremendously in both scope and significance. In various ways, the federal government encourages businesses to set aside retirement funds for their employees and provides incentives for individuals to do likewise. There are many kinds of *retirement plans,* each designed to fulfill specific needs. Life insurance companies play a major role in the retirement planning arena, as the products and contracts they offer provide ideal funding or financing vehicles for both individual plans and employer-sponsored plans.

Broadly speaking, retirement plans can be divided into two categories: *qualified plans* and *nonqualified plans*. Qualified plans are those that, by design or by definition, meet certain requirements established by the federal government and, consequently, receive favorable tax treatment.

- Employer contributions to a qualified retirement plan are considered a deductible business expense, which lowers the business's income taxes.

- The earnings of a qualified plan are exempt from income taxation.

157

- Employer contributions to a qualified plan are not currently taxable to the employee in the years they are contributed, but are taxable when they are paid out as a benefit (and, typically, when the employee is retired and in a lower tax bracket).

- Contributions to an individual qualified plan, such as an individual retirement account or annuity (IRA), are deductible from income under certain conditions (which will be discussed shortly).

If a plan does not meet the specific requirements set forth by the federal government, it is termed a *nonqualified* plan and, thus, is not eligible for favorable tax treatment. For example, Bill, age 42, decides he wants to start a retirement fund. He opens a new savings account at his local bank, deposits $150 a month in that account and vows not to touch that money until he reaches age 65. Although his intentions are good, they will not serve to "qualify" his plan. The income he deposits and the interest he earns are still taxable every year. Our discussion in this chapter will focus on qualified retirement plans, both individual and employer-sponsored.

Qualified Employer Retirement Plans

An *employer retirement plan* is one that a business makes available to its employees. Typically, the employer makes all or a portion of the contributions on behalf of its employees and is able to deduct these contributions as ordinary and necessary business expenses. The employees are not taxed on the contributions made on their behalf, nor are they taxed on the benefit fund accruing to them until it actually is paid out. By the same token, contributions made by an individual employee to a qualified employer retirement plan are not included in his or her ordinary income and therefore are not taxable.

Basic Concepts

Many of the basic concepts associated with qualified employer plans can be traced to the *Employee Retirement Income Security Act of 1974,* commonly called ERISA. The purpose of ERISA is to protect the rights of workers covered under an employer-sponsored plan. Prior to the passage of ERISA, workers had few guarantees to assure them that they would receive the pension benefit they thought they had earned. A sad but common plight was the worker who had devoted many years to one employer, only to be terminated within a few years of retirement—and not be entitled to a pension benefit.

ERISA imposes a number of requirements that retirement plans must follow to obtain Internal Revenue Service (IRS) approval as a qualified plan eligible for favorable tax treatment. (See Ill. 12.1.) While an in-depth discussion of these requirements is beyond the scope of this text, the basic concepts of *participation, coverage, vesting, funding* and *contributions* should be noted.

Participation Standards

All qualified employer plans must comply with minimum *participation standards* designed to determine employee eligibility. In general, employees who have reached age 21 and have completed one year of service must be allowed to enroll in a qualified plan. Or, if the plan provides for 100 percent vesting

Ill. 12.1

General Qualification Requirements for Employer-Sponsored Retirement Plans

1. A plan must be written.
2. A plan must be in effect.
3. A plan must be communicated to employees.
4. A plan must be established by the employer.
5. Contributions must be made by the employer or the employees, or both.
6. A plan must be for the exclusive benefit of the employees.
7. A plan must be permanent.
8. Any life insurance benefits must be incidental to retirement benefits.
9. Minimum participation standards must be met.
10. A plan must not discriminate in coverage.
11. A plan must not discriminate in contributions or benefits on the basis of income or gender.
12. Annuity payments under a plan must be available in the form of a joint and survivor annuity.
13. Comprehensive vesting standards concerning the vesting of an employee's benefits must be followed.
14. Minimum funding standards must be met.
15. A plan must comply with limitations on contributions and benefits.
16. There must be no assignment or alienation of benefits.
17. A plan must meet Social Security integration rules.
18. A plan must meet rules for mergers and consolidations.
19. A plan must meet rules for multi-employer plans.
20. A plan must meet rules pertaining to the reduction of benefits because of Social Security.
21. A plan must fulfill plan termination requirements.
22. A plan must fulfill special requirements for particular plans.
23. A top-heavy plan must contain contingency provisions.

upon participation, they may be required to complete two years of service before enrolling.

Coverage Requirements

The purpose of *coverage requirements* is to prevent a plan from discriminating against rank-and-file employees in favor of the "elite"—shareholders, officers and highly compensated employees—whose positions often enable them to make basic policy decisions regarding the plan. The IRS will subject qualified employer plans to *coverage tests* to determine if they are discriminatory. A qualified plan cannot discriminate in favor of highly paid employees in its coverage provisions nor in its contributions/benefits provisions.

Vesting Schedules

All qualified plans must meet standards that set forth the employee *vesting schedule* and nonforfeitable rights at any specified time. "Vesting" means the right each employee has to his or her fund; benefits that have "vested" belong to the employee even if he or she terminates employment prior to retirement. For all plans, an employee always has a 100 percent vested interest in benefits that accrue from his or her *own* contributions. Benefits that accrue from employer contributions must vest according to vesting schedules established by law. (See Ill. 12.2.)

Ill. 12.2

Vesting Schedules for Qualified Plans

In order to meet IRS qualification standards, an employer retirement plan must provide for a specific *vesting schedule,* which sets forth the time period by which an employee-participant becomes entitled to nonforfeitable benefits under the plan. Generally speaking, there are two schedules available:

1. Cliff Vesting:

Years of Service	Vested Percentage
1	0
2	0
3	0
4	0
5	100

2. Graded Vesting:

Years of Service	Vested Percentage
1	0
2	0
3	20
4	40
5	60
6	80
7	100

As an alternative, a plan can provide for a different vesting schedule, as long as it is no less favorable to the participants than those above.

Funding Standards

For a plan to be qualified, it must be *funded*. In other words, there must be real contributions on the part of the employer, the employee or both, and these funds must be held by a third party and invested. The *funding vehicle* is the method for investing the funds as they accumulate. Federal minimum funding requirements are set to ensure that an employer's annual contributions to a pension plan are sufficient to cover the costs of benefits payable during the year, plus administrative expenses.

Contributions

Qualification standards regarding the amount and type of *contributions* that can be made to a plan vary, depending on whether the plan is a *defined contribution plan* or a *defined benefit plan*, discussed below. Suffice it to say, all plans must restrict the amount of contributions that can be made for or accrue to any one plan participant.

With these basics in mind, let's turn to the two major categories of qualified employer retirement plans, used primarily by *corporate* employers. They are the *defined contribution plan*, which obligates the plan sponsor to make periodic contributions for each participant per a defined formula, and the *defined benefit plan*, which defines the amount of retirement income each participant will receive.

Defined Contribution Plans

The provisions of a *defined contribution plan* address the amounts going *into* the plan currently and identify the participant's vested (nonforfeitable) account. These predetermined amounts contributed to the participant's account accumulate to a future point (i.e., retirement) and the final fund available to any one participant depends on total amounts contributed, plus interest and dividends earned.

There are three types of defined contribution plans: *profit-sharing plans, stock bonus plans* and *money-purchase plans*.

Profit-Sharing Plans

Profit-sharing plans are established and maintained by an employer that allow employees to participate in the profits of the company. They provide for a definite predetermined formula for allocating plan contributions among the participants and for distributing the funds upon retirement, death, disability or termination. Since contributions are tied to the company's profits, it is not necessary that the employer contribute every year nor that the amount of contribution be the same. However, the IRS states that to qualify for favorable tax treatment, the plan must be maintained with "recurring and substantial" contributions.

Stock Bonus Plans

A *stock bonus plan* is similar to a profit-sharing plan, except that contributions by the employer do not depend on profits, and benefits are distributed in the form of company stock.

Money-Purchase Plans

Money-purchase plans provide for fixed contributions with future benefits to be determined and thus most truly represent a defined contribution plan. A money-purchase plan must meet three requirements:

1. Contributions and earnings must be allocated to participants in accordance with a definite formula.

2. Distributions can be made only in accordance with amounts credited to participants.

3. Plan assets must be valued at least once a year, with participants' accounts being adjusted accordingly.

Defined Benefit Plans

In contrast to a defined contribution plan that sets up predetermined contributions, a *defined benefit plan* establishes a definite future *benefit,* predetermined by a specific formula. When the term "pension" is used, the reference is typically to a defined benefit plan. Usually the benefits are tied to the employee's years of service, amount of compensation or both. For example, a defined benefit plan may provide for a retirement benefit equal to 2 percent of the employee's highest consecutive five-year earnings, multiplied by the number of years of service. Or the benefit may be defined as simply as $100 a month for life.

In order to qualify for federal tax purposes, a defined benefit plan must meet the following basic requirements:

- The plan must provide for *definitely determinable benefits,* either by a formula specified in the plan or by actuarial computation.

- The plan must provide for *systematic payment of benefits* to employees over a period of years (usually for life) after retirement. Thus, the plan has to detail the conditions under which benefits are payable and the options under which benefits are paid.

- The plan must provide *primarily retirement benefits.* The IRS will allow provisions for death or disability benefits, but these benefits must be incidental to retirement.

- The *maximum annual benefit* an employee may receive in any one year is limited to an amount set by the tax law. This amount is indexed for inflation. In 1994, the indexed amount was $118,800.

The appropriate choice of qualified corporate retirement plan—defined contribution or defined benefit—requires an understanding of the operation and characteristics of each plan as they relate to the employer's objectives.

Cash or Deferred Arrangements (401(k) Plans)

Another form of qualified employer retirement plan growing in popularity is commonly known as the *401(k) plan,* whereby employees can elect to take a reduction in their current salaries by deferring amounts into a retirement plan.

These plans are called *"cash or deferred arrangements"* because employees cannot be forced to participate; they may take their income currently as cash, or defer a portion of it until retirement, with favorable tax advantages.

The amounts deferred are not included in the employees' gross income and earnings credited to the deferrals grow tax-free until distribution. Typically, 401(k) plans include matching employer contributions: for every dollar the employee defers, for example, the employer will contribute 50 cents. The maximum annual amount an employee could defer was $9,240 in 1994. (This amount is indexed for inflation and may vary from year to year.)

A cash or deferred arrangement must be part of a profit-sharing or stock bonus plan. In addition to meeting the qualification rules applicable to defined contribution plans, 401(k) plans also must qualify under a special set of rules:

- Amounts deferred can be distributed only by reason of retirement, death, disability, separation from service, "severe hardship" or attainment of age 59½.

- Employee deferred contributions are nonforfeitable.

- Special nondiscrimination requirements must be met to prevent highly compensated employees from deferring disproportionately higher amounts of their salaries.

Employer contributions to a qualified cash or deferred profit-sharing plan are not currently taxed to the employee.

Tax-Sheltered Annuities (403(b) Plans)

Another type of employer retirement plan is the *tax-sheltered annuity* or *403(b) plan*. This was explained in Chapter 10, but it is appropriate to review it here.

A tax-sheltered annuity is a special tax-favored retirement plan available only to certain groups of employees. Tax-sheltered annuities may be established for the employees of specified nonprofit charitable, educational, religious and other 501(c)(3) organizations, including teachers in public school systems. Such plans generally are not available to other kinds of employees.

Funds are contributed by the employer or by the employees (usually through payroll deductions) to tax-sheltered annuities and, thus, are excluded from the employees' current taxable income.

Code Section 457 Deferred Compensation Plans

Deferred compensation plans for employees of state and local governments and nonprofit organizations became popular in the 1970s. Congress enacted Internal Revenue Code Section 457 to allow participants in such plans to defer compensation without current taxation as long as certain conditions are met.

If a plan is eligible under Section 457, amounts deferred will not be included in gross income until they are actually received or made available. Life insurance and annuities are authorized investments for these plans.

Under Section 457, the amount an employee defers may not exceed the *lesser* of $7,500 or 33⅓ percent of includable compensation. "Includable compensation" means compensation that is currently includable in gross income. In general, 33⅓ percent of includable compensation equals 25 percent of total compensation. For example, a person earning $30,000 per year enters into an agreement to defer $7,500. The person's includable compensation will be $22,500 ($30,000 total compensation minus the $7,500 not currently includable in gross income).

Qualified Plans for the Small Employer

Prior to 1962, many small business owners found that their employees could participate in, and benefit from, a qualified retirement plan, but the owners themselves could not. Self-employed individuals were in the same predicament. The reason was that qualified plans had to benefit "employees." Because business owners were considered "employers," they were excluded from participating in a qualified plan.

The *Self-Employed Individuals Retirement Act,* signed into law in 1962, rectified this situation by treating small business owners and self-employed individuals as "employees," thus enabling them to participate in a qualified plan, if they chose to do so, just as their employees. The result was the Keogh or HR-10 retirement plan.

Keogh Plans (HR-10s)

A *Keogh plan* is a qualified retirement plan designed for unincorporated businesses that allows the business owner (or partner in a business) to participate as an "employee." These plans may be set up as either defined contribution or defined benefit plans.

In the first years following enactment of the Keogh bill, there was a great deal of disparity between the rules for Keogh plans and those for corporate plans. However, in 1982, as part of TEFRA, the law eliminated most of the rules unique to Keogh plans, thereby establishing parity between qualified corporate employer retirement plans and noncorporate plans. Basically speaking:

- Keogh plans are subject to the same maximum contribution limits and benefit limits as qualified corporate plans.

- Keogh plans must comply with the same participation and coverage requirements as qualified corporate plans.

- Keogh plans are subject to the same nondiscrimination rules as qualified corporate plans.

Simplified Employee Pensions (SEPs)

Another type of qualified plan suited for the small employer is the *simplified employee pension* (SEP) plan. Due to the many administrative burdens and the costs involved with establishing a qualified defined contribution or defined benefit plan as well as maintaining compliance with ERISA, many small businesses have been reluctant to set up retirement plans for their employees. SEPs were introduced in 1978 specifically for small businesses to overcome these cost, compliance and administrative hurdles.

Basically, a SEP is an arrangement whereby an employee (including a self-employed individual) establishes and maintains an *individual retirement account* (IRA) to which the employer contributes. Employer contributions are not included in the employee's gross income. A primary difference between a SEP and an IRA is the much larger amount that can be contributed each year to a SEP—$30,000 or 15 percent of the employee's compensation.

In accordance with the rules that govern other qualified plans, SEPs must not discriminate in favor of highly compensated employees with regard to contributions or participation.

Salary reduction SEPs are a popular variation of the traditional employer-provided SEP. Salary reduction SEPs allow employees to defer a portion of their pretax income to the plan, thereby lowering their taxable income. (The maximum deferral amount was $9,240 in 1994.) Salary reduction SEPs are reserved for small companies with 25 or fewer employees.

Individual Retirement Plans

In much the same way that it encourages businesses to establish retirement plans for their employees, the federal government provides incentives for *individuals* to save for their retirement by allowing certain kinds of plans to receive favorable tax treatment. Most notable of these individual plans are *individual retirement accounts, spousal retirement accounts* and *rollover retirement accounts.*

Individual Retirement Accounts (IRAs)

An *individual retirement account,* commonly called an IRA, is a means by which individuals can save money for retirement and receive a current tax break. Basically, the amount contributed to an IRA accumulates and grows tax deferred. IRA funds are not taxed until they are taken out at retirement. In addition, depending on the individual's earnings and whether or not he or she is covered by an employer-sponsored retirement plan, the amount he or she contributes to an IRA may be fully or partially deducted from current income, resulting in lower current income taxes.

IRA Participation

Basically, anyone under the age of 70½ who has earned income may open an IRA and contribute each year an amount up to $2,000 or 100 percent of compensation, whichever is less. Contributions grow tax free until they are withdrawn.

Deduction of IRA Contributions

In many cases, the amount an individual contributes to an IRA can be deducted from his or her income in the year it is contributed. The ability of an

IRA participant to take a deduction for his or her contribution rests on two factors:

1. whether or not he or she is covered by an employer-sponsored retirement plan and

2. the amount of income he or she makes.

Individuals who are *not* covered by an employer-sponsored plan may contribute up to $2,000 to an IRA and deduct from their current income the full amount of the contribution, no matter what their level of income is. Married couples who both work and have no employer-sponsored plan can contribute and deduct up to $4,000 a year to an IRA.

Individuals who *are* covered by an employer-sponsored plan are subject to different rules regarding deductibility of IRA contributions. For them, the amount of income they make is the determining factor: the more they make, the less IRA deduction they can take. For example, single taxpayers covered by an employer plan, whose adjusted gross income is $25,000 or less may take up to the $2,000 maximum deduction. As income exceeds $25,000, the amount of allowable IRA deduction is phased down gradually. Single taxpayers covered by an employer plan lose IRA deductibility completely when adjusted gross income reaches $35,000.

For married individuals filing jointly, when either or both are covered by an employer plan, the full deduction is available if their adjusted gross income is less than $40,000. Again, the deduction is phased down gradually as income rises. Once joint income reaches $50,000, there is no deduction allowed for IRA contributions.

Do not confuse deductibility of contributions with the ability to make contributions. Again, anyone under age 70½ who has earned income can *contribute* to an IRA. However, level of income and participation in an employer plan may affect the IRA owner's ability to *deduct* the contributions.

IRA Withdrawals

Because the purpose of an IRA is to provide a way to accumulate retirement funds, there are a number of rules that discourage IRA owners from withdrawing these funds prior to retirement. By the same token, IRA owners are discouraged from perpetually sheltering their accounts from taxes by rules that mandate when the funds must be withdrawn.

- IRA owners must begin to receive payment from their accounts no later than April 1 following the year in which they reach age 70½. A heavy penalty is assessed if distribution is delayed beyond that time. In addition, the law specifies a minimum amount that must be withdrawn every year if the penalty tax is to be avoided.

- Any withdrawal from an IRA before the owner is 59½ years old (except in cases of death, disability or as a result of a divorce decree) generally will have adverse income tax consequences. A tax penalty equal to 10 percent of the amount received is imposed, and the entire amount withdrawn is included in gross income. (This penalty is similar to that imposed on early withdrawals from deferred annuities.) However, there is an exception to this rule: withdrawals taken as a *life annuity* are not subject to the early withdrawal penalty. After age 59½ (or in the case of disability), an IRA distribution is subject to tax as ordinary income with no penalty.

- At retirement, or any time after age 59½, the IRA owner can elect to receive either a lump-sum payment or periodic installment payments from his or her fund. IRA distributions are taxed in much the same way as annuity benefit payments are taxed. That is, the portion of an IRA distribution that is attributed to nondeductible contributions is received tax free; the portion that is attributed to interest earnings or deductible contributions is taxed. The result is a tax-free return of the IRA owner's cost basis and a taxing of the balance.

- If an IRA owner dies before receiving full payment, the remaining funds in the deceased's IRA will be paid to the named beneficiary.

IRA Funding

An ideal funding vehicle for IRAs is a *flexible premium deferred annuity.* Other acceptable IRA funding vehicles include bank time deposit open accounts, bank certificates of deposit, insured credit union accounts, mutual fund shares, face amount certificates, real estate investment trust units and certain U.S. gold and silver coins.

Spousal IRAs

Persons eligible to set up IRAs for themselves may create a *"spousal IRA"* with a nonworking spouse. A marginally employed spouse (one with annual income of less than $250) is considered as having no earned income for the year and is eligible for a spousal IRA.

The maximum deductible contribution that can be made to a spousal IRA is $2,250. Thus, for example, a worker who is not covered by an employer retirement plan and who has a nonworking spouse would qualify for a combined maximum deductible contribution of up to $2,250, or 100 percent of the earned income of the working spouse, whichever is less. The $2,250 is not required to be split evenly between the spouses, but the contributions credited to either spouse's fund may not exceed $2,000. The spousal IRA contribution also must be reported on a joint tax return.

Rollover IRAs

Normally, benefits withdrawn from any qualified retirement plan are taxable the year in which they are received. However, certain tax-free "rollover" provisions of the tax law provide some degree of portability when an individual wishes to transfer funds from one plan to another, specifically to a *rollover IRA.*

Essentially, rollover IRAs provide a way for individuals who have received a distribution from a qualified plan to reinvest the funds in a new tax-deferred account and continue to shelter those funds and their earnings from current taxes. Rollover IRAs are used by individuals who, for example, have left one employer for another and have received a complete distribution from their previous employer's plan or by those who had invested funds in an individual IRA of one kind and want to roll over to another IRA for a higher rate of return.

A distribution received from an employer-sponsored retirement plan or from an IRA is eligible for a tax-free "rollover" if it is reinvested in an IRA within 60 days following receipt of the distribution and if the plan participant does not actually take physical receipt of the distribution. The entire amount need not be rolled over; a partial distribution may be rolled over from one IRA or eligible plan to another IRA. However, if a partial rollover is executed, the part retained will be taxed as ordinary income.

Only the person who established an IRA is eligible to benefit from the rollover treatment—with one exception. A surviving spouse who inherits IRA benefits or benefits from the deceased spouse's qualified plan *is* eligible for a rollover IRA, established in his or her own name.

Summary

Individuals prepare for the financial challenges of retirement in a variety of ways. They may be covered under any one (or more) of a variety of employer-sponsored *qualified retirement plans,* including *defined benefit* and *defined contribution* pension plans, *403(b) plans, 457 deferred compensation plans, simplified employee pension* (SEP) *plans, Keogh plans* and *401(k) plans.* Even if they are not covered under an employer-sponsored plan, individuals can save for retirement with an *individual retirement account* or *annuity* (IRA).

Key Concepts

In preparing for their licensing examination, students should be familiar with the following concepts:

qualified vs. nonqualified retirement plans	457 plans
	Keogh plans
defined contribution plans	SEP plans
defined benefit plans	tax-sheltered annuity (403(b)) plans
vesting	IRAs
minimum participation standards	spousal IRAs
401(k) plans	rollover IRAs

Chapter 12
Questions for Review *(Answers are located at the end of the book.)*

1. All of the following employed persons who have no employer-sponsored retirement plan would be eligible to set up and contribute to an IRA, EXCEPT:

   a. Miriam, age 26, secretary.
   b. Brent, age 40, medical technician.
   c. Edna, age 72, nurse.
   d. Jack, age 60, plumber.

2. David is age 40 and single. He earns $45,000 annually as an engineer with a company that has a group life plan but no employer-sponsored retirement plan. If David sets up an IRA, what is the maximum contribution he can make and deduct from taxes per year?

   a. $1,000
   b. $2,000
   c. $2,250
   d. $0

3. Herbert and Olga have been married ten years. They have no children and each has a well-paying job. However, neither is covered by an employer retirement plan. What is the maximum amount they may set aside in tax-deductible IRA funds each year for retirement?

   a. $2,200
   b. $2,250
   c. $3,000
   d. $4,000

4. All of the following statements pertaining to IRAs are correct, EXCEPT:

   a. June has accumulated $30,000 in her IRA. At age 55 she withdraws $2,500 to take a vacation. She will have to include the $2,500 in her taxable income for the year and pay a $250 penalty.
   b. Bradley, age 72, is covered by an employer-sponsored retirement plan. He cannot establish an IRA.
   c. Peter inherits $15,000 in IRA benefits from his father, who died in 1994. Peter can set up a tax-favored rollover IRA with the money and defer current income tax on the benefits received.
   d. Walter is age 60 and not disabled. If he takes a distribution from his IRA, it will not be subject to an early withdrawal penalty.

5. An employer's maximum annual contribution for an employee to a simplified employee pension (SEP) is

   a. the lesser of 15 percent of compensation or $30,000.
   b. $30,000.
   c. the lesser of 25 percent of compensation or $30,000.
   d. 25 percent of compensation or $25,000, whichever is less.

6. All of the following statements regarding Keogh plans are true, EXCEPT:

   a. They must comply with the same participation and coverage requirements as qualified corporate plans.
   b. They apply to self-employed persons.
   c. They may be funded by an individual retirement annuity.
   d. Distributions prior to age 59½ are tax deductible.

7. Which of the following statements correctly describe(s) tax advantages of a qualified retirement plan?

   I. The earnings of a qualified plan are exempt from the employee's current income taxation.
   II. Employer contributions to a qualified plan are considered to be a deductible business expense.

   a. I only
   b. II only
   c. Both I and II
   d. Neither I nor II

8. Which of the following phrases best describes vesting?

   a. The time at which a worker meets the eligibility requirements for plan participation
   b. The age at which an employee must begin to make withdrawals from retirement plans
   c. The right of a worker's spouse to be considered in retirement income needs
   d. The employee's right to funds or benefits, contributed by the employer, should he/she leave that employer

9. Marvin is single and earns $24,000 per year. The company where he is employed has a pension plan in which he participates. He is eligible to set up an IRA and deduct annual contributions of up to

   a. $0.
   b. $1,000.
   c. $2,000.
   d. $4,000.

10. All of the following should be eligible to establish a Keogh retirement plan, EXCEPT:

    a. a dentist in private practice.
    b. partners in a furniture store.
    c. a sole proprietor of a jewelry store.
    d. a major stockholder-employee in a family corporation.

13 Uses of Life Insurance

Determining Proper Insurance Amounts • Individual Uses for Life Insurance • Business Uses for Life Insurance

The valuable role life insurance plays in providing a death benefit is easily recognized. What is often overlooked or not understood are the many "living benefits" of life insurance—especially whole life insurance. The cash value feature of permanent insurance and the owner's right to borrow from the cash value make these policies an important source of funds to meet living needs. This chapter reviews the more common uses of life insurance in meeting individual needs as well as business needs, not only at the death of the policyowner but during the owner's life, too.

Determining Proper Insurance Amounts

There are many uses for life insurance, some of which are easily recognized, others of which aren't so apparent. A family's desire to provide protection against the loss of its breadwinner (or breadwinners) is certainly understood to involve life insurance. A small business's need to protect itself against the death of a key employee is also easily solved with life insurance. But how many people recognize whole life insurance as a means of saving for retirement or a child's education? The uses of life insurance extend far beyond the realm of "death benefits."

How much life insurance is enough? Professional insurance producers know that the answer is *not,* "How much can the owner afford?" Determining the proper amount of life insurance depends on a number of factors. The ability of the policyowner to comfortably afford the premium payments is, of course, an important consideration. Other questions must be asked, though. What are the planned uses for the insurance? What are the owner's long-range goals and can life insurance help meet those goals? These are just a few of the questions that the insurance producer should ask before recommending the purchase of a policy.

There are two basic approaches used today to help insurance buyers and producers determine the proper amount of life insurance. The older method, known as the *human life value approach,* has since been largely replaced by the more practical *needs approach*—but both methods can be effective in answering the primary question, "How much life insurance is needed?"

Human Life Value Approach

The concept of *human life value* was first mentioned in Chapter 1, where we discussed the purpose and function of insurance. This concept was formulated by the late Dr. Solomon S. Heubner in 1924 as a philosophical framework for understanding the services that can be performed by life and health insurance, for people both in and out of the insurance business. The result of Dr. Heubner's work is that everyone can have a better idea of how an insurance plan can be tailor-made to meet specific objectives.

Dr. Heubner pointed out that the value of a human life can and should be expressed as a *dollar valuation;* that is, determining the economic value of a person by *discounting estimated future net earnings* used for family purposes at a reasonable rate of interest.

A relatively simple method of accomplishing this is to

1. estimate an individual's average annual future earnings after deducting taxes and personal living costs;

2. estimate the number of years the individual expects to work until retirement;

3. select a reasonable interest rate (comparable to current rates paid on insurance proceeds held by insurers) at which future earnings should be discounted; and

4. multiply the present value of one dollar payable annually for the number of years until expected retirement (#2), using the selected interest rate (#3), by the estimated average future annual earnings (#1). The result is a reasonably accurate estimate of the individual's economic value to his or her family. (Tables are available that show the present value of one dollar at various interest rates.)

Example of the Human Life Value Approach

As a simple example of the human value approach, take 35-year-old George who estimates that he will earn an average of $40,000 a year until retirement at age 65. Of that $40,000, $25,000 is devoted to the care and maintenance of his family; the remaining $15,000 goes for taxes and his personal living costs.

Based on these assumptions, we can see that George's family will need and use $750,000 over George's working lifetime ($25,000 per year × 30 years). Essentially, this is George's economic value to his family over the next 30 years. However, what if today George were to die or become so severely disabled that he could not work? What source could his family rely on to continue to provide them with $25,000 a year for the next 30 years? What George needs today is a fund that, when compounded at a certain rate of interest, will produce a constant $25,000 a year for the next 30 years.

Ill. 13.1 Amounts Necessary to Produce Future Income Streams

This table illustrates the amount of capital that must be on hand today to produce various annual incomes for specified time periods. The assumed interest rate is 4 percent.

Number of Years of Income	Annual Income Streams (4 Percent Interest)			
	$10,000	$15,000	$20,000	$25,000
40	$197,928	$296,892	$395,856	$494,820
35	$186,646	$279,969	$373,292	$466,615
30	$172,920	$259,380	$345,840	$432,300
25	$156,221	$234,332	$312,442	$390,553
20	$135,903	$203,855	$271,306	$339,758

For example, in order to generate $25,000 a year for 30 years, one needs $432,300 on hand today, earning 4 percent interest.

Illustration 13.1 shows the amount of money that must be on hand today to produce annual incomes of $10,000, $15,000, $20,000 and $25,000 for various terms, assuming a 4 percent interest factor. For George, who needs a fund that will generate $25,000 a year for 30 years, the amount needed today is $432,300. Thus, George's human life value to his family is $432,300—the amount required today that, at 4 percent interest, would produce the same annual income his family consumes over the same length of time that George plans to work. This $432,300 is a measurement of how much financial protection—insurance—George's family needs in order to replace the income that will be lost if he dies or becomes disabled.

Calculating human life value is one method of determining the amount of life insurance an individual should have. It should be noted, however, that this approach has come under criticism by some industry experts who point out that it does not take into account inflation or the likelihood of increases in wages or standards of living. In other cases, it may actually overstate the amount of insurance needed if it does not take into consideration other sources of income or family situations changing. Consequently, the method most typically used today is the *needs approach.*

Needs Approach

Fundamentally, the *needs approach* for determining how much insurance protection a person should have requires first analyzing the family's (or business's) financial needs and objectives should the breadwinner (or businessperson) die or become disabled. Then, those needs are weighed against the ability of the family (or business) to meet them out of current or anticipated assets. For example, the death of a family's breadwinner will necessitate a new source of funds to replace the earnings that are now lost. The obvious answer is life insurance. However, the amount of life insurance required must take into account the amount of monthly benefits the family will be receiving from Social Security, from the deceased's pension plan, from personal savings and any other source. The difference between what is now owned (or will ultimately be available) and what is needed in terms of funds is then used to help the insurance producer recommend an insurance program that may involve the use of term insurance, permanent insurance, annuities or a combination of all three.

The needs approach is not limited to fulfilling objectives in the event of death only. It also considers a family's (or business's) *living* needs, such as providing for a child's education and planning for retirement. Again, the amount of life insurance required to meet these needs is coordinated with other assets that may be available.

In the remainder of this chapter, we will look at the many uses for life insurance. Insurance producers should consider all these concerns when helping a person or a business determine the proper insurance program to meet anticipated needs. In some cases, such as planning for education or retirement, the producer must consider the need for funds not only if the insured dies, but lives, as well. A whole life policy, in this example, can provide funds either in the form of a death benefit or cash value when those funds are needed. If the insured should die prematurely, the beneficiary can take comfort in knowing that funds will be available to meet the planned objectives. If the insured lives, the policy's cash value can be used to meet the same objectives.

A family's or business's ability to pay for the insurance deemed necessary to meet its objectives is, of course, an important consideration. It may be decided that only part of the insurance plan can be purchased immediately and the rest will be put into effect at a later date. For this reason, and because a family's or business's needs change over time, a needs approach insurance program usually includes plans for periodic reviews (usually annually) to update the program as needed.

Individual Uses for Life Insurance

The number of uses for life insurance in meeting personal and family financial needs is really quite impressive. The following list of common uses can be met with *term insurance* if the need is temporary (such as providing an additional protection fund while the children are growing up and living at home), with *whole life insurance* if the need is permanent (such as meeting estate planning objectives and for any "living" financial need) or with *annuities* if the need is for future income (such as retirement income).

In some cases, different products can be mixed to strengthen the protection. For example, a person may use a deferred annuity to plan for retirement, but also use a whole life policy to provide protection before retirement and additional retirement funds, through the policy's cash value, at retirement. Health insurance, covered later in this text, also plays an important role in a balanced insurance program.

When working with a client, the insurance producer should consider the following individual needs.

Final Expense Fund

A *final expense fund* is the amount of cash that is required (and should be on hand) at death to pay for a deceased breadwinner's last illness and funeral costs, outstanding debts, federal and state death taxes and any other unpaid taxes, legal fees, court costs and executor's fees, etc. These last expenses usually will total at least several thousand dollars. Social Security provides only a very small amount—a maximum lump-sum of $255—and only to an eligible surviving spouse or child.

Housing Fund

In the case of a breadwinner's death, there may be the need for a *home mortgage* or *rental allowance fund.* With this cash fund, a surviving family can, for example, pay off the mortgage or continue mortgage payments. If the family rents its home, the need may be for a monthly amount that will continue rental payments for a certain number of years.

Education Fund

How much, where and how expensive a child's *education* will be—together with how it is to be paid for—are goals that vary widely from family to family. However, most people want their children to obtain a "good education" and studies prove that a college education is vitally important for today's young people.

The cost of college educations have continued to spiral in recent years, currently ranging from about $24,000 or more for four years in state universities to approximately $50,000 or more in private institutions. An adequate education fund is a typical family need.

Monthly Income

The income a breadwinner provides for his or her family will obviously cease upon his or her death. However, the *income needs* of the surviving family continue. Monthly income will be needed during the years that the children are growing and living at home and then for the surviving spouse after the children are self-supporting. Thus, there are two distinct income needs periods: the *dependency period* and the *blackout period.* Ensuring a source of monthly income during these two critical periods is another use for life insurance.

Dependency Period

The *"dependency period"* refers to that period following the death of a breadwinner during which the children are living at home. The need for family income is greatest while the children are growing up. When a breadwinner dies, a surviving spouse with small children usually will be eligible for Social Security benefits. However, as we have seen, Social Security benefits, while helpful, generally will not meet the total family need.

Moreover, an eligible spouse with an eligible child receives Social Security income only while the child is under age 16 (or disabled). Once the child turns 16, his or her Social Security benefits will continue another two years, but income to the spouse ceases and will not resume until, at the earliest, the spouse reaches age 60.

Blackout Period

The period in which there are no Social Security benefits for the surviving spouse is known as the *"blackout period."* Again, the blackout period begins when the youngest child turns 16. If there are no eligible children with the surviving spouse when the breadwinner dies, the blackout period starts immediately and continues until, at the earliest, the spouse reaches age 60.

Emergency Fund

Every family faces emergencies from time to time, so a fund is needed to provide money for various miscellaneous costs and expenses that may arise, but cannot be foreseen.

Income Needs if Disabled

Basically, the same cash (except a final expense fund) and monthly income needs that arise at the death of a breadwinner exist when disability strikes a breadwinner. In both cases, the family loses the breadwinner's earnings. However, the need for income is often greater with disability because most of the disabled person's expenses continue and the family is generally faced with additional medical expenses. Medical expense insurance and disability income insurance (discussed in Chapters 16 and 17), should also be considered in a personal insurance program.

Retirement Income

The happy eventuality is that both spouses will live to a ripe old age. If so, they also will need income to supplement their Social Security or other retirement benefits. The same holds true for single individuals as well.

Business Uses for Life Insurance

Continued financial well-being for families depends not only upon income from breadwinners, but also upon the continued good health of the businesses in which they are engaged. So life insurance also plays an important role in the business world. The reasons for buying life insurance for business uses are the same as those for buying personal insurance—in one word, *protection*. Business owners wish to protect the condition of their businesses in order to provide security for their families. When people buy insurance for personal reasons their families are concerned; when they buy it for business reasons, their employees, their associates and their families are involved.

Life insurance is used in businesses in a variety of ways:

1. *As a funding medium.* For example, life insurance can be used to fund a business continuation (buy-sell) agreement to transfer ownership between partners or stockholders or to fund a deferred compensation plan.

2. *As a form of business interruption insurance.* Life insurance cannot prevent the interruption of business activity caused by death or disability; however, it can indemnify the business for losses created by these interruptions.

3. *As an employee benefit.* Life insurance can protect employees and their families from the financial problems of death, disability, illness and retirement.

Health insurance also plays a vital role in the business arena, primarily as an employee benefit. In this chapter, we will focus on business uses of life insurance; Chapter 23 covers business (and personal) uses of health insurance.

A Funding Medium

When a business owner dies, the business itself may terminate, or at least its ownership and management personnel will change. The death of a business owner often creates havoc—not only with the business, but also with the deceased owner's estate.

Insured buy-sell agreements can assure the orderly continuation of a business, while family survivors receive a fair cash settlement for a deceased owner's interest in the business. Such an agreement guarantees that cash will be available at the owner's death to purchase the deceased owner's interest, so the business can continue without financial disruption. Buy-sell plans may be used in any form of business—sole proprietorship, partnership or close corporation—so long as there are potential buyers.

Sole Proprietor Buy-Sell Plans

When a sole proprietor dies, his or her business generally comes to a sudden halt unless some arrangement has been made beforehand to continue the business. There are three alternatives. First, a member of the proprietor's family may be willing and able to pick up the reins and operate the business at the proprietor's death. If so, the proprietor may wish to leave the business to one or more family survivors as a gift. Second, there may be no interested taker, so the only thing to do is close down the business at the proprietor's death. The third, and often most desirable alternative, is for the business to be sold to a competent and faithful employee.

Employees who have been active in the operation or the management of the business are the most likely buyers. Many times, the employee's talent is recognized by customers, creditors and suppliers, and it is obvious that the employee has helped build the good reputation enjoyed by the business. As a result, there is every indication that the business can continue successfully under the employee's direction.

A two-step *buy-sell plan* then can be arranged to sell the business to the employee at the proprietor's death:

1. A *buy-sell agreement* is drafted by an attorney, setting forth the employee's obligation to buy and the responsibility of the proprietor's estate to sell the business interest at an agreed-upon price.

2. An *insurance policy* is purchased by the employee on the life of the proprietor. The employee is the owner, premium-payor and beneficiary of the policy, the proceeds from which will be used to buy the business at the proprietor's death.

In addition, when cash value life insurance is used to fund the agreement, the plan may call for a transfer of ownership should the proprietor prefer to retire at some future time. The employee then could use the policy's cash value to make a substantial down payment toward the purchase of the business. The balance of the purchase price might be paid in installments over a period of years.

Partnership Buy-Sell Plans

By law, *partnerships* are dissolved automatically upon the death of a partner. Thus, it is vital that a binding buy-sell agreement be established by the partners while they are living. Under such an agreement, the interest of any partner who dies will be sold to and purchased by the surviving partners. The price (or a formula to determine one) is agreed upon in advance and stipulated in the buy-sell plan.

When properly executed—and funded with life insurance—a partnership buy-sell plan benefits all parties involved and there is no uncertainty as to the outcome. The deceased has agreed beforehand to the sale of his or her interest. The surviving partners know they will have a legal right to buy, and the deceased's family and heirs are certain that the partnership interest will be disposed of at a fair price. Furthermore, with life insurance as the funding vehicle, the money needed to purchase the deceased partner's interest will be available at precisely the moment it is needed. So, at the death of any partner, the surviving partners are able to maintain the business while the deceased partner's estate receives full value for the deceased's interest.

There are two kinds of partnership insured buy-sell agreements: the *cross-purchase plan* and the *entity plan*.

Partnership Cross-Purchase Plan

Under the *cross-purchase buy-sell plan,* which is the more common approach to a buy-out, the partners individually agree to purchase the interest of a deceased partner, and the executor of the deceased partner's estate is directed to sell the interest to the surviving partners. The partnership itself is not a party to the agreement.

With these plans, each partner owns, is the beneficiary of and pays the premiums for life insurance on the other partner or partners in an amount equal to his or her share of the purchase price. For example, assume that a partnership worth $300,000 is owned equally by Partners A, B and C. Under an

Ill. 13.2 Partnership Cross-Purchase Buy-Sell Plan

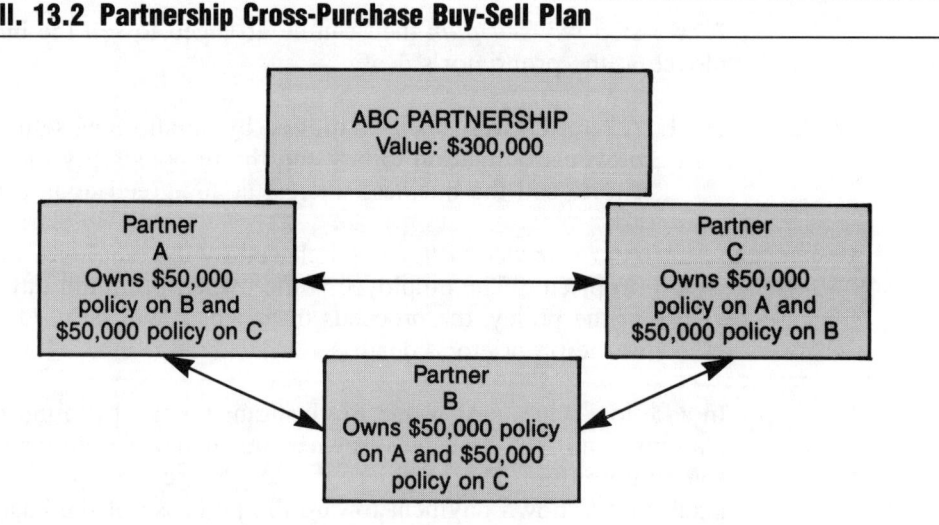

Ill. 13.3 Partnership Entity Buy-Sell Plan

```
                    XYZ PARTNERSHIP
                     Value: $600,000
        Owns $200,000  Owns $200,000  Owns $200,000
         policy on X    policy on Y    policy on Z

    Partner                                  Partner
       X                                        Z

                       Partner
                          Y
```

insured cross-purchase plan, each partner insures the life of each of the other partners for $50,000. As a result, the total insurance on each partner's life equals his or her share—$100,000—which would approximate the total purchase price the surviving partners would pay to the deceased's estate. (See Ill. 13.2.)

Partnership Entity Plan

Under the *entity buy-sell plan,* the business itself—the partnership—owns, pays for and is the beneficiary of the policies that insure the lives of the individual partners. The partnership is a party to the buy-sell agreement.

With an entity plan, when a partner dies, his or her interest is purchased from his or her estate by the partnership. This interest is then divided among the surviving partners in proportion to their own interest. For example, assume the XYZ Partnership is worth $600,000 and each partner has an equal interest. The partnership purchases a $200,000 insurance policy on the life of each partner. If Partner X dies first, the partnership buys X's interest from his estate with the $200,000 insurance proceeds and divides this interest equally between Partners Y and Z. The proportionate share of Y and Z would then be increased from $33\frac{1}{3}$ percent to 50 percent. (See Ill. 13.3.)

Close Corporation Buy-Sell Plans

In a *close corporation* (generally an incorporated family business), an insured buy-sell agreement can provide multiple advantages for all concerned. Unlike a partnership, a corporation does not cease to exist after the death of one of its owners. It is, by law, a separate entity apart from its owners, the stockholders. Nevertheless, problems are certain to develop if an agreement is not made in advance as to the disposition of a deceased stockholder's interest.

So buy-sell agreements are every bit as important to a close corporation as to a partnership. Just as in partnerships, the corporate insured buy-sell plan can take one of two forms, *cross-purchase* or *entity*. In a corporate plan, however, the entity type of agreement is known as a *stock redemption* plan. It does not matter which plan—cross-purchase or stock redemption—is used, although a close corporation with a relatively large number of stockholders usually will find the stock redemption plan more suitable. The decision about the type of plan should be left to the stockholders themselves, their attorney and their accountant.

Close Corporation Cross-Purchase Plan

The close corporation *cross-purchase agreement* is similar to that used in a partnership. The agreement calls for the surviving stockholders, as individuals, to purchase the interest of the deceased stockholder and for the estate of the deceased stockholder to sell the interest directly to the surviving stockholders. The corporation itself is not a party to the agreement. To fund a cross-purchase plan, each stockholder owns, pays for and is the beneficiary of insurance on the life of each of the other stockholders in amounts equivalent to his or her share of the purchase price.

Close Corporation Stock Redemption Plan

The corporate *stock redemption plan* operates in much the same manner as an entity plan in a partnership. The corporation, rather than the individual stockholders, is owner, premium-payor and beneficiary of policies on the lives of the stockholders. The corporation is a party to the agreement.

The amount of insurance carried by the corporation on the lives of the stockholders is equal to each stockholder's proportionate share of the purchase price. When a stockholder dies, the proceeds of the policy insuring that person are paid to the corporation. The corporation then uses the proceeds to buy the deceased's business interest represented by the stock in the deceased's estate. As with other life insurance, the premiums paid by the corporation are *not* tax deductible. The proceeds, however, are generally received income tax free, as is the case in a partnership plan.

Key-Person Insurance

Another important use of life insurance is to protect a business against interruptions caused by the loss of one of its valuable assets—a *key employee* or *key executive*.

When an individual dies, the primary function of life insurance is to offset the economic loss. We have noted how important life insurance is to the family. Key-employee or key-executive life insurance provides similar benefits—not to the family, but to the business. For example, when an insured key person dies, the insurance beneficiary is the business itself.

A key person is any person in an organization whose contribution to the operation and success of the business is essential. Therefore, an owner-executive or highly skilled employee generally may be considered a key person.

With key-person insurance, the owner, premium-payor and beneficiary of the policy is the business organization. Complete control of the policy rests with the business, which means key-person insurance can be considered a company-owned asset not earmarked for any specific purpose. The death proceeds, or even the policy's cash value, may be used for a variety of business purposes. In fact, flexibility is one of the outstanding features of this type of insurance. However, it usually is employed for some major purposes that, rather than being distinct from one another, actually work together to make the life insurance a practical company investment.

Generally speaking, the following are the primary purposes that key-person insurance serves:

1. *Business indemnification.* Key-person insurance indemnifies a business; that is, it compensates a business for any financial loss caused by the death of a valuable key person. For example, the death of a key person—whether an owner or employee—may result in less liberal credit terms from suppliers; banks may be less willing to lend the business money; valuable accounts once served by the key person may be lost. The proceeds from a key-person policy can be utilized to avoid some or all of these problems before they occur or to ease the financial burden they bring about.

2. *A reserve fund.* Key-person life insurance also provides a business with a "living benefit." When a business purchases key-person insurance, it automatically acquires an asset that can perform valuable services for the business while the key person is still alive. For example, when whole life insurance is purchased, the cash values increase steadily to provide a cash reserve fund for the business, which appears each year as an asset on the company's balance sheet.

3. *Business credit.* Disruption of a business by the death of a key person can seriously affect a business's credit. Key-person life insurance, however, can offset this danger in two ways: as tangible evidence of business character and as a guarantee of loan repayment at the death of the key person.

4. *Favorable tax treatment.* Finally, key-person life insurance receives favorable tax treatment. The death proceeds received by the business are *not* taxable. Premiums, of course, are not deductible for income purposes.

Employee Benefit Plans

Life insurance also serves an important role in the area of *employee benefits*. Basically, employee benefits are plans established by employers who pay all or a portion of the cost of the plans to benefit their employees and, in some cases, to obtain favorable tax treatment. Let's review a few of these plans.

Split-Dollar Plans

Many business organizations have found *split-dollar life insurance plans* to be an effective and economical way to encourage young employees to join the organization and to discourage the established executive from taking his or her talents and knowledge elsewhere.

Split-dollar insurance plans enable an employer and any employee of the employer's choosing to share premium payments toward the purchase of insurance on the employee's life. Therefore, the split-dollar policy is a *method* of buying life insurance rather than a reason for buying it. The employee already has determined the need for the insurance, but cannot afford the entire premium. The employer has the funds to help finance the purchase of the insurance and has a specific reason for doing so—the desire to attract and hold key employees.

The split-dollar plan is informal in nature; it requires no qualification or approval by the Internal Revenue Service. A split-dollar plan has a low premium outlay. It is a single contract that uses cash value whole life and term insurance protection (generally dividends are used to purchase one-year term; any dividend excess is applied to the year's premium) to guarantee the return of the premium money to one party while assuring a death benefit to the policy beneficiary.

In a typical split-dollar plan, the employer and the employee share the premium cost. Though there are variations, generally the employer contributes to the premium each year the amount equal to the increase in the policy's cash value. The employee pays only the balance of the premium. Upon the insured employee's death, the amount of death proceeds equal to the cash value generally goes to the employer, and the balance of the proceeds goes to the insured's beneficiary. On the other hand, if the plan is terminated while the insured is living, the cash value generally goes to the employer to compensate for the portion of premiums paid.

This method permits a financially able person or entity to help another person buy insurance, generally in the favorable interest of both parties. For example, split-dollar may be used as an incentive plan by an employer for an employee, by an employer for a stockholder/employee, for business partners, for business co-owners or by a parent for a child or child-in-law.

Deferred Compensation Plans

Deferred compensation plans are a popular way for businesses to provide an important benefit for their owners or for select employees. Basically speaking, a deferred compensation plan is an arrangement whereby an employee (or owner) agrees to forgo some portion of his or her current income (such as annual raises or bonuses) until a specified future date, typically retirement. Life insurance is a popular funding vehicle for deferred compensation plans, in that the amounts deferred are used to pay premiums on cash value life insurance. At retirement, the cash values are available to the employee to supplement income. If the employee dies prior to retirement, his or her beneficiary will receive the policy's proceeds. Deferred compensation plans can be employer-motivated or established at the employee's request.

A deferred compensation plan is an example of a *nonqualified* plan. Recall that a nonqualified plan does not receive favorable tax treatment by the IRS. On the other hand, because it is nonqualified, it allows a company to pick and choose who among its employees and/or owners may participate in the plan, without regard to years of service, salary levels or any other criteria. A nonqualified plan allows a business to provide proportionate benefits for officers, executives and other highly paid employees; a qualified plan is not nearly as flexible.

Salary Continuation Plans

Deferred compensation and *salary continuation plans* appear similar in nature, but in fact, are quite different. Deferred compensation gives employees deferred benefits in lieu of a current raise or bonus. Salary continuation, on the other hand, is an additional fringe benefit, rather than a "salary reduction" type plan. In simple terms, the *employee* funds the deferred compensation plan; the *employer* funds the salary continuation plan.

A salary continuation plan may be set up between an employer and its employees or between a business and an independent contractor. Typically, the employer agrees to pay the employee (or his or her assignee) continuing payments at retirement, death or disability. This is subject to the condition that the employee continues employment with the employer. Or the plan may require that the employee provide continuing consulting-type services after his or her retirement. The plan is informally funded through life insurance.

Other Employee Benefit Plans

There are many other types of employee benefit plans and programs. These programs include *retirement plans* (pensions, profit-sharing plans, employer-sponsored IRAs, 401(k) and 403(b) plans), *group life and health plans, child care plans, educational assistance programs, disability plans, survivor benefit plans* and *wellness programs,* to name just a few. Some might even argue that an employer's FICA contributions to the Social Security system and payments to workers' compensation programs, though they are mandatory, are forms of employee benefits.

Throughout this text, we have discussed many of these benefit plans and in the next section, we will focus specifically on health and disability programs; therefore, we will not go into any additional detail here, other than to emphasize that insurance helps make a lot of these employee benefits possible, either as the funding vehicle or as the benefit itself.

Summary

Beyond the obvious use for life insurance—to provide a source of funds for an insured's beneficiary—there are a number of other uses for this versatile product in meeting individual needs as well as business needs. Some producers find that they are most comfortable working in the individual or "family" market, while others prefer the business market.

An important duty of the professional insurance producer is to determine the proper amount of insurance needed to meet a client's needs. The two most common methods used in answering the question "How much?" are the *human life value* and the *needs* approaches.

Life insurance can be used in a variety of ways to meet personal and family financial needs. The cash values of a *whole life* insurance policy make it especially helpful in meeting permanent insurance needs such as estate planning objectives as well as financial needs that arise at death. On the other hand, *term* insurance is ideally suited for meeting temporary needs. *Annuities* are the perfect answer to a future income need, such as retirement.

Businesses also have many needs for life insurance. It can provide the foundation for business *continuation agreements* or *buy-sell plans,* for *key-person protection* or for any number of *employee benefit programs.*

Key Concepts

In preparing for their licensing examination, students should be familiar with the following concepts:

human life value approach
needs approach
individual uses for life insurance
business uses for life insurance
buy-sell plans

key-person insurance
split-dollar life insurance
deferred compensation plans
employee benefits

Chapter 13
Questions for Review *(Answers are located at the end of the book.)*

1. Which of the following statements regarding ways to determine the proper amount of life insurance are correct?

    I. The most popular method today for determining the proper amount of life insurance is the human life value approach.
    II. The needs approach takes into account family financial goals such as college education for children or retirement income for a surviving spouse.
    III. When using the needs approach to determine the proper amount of life insurance to purchase, non-insurance-type assets, such as pension benefits or personal savings, are not factors in the calculation.
    IV. Because of its available cash value, whole life insurance can be used as a means to address family financial needs while the insured still lives.

    a. I and II only
    b. I and III only
    c. II and III only
    d. II and IV only

2. All the following statements regarding survivor financial needs are correct, EXCEPT:

    a. The term "dependency period" refers to the 20-year period immediately following the insured's death during which the widowed spouse must depend on Social Security.
    b. The period for which there are no Social Security benefits for the surviving spouse is known as the blackout period.
    c. A final expense fund addresses a deceased breadwinner's last illness and funeral costs, death taxes, outstanding debts and more.
    d. A housing fund addresses a family's rental or home mortgage needs.

3. Three business partners individually agree to acquire the interest of a deceased partner and own life insurance on each of the other partners in the amount of his or her share of the business's buy-out value. What is described here is

   a. an entity buy-sell plan.
   b. a stock redemption buy-sell plan.
   c. a cross-purchase buy-sell plan.
   d. a 401(k) plan.

4. Which of the following statements regarding key-person insurance is NOT correct?

   a. Key-person life insurance indemnifies a business for financial loss caused by the death of a key employee or key executive.
   b. The business may borrow from the cash value of a permanent key-person life insurance policy.
   c. The policy's death proceeds received by the business are not taxable.
   d. Premiums for a key-person life insurance policy are a tax deductible expense to the business.

5. Which of the following statements regarding deferred compensation plans is correct?

   a. A deferred compensation plan must always be designed as a qualified plan.
   b. Life insurance is not a permissible funding vehicle, but annuities are.
   c. They permit a business to provide extra benefits to officers, executives and other highly paid employees.
   d. A deferred compensation plan must be made available to all employees who are at least 21 years old and have one year of service to the business.

6. With three partners in a business, how many life insurance policies would be required to insure a cross-purchase buy-sell plan?

   a. 3   c. 9
   b. 6   d. 12

7. Robert and his employer agree on the purchase of a split-dollar life insurance policy and the usual split-dollar approach to premium payments. Each year, the employer will contribute to the premium an amount equal to:

   a. one-half the premium.
   b. the annual dividend.
   c. the increase in the policy's cash value.
   d. two-thirds of the premium.

8. Roland is 45 years old and married. He has a son, age 19, a freshman at a local university and a daughter, age 8. Decreasing term insurance could be recommended for Roland for which of the following reasons?

   a. To supplement retirement income
   b. To guarantee a college education for the son
   c. To provide payment protection
   d. To provide a college education fund for the daughter

III PRINCIPLES OF HEALTH INSURANCE

14 Introduction to Health Insurance

Basic Forms of Coverage • How Health Insurance Is Purchased • Characteristics

The terms "health and accident insurance," "accident and sickness insurance" and "health insurance" are used interchangeably in the health insurance industry, from state to state and company to company. No matter what it is called in the industry, it all means the same thing to consumers—a critically important type of insurance that provides financial protection from the high costs of illness and injury.

The remainder of this text is devoted to the principles of health insurance. We will take a look at the types of health insurance plans, including plans for the elderly; the providers of health insurance coverages; policy provisions; underwriting standards; and more. This chapter is designed to provide an overview of the broad field of health insurance, focusing on the basics.

Basic Forms of Health Insurance Coverage

Health insurance (as it will be called in this text) refers to the broad field of insurance plans that provide protection against the financial consequences of illness, accidents, injury and disability. Statistics reveal that approximately 214 million Americans are protected by one or more forms of health coverage. Health insurance claims payments made to insureds amount to billions of dollars every year, and approximately half of these claims payments are made by commercial insurance companies.

Within the broad field of health insurance, there are three distinct categories of health coverage: *medical expense insurance, disability income insurance* and *accidental death and dismemberment insurance.* Each of these coverages will be discussed in detail in subsequent chapters, but an introduction is appropriate here.

Medical Expense Insurance

Medical expense insurance provides financial protection against the cost of medical care by reimbursing the insured, fully or in part, for these costs. It

Ill. 14.1

Health Coverages and What They Provide

Type of Coverage	Provisions and Benefits
Medical Expense Insurance	Provides benefits for the cost of medical care. Depending on the type of policy (and its specific provisions), coverage can range from limited (coverage for hospital costs only, for example) to very broad (coverage for all aspects of medical services and care).
Disability Income Insurance	Provides a specified periodic income to the insured—usually on a monthly basis—in the event he or she becomes disabled.
Accidental Death and Dismemberment Insurance	Provides a lump-sum payment in the event the insured dies due to an accident or suffers the loss of one or more body members due to an accident.

includes many kinds of plans that cover hospital care, surgical expenses, physician expenses, medical treatment programs, outpatient care and the like.

Disability Income Insurance

Disability income insurance is designed to provide a replacement income when wages are lost due to a disability. As such, it does not cover the medical expenses associated with a disability; rather, it provides the disabled insured with a guaranteed flow of periodic income payments while he or she is disabled.

Accidental Death and Dismemberment Insurance

Accidental death and dismemberment insurance, commonly referred to as AD&D, is the purest form of accident insurance, providing the insured with a lump-sum benefit amount in the event of accidental death *or* dismemberment under accidental circumstances. Typically, AD&D coverage is a part of a group insurance plan.

Within each of the above three categories are many forms and variations of coverage that have evolved to meet unique insurance needs. Even the type of health insurance provider—of which there are many—can make a difference in the basic makeup of any of these kinds of coverages. Each of these basic coverages, as well as the many types of health insurance providers, will be discussed in later chapters. They are introduced here to help acquaint you with the health insurance field in general.

How Health Insurance Is Purchased

As is the case with life insurance, health insurance is available to individuals and families through individual plans and policies or group plans and policies, including blanket policies and franchise policies.

Individual health insurance is issued by commercial insurers and service organizations as contracts between the insured and the company. Though all companies have standard policies for the coverages they offer, most allow an individual to select various options or benefit levels that will most precisely meet his or her needs. Individual health contracts require an application and usually the proposed insured must provide evidence of insurability.

Group health insurance, also issued by commercial insurers and service organizations, provides coverage under a master contract to members of a specified group. Like group life, group health plans are available to employers, trade and professional associations, labor unions, credit unions and other organizations. Insurance is extended to the individuals in the group through the master contract, usually without individual underwriting and usually without requiring group members to provide evidence of insurability. The employer or the association is the policyowner and is responsible for premium payments. The employer may pay the entire premium or may require some contribution from each member to cover the insurance cost. Generally speaking, the provisions and coverages of group health insurance contracts are more liberal than individual health contracts.

Health insurance is also provided through *state and federal government* programs. At the state level, *Medicaid* is available to assist low-income individuals in meeting the costs of medical care. The federal government offers health insurance protection through *Medicare* and *OASDI disability* provisions, components of the Social Security system.

Characteristics of Health Insurance

Though closely related to life insurance in purpose, health insurance differs from its life cousin in several important ways. A review here of the distinguishing characteristics of health insurance will set the stage for the more in-depth discussion to follow in later chapters.

Renewability Provisions

Life insurance (particularly whole life insurance) and annuities are characterized by their permanence; the policies cannot be canceled by the insurer unless the policyowner fails to make a required premium payment. Even term life policies are guaranteed effective for the duration of the term, as long as premiums are paid. Health insurance is not so permanent in nature. Health insurance policies may contain any one of a wide range of *renewability provisions,* which define the rights of the insurer to cancel the policy at different points during the life of the policy. There are five principal renewability classifications: *cancelable, optionally renewable, conditionally renewable, guaranteed renewable* and *noncancelable.* The distinguishing characteristics of each type will be covered in Chapter 20, but generally speaking, the more advantageous the renewability provisions to the insured, the more expensive the coverage.

Premium Factors

Like life insurance, health insurance is funded by the regular payment of premiums. Unlike life insurance, however, there are relatively few payment options available with a health policy. For example, health policies do not offer any sort of "limited payment" option, as one would find with, say, a ten-pay or paid-up at 65 life policy. Health insurance policies are paid for on a year-by-year basis. Furthermore, except for the noncancelable type of policy cited previously, health insurance premium rates *are* subject to periodic increases. Health premiums can be paid under one of several different payment modes, including annual, semi-annual, quarterly and monthly. Monthly premiums are often paid through some form of preauthorized check method, by which the insurer automatically obtains the premium directly from the policyholder's checking account.

There are various factors that enter into premium calculations for health insurance. These include interest, expense, types of benefits and *morbidity*. Morbidity is the expected incidence of sickness or disability within a given age group during a given period of time; it is to health insurance what mortality is to life insurance. Other health insurance premium factors are claims experience and the age, sex and occupation of the insured. All of these factors are discussed in detail in Chapter 21.

Participating vs. Nonparticipating Policies

Health insurance policies may be written on either a *participating* or *nonparticipating* basis. Most individual health insurance is issued on a nonparticipating basis. Group health insurance, on the other hand, is generally participating and provides for *dividends* or *experience rating*.

Group health plans issued by mutual companies usually provide for dividends, while stock companies frequently issue experience-rated plans. A group policy that is experience-rated may make premium reductions retroactive for 12 months. Premium increases for such policies are not retroactive. Experience-rated refunds may be contingent upon renewal of the master policy, but the payment of dividends usually is not contingent upon renewal.

Cost-accounting formulas are complex and vary from insurer to insurer; however, the two major factors that influence whether or not dividends or experience-rated refunds are payable are *expenses* and *claims costs* of the insurer. If these cost items are less than anticipated, the group policyowner benefits by receiving a dividend or refund credit. If expenses and claims costs are higher than expected, the group policyowner may not qualify for a dividend or refund credit.

Reserves

Reserves are set aside by an insurance company and designated for the payment of future claims. Part of each premium is designated for the reserves.

Two types of health insurance reserves are *premium reserves* and *loss (or claims) reserves*. Premium reserves reflect the liability of the insurer for losses that have not occurred but for which premiums have been paid. Reserves earmarked as loss (or claims) reserves represent the insurer's liability for losses that have occurred, but for which settlement is not yet complete. The details of how reserves are handled and recorded by the company are very technical. State laws dictate the minimum requirements for reserves for both life and health insurance. The annual statements required by state insurance departments break down a company's reserves in considerable detail.

Claims

The role of the health insurance claims examiner differs somewhat from that of the life insurance claims examiner. In the case of life insurance, most *claims* are fairly well defined: the amount of insurance coverage is readily determined by the policy and benefits are payable if the insured has died. With health insurance, though, the claims process is not so clearly defined. Medical expense insurance, for example, is typically based on a *contract of reimbursement* meaning that the benefit an insured receives is not fixed, but instead is dependent on the amount of the loss. Its purpose is to reimburse the insured for the amount of loss sustained (within limits). This is in contrast to life insurance, AD&D and disability income insurance that are all *valued contracts*—they pay the amount stated in the contract if a defined event, such as death or disability, occurs.

The health claims examiner must also decide if, in fact, a loss has actually occurred. This is especially challenging in disability income cases, where a subjective assessment of "disabled" can create misunderstandings.

Summary

This chapter introduced the important field of health insurance. There are many hybrid plans that offer health protection in three different forms: *medical expense, disability income* and *accidental death and dismemberment.* Health insurance is available to individuals and families on an *individual basis,* through a *group plan* or by the *federal government.* It is distinguished by many factors, including its provisions for renewability, premium factors, whether or not the contract is participating, reserves and its claims procedures. In the following chapters, we'll review the different types of health insurance and health insurance providers in greater detail.

Key Concepts

In preparing for their licensing examination, students should be familiar with the following concepts:

medical expense insurance
disability income insurance

accidental death and
    dismemberment insurance
valued vs. reimbursement contracts

Chapter 14
Questions for Review *(Answers are located at the end of the book.)*

1. Which of the following statements pertaining to health insurance policy premium factors is correct?

    a. A "policy fee" is another term for policy premium.
    b. A policyowner has an individual health plan; therefore, the policy is most likely a participating policy.
    c. Age and sex of the individual insureds would have the most influence on a group health insurance policy's experience rating refund credit.
    d. Pearl files a claim against her major medical policy for a $9,800 hospital bill. The claim will likely be paid out of the insurer's reserves.

2. All of the following are basic forms of health insurance coverage, EXCEPT:

    a. medical expense.
    b. limited pay health.
    c. disability income.
    d. accidental death and dismemberment.

3. Which of the following premium factors is unique to health insurance (as opposed to life insurance)?

    a. Age
    b. Sex
    c. Morbidity
    d. Interest

4. Which of the following statements regarding health insurance is true?

    a. Once issued, health insurance policies cannot be canceled by the insurer.
    b. There are a variety of premium-payment options available with health insurance policies.
    c. Medical expense reimbursement policies are indemnity contracts.
    d. Disability income policies are designed to pay the medical expenses associated with a disability.

5. Assume a health insurance contract states that it will pay $350 a month to the insured, should he or she become totally disabled. Which term most aptly defines this kind of contract?

    a. Participating
    b. Valued
    c. Inclusive
    d. Reimbursement

15 Health Insurance Providers

Commercial Insurers • Service Providers
• Government Insurance Programs • Alternatives

When it comes to obtaining health insurance coverage, Americans have a variety of providers from which to choose. On a very broad plane, the entire field of health insurance providers can be divided into three general categories: commercial insurers, service providers and state and federal government. It is from these three general groups that the variety of providers emerge. In all cases, though, the objective is the same: to provide protection against the costs associated with illness, injury or disability. How each provider goes about this task is unique. In this chapter we will review the prominent types of health providers and introduce Medicare, which plays an important role in providing health insurance for a large segment of our population.

Commercial Insurance Providers

Health insurance may be written by a number of *commercial insurers,* including life insurance companies, casualty insurance companies or monoline companies that specialize in one or more types of medical expense and disability income insurance. This includes both individual and group insurance policies. Among life insurance companies, health insurance is offered by "ordinary" companies as well as "debit" (or home service) companies. (Recall that debit companies sell what are known as "industrial" policies.)

Commercial insurance companies function on the *reimbursement approach;* that is, policyowners obtain medical treatment from whatever source they feel is most appropriate and, per the terms of their policy, submit their charges to their insurer for reimbursement. The *right of assignment* built into most commercial health policies lets policyowners assign benefit payments from the insurer directly to the health care provider, thus relieving the policyowner of first having to pay the medical care provider. The right to assign a policy's benefits, however, does not change the fact that the policy is reimbursing the insured for covered medical expenses.

Service Providers

Service providers are not insurers per se; rather, they operate on the principle that their *subscribers* (the term used in place of policyholders) receive medical care *services* as a result of their payment of premiums. Subscribers typically are not billed for services rendered by a medical care provider. Instead, the care provider—who has entered into an agreement with the service organization to provide medical care—is paid directly by the service organization. As you can see, this is the opposite of the cash reimbursement approach taken by commercial insurers. Under the service approach, the subscriber receives "benefits" in the form of medical services for which payment has already been made (via the premium).

This service approach is used primarily by three types of organizations: *Blue Cross* and *Blue Shield organizations, health maintenance organizations* (HMOs) and *preferred provider organizations* (PPOs).

Blue Cross and Blue Shield

Blue Cross and *Blue Shield* are voluntary not-for-profit health care service organizations. Blue Cross offers prepayment plans designed to cover hospital services; Blue Shield covers surgical expenses and other medical services performed by physicians.

Generally, Blue Cross and Blue Shield plans work in close cooperation with each other, within a given state or region within a state. In fact, in the past few years, most Blue Cross and Blue Shield plans have merged into single plans. Unlike commercial insurance companies, Blue Cross and Blue Shield organizations have contractual arrangements with hospitals and physicians. These contracts provide for payments for services rendered to subscribers with agreed-upon rate or fee schedules.

Consequently, in order to obtain full value from their service plans, subscribers are usually required to utilize the contracted hospitals and physicians for medical care. Payments for services are made directly by Blue Cross or Blue Shield to the hospitals and physicians; subscribers are responsible only for services not covered by their particular plans. (Blue Cross and Blue Shield plans offer a broad and comprehensive range of services from which the subscriber can choose.)

Blue Cross and Blue Shield plans are available on an individual, family or group basis.

Health Maintenance Organizations

A *health maintenance organization,* or HMO, is another type of organization offering comprehensive prepaid health care services to its subscribing members. HMO participants can be members under a group insurance plan or they can be individual or family members.

HMOs are distinguished by the fact that they not only finance health care services for their subscribers on a prepayment basis, but they also organize and deliver the health services as well. Subscribers pay a fixed periodic fee to the HMO (as opposed to paying for services only when needed) and are provided with a broad range of health services, from routine doctor visits to emergency and hospital care. This care is rendered by physicians and hospitals who participate in the HMO. HMOs are known for stressing preventive care, the objective being to reduce the number of unnecessary hospital admissions and duplication of services. Unlike commercial insurers and Blue Cross/Blue Shield organizations, HMOs rarely assess deductibles; when they do, the charges are nominal, such as $2 for prescription drugs or $5 for an office visit.

There are two basic types of HMOs: an *open-panel* HMO and a *closed-panel* HMO.

1. *Open-panel HMO.* An open-panel HMO is characterized by a network of physicians who work out of their own private offices and participate in the HMO on a part-time basis.

2. *Closed-panel HMO.* A closed-panel HMO is represented by a group of physicians who are salaried employees of the HMO and work out of its facilities.

Health maintenance organizations may be self-contained and self-funded based on dues or fees from their subscribers, or they may contract for excess insurance or administrative services provided by insurance companies. In fact, some HMOs are sponsored by insurance companies.

The Health Maintenance Act of 1973, which provided some federal funding for these organizations, spurred the HMO movement forward. One of its provisions requires employers with 25 or more employees to offer enrollment in an HMO if they provide health care benefits for their workers.

Preferred Provider Organizations

Another type of health insurance provider, a recent entrant to the field of health insurers, is the *preferred provider organization* or PPO. A preferred provider organization is a collection of health care providers, such as physicians, hospitals and clinics, who offer their services to certain groups at prearranged prices. In exchange, the group refers its members to the preferred providers for health care services.

Unlike HMOs, preferred provider organizations usually operate on a fee-for-service-rendered basis, not on a prepaid basis. Members of the PPO select from among the preferred providers for needed services. Also in contrast to HMOs, PPO health care providers are normally in private practice. They have agreed to offer their services to the group and its members at fees that are typically less than what they normally charge. In exchange, because the group refers its members to the PPO, the providers broaden their patient/service base. One of the features that attracts groups to PPOs is the discounted fees that are negotiated in advance.

Groups that contract with PPOs are very often employers, insurance companies or other health insurance benefits providers. While these groups do not mandate that individual members must use the PPO, a reduced benefit is typical if they do not. For instance, individuals may pay a $100 deductible if they use PPO services and a $500 deductible if they go outside the PPO for health care services.

Government Insurance Programs

For many people, health care cost protection is made available through a state or federal government program. At the federal level, *Medicare* is the primary source of health insurance. It is a part of the Social Security program that also provides *disability income* to qualified workers under OASDI. At the state level, *Medicaid* offers protection to financially needy individuals, and *state workers' compensation* programs provide benefits for workers who suffer from occupational injuries or illnesses. Let's take a brief look at each. Because of their significance to the health care needs of seniors, a detailed discussion of Medicare and Medicaid is included in Chapter 19.

Medicare

The federally administered *Medicare* program took effect in 1966. Its purpose is to provide hospital and medical expense insurance protection to those aged 65 and older, to those of any age who suffer from chronic kidney disease or to those who are receiving Social Security disability benefits.

Social Security Disability Income

In addition to Medicare, the federal government also provides *disability-related benefits* through the Social Security OASDI program. Though this subject was covered in Chapter 11, let's review some of the important points here.

Disability income benefits are available to covered workers who qualify under Social Security requirements. One of the requirements is that the individual must be so mentally or physically disabled that he or she cannot perform any substantial gainful work. In addition, the impairment must be expected to last at least 12 months or result in an earlier death. The determination of disability for Social Security purposes is usually made by a government agency. In addition to meeting the definition of disabled, the individual must have earned a certain minimum number of quarters of coverage under Social Security.

A five-month waiting period is required before an individual will qualify for benefits, during which time he or she must remain disabled. For example, if Jerry became disabled in January, he must wait five full months—February through June—before he will qualify for disability benefits. His first benefit payment would be for July, and it would be paid in August. No second five-month waiting period is required if the disabled worker recovers and then is disabled again within five years.

Medicaid

Medicaid is Title XIX of the Social Security Act, added to the Social Security program in 1965. Its purpose is to provide matching federal funds to states for their medical public assistance plans to help needy persons, regardless of age. If family income is below a specified level, Medicaid benefits generally are available. Although each state has some leeway in establishing eligibility requirements, Medicaid benefits are generally payable to low income individuals who are blind, disabled or under 21 years of age. The benefits may be applied to Medicare deductibles and copayment requirements.

State Workers' Compensation Programs

All states have *workers' compensation laws,* which were enacted to provide mandatory benefits to employees for work-related injuries, illness or death. Employers are responsible for providing workers' compensation benefits to their employees and do so by purchasing coverage through state programs, private insurers or by self-insuring.

Although each state's laws differ with regard to procedures, requirements and minimum benefits, there is uniformity to the following extent:

- If a worker is killed in an industrial accident, the law provides for payment of burial expenses, subject to a maximum amount, and compensation for the surviving spouse or other dependents of the worker at the time of death.

- Regardless of any negligence by the employer, he or she is liable for work-related disabilities that employees suffer.

- Under the law, a disabled employee is entitled to benefits as a matter of right, without having to sue the employer for benefits. However, in return for the benefits provided under the law, the employee gives up the right to sue the employer.

- Under most laws, a disabled employee is paid benefits on a weekly or monthly basis, rather than in a lump sum.

- The employer must provide the required benefits; the employee does not contribute to the plan.

The law provides for a schedule of benefits, the size of which is based on such factors as the severity of the disability and the employee's wages.

Alternative Methods of Providing Health Insurance

For businesses and individuals, an alternative to a commercial or service health insurance plan is *self-insurance.* Large corporations especially will self-insure their sick-leave plans for their employees. Labor unions, fraternal associations and other groups often self-insure their medical expense plans through dues or contributions from members. Others may self-insure part of a plan and use insurance to protect against large, unpredictable losses.

Many of these self-insured plans are administered by insurance companies or other organizations that are paid a fee for handling the paperwork and processing the claims. When an outside organization provides these functions, it is called an *administrative-services-only* (ASO) or *third-party administrator* (TPA) arrangement.

To bolster a self-insured plan, some groups adopt a *minimum premium plan* (MPP). These plans are designed to insure against a certain level of large, unpredictable losses, above and beyond the self-insured level. As the name implies, MPPs are available for a fraction of the insurer's normal premium.

Summary

A number of sources are available for people seeking health insurance protection. *Commercial insurance companies,* which include life insurance companies as well as mono-line and casualty insurance companies, are one source. *Service providers,* including the *Blue Cross* and *Blue Shield organizations* and the more recently introduced *health maintenance organizations,* are others. *Preferred provider organizations* provide an additional option by contracting their services with employer groups or insurers.

For many people, health insurance protection is obtained through a *government-sponsored program.* At the federal level, the Social Security program (OASDI) provides both disability income benefits and medical expense protection, the latter through the *Medicare* program.

At the state level, medical expense insurance is provided to financially needy citizens who are blind, disabled or under age 21 through the *Medicaid* program. Because Medicaid is state-administered (and only partially federally supported), each state has some leeway in setting the qualification standards for its program. All states have also enacted *workers' compensation* programs, which provide benefits to workers for occupational illnesses and disabilities.

Some large employers prefer to retain the risk of covering their employees' medical care expenses, or at least part of the expenses, and thus *self-insure* their plan.

Key Concepts

In preparing for their licensing examination, students should be familiar with the following concepts:

commercial health insurers
service providers
health maintenance organizations (HMOs)
preferred provider organizations (PPOs)
self-insured plans
administrative-services-only (ASO) plans
third-party administrator (TPA) plans
Medicare
Social Security disability income
Medicaid
workers' compensation

Chapter 15
Questions for Review *(Answers are located at the end of the book.)*

1. HMOs are known for stressing

    a. preventive medicine and early treatment.
    b. state-sponsored health care plans.
    c. in-hospital care and services.
    d. health care services for government employees.

2. Which of the following statements regarding Blue Cross and Blue Shield organizations is/are correct?

   I. Blue Cross provides surgical expense prepayment plans.
   II. Blue Shield provides hospital expense prepayment plans.
   III. Reimbursement for hospital and medical expenses is made directly by Blue Cross and Blue Shield to the subscriber.
   IV. Both Blue Cross and Blue Shield plans are available on a group basis.

   a. I, II and III
   b. III only
   c. IV only
   d. All of the above

3. Which of the following organizations would make reimbursement payments directly to the insured individual for covered medical expenditures?

   a. Blue Cross/Blue Shield
   b. Commercial insurer
   c. Preferred provider organization
   d. Health maintenance organization

4. Marty just received his first Social Security disability payment. From this, we can assume

   a. he had previously applied for Medicaid.
   b. he is at least 65 years of age.
   c. his disability is expected to last at least 12 months.
   d. his disability commenced three months ago.

5. Which of the following statements pertaining to health maintenance organizations (HMOs) is/are correct?

   a. An insurance company that also markets group health insurance is known as an HMO.
   b. If a person joins an HMO and undergoes a physical examination, he or she will be billed for the exam and each subsequent medical service as it is performed.
   c. An insurance company may sponsor an HMO or assist an HMO by providing contractual services.
   d. All of the above

6. The waiting period before qualifying for Social Security disability benefits is

   a. 3 months.
   b. 5 months.
   c. 6 months.
   d. 12 months.

7. Which of the following statements regarding workers' compensation plans is/are correct?

   a. Benefit amounts are mandated by the federal government.
   b. A worker will qualify for benefits only if his or her disability or illness was a result of employer negligence.
   c. Benefits may be financed by private insurers, state funds or self-insurance.
   d. All of the above

8. All of the following statements pertaining to Medicaid are correct, EXCEPT:

   a. It provides federal matching funds to states for medical public assistance plans.
   b. Its purpose is to help eligible needy persons with medical assistance.
   c. Medicaid benefits may be used to pay the deductible and coinsurance amounts of Medicare.
   d. It limits financial assistance to persons age 65 or over who are in need of medical services they cannot afford.

16 MEDICAL EXPENSE INSURANCE

Purpose • Basic Medical Expense Plans • Major Medical Expense Plans • Other Types of Medical Expense Plans

When people speak of their "health insurance," they are usually referring to insurance that protects against the costs of medical care. Medical expense insurance, which is available in several different forms, reimburses policyowners for part or all of the costs of obtaining medical care. It is a vital form of insurance considered by many to be the one type of insurance they cannot do without.

Purpose of Medical Expense Insurance

Medical expense insurance provides financial protection against the cost of medical care for accidents and sickness. In this broad context, "medical care" includes hospital care, physician services, surgical expenses, drugs, nursing and convalescent care, diagnostic treatment, laboratory services, rehabilitative services, dental care, physical therapy—in short, all medical treatment and services. To what extent a given medical expense policy covers medical care—the specific types of services and treatments covered and the benefits provided—depends on the policy. Generally speaking, medical expense insurance is available through one of two different policy plans: *basic medical insurance* or *major medical insurance*. Basic medical insurance limits coverage to select types of medical care; major medical insurance, which can work either as a supplement to a basic plan or as a comprehensive stand-alone plan, provides broader, more complete coverage.

Reimbursement vs. Indemnity Approach

Medical expense plans typically pay benefits as a *reimbursement* of actual expenses, although some benefits are paid as fixed *indemnities*, irrespective of the extent of actual loss. The distinction can be clarified with an example.

Assume Karl owns a reimbursement-type medical expense policy that pays a maximum benefit of $200,000. He is hospitalized for ten days and incurs covered medical expenses totaling $10,000. The policy would provide benefits of $10,000—the expenses *incurred*.

Assume Doris owns an indemnity-type medical expense policy that provides a $100-per-day benefit for each day of hospitalization. She is hospitalized for ten days, incurring medical expenses of $10,000. Her policy will *indemnify* her by providing benefits of $1,000: ten days at $100 per day. Indemnity medical expense policies do not pay expenses or bills; they merely provide the insured with a stated benefit amount for each day he or she is confined to a hospital as an inpatient. The money may be used by the insured for any purpose.

With this foundation, we're ready to take a look at the two kinds of medical expense insurance policies: *basic* and *major medical*. Within these two categories are many types of plans.

Basic Medical Expense Plans

Basic medical expense insurance is sometimes called "first dollar insurance" because, unlike major medical expense insurance, it provides benefits "up front," without requiring the insured to first satisfy a deductible. For many years it was the leading type of medical expense insurance sold, but today it is overshadowed by major medical insurance. This is due largely to the fact that basic medical expense policies limit the type and duration of services covered and dollar amounts that will be paid (or reimbursed) to the insured. Major medical plans are not so limiting.

Basic medical expense policies classify their coverages according to general categories of medical care: *hospital expense, surgical expense* and *physicians' (nonsurgical) expense*. Additional plans cover *nursing expenses* and *convalescent care*. While it is common to find all categories contained under the umbrella of one policy, they can be written as separate coverages.

Basic Hospital Expense

Basic hospital expense insurance reimburses policyowners for the cost of hospital confinement. (Many policies today also provide coverage for outpatient care if it is provided in lieu of hospitalized care.) Basic hospital policies cover costs associated with daily room and board and other miscellaneous expenses.

Daily Room and Board

Basic hospital expense policies cover the daily cost of *room and board.* There are no set standards these policies follow; they vary by daily amount payable and by the length of time the benefits are payable. For example, some policies will pay an in-hospital benefit for as long as 365 days, while others pay benefits for only 90 days or 30 days. Some policies reimburse the insured for the daily room and board charge up to a specified dollar amount. Others provide a service type of benefit, paying an amount equal to the hospital's daily charge for a semiprivate room.

Miscellaneous Expenses

In addition to room and board, basic hospital expense policies cover *hospital "extras"* or *miscellaneous charges,* up to a specified limit. Covered miscellaneous expenses include drugs, X rays, anesthesia, lab fees, dressings, use of the operating room and supplies.

Generally, the maximum miscellaneous expense benefit is expressed as a multiple of the daily room and board benefit (ten times room and board or 20 times room and board, for example) or it may be a stated dollar amount. Some policies may even specify individual maximums for certain expenses within the maximum miscellaneous benefit. For example, the overall maximum for miscellaneous expenses may be $1,000, with maximums of $150 for use of the operating room, $125 for anesthesia, $75 for drugs and so on. But the total miscellaneous benefit would be limited to $1,000.

It is important to note that physicians' services are not covered under a basic hospital expense policy, even in the case of surgery. The cost for a physician is covered under a basic surgical expense or basic physicians' (nonsurgical) expense policy.

Basic Surgical Expense

Basic surgical expense policies provide coverage for the cost of a surgeon's services, whether the surgery is performed in the hospital or out. Generally included in the coverage is the surgeon's fees as well as the fees of the anesthesiologist and any postoperative care.

There are three different approaches used by insurers in providing this type of coverage and determining the benefits payable. These are the *surgical schedule* approach, the *"reasonable and customary"* approach and the *relative value scale* approach.

Surgical Schedule

Under the *surgical schedule* method, every surgical procedure is assigned a dollar amount by the insurer. Although the policy itself will only contain a representative sampling of common surgical procedures and their "prices," a complete listing of all established surgical procedures is maintained in the insurer's claims department, for use by its claims examiners. When a claim is submitted to the insurer, the claims examiner reviews the policy to determine what amount is payable; if the surgeon's bill is more than the allowed charge set by the insurer, it is up to the insured to pay the surgeon the difference. If the surgeon's bill is less than the allowed charge, the insurer will pay only the full amount billed; the claim payment will never exceed the amount charged.

Reasonable and Customary Approach

Whereas the surgical schedule method pays up to a stated dollar amount regardless of the actual charge, the *"reasonable and customary" approach* is more open in its determination of benefits payable. Under this approach, the surgical expense is compared to what is deemed "reasonable and customary" for the geographical part of the country where the surgery was performed. If the charge is within the "reasonable and customary" parameters, the expense is paid, usually in full.

Relative Value Scale

The *relative value scale* is similar to the surgical schedule method, except that instead of a flat dollar amount being assigned to every surgical procedure, a set of *points* is assigned.

The number of points assigned to any one procedure is relative to the number of points assigned to a *maximum procedure.* Typically, something like a triple heart bypass would be considered a maximum procedure and assigned a high number of points (usually 500 or 1,000). Every other procedure is also assigned a set of points relative to that; an appendectomy, which is a major procedure but not as serious as a triple bypass, might be assigned 200 points. Setting a broken finger might rate five points.

How are benefit amounts determined? The policy will carry a stated dollar-per-point amount, known as the *conversion factor,* to determine the benefit. For example, a plan with a $5-per-point conversion factor would pay $1,000 for a 200-point procedure. Generally the larger the conversion factor, the larger the policy's premium.

Basic Physicians' (Nonsurgical) Expense

Basic physicians' expense insurance provides benefits for nonsurgical physicians' services. Examples of services covered include office visits and the care by a physician while the insured is hospitalized for a nonsurgical reason. Benefits are usually based on the indemnity approach; for example, a plan might pay a flat fee of $50 per visit (but not to exceed the actual charge, if less). These policies typically carry a number of exclusions, such as X rays, drugs and dental treatment.

Other Basic Plans

Two other basic medical expense plans are worth noting: *nurses' expense benefits* and *convalescent care facility benefits.*

Nurses' expense benefits coverage generally is limited to private duty nursing care arranged in accordance with a doctor's order while the insured is a hospital patient. It may cover both registered professional and licensed practical nurses.

Ill. 16.1

Basic Medical Expense Coverages

Category of Medical Expense	What Is Covered
Hospital expense	• Daily room and board • Miscellaneous expenses
Surgical expense	• Cost of surgeon's services • Anesthesiologist
Physicians' expense	• Office visits • Nonsurgical care by a physician while hospitalized
Nurses' expense	• Private duty nursing care
Convalescent care expense	• Skilled nursing facility expenses

Basic medical expense policies provide coverage according to general categories of medical care. Policies covering all categories are available, as are policies that cover only select categories.

Convalescent care facility benefit coverage provides a maximum daily benefit for confinement in a skilled nursing facility for a specified recovery period following discharge from a hospital. Rest cures and normal custodial care are not covered.

Major Medical Expense Plans

Major medical expense insurance, often called *"major medical,"* has made it possible for many people to achieve substantial protection against the high cost of medical care. It offers broad coverage under one policy, typically paying benefits for hospital room and board, hospital extras, nursing services in-hospital or at home, blood, oxygen, prosthetic devices, surgery, physicians' fees, ambulance services and more. In addition, it provides for high benefit limits. It generally is available on both an individual basis and a group basis.

The services and supplies covered under a major medical policy must be performed or prescribed by a licensed physician and necessary for the treatment of an insured's illness or injury. The benefit period may be defined on a calendar-year basis or may be specified as a two-year to five-year period. In contrast to basic medical expense insurance, major medical policies provide total maximum lifetime benefits to individual insureds from about $250,000 to $1,000,000 or more.

Major medical expense insurance usually picks up where basic medical expense insurance leaves off, in one of two ways: as a *supplement* to a basic plan or as a *compenhensive stand-alone plan.*

Supplementary Major Medical

A *supplementary major medical plan* covers expenses not included at all under a basic plan. It also provides coverage for expenses that are in excess of the dollar maximums specified in the basic policy as well as those expenses no longer covered by the basic plan because the benefits have been exhausted.

With a supplemental plan, major medical coverage is coordinated with various basic medical expense coverages, picking up where the basic plan leaves off. For example, a basic plan may provide for hospital room and board benefits for a maximum of 45 days. If that basic plan were supplemented with a major medical plan, the supplementary major medical plan would cover hospital room and board expenses beginning on the 46th day. Or, if a basic plan provides a maximum benefit of $1,500 for a specific surgical procedure and the actual cost of the procedure was $2,000, a major medical supplement would cover the additional $500. In addition, because of the broad coverage associated with most major medical supplements, a supplement will likely cover expenses that are either beyond the scope of the basic plan or excluded from its coverage.

Comprehensive Major Medical

The second type of major medical plan is the *comprehensive major medical plan.* Comprehensive plans are distinguished by the fact that they cover virtually all medical expenses—hospital expenses, physician and surgeon expenses, nursing care, drugs, physical therapy, diagnostic X rays and laboratory services, medical supplies and equipment, transfusions and more—under a *single policy*.

Major medical plans, whether supplementary or comprehensive, typically include two important features: *deductibles* and *coinsurance*. Both of these features require the insured to absorb some of the cost of his or her medical expenses, thus allowing the insurer to avoid small claims and keep the cost of premiums down. In contrast, a basic medical plan usually does not include either of these features; instead it imposes limitations in the form of maximum benefit amounts that will be paid.

Deductibles

A *deductible* is a stated initial dollar amount that the individual insured is required to pay before insurance benefits are paid. For example, if a plan has a flat $250 annual deductible, the insured is responsible for the first $250 of medical expenses every year. Covered expenses in excess of $250 are then paid by the major plan (subject to any coinsurance).

Depending on the type of major medical policy, the deductible may be one of three kinds: *flat, corridor* or *integrated*.

Flat Deductible

A *flat deductible* is a stated amount that the insured must pay before policy benefits become payable. For example, if an insured has a policy with a $500 deductible and incurs $2,000 of covered medical expenses, he or she must pay $500 toward the total. The insurer will then base its payments on the remaining $1,500. Quite often, policies will include a *family deductible,* usually equal to three times the individual deductible amount. In a family of four, for example, if three members each satisfied the individual deductible in one year, no deductible would be applied to medical expenses incurred by the fourth member.

Corridor Deductible

A *corridor deductible* is typical for a supplementary major medical policy that works in conjunction with a basic medical expense policy. The first covered medical expenses the insured incurs are paid by the basic policy. After the basic policy benefits are exhausted, the insured pays the full deductible, and then the major medical benefits are payable.

Integrated Deductible

An *integrated deductible* is also used with a supplementary major medical plan, but it is "integrated" into the amounts covered by the basic plan. For example, if a supplementary plan carries a $500 deductible and the insured incurs $500 or more of covered expenses under the basic plan, the deductible is satisfied. If the basic policy benefits do not cover the entire deductible amount specified in the major medical policy, the insured is compelled to make up the difference.

Each of the preceding deductibles may be figured on one of two bases. If a major medical plan provides for a *calendar year deductible,* the deductible amount is applied only once during each calendar year. Once the deductible

Ill. 16.2 Types of Major Medical Deductibles

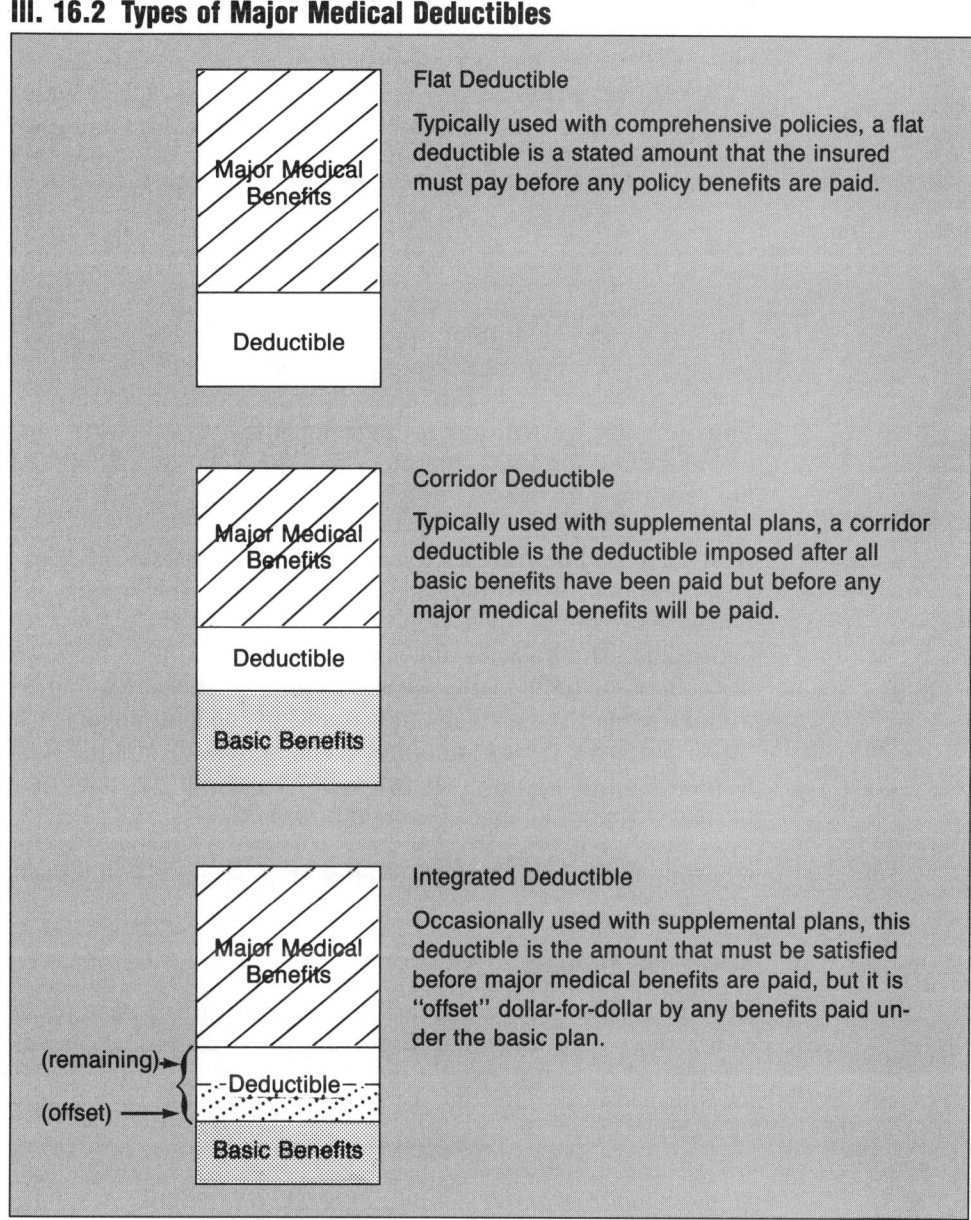

Flat Deductible

Typically used with comprehensive policies, a flat deductible is a stated amount that the insured must pay before any policy benefits are paid.

Corridor Deductible

Typically used with supplemental plans, a corridor deductible is the deductible imposed after all basic benefits have been paid but before any major medical benefits will be paid.

Integrated Deductible

Occasionally used with supplemental plans, this deductible is the amount that must be satisfied before major medical benefits are paid, but it is "offset" dollar-for-dollar by any benefits paid under the basic plan.

has been met in a calendar year, all claims submitted will be treated for the balance of the year without regard to any deductibles.

If a major medical plan has a *per cause deductible,* separate deductibles are required for each separate illness or each separate accident. Per cause deductibles are common in policies that define causes of loss as "each sickness or each injury."

Coinsurance

Coinsurance, or percentage participation, is another characteristic of major medical policies. It is, simply, a sharing of expenses by the insured and the insurer. After the insured satisfies the deductible, the insurance company pays a high percentage of the additional (covered) expenses—usually 75 percent or 80 percent—and the insured pays the remainder. For example, Joe has an 80 percent/20 percent major medical policy, with a $200 flat annual deductible. This year, he incurs $1,200 in medical expenses, all of which are covered by his policy. The responsibility for payment would be as follows:

Total expenses:	$1,200
Deductible Joe pays:	−$200
Basis for insurer's payment:	$1,000
	× .80
Amount insurer pays:	$800
Coinsurance amount Joe pays:	$200

Thus, the insurer will pay 80 percent of the charges after the deductible has been satisfied, or $800. Joe must pay the $200 deductible and 20 percent of the remaining expenses, for a total cost share of $400.

Now let's assume that Joe experiences two separate medical problems this year. The first, which required hospitalization and surgery, totaled $7,500. Under his major medical policy, Joe submitted his claim and paid his $200 deductible. The policy would pay 80 percent of the charges above the deductible, or $5,840; Joe is responsible for the remaining $1,460. Three months later, Joe incurs another round of medical expenses amounting to $900. Since his policy stipulates a flat annual deductible, which Joe has already paid, the policy will base its 80 percent payment on the full $900; Joe must pay the remaining 20 percent, or $180.

Coinsurance provisions are effective throughout the duration of a policy.

Stop-Loss Feature

In order to provide a safeguard for insureds, many major medical policies contain a *stop-loss feature* that limits the insured's out-of-pocket expenses. This means that once the insured has paid a specified amount toward his or her covered expenses—usually $1,000 to $2,000—the company pays 100 percent of covered expenses after that point.

How a stop-loss cap is defined depends on the policy. For example, one policy may stipulate that the contract will cover 100 percent of eligible expenses after the insured incurs $1,000 in out-of-pocket costs. Another policy may specify that the coinsurance provision applies only to the next $3,000 of covered expenses after the deductible is paid, with full coverage for any remaining expenses.

Preexisting Conditions

Another feature characteristic of most major medical policies is the exclusion for *preexisting conditions*. For individual plans, a preexisting condition is an illness or physical condition that existed before the policy's effective date and one that the applicant did not disclose on the application. (A condition that *is* noted on the application may be excluded by rider or waiver.) Consequently, medical costs incurred due to a preexisting condition are excluded from coverage under plans that contain this exclusion. However, the exclusion applies for only a limited time. After that time limit passes, any existing conditions are no longer considered "preexisting" and will be covered in full, subject to any other policy limitations. (See also "Time Limit on Certain Defenses," Chapter 20.)

The exclusion for preexisting conditions is designed to protect insurers against adverse selection by those who know they have a medical ailment and are facing certain medical costs.

Other Types of Medical Expense Coverage

As we've discussed, basic medical expense plans and major medical expense plans are the two primary kinds of health policies that provide coverage for accidents and illness. However, a discussion of medical expense plans would not be complete without mentioning a couple of other plans, most notably *hospital indemnity policies* and *limited risk (or "dread disease") policies*.

Hospital Indemnity Policies

A *hospital indemnity policy* simply provides a daily, weekly or monthly indemnity of a specified amount based on the number of days the insured is hospitalized. For example, a hospital indemnity plan may provide the insured $100 a day for every day he or she is confined in a hospital. This insurance has been available for many years, but has been promoted more heavily in recent years largely due to skyrocketing health care costs. Many companies can offer high benefit indemnity plans at reasonable premiums because underwriting and administration are greatly simplified and claim costs are not affected by increases in medical costs.

Benefits may run as high as $4,500 per month, based on a daily hospital confinement benefit of $150, and some are even higher. Maximum benefit periods range from about six months to several years or for a lifetime. Benefits are payable directly to the insureds and may be used for any purpose. Hospital indemnity policies also are usually exempt from most state laws that apply to specific kinds of insurance contracts.

Limited Risk Policies

Policies that provide medical expense coverage for specific kinds of illnesses are known as *limited risk* or *dread disease* policies. They are available primarily due to the high costs associated with certain illnesses, such as cancer or heart disease. It should be noted, however, that some states prohibit the sale of these policies, since they invite questionable sales and marketing practices that take advantage of people's fear of these diseases.

Limited risk policies that cover specified accidents are also available and are discussed in Chapter 18.

Summary

The need for medical expense insurance—"health care insurance" in current vernacular—is greater today than at any time in the past, because of the high cost of medical care. *Basic medical expense insurance,* once the predominant form of health insurance, is now overshadowed by *major medical insurance* in terms of premium dollars and total coverage. Offered as individual and group policies, medical expense insurance is an indispensable part of a total insurance portfolio.

Key Concepts

In preparing for their licensing examination, students should be familiar with the following concepts:

basic medical expense policies
basic hospital expense
basic surgical expense
basic physicians' (nonsurgical) expense
supplementary and comprehensive major medical expense policies

deductibles
coinsurance
stop-loss feature
preexisting condition
hospital indemnity policy
limited risk policy

Chapter 16
Questions for Review *(Answers are located at the end of the book.)*

1. The "miscellaneous expense" benefit in a basic hospital expense policy normally will cover

   a. physicians' bedside visits.
   b. the administering of anesthesia.
   c. drugs and medicine administered in the hospital.
   d. hospital room and board.

2. Clarence is to enter the hospital for a thyroidectomy. His basic medical expense policy includes a relative value schedule for surgical expense. The schedule lists 55 units for a thyroidectomy and a conversion factor of $8. How much will the policy pay?

   a. $400   c. $540
   b. $440   d. $550

3. All of the following statements pertaining to deductible provisions in medical insurance policies are correct, EXCEPT:

   a. They help to eliminate small claims.
   b. They provide that initial expenses up to a specified amount are to be paid by the insured.
   c. They are most common in basic medical expense policies.
   d. They help to hold down premium rates.

4. An insured has a basic hospital/surgical expense policy, which provides benefits of $50 per day for up to 30 days of hospitalization and $750 for miscellaneous charges. It bases its surgical benefits on a schedule approach. The insured is hospitalized for a severely broken leg that requires surgery. The surgical procedure has been assigned $500 by the policy, though the customary charge in the area is $600. The insured incurs the following covered expenses:

   $80 per day for 7 days hospital charge
   $675 for the surgical procedure
   $800 for miscellaneous expenses

   The insured's policy will pay

   a. $2,035. c. $1,700.
   b. $1,810. d. $1,600.

5. When a medical expense policy pays benefits on an indemnity basis, it pays

   a. a certain percentage of whatever the hospital room charges are.
   b. for total hospital expenses, less a deductible.
   c. a flat amount per day for hospital room and board.
   d. only for surgery and miscellaneous hospital expenses.

6. Wilbur's basic medical expense policy limits the miscellaneous expense benefit to 20 times the $90 daily room and board benefit. During his recent hospital stay, miscellaneous expenses totaled $2,100. How much, if any, of this amount will Wilbur have to pay?

   a. $0   c. $300
   b. $210 d. $2,100

7. Which of the following examples pertaining to major medical policy deductibles is correct?

   a. Eldon's major medical policy has a $500 flat deductible provision. He incurs covered expenses totaling $350. He will pay nothing and his major medical policy will pay $350.
   b. Sarah has a major medical policy with a $500 flat deductible and an 80/20 coinsurance provision. Her covered expenses total $1,800. Of that amount, she will pay $500 and her insurance will pay $1,300.
   c. Valerie incurs a hospital bill of $8,300. Her basic medical expense insurance pays $2,400. Valerie pays a $200 deductible and her major medical plan takes care of the balance of covered expenses. Her deductible would be classified as a corridor deductible.
   d. An integrated deductible amount is $2,000. With this deductible, after the basic policy benefits are exhausted, the insured pays the full $2,000 deductible and then the major medical benefits are payable.

8. Arthur incurs total hospital expenses of $9,500, all of which are covered by his major medical policy. The policy includes a $500 deductible and a 75/25 coinsurance feature. Of the total expense, how much will Arthur have to pay?

   a. $2,375 c. $2,875
   b. $2,750 d. $6,675

9. All of the following are types of deductible provisions associated with major medical policies, EXCEPT:

   a. corridor.
   b. integrated.
   c. flat.
   d. stop-loss.

10. If the coinsurance feature in a major medical insurance policy is 75/25 with a $100 deductible, how much of a $2,100 bill would the insured pay?

    a. $1,500
    b. $100
    c. $500
    d. $600

17 Disability Income Insurance

*Purpose • Disability Income Benefits
• Policy Provisions • Policy Riders*

Disability income insurance is often called "the forgotten need." All too frequently, what is thought to be a well-planned insurance program—a program consisting of life insurance, annuities and medical expense coverage—is proven completely inadequate when the one risk not covered materializes. The risk associated with disability is *loss of income:* if an individual can't work due to a disability, he or she won't be able to earn a living. The purpose of this chapter is to describe the important role disability income insurance serves and to explain the features of these kinds of policies.

Purpose of Disability Income Insurance

Disability income insurance is designed to provide an individual with a stated amount of periodic income in the event he or she cannot work due to a disabling illness or accident. Statistics prove that the probability of disability greatly exceeds the probability of death during an individual's working years. The need for protection against the *economic death* of a wage earner cannot be overemphasized and it is this need that disability income insurance fills.

Disability income policies provide coverage for disabilities resulting from either accidents alone or from accidents and sickness. Because sickness-related disabilities represent only a small fraction of all disabilities, it is not economically feasible to issue sickness-only disability policies. To obtain sickness income protection, one normally has to purchase accident income coverage as well.

Disability income policies are available as individual plans and group plans. They also serve a very important function for businesses and business owners. In this chapter, we will focus on the basics of individual disability policies; group disability is discussed in Chapter 22 and business uses of disability income insurance are discussed in Chapter 23.

Disability Income Benefits

The benefits paid under a disability income policy are in the form of monthly *income payments.* Unlike life insurance, which insurers will issue for almost any amount the applicant applies for (and qualifies for), disability income insurance is characterized by benefit limits. Insurers typically place a ceiling on the amount of disability income protection they will issue on any one applicant, defined in terms of the insured's earnings. And with few exceptions, this benefit ceiling is *less* than the insured's regular income. Without such restrictions, a disabled insured could conceivably receive as much income as he or she did while working, with little incentive to return to work and much incentive to prolong the disability.

Insurers use two methods to determine the amount of benefits payable under their disability income policies. The first method determines the benefit using a *percentage* of the insured's predisability earnings, and takes into account other sources of disability income. For example, an individual earning $2,000 a month may be limited by Company A to a monthly benefit of 60 percent of income, or $1,200. If that individual already has an existing disability income policy from Company X that provides for $400 in monthly income, the amount payable by Company A would be limited to $800 a month. Some policies that use the percent-of-earnings formula provide a benefit that varies with the length of the disability. For instance, the benefit amount may equal 100 percent of the insured's predisability earnings for the first month and then reduce the benefit amount to 70 percent thereafter.

The second method used to establish disability benefits is the *flat-amount* method. Under this approach, the policy specifies a flat income benefit amount that will be paid if the insured becomes totally disabled. Normally, this amount is payable regardless of any other income benefits the insured may receive.

The percent-of-earnings approach is typically used in group disability income plans; the flat-amount method is more common in individual plans.

Disability Defined

Before benefits under a disability income policy are payable, the insured must be *totally disabled.* What constitutes "total disability" varies from policy to policy and the insured must meet the definition as set forth in his or her policy.

Years ago, it was common for insurers to define total disability as "the inability to engage in any occupation for wage or profit." Since this restrictive definition prevented many people from qualifying for benefits, it has since been replaced with more liberal terms. Today, most disability income policies use one of two approaches to define total disability: "any occupation" or "own occupation."

Any Occupation

The "any occupation" definition of total disability requires the insured to be unable to perform *"any occupation for which he or she is reasonably suited by reason of education, training or experience"* in order to qualify for disability income benefits.

Ill. 17.1 Probability of Disability

From Age 20 To Age:	Probability of Disability	
	Males	Females
21	0.1 percent	0.0 percent
25	0.5	0.3
30	1.3	0.7
35	2.3	1.5
40	3.5	2.6
45	5.2	4.1
50	7.8	6.4
55	12.0	9.9
60	19.1	15.3
65	29.2	22.1

This table shows the probability of a disability from age 20 (based on attainment of age 20 in 1986).

Source: *1992 Sourcebook of Health Insurance Data*

Own Occupation

The "own occupation" definition of total disability requires that the insured be unable to work at his or her *own* occupation as a result of an accident or sickness. Obviously from a policyowner's point of view, an "own occupation" disability income policy is more advantageous—it is also more expensive and difficult to qualify for. Often, disability income policies qualify total disability in two stages, using both the own occupation and any occupation definitions. These policies will provide initial benefits based on the own occupation definition for a specified period of time (for example, during the first two years of the disability), then change the qualifying basis to the any occupation definition.

Presumptive Disability

Most policies today contain a *presumption of disability* provision. Basically, this provision specifies certain conditions that automatically qualify the insured for the full benefit, since the severity of the conditions *presumes* the insured is totally disabled even if he or she is able to work. Presumptive disabilities include blindness, deafness, loss of speech and loss of two or more limbs.

Partial Disability

Not all disabilities result in the total loss of wages; therefore, it is common for most disability income policies to make a provision for *partial disability,* either as part of the basic coverage or as an optional rider for an additional premium. By most definitions, partial disability is the inability of the insured to perform *one or more important duties of his or her job* or the inability to work at that job on a *full-time basis,* either of which results in a decrease in income. Depending on the policy, a partial disability may have to be preceded by a total disability in order for the insured to receive partial disability benefits. The purpose of partial disability benefits is to reduce the frequency—and length—of total disability payments in cases where the insured is capable of some work and to encourage him or her to return to work without the fear of losing all disability benefits.

Benefits paid during a period of partial disability are classified as either *partial* or *residual*, depending on how the amount is calculated.

Partial Disability Benefit

A *partial disability benefit* is a flat amount specified in the policy. It is usually 50 percent of the full disability income benefit. For example, let's assume Helen, who has a disability income policy with an own-occupation definition, is severely injured after falling down a flight of stairs. She is unable to work for four months, during which time her disability income policy pays a full benefit. After four months she is able to return to work, but only on a part-time basis, earning substantially less than she did before her injury. If her policy did not contain a partial disability provision, her benefits would cease entirely since she no longer meets the definition of totally disabled. However, if her policy provides for partial disability benefits, she will be able to work on a part-time basis and continue to receive half of her disability benefits. Most partial disability provisions require that the insured first be totally disabled before partial benefits are payable.

Residual Disability Benefit

A *residual disability benefit* reflects the proportional amount of income actually lost due to the partial disability, taking into account the fact that the insured is able to work and earn some income. For example, if the insured suffered a 40 percent loss of income because of the partial disability, the residual disability benefit payable would be 40 percent of the total disability benefit. This percentage is subject to change as the disabled insured's income varies. Generally, residual benefits are provided through a rider to the policy and will be paid as long as the insured's earnings are reduced at least 20 to 25 percent below his or her predisability earnings. In most cases, residual benefits are payable even if the insured was not first totally disabled.

Let's look at an example. Larry, a printer, suffered a severe back injury following a car accident. Though he was able to continue working, it was on a limited part-time basis, at only 60 percent of his predisability salary. If Larry's disability income policy provided for residual disability benefits, he would receive monthly payments from the insurer equal to 40 percent of the total disability benefit.

Cause of Disability

Another important aspect of disability income policies is the way in which they define the *cause* of disability. As noted above, disability income insurance policies cover accidents only or accidents and sickness. Thus, how a disability occurs is an important consideration for disability income policies, as well as any other kind of policy covering injury due to accident.

Generally, disability income policies state that benefits are payable when injuries are caused by either "external, violent and *accidental means*" or result in "*accidental bodily injury*."

Policies that use the *accidental means* provision require that the *cause* of the injury must have been unexpected and accidental. Policies that use the *accidental bodily injury* provision require that the *result* of the injury—in other words, the injury itself—has to be unexpected and accidental. This is also known as the "results" provision.

For example, assume Jim, the insured, took an intentional dive off a high, rocky ledge into a lake. He struck his head on some rocks and ended up partially paralyzed. If his policy had an accidental means provision, the benefits would probably not be payable since the cause of his injury—the dive—was intentional. However, if his policy had an accidental bodily injury (or results) provision, benefits would be payable since the result of the accident—his injury—was unintentional and accidental.

Today, most disability income policies (and other policies providing accident protection) use the accidental bodily injury or results provision, which is far less restrictive than the accidental means provision. In fact, many states now require all accident-based insurance benefits to be based on the accidental bodily injury provision.

Disability Income Policy Provisions

In addition to specifying the amount of benefit payable and the circumstances under which a benefit is payable (plus complying with required provisions standards), disability income policies contain a number of other important provisions. The most notable of these are as follows.

Probationary Period

The *probationary period* specified in a disability insurance policy is the period of time that must elapse *following the effective date of the policy* before benefits are payable. It is a one-time-only period that begins on the policy's effective date and ends 15 or 30 days after the policy has been in force. The purpose of the probationary period is to exclude *preexisting sicknesses* from coverage and provide a guidepost in borderline cases when there is a question as to whether an insured became ill before or after the effective date of the policy. Just as important, it helps protect the insurer against adverse selection, since those who know they are ill are more likely to try to obtain insurance coverage.

Note that a disability income probationary period applies to sickness only; it does not apply to accidents. Whereas a person may be able to anticipate a sickness-related disability (after a visit to the doctor, for example), it is not possible to anticipate an accident.

Elimination Period

Similar in concept to a deductible, the *elimination period* is the time immediately *following the start of a disability* when benefits are *not* payable. Elimination periods eliminate claims for short-term disabilities for which the insured can usually manage without financial hardship and save the insurance company from the expense of processing and settling small claims. This, in turn, helps keep premiums down. The longer the elimination period, the lower the premium for comparable disability benefits. An elimination period can be compared to a deductible since both are cost-sharing devices that can have a direct bearing on the amount of premium required of the policyowner.

Depending on the policy, elimination periods may apply only to disabilities caused by sickness and not to disabilities caused by accident. In either event, elimination periods usually range from one week to one year or longer, but most are at least 30 days.

Benefit Period

The *benefit period* is the maximum length of time that disability income benefits will be paid to the disabled insured. The longer the benefit period, the higher the cost of the policy. For individual policies, there are basically two types of benefit periods and accordingly they serve to classify a disability income policy as either "short term" or "long term." Individual short-term policies provide benefits for six months to two years, after which payments cease. Individual long-term policies are characterized by benefit periods of more than two years, such as five, ten or 20. In some cases, a long-term policy will provide for benefits until the insured reaches age 65. The classifications of short term and long term are not necessarily the same for individual and group plans. See Chapter 22 for a discussion of group disability plans.

Delayed Disability Provision

In some cases, total disability does not occur immediately after an accident, but develops some days or weeks later. Most policies allow a certain amount of time during which total disability may result from an accident and the insured will still be eligible for benefits. The amount of time allowed for a *delayed disability* may be 30, 60 or 90 days, for example.

Recurrent Disability Provision

It is not unusual for a person who experienced a total disability to recover and then, weeks or months later, undergo a recurrence of the same disability. Most policies provide for *recurrent disabilities* by specifying a period of time during which the recurrence of a disability is considered a continuation of the prior disability. If the recurrence takes place after that period, it is considered a new disability and will be subject to a new elimination period before benefits are again payable.

For example, Rachael has a short-term disability policy that stipulates a new benefit-paying period begins if the insured is disabled, recovers and returns to work for six months and then becomes disabled again. Rachael is totally disabled and off work from January 15 to April 15, when she returns to work. She is stricken again the same year and is off work from September 1 to November 10. Rachael's policy would resume paying benefits, classifying her recurrence as a continuation of her prior disability, since her return to work did not last six months. She would not be subject to a new elimination period.

Nondisabling Injury

Frequently, a person covered by a disability income policy will suffer an injury that does not qualify for income benefits. Many such policies include a provision for a medical expense benefit that pays the actual cost of medical treatment for *nondisabling injuries* that result from an accident.

The benefit is generally limited to a percentage of the weekly or monthly income benefit specified in the policy. It is payable to eligible insureds in lieu of other benefits under the policy.

Disability Income Policy Riders

As is true with life insurance policies, disability income policies may be purchased with riders or options that will enhance their value to the insured. Some of the more common riders are discussed below.

Waiver of Premium Rider

A *waiver of premium rider* generally is included with guaranteed renewable and noncancelable individual disability income policies. It is a valuable provision because it exempts the policyowner from paying the policy's premiums during periods of total disability. To qualify for the exemption, the insured must experience total disability for more than a specified period, commonly three or six months. In some cases, the waiver retroactively applies to the original date of disability and any premiums paid for that period are refunded. The trend is to have the waiver apply to the entire period of total disability, rather than to just the benefit period.

The waiver of premium generally does not extend past the insured's age 60 or 65. When the waiver is added, policy premiums are adjusted upward to cover the additional risk. Premiums then are reduced when the waiver is dropped due to the insured reaching the specified age limit.

Social Security Rider

The *Social Security rider,* sometimes called the *"social insurance substitute" rider,* provides for the payment of additional income when the insured is eligible for social insurance benefits but those benefits have not yet begun, have been denied or have begun in an amount less than the benefit amount of the rider. Usually covered under the definition "social insurance" are disability benefits from Social Security as well as state and local government programs or workers' compensation programs.

When applying for the rider, the applicant states the amount of benefit expected from Social Security and any other programs for which he or she might be eligible. Of course, the level of expected benefits must be realistic in light of the applicant's earnings level. When total disability strikes, the applicant must show that social insurance benefits have been applied for. After the Social Security Administration (or comparable administrative body of a state or local program) determines the benefit payable, the *difference* between the actual benefit and the "expected" benefit listed in the rider is payable as an additional disability income benefit.

Cost of Living Adjustment Rider

The *cost of living adjustment* (COLA) *rider* provides for indexing the monthly or weekly benefit payable under a disability policy to changes in the Consumer Price Index. Typically, the benefit amount is adjusted on each disability anniversary date to reflect changes in the CPI (though often a minimum CPI change, such as 4 percent, is required to trigger a disability income benefit increase). When the disability ceases, the policyowner can elect to maintain the policy at the new (increased) benefit level by paying additional premiums or can choose to let the benefit return to the originally scheduled amount for the same premium as was paid before the disability commenced.

Guaranteed Insurability Rider

A disability income policy is the only type of health insurance policy to which a *guaranteed insurability rider* may be attached. This option guarantees the insured the right to purchase additional amounts of disability income coverage at predetermined times in the future *without evidence of insurability*. The guarantee may be contingent upon the insured meeting an earnings test prior to each purchase—a condition stipulated by the insurer to avoid overinsurance.

Most guaranteed insurability riders require the insured to exercise the option for additional coverage prior to a specific age, such as age 50.

Summary

Often called "the forgotten need," disability income insurance is an important part of a complete insurance program. Monthly or weekly benefits are paid when the insured is *totally disabled,* as determined by either the "any occupation" or the more liberal "own occupation" definition. If the policy has a *partial disability provision,* benefits may be payable if the insured is able to work only part time or suffers a less-than-total disability. Another feature of disability income policies is that they define the cause of a disabling accident on an *accidental means* or *accidental results* basis.

Disability income contracts are characterized by *probationary periods,* which exclude preexisting sickness from immediate coverage, and *elimination periods,* which specify the time after the start of a disability when benefits are not payable, thereby excluding very short-term disabilities from coverage. Like life insurance, disability income policies may be purchased with policy riders that can increase their value to the insured.

Disability income coverage may be purchased as individual or group policies. Its uses for businesses and business owners will be discussed in Chapter 23.

Key Concepts

In preparing for their licensing examination, students should be familiar with the following concepts:

total disability	probationary period
any occupation	elimination period
own occupation	waiver of premium rider
partial disability	Social Security rider
presumptive disability	cost of living adjustment rider
residual disability	guaranteed insurability rider

Chapter 17
Questions for Review *(Answers are located at the end of the book.)*

1. Assume an insurer will issue a maximum monthly disability income benefit of $5,000, provided the total of such benefits payable by all companies does not exceed 60 percent of the insured's regular monthly income. Ted earns $4,500 per month and has no existing disability income policy. The maximum monthly disability income benefit this insurer would issue to Ted is

    a. $2,500.
    b. $2,700.
    c. $4,500.
    d. $5,000.

2. Total disability typically means that an individual is unable to perform the duties of the occupation for which he or she is suited by

    a. education.
    b. training.
    c. experience.
    d. All of the above

3. All of the following statements pertaining to elimination periods in disability income policies are correct, EXCEPT:

    a. Elimination periods apply to disabilities due to sickness and not accidents.
    b. Benefits are not payable during an elimination period, but are paid retroactively to the beginning of the period if the insured remains disabled throughout the period.
    c. An elimination period follows the start of a disability.
    d. Elimination periods help keep premiums down.

4. Which of the following riders provides for changes in the benefit payable based on changes in the consumer price index (CPI)?

    a. Guaranteed insurability rider
    b. Cost of living adjustment rider
    c. Social Security rider
    d. Waiver of premium rider

5. Benefit periods for individual short-term disability policies typically vary from

    a. 1 to 12 months.
    b. 3 months to 3 years.
    c. 6 months to 2 years.
    d. 1 to 5 years.

6. All of the following statements pertaining to waiver of premium in health insurance policies are correct, EXCEPT:

    a. It exempts an insured from paying premiums during periods of permanent and total disability.
    b. It may apply retroactively.
    c. It generally drops off after the insured reaches age 60 or 65.
    d. It normally applies to both medical expense and disability income policies.

7. Which of the following terms relates to disability income insurance?

   a. Service basis
   b. First-dollar
   c. Residual basis
   d. Coinsurance

8. All of the following statements pertaining to recurrent disabilities for disability insurance are correct, EXCEPT:

   a. A recurrent disability is one that the insured experiences more than once.
   b. Recurrent disability policy provisions have no effect on the payment of benefits.
   c. A new elimination period may or may not be required for a recurrent disability.
   d. A recurrent disability may begin a new benefit period.

9. Sidney has a monthly benefit of $2,500 for total disability under a residual disability income policy. If Sidney suffers a 40 percent loss of his pre-disability income, how much will his benefit be?

   a. $2,500
   b. $1,500
   c. $1,000
   d. $0

10. What is the initial period of time specified in a disability income policy that must pass, after a policy is in force, before a loss due to sickness can be covered?

    a. Preexisting term
    b. Probationary period
    c. Temporary interval
    d. Elimination period

18 Accidental Death and Dismemberment Insurance

Nature of AD&D • AD&D Benefits • Other AD&D Forms

The third major form of health insurance coverage is accidental death and dismemberment insurance, commonly referred to as AD&D. Actually, it is something of a hybrid, paying benefits in the event of death or dismemberment. Though the circumstances under which it pays these benefits are somewhat limited, it is a popular form of insurance protection and is widely utilized in group insurance plans. In this chapter we will review the nature and principles of AD&D policies and benefits.

Nature of AD&D Policies

Accidental death and dismemberment insurance is the primary form of pure *accident coverage.* As such, it serves a somewhat limited purpose: it provides a stated lump-sum benefit in the event of accidental death *or* in the event of loss of body members due to accidental injury. This latter includes loss of hands or feet or the loss of sight in one or both eyes. ("Loss of body member" is typically defined as actual severance from the body, though it may include loss of use, depending on the policy.) Separate benefits for hospital, surgical and other medical expenses are generally not included in AD&D policies, although some may pay a medical reimbursement benefit up to a stated amount.

AD&D Benefits

Since an AD&D policy pays a specified benefit to the insured in the event of accidental death or dismemberment due to accidental injury, it is necessary for the policy to make distinctions between these two contingencies and to define the benefits accordingly. Consequently, AD&D policies make benefits payable in the form of a *principal sum* and a *capital sum.*

1. **Principal Sum.** The principal sum under an AD&D policy is the amount payable as a *death benefit.* It is the amount of insurance purchased—$10,000, $25,000, $50,000, $100,000 or more. The principal sum represents the maximum amount the policy will pay.

2. ***Capital Sum.*** The capital sum paid under an AD&D policy is the amount payable for the accidental loss of sight or accidental dismemberment. It is a specified amount, usually expressed as a percentage of the principal sum, that varies according to the severity of the injury. For example, the benefit for the loss of one foot or one hand is typically 50 percent of the principal sum. The benefit for the loss of one arm or one leg is usually two-thirds of the principal sum. The most extreme losses, such as both feet or sight in both eyes, generally qualify for payment of the full benefit, which is 100 percent of the principal sum.

Let's say, for example, Kevin has an accidental death and dismemberment policy that pays $50,000 for accidental loss of life and the same for accidental loss of two limbs or the sight in both eyes. Thus, $50,000 is the policy's principal sum. The same policy pays $25,000 for accidental loss of sight of one eye or dismemberment of one limb. Therefore, $25,000 is the policy's capital sum.

Some AD&D policies provide for payment of double, triple or even quadruple the principal sum if the insured dies under specified circumstances. A double payment is referred to as *"double indemnity."* If three times the principal sum is payable, it is called *"triple indemnity."* However, do not let these terms confuse you. AD&D policies, because they pay a stated benefit, are *valued contracts.* They are not contracts of indemnity.

Accidental Means vs. Accidental Results

As we learned in the last chapter, an insurance policy that provides benefits in the event of an injury due to an accident must define "accident." In all cases, an accident is "external and violent," but accidental death and dismemberment policies (like disability income policies) make a distinction between injuries due to *accidental means* and those due to *accidental results* (or accidental bodily injury).

By way of a review, policies that base their benefit payments on accidental means require that both the cause and the result of an accident must be unintentional. Policies that use the more liberal accidental results definition stipulate that only the injury resulting from an accident must be unintentional. If Ted, the insured under an AD&D policy, intentionally jumps from the roof of his house after fixing his antenna (instead of climbing down the ladder) and so severely injures his leg that it must be amputated, he would be paid the appropriate percentage of the capital sum only if his policy used the "results" definition. If his policy used the "means" definition, no benefit would be payable because Ted intentionally performed the action (the jump) that resulted in the injury.

As noted in the discussion of disability income policies, most states require that policies that provide any form of accident benefit, as do AD&D policies, base the definition of "accident" on the results definition, not the means definition.

Other Forms of AD&D

Accidental death and dismemberment coverage is made available in a variety of ways. It can be purchased by individuals as a single policy or it may be a part of an individual disability income policy. Quite typically, however, it is an aspect of a group insurance plan—either group life or group health—or it may in and of itself comprise a group plan. Usually, AD&D benefits are payable whether the injury resulted on the job or off.

By their very nature, AD&D policies are somewhat narrow, providing benefits only in the event of death or dismemberment due to an accident. There is another type of AD&D coverage, even more narrow in scope, that provides protection against accidental death or dismemberment only in the event of certain *specified* accidents. These are *limited risk policies* and *special risk policies*.

Limited Risk Policies

As noted in Chapter 16, *limited risk policies* set forth a specific risk and provide benefits to cover death or dismemberment due to that risk. For example, an *aviation policy* provides benefits for accidental death or dismemberment if death or injury results from an aviation accident during a specified trip. An *automobile policy* provides benefits for accidental death or injury while riding in a car. *Travel accident* covers most kinds of travel accidents, but only for a specified period of time, such as one year.

Special Risk Policies

A distinction should be made between limited risk and *special risk* policies. A special risk policy covers unusual hazards normally not covered under ordinary accident and health insurance. An actress who insures her legs for $1 million or a pilot test-flying an experimental airplane who obtains a policy covering his life while flying that particular plane, are both purchasing special risk policies. But a traveler who purchases an accident policy at the airport to provide coverage while he or she is a passenger on a commercial airlines flight is purchasing a limited risk policy.

Summary

Accidental death and dismemberment insurance, known as AD&D, represents the purest form of accident coverage. It provides a stated sum benefit in the event of accidental death or accidental loss of one or more body members or accidental loss of sight. The benefit payable in the event of death is known as the *principal sum;* the benefit payable in the event of dismemberment or loss of sight is the *capital sum.*

Like all policies that provide accident benefits, AD&D policies must define the term "accident" on either a *means basis* (in which both the cause and the result of the accident must be unintentional) or on a *results basis* (requiring only that the injury itself be accidental). Most states stipulate the use of the results definition.

AD&D coverage may be purchased as an individual policy, but usually is part of a larger group life or health plan. In some cases, it is offered as a separate group plan. Specialized forms of AD&D coverage, known as *limited risk* and *special risk insurance,* provide accident protection in the event of specified limited risks, such as travel or aviation.

Key Concepts

In preparing for their licensing examination, students should be familiar with the following concepts:

accidental death and
  dismemberment coverage
principal sum

capital sum
limited risk policies
special risk policies

Chapter 18
Questions for Review *(Answers are located at the end of the book.)*

1. The amount payable as a death benefit in an accidental death and dismemberment policy is known as the

   a. primary amount.
   b. capital sum.
   c. indemnity amount.
   d. principal sum.

2. Theodore received a $15,000 cash benefit from his $50,000 accidental death and dismemberment policy for the accidental loss of one eye. The amount he received could be identified as the policy's

   a. principal sum.
   b. secondary sum.
   c. capital sum.
   d. contingent amount.

3. Which of the following examples pertaining to accidental death and dismemberment insurance is correct?

   a. Merrill is the insured under a $50,000 AD&D policy and dies unexpectedly of a heart attack. His beneficiary will receive $50,000 as the death benefit.
   b. Linda has a $40,000 AD&D policy that pays triple indemnity. If she should be killed in a train wreck, her beneficiary would receive $120,000.
   c. Paula has an AD&D policy that pays $15,000 for the loss of one hand or foot or the sight of one eye. That benefit is called the principal sum.
   d. Eric has an AD&D policy. He is killed in an auto accident. The $30,000 his beneficiary receives as a death benefit is the policy's capital sum.

4. Agnes purchases a round-trip travel accident policy at the airport before leaving on a business trip. Her policy would be which type of insurance?

   a. Limited risk
   b. Business overhead expense
   c. Credit accident and health
   d. Industrial health

19 Senior Health Insurance Plans

Medicare • Medicare Supplement Policies • Medicaid
• Long-Term Care

Modern medical science is one of the miracles of the twentieth century. Illnesses and diseases considered fatal or incurable only a few decades ago are now routinely treated with simple injections or tablets. One result of these medical breakthroughs is that people live longer. However, as individuals live longer, they encounter more medical problems and require more care. The cost of treating these problems has spiraled at a dizzying rate, leading to an ever-growing concern over how these costs will be paid. The concern is especially great for the elderly since, as a group, seniors are some of the heaviest users of medical and health care services.

In this chapter, we examine a number of plans—public and private—designed to provide health care insurance or health care financing for the elderly.

Medicare

As discussed in Chapter 15, the federally administered *Medicare* program took effect in 1966. Its purpose is to provide hospital and medical expense insurance protection to those aged 65 or older, to those of any age who suffer from chronic kidney disease or to those who are receiving Social Security disability benefits.

Medicare consists of two parts: *Medicare Part A* and *Medicare Part B*. *Medicare Part A* is compulsory hospitalization insurance (HI) that provides specified in-hospital and related benefits. It is compulsory in that all workers covered by Social Security finance its operation through a portion of their FICA taxes and are automatically provided with benefits once they qualify for Social Security benefits.

Medicare Part B is a voluntary program designed to provide supplementary medical insurance (SMI) to cover physician services, medical services and supplies not covered under Part A. Those who desire the coverage must enroll and pay a monthly premium. Medicare Part B is financed by monthly premiums from those who participate and by tax revenues.

Medicare Part A Coverages

Medicare Part A provides coverage for inpatient hospitalization and post-hospital skilled facility care and home care. For the first 60 days of hospitalization during any one benefit period, Medicare pays for all covered services, except for an initial deductible ($696 in 1994). Covered services include semi-private room, nursing services and other inpatient hospital services.

For the 61st through the 90th day of hospitalization, Medicare pays a reduced amount of the covered services. The patient is responsible for a daily copayment ($174 per day in 1994).

This 90-day hospitalization coverage is renewed with each benefit period. A *benefit period* starts when a patient enters the hospital and ends when the patient has been out of the hospital for 60 days. If a patient reenters a hospital before the end of a benefit period, the deductible is not reapplied, but the 90-day hospital coverage period is not renewed. However, if the patient reenters a hospital after a benefit period ends, a new deductible is required and the 90-day hospital coverage period is renewed.

Medicare patients also have a *lifetime reserve* of 60 days of hospital coverage. If a patient is hospitalized longer than 90 days in a benefit period, he or she can tap into the 60-day reserve. The lifetime reserve is a one-time benefit; it does not renew with a new benefit period. If a patient is hospitalized and taps into the reserve days, he or she is required to pay a higher copayment ($348 per day in 1994). If a patient is hospitalized beyond the 60th lifetime reserve day, thereby exhausting the reserve, he or she is responsible for all hospital charges.

Medicare Part A is available when an individual turns 65 and is automatically provided when he or she applies for Social Security benefits.

In addition, Part A provides benefits for skilled nursing facility care, hospice care, home health services and, to a limited degree, inpatient psychiatric care. In all cases, Part A covers only those services that are medically necessary and only up to amounts deemed "reasonable" by Medicare.

Part A covers the costs of care in a skilled nursing facility as long as the patient was first hospitalized for three consecutive days. Treatment in a skilled nursing facility is covered in full for the first 20 days. From the 21st to the 100th day, the patient must pay the daily copayment ($87 per day in 1994). There are no Medicare benefits provided for treatment in a skilled nursing facility beyond 100 days.

Medicare Part B Coverages

For those who desire, additional coverage is available under Medicare Part B for physician services, diagnostic tests, physical and occupational therapy, medical supplies and the like. Part B participants are required to pay a monthly premium ($41.10 in 1994) and are responsible for an annual deductible ($100 in 1994). After the deductible, Part B will pay 80 percent of covered expenses, subject to Medicare's standards for reasonable charges.

Ill. 19.1

What Medicare Covers

Part A

- Inpatient hospital services, including semiprivate room and board and nursing services
- Posthospital skilled nursing care, in an accredited care facility
- Posthospital home health services, including nursing care, therapy and part-time home health aides
- Hospice benefits for the care of terminally ill patients (to the exclusion of all other Medicare benefits, except for physician services)
- Inpatient psychiatric care, on a limited basis

Part B

- Physicians' and surgeons' services, whether in a hospital, clinic or elsewhere
- Medical and health services, such as X rays, diagnostic lab tests, ambulance services, medical supplies, medical equipment rental and physical and occupational therapy

Primary Payor; Secondary Payor

Anyone aged 65, who is eligible for Medicare and who works for an employer of 20 or more employees, is entitled to the same health insurance benefits as the employer offers to younger employees. In these cases, the employer-sponsored plan is the *primary payor* and Medicare is the *secondary payor*. This means that Medicare pays only those charges that the employer-sponsored plan does not cover. This also applies to any disabled Medicare enrollee who is also covered by an employer-provided health care plan as a "current employee" or as a family member of an employee, but only if the employer plan covers 100 or more employees.

Medicare Supplement Policies

As is apparent from the above discussion, Medicare leaves many "gaps" in its coverage. With its structure of limited benefit periods, deductibles, copayments and exclusions, the coverage it provides is limited at best. To help fill these gaps, private insurance companies market Medicare supplement insurance policies to consumers. *Medicare supplement* (or *"Medigap"*) policies are designed to pick up coverage where Medicare leaves off.

The term "Medicare supplement" implies that the policy is supposed to cover what Medicare doesn't. Unfortunately, until recently some policies did not live up to what was expected of them. To combat this, in 1990 Congress passed a far-reaching "Medigap" law that required the National Association of Insurance Commissioners (NAIC) to address the subject of Medicare supplement policies. Specifically, the NAIC's task was to develop a standardized model Medicare supplement policy, which would provide certain "core" benefits, plus as many as nine other supplement policies that would provide increasingly more comprehensive benefits. These ten "model" policies could then be adopted by the states as prototype policies for their insurers. (See Ill. 19.2)

The purpose of this law was to reduce the number of Medicare supplement policies being offered for sale and to eliminate some of the questionable marketing practices associated with these policies. It was intended that these model policies would help consumers better understand Medicare supplement policies, thereby allowing them to make more informed buying decisions by

- standardizing coverages and benefits from one policy to the next;

- simplifying the terms used in these policies;

Ill. 19.2 NAIC's Ten Standard Medicare Supplement Policies

The NAIC has developed ten standard Medicare supplement policies. At a minimum, all Medicare supplement policies must contain the provisions of Plan A—the "core" plan. This plan includes coverage for Part A copayment amounts; 365 additional (lifetime) days of Medicare-eligible expenses once the Medicare lifetime reserve days are exhausted; the 20 percent Part B copayment amounts (for Medicare-approved services); and the first three pints of blood each year. At a minimum, all Medicare supplement policies must contain these "core" benefits.

The NAIC recommends that if a state authorizes the sale of only some of these plans, the letter codes of each plan—A, B, C, D, E, F, G, H, I and J—should be preserved. This uniform "naming" system will enable consumers to compare specific policy plans.

The chart below summarizes all ten standard plans, each of which includes the core benefits of Plan A.

A	B	C	D	E	F	G	H	I	J
Basic Benefits	Basic Benefits	Basic Benefits	Basic Benefits	Basic Benefits	Basic Benefits	Basic Benefits	Basic Benefits	Basic Benefits	Basic Benefits
		Skilled Nursing Copayment	Skilled Nursing Copayment	Skilled Nursing Copayment	Skilled Nursing Copayment	Skilled Nursing Copayment	Skilled Nursing Copayment	Skilled Nursing Copayment	Skilled Nursing Copayment
	Part A Deductible	Part A Deductible	Part A Deductible	Part A Deductible	Part A Deductible	Part A Deductible	Part A Deductible	Part A Deductible	Part A Deductible
		Part B Deductible			Part B Deductible				Part B Deductible
					Part B Excess (100%)	Part B Excess (80%)		Part B Excess (100%)	Part B Excess (100%)
		Foreign Travel Emergency	Foreign Travel Emergency	Foreign Travel Emergency	Foreign Travel Emergency	Foreign Travel Emergency	Foreign Travel Emergency	Foreign Travel Emergency	Foreign Travel Emergency
			At-Home Recovery			At-Home Recovery		At-Home Recovery	At-Home Recovery
							Basic Drugs ($1,250 Limit)	Basic Drugs ($1,250 Limit)	Extended Drugs ($3,000 Limit)
				Preventive Care					Preventive Care

Source: NAIC

- facilitating policy comparisons; and

- eliminating policy provisions that may be misleading or confusing.

Medicaid

As the longevity of the U.S. population has increased, more people than ever are faced with the rapidly rising costs of long-term health care. Government officials have long struggled to find a solution to the problem of affordable health care. In the early 1960s, President Kennedy proposed legislation to cover medical care for the poor and elderly. After many compromises, the problem of providing medical care was solved, in part, by the passage of the *Social Security Amendments of 1965*. Part of that legislation, called *Title XIX*, created a medical assistance program called Medicaid.

Medicaid is a government-funded, *means-tested* program designed to provide health care to poor people of all ages. The goal of Medicaid is to offer medical assistance to those whose income and resources are insufficient to meet the costs of necessary medical care. Individuals claiming benefits must prove they do not have the ability or *means* to pay for their own medical care.

Applicants must complete a lengthy questionnaire, disclosing all assets and income. To qualify for Medicaid, a person must be poor or become poor. Such people frequently include children born to low-income mothers, babies born addicted to drugs, AIDS patients and the indigent elderly.

Individual states design and administer the Medicaid programs under broad guidelines established by the federal government. On average, the federal government contributes about 56 cents for every Medicaid dollar spent; however, the amount contributed may be lower or higher. State governments contribute the balance and the extent of coverage and the quality of services vary widely from state to state.

Qualifying for Medicaid Nursing Home Benefits

Unlike Medicare, Medicaid does provide for custodial care or assisted care in a nursing home. However, as explained earlier, individuals claiming a need for Medicaid must prove that they cannot pay for their own nursing home care. In addition, the potential recipient must

- be at least age 65, blind or disabled (as defined by the recipient's state);

- be a U.S. citizen or permanent resident alien;

- need the type of care that is provided only in a nursing home; and

- meet certain asset and income tests.

People meeting these basic criteria will usually have their long-term nursing home care paid for by Medicaid. However, each state (and even some counties within certain states) evaluates an individual's ability to pay by looking at the nursing home resident's (and spouse's) income and assets. The specific limits for each of these sources vary by state and change annually.

Long-Term Care

Americans are living longer and many can expect to live a substantial portion of their lives in retirement. That's the good news. The bad news is, although statistics regarding longevity for older Americans may be improving, many individuals over age 65 still have to deal with poor health during their retirement years. As people age, they consume a larger proportion of health care services because of chronic illness, such as Alzheimer's disease, heart disease and stroke. The cost of the extended day in, day out care some older people need can be staggering: as much as $25,000 or $30,000 a year or more for nursing home care and upwards of $1,000 a month—or more—for aides who come to one's home.

As beneficial as Medicare and Medicare supplement insurance are to the elderly in protecting them against the costs of medical care, neither of these programs covers long-term custodial or nursing home care. Medicaid covers some of the costs associated with long-term care but a person is ineligible for Medicaid until he or she is practically destitute. How can these costs be paid? The solution for many is *long-term care insurance.*

What Is Long-Term Care?

You'll often see nursing home care referred to as "long-term care." However, long-term care (LTC) refers to a broad range of medical, personal and environmental services designed to assist individuals who have lost their ability to remain completely independent in the community. Although care may be provided for short periods of time while a patient is recuperating from an accident or illness, LTC refers to care provided for an extended period of time, normally more than 90 days. And, depending on the severity of the impairment, assistance may be given at home, at an adult care center or in a nursing home.

A large percentage of the elderly population will spend time in a nursing home. In fact, the Department of Health and Human Services estimates that in 1993 about 1.7 million people received services in nursing homes at a cost of over $53 billion. An additional 4.4 million elderly or disabled people remained at home but required some type of home care at a cost of about $8 billion.

What Is Long-Term Care Insurance?

Long-term care insurance is a relatively new type of insurance product. However, more and more insurance companies are beginning to offer this coverage as the need for it grows. It is similar to most insurance plans, in that the insured, in exchange for a certain premium, receives specified benefits in the event he or she requires LTC, as defined by the policy. Most LTC policies pay the insured a fixed dollar amount for each day he or she receives the kind of care the policy covers, regardless of what the care costs.

Insurers offer a wide range of benefit amounts, ranging from, for example, $40 a day to $100 a day for nursing home care. The daily benefit for at-home care is typically half the nursing home benefit. Many policies include an inflation rider or option to purchase additional coverage, enabling the policies to keep pace with increases in LTC costs.

Long-Term Care Coverages

As individuals age, they are likely to suffer from acute and/or chronic illnesses or conditions. An *acute illness* is a serious condition, such as pneumonia or influenza, from which the body can fully recover with proper medical attention. The patient may also need some assistance with chores for short periods of time until recovery and rehabilitation from the illness are complete.

Some people will suffer from *chronic conditions,* such as arthritis, heart disease or hypertension, that are treatable but not curable illnesses. When chronic conditions such as diabetes or heart disease initially manifest, many people ignore the inconvenience or pain they cause. Over time, however, a chronic condition frequently goes beyond being a nuisance and begins to inhibit a person's independence.

Typically, the need for LTC arises when physical or mental conditions, whether acute or chronic, impair a person's ability to perform the basic activities of everyday life—feeding, toileting, bathing, dressing and walking. This is the risk that long-term care insurance is designed to protect.

Broadly speaking, the kinds of services and support associated with long-term care are provided at three levels: *institutional care, home-based care* and *community care.* The appropriate level of care depends, of course, on the individual's medical or health care needs. Within each of these broad levels are many types of care, any or all of which may be covered by a long-term care insurance policy. Typical types of coverages are explained below.

Skilled Nursing Care

Skilled nursing care is continuous around-the-clock care provided by licensed medical professionals under the direct supervision of a physician. Skilled nursing care is usually administered in nursing homes.

Intermediate Nursing Care

Intermediate nursing care is provided by registered nurses, licensed practical nurses and nurse's aides under the supervision of a physician. Intermediate care is provided in nursing homes for stable medical conditions that require daily, but not 24-hour, supervision.

Custodial Care

Custodial care provides assistance in meeting daily living requirements, such as bathing, dressing, getting out of bed, toileting, etc. Such care does not require specialized medical training, but it must be given under a doctor's order. Custodial care is usually provided by nursing homes, but can also be given by adult day-care centers, respite centers or at home.

Home Health Care

Home health care is care provided in the insured's home, usually on a part-time basis. It can include skilled care (such as nursing, rehabilitative or physical therapy care ordered by a doctor) or unskilled care (such as help with cooking or cleaning).

Adult Day Care

Adult day care is designed for those who require assistance with various activities of daily living, while their primary caregivers (usually family or friends) are absent. These day care centers offer skilled medical care in conjunction with social and personal services, but custodial care is usually their primary focus.

Respite Care

Respite care is designed to provide a short rest period for a family caregiver. There are two options: either the insured is moved to a full-time care facility or a substitute care provider moves into the insured's home for a temporary period, giving the family member a rest from his or her caregiving activities.

Residential Care

A fairly new kind of LTC coverage, *residential care coverage,* is designed to provide a benefit for elderly individuals who live in a retirement community. Retirement communities are geared to senior citizens' full-time needs, both medical and social, and are often sponsored by religious or nonprofit organizations.

LTC Policy Provisions and Limits

As we have stated, there are a number of LTC policies on the market today, each characterized by some distinguishing feature or benefit that sets it apart from the rest. However, there are enough similarities to allow us to discuss the basic provisions of these policies and their typical limits or exclusions.

Qualifying for Benefits

When LTC policies were introduced, insurers frequently required at least three days of prior hospitalization or skilled nursing home stays before the LTC policy benefits were "triggered." The *benefit trigger* is an event or condition that must occur before benefits are paid.

Although most LTC policies require a physician's certification that nursing home or home care is required because of illness, injury or medical emergency, most policies no longer require prior hospitalization. Currently, two models are used to trigger benefits: the functional model and the medical model.

The *functional model* measures the insured's ability to function independently in the community. Ideally, this should encompass both physical and mental measurements, but some companies measure only physical abilities using activities of daily living (ADLs) without a mental measure. This could result in denied benefits for Alzheimer's disease patients who may be able to complete most ADLs but who will need assistance and supervision throughout the day.

A more comprehensive (and a more common) LTC benefit trigger is the *medical model* that uses "medically necessary care" to trigger benefits. What is medically necessary care? Some insurers attempt to define it in their contracts; others purposefully leave the language vague, and will allow the claimant's physician to determine if the care is medically necessary.

Benefit Limits

Almost all LTC policies set *benefit limits,* in terms of how long the benefits are paid or how much the dollar benefit will be for any one covered care service or a combination of services. Maximum dollar amounts vary considerably from policy to policy. Maximum coverage periods also vary.

In fact, with LTC policies, it is not unusual for one policy to include separate maximum coverage periods for nursing home care and home health care. Generally speaking, maximum coverage periods extend anywhere from two to six years. Some policies offer unlimited lifetime coverage.

Age Limits

LTC policies typically set *age limits* for issue, the average age being about 79. However, some newer policies can be sold to people up through age 89. Many policies also set a minimum purchase age, the average being age 50.

Renewability

Most LTC policies are guaranteed renewable, meaning the insurance company cannot cancel the policy and must renew coverage each year, as long as premiums are paid. A guaranteed renewable policy allows the insurer to raise premiums, but only for entire classes of insureds.

Probationary Periods

LTC *probationary periods* can range from 0 to 365 days, and many insurers give the insured the option of selecting the period that best serves his or her needs. The longer the deductible or probationary period, the lower the premium.

Specified Exclusions

Most LTC policies exclude coverage for drug and alcohol dependency, acts of war, self-inflicted injuries and nonorganic mental conditions. Organic cogni-

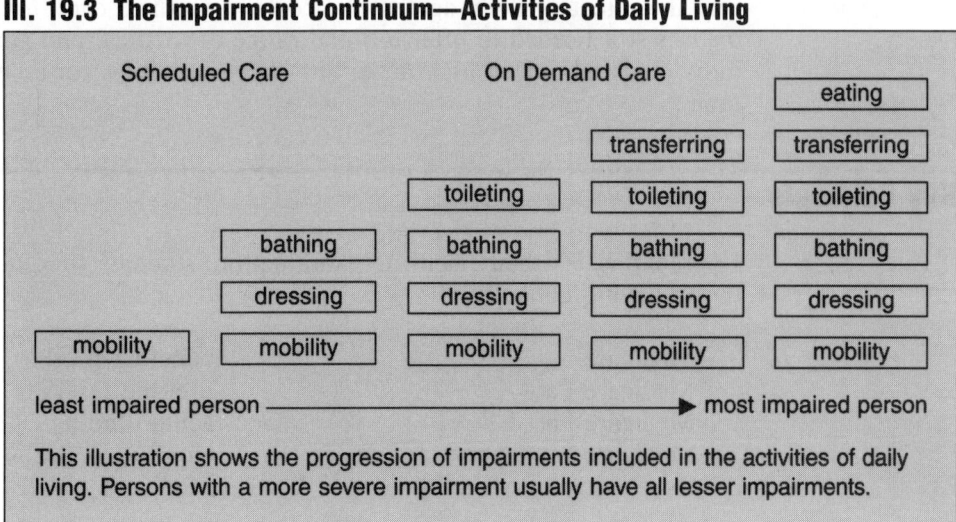

Ill. 19.3 The Impairment Continuum—Activities of Daily Living

This illustration shows the progression of impairments included in the activities of daily living. Persons with a more severe impairment usually have all lesser impairments.

tive disorders, such as Alzheimer's disease, senile dementia and Parkinson's disease are almost always included.

Premiums

The cost for a LTC policy is based on a number of factors: the insured's age and health, the type and level of benefits provided, the inclusion or absence of a deductible or probationary period and the length of that period, and whether or not options or riders are included with the policy (such as the option to purchase additional coverage in the future or the inflation-adjustment rider, which automatically increases the policy's coverage to match inflation levels).

Summary

As people live longer, senior health care issues are receiving more attention from the government, from private insurers and from the public at large. *Medicare,* which provides medical and hospital care for people age 65 and older, serves to control some health care costs through a framework of regulations and guidelines aimed at the health care industry. Medicare consists of two parts: *Part A,* which provides primarily hospital care, skilled nursing facility care and home health care; and *Part B,* which covers most medical expenses not covered by Part A.

Medicare supplement (or *"Medigap") policies,* designed to make up for what Medicare doesn't cover, are also becoming increasingly popular. In 1990, the NAIC developed ten Medicare standard supplement plans, ranging from the basic "core" policy, *Plan A,* to those with more comprehensive coverage.

Medicaid is a joint federal and state program to pay health care expenses for the poor. To qualify for Medicaid benefits, an individual must meet certain asset and income limitation tests. However, even if a person qualifies for Medicaid, finding an adequate nursing home is difficult because Medicaid does not pay for the full cost of care. Medicaid patients are limited in choice as to which nursing home they go to.

As beneficial as Medicare and Medicare supplement insurance are to the elderly in protecting them against the costs of medical care, *long-term care insurance* is still needed to offer a broad range of medical and personal services for individuals who need assistance with daily activities, for an extended period of time.

Key Concepts

In preparing for their licensing examination, students should be familiar with the following concepts:

Medicare	benefit period
Medicare Part A	lifetime reserve
Medicare Part B	acute illness
Medicare supplement policies	chronic condition
long-term care policies	Medicaid

Chapter 19
Questions for Review *(Answers are located at the end of the book.)*

1. Which of the following statements pertaining to Medicare is correct?

    a. Bob is covered under Medicare Part B. He submitted a total of $1,100 of approved medical charges to Medicare after paying the required deductible. Of that total, Bob must pay $880.
    b. Each individual covered by Medicare Part A is allowed one 90-day benefit period per year.
    c. For the first 90 days of hospitalization, Medicare Part A pays 100 percent of all covered services, except for an initial deductible.
    d. Medicare Part A is automatically provided when a qualified individual applies for Social Security benefits.

2. Under Medicare Part B, the participant must

    I. pay an annual deductible.
    II. pay a per benefit deductible.
    III. pay 20 percent of covered charges above the deductible.
    IV. pay 80 percent of covered charges above the deductible.

    a. I only
    b. II and III only
    c. I and III only
    d. II and IV only

3. For how many days of skilled nursing facility care will Medicare pay benefits?

    a. 25
    b. 60
    c. 75
    d. 100

4. The "core policy" (Plan A) developed by the NAIC as a standard Medicare supplement policy includes all of the following, EXCEPT:

    a. the Medicare Part A deductible.
    b. Part A coinsurance amounts.
    c. the first three pints of blood each year.
    d. the 20 percent Part B coinsurance amounts for Medicare-approved services.

5. A/an _____ is a serious condition from which a patient can fully recover with proper medical attention.

    a. chronic condition
    b. long-term condition
    c. acute illness
    d. severe illness

6. Skilled nursing care differs from intermediate care in which of the following ways?

   a. Skilled care must be performed by skilled medical professionals whereas intermediate care does not require medical training.
   b. Skilled care must be available 24 hours a day while intermediate care is daily, but not 24-hour care.
   c. Skilled care is typically given in a nursing home, while intermediate care is usually given at home.
   d. Skilled care encompasses rehabilitation, while intermediate care is for meeting daily personal needs, such as bathing and dressing.

7. All of the following conditions are typically covered in a long-term insurance policy, EXCEPT:

   a. Alzheimer's disease.
   b. senile dementia.
   c. alcohol dependency.
   d. Parkinson's disease.

20 HEALTH INSURANCE POLICY PROVISIONS

NAIC Policy Provisions • Common Exclusions
• Renewability Provisions

To understand health insurance, one must have a firm knowledge of the contract provisions that distinguish it from other insurance policies. Health insurance, more so than life insurance, is characterized by a number of mandatory provisions that must be included in the contract. The 12 mandatory provisions and 11 optional provisions covered in this chapter evolved for the purpose of adding a uniformity to contracts that present themselves as "health insurance policies," thus elevating health insurance to a very high level of regulatory protection. (It may be helpful to review the sample health policy in the Appendix as you read this chapter.)

NAIC Model Health Insurance Policy Provisions

Years ago, the National Association of Insurance Commissioners (NAIC) developed a model "Uniform Individual Accident and Sickness Policy Provisions Law." Almost all states have adopted this model law or similar legislation or regulations.

The purpose of the NAIC law was to establish uniform or model terms, provisions and wording standards for inclusion in all individual health insurance contracts or all contracts that provide insurance against loss "resulting from sickness or from bodily injury or death by accident or both." The result was *12 mandatory policy provisions* and *11 optional policy provisions*. Because these provisions are to be followed "in substance," insurers may employ different wording from that of the law, as long as the protection is provided and is no less favorable to the insured than the law stipulates.

Similar to a life insurance contract, a health insurance contract obligates the insurer to pay the insured (or a beneficiary) a stipulated benefit under circumstances specified in the contract. The specifics of the benefit and the requisite circumstances are set forth in the contract's provisions. Let's take a look at these provisions.

Twelve Mandatory Policy Provisions

In accordance with the NAIC model law, there are *12 mandatory* provisions that are required to be in all health insurance contracts. These are as follows.

#1: Entire Contract

Like its counterpart in a life insurance policy, the *entire contract* provision in a health insurance policy protects the policyowner in two ways. First, it states that nothing outside of the contract—which includes the signed application and any attached policy riders—can be considered part of the contract; that is, nothing can be "incorporated by reference." Second, it assures the policyowner that no changes will be made to the contract after it has been issued, even if the insurer makes policy changes that affect all policy sales in the future.

#2: Time Limit on Certain Defenses

Under the *time limit on certain defenses* provision, the policy is incontestable after it has been in force a certain period of time, usually two years. This is similar to the "incontestable clause" in a life insurance policy. However, unlike life policies, a fraudulent statement on a health insurance application is grounds for contest at any time, unless the policy is guaranteed renewable, in which case it cannot be contested for any reason after the contestable period expires.

Another part of this provision concerns any preexisting conditions (conditions that existed prior to the policy's effective date) an insured may have. Under the provision, the insurance company cannot deny a claim on the basis of a preexisting condition after expiration of the stated contestable period—unless such preexisting condition has been excluded specifically from the policy by name or description.

#3: Grace Period

Per the *grace period* provision, the policyowner is given a number of days after the premium due date during which time the premium payment may be delayed without penalty and the policy continues in force. Depending on the state, the minimum grace periods that may be specified are typically seven days for policies with weekly premium payments (i.e., industrial policies), ten days for policies with premiums payable on a monthly basis and 31 days for other policies. (Some states, however, require a standard grace period of 31 days, regardless of the frequency of premium payment or policy term.)

#4: Reinstatement

Under certain conditions, a policy that has lapsed may be *reinstated*. Reinstatement is automatic if the delinquent premium is accepted by the company or its authorized agent and the company does not require an application for reinstatement.

If a company does require such an application, it may or may not approve the application. If it takes no action on the application for 45 days, the policy is reinstated automatically. To protect the company against *adverse selection*, losses resulting from sickness are covered only if the sickness occurs at least ten days after the reinstatement date.

#5: Notice of Claims

The *notice of claims* provision describes the policyowner's obligation to the insurer to provide notification of loss within a reasonable period of time. Typically, this period is 20 days after the occurrence or a commencement of the loss, or as soon thereafter as is reasonably possible. If the loss involves disability income payments that are payable for two or more years, the disabled claimant must submit proof of loss every six months. Such proof may be submitted to either the company or an authorized agent of the company.

#6: Claims Forms

It is the company's responsibility to supply a *claims form* to an insured within 15 days after receiving notice of claim. If it fails to do so within the time limit, the claimant may submit proof of loss in any form, explaining the occurrence, the character and the extent of the loss for which the claim is submitted.

#7: Proof of Loss

After a loss occurs, or after the company becomes liable for periodic payments (e.g., disability income benefits), the claimant has 90 days in which to submit *proof of loss*. The claim will not be affected in any way, however, if it is not reasonably possible for the claimant to comply with the 90-day provision.

There is a time limit for submitting proof of loss—whether or not it is "reasonably possible" to do so—and that is one year after the company becomes liable for the loss. The only exception to the one-year limit is if the claimant does not have the "legal capacity" to comply.

#8: Time of Payment of Claims

The *time of payment of claims* provision provides for immediate payment of the claim after the insurer receives notification and proof of loss. If the claim involves disability income payments, they must be paid at least monthly, if not at more frequent intervals specified in the policy. In many states, the time payment of claims is 60 days.

#9: Payment of Claims

The *payment of claims* provision in a health insurance contract specifies how and to whom claim payments are to be made. Payments for loss of life are to be made to the designated beneficiary. If no beneficiary has been named, death proceeds are to be paid to the deceased insured's estate. Claims other than death benefits are to be paid to the insured.

In accordance with this required provision are two optional provisions that insurers may add. One gives the insurer the right to expedite payment of urgently needed claim funds and pay up to $1,000 in benefits to a relative or individual who is considered to be equitably entitled to payment. The other optional provision allows the insured to have medical benefits assigned—or paid directly—to the hospital or physician rendering the covered services.

#10: Physical Exam and Autopsy

The *physical exam and autopsy* provision entitles a company, at its own expense, to make physical examinations of the insured at reasonable intervals during the period of a claim. In the case of death, the insurer has the right to conduct an autopsy on the body of the insured, provided it is not forbidden by state law.

#11: Legal Actions

The insured cannot take *legal action* against the company in a claim dispute until after 60 days from the time the insured submits proof of loss. The same rule applies to beneficiaries. Also, if legal action is to be taken against the company, it must be done within a certain time after proof of loss is submitted (usually two or three years).

#12: Change of Beneficiary

The insured, as policyowner, may change the *beneficiary designation* at any time, unless a beneficiary has been named irrevocably. So long as the insured reserves the right to change beneficiaries, he or she also may surrender or assign the policy without obtaining the consent of the beneficiary.

Eleven Optional Provisions

There are *11 optional* health policy provisions, and companies may ignore them or use only those that are needed in their policy forms. The provisions pertaining to "other insurance in this insurer," "insurance with other insurers," and "relation of earnings to insurance" seldom are used. They were intended to deal with the problem of overinsurance, but generally proved to be ineffective.

#1: Change of Occupation

The *change of occupation* provision sets forth the changes that may be made to premium rates or benefits payable should the insured change occupations. Many insurers include this provision in their disability income policies because an individual's occupation has a direct bearing on his or her risk profile and one's risk profile has a direct bearing on premium charges. Consequently, this provision allows the insurer to reduce the maximum benefit payable under the policy if the insured switches to a *more* hazardous occupation or to reduce the premium rate charged if the insured changes to a *less* hazardous occupation. These benefit and premium changes take effect at the time the insured changes occupations; if a change in jobs is discovered after a disability begins, the changes are made retroactively.

#2: Misstatement of Age

The *misstatement of age* provision allows the insurer to adjust the benefit payable if the age of the insured was misstated when application for the policy was made. Benefit amounts payable in such cases will be what the premiums paid would have purchased at the correct age. As we know, the older the applicant, the higher the premium; therefore, if the insured was older at the time of application than is shown in the policy, benefits would be reduced accordingly. The reverse would be true if the insured were younger than listed in the application.

#3: Other Insurance in This Insurer

The purpose of the *other insurance in this insurer* provision is to limit the company's risk with any individual insured. Under this provision, the total amount of coverage to be underwritten by a company for one person is restricted to a specified maximum amount, regardless of the number of policies issued. Premiums that apply to any such excess of coverage must be returned to the insured or the insured's estate.

#4: Insurance with Other Insurer

In attempting to deal with the potential problem of overinsurance, the *insurance with other insurer* provision states that benefits payable for "expenses incurred" will be prorated in cases where the company accepted the risk without being notified of other existing coverage for the same risk. When premiums are paid that exceed the amount needed to cover what the company determines it will pay, the excess premiums must be refunded to the policyowner.

#5: Insurance with Other Insurers

Similar to the above, the *insurance with other insurers* provision calls for the prorating of benefits that are payable on any basis other than "expenses incurred." It also provides for a return of premiums that exceed the amount needed to pay for the company's portion of prorated benefits.

#6: Relation of Earnings to Insurance

If disability income benefits from *all* disability income policies for the same loss exceed the insured's monthly earnings at the time of disability (or the average monthly earnings for two years preceding disability), the *relation of earnings* provision states that the insurer is liable only for that *proportionate* amount of benefits as the insured's earnings bear to the total benefits under all such coverage.

Total indemnities payable to the insured may not be reduced below $200 or the sum total benefits under all applicable coverage, whichever is less. Any premiums paid for the excess coverage are refunded.

#7: Unpaid Premiums

If there is an *unpaid premium* at the time a claim becomes payable, the amount of the premium is to be deducted from the sum payable to the insured or beneficiary. Or, if the premium is covered by a note when a claim is submitted, the note payment will be subtracted from the amount payable for the claim.

#8: Cancelation

Though prohibited in a number of states, the provision for *cancelation* gives the company the right to cancel the policy at any time with five days' written notice to the insured. It also provides that the insured may cancel the policy anytime after the policy's original term has expired. Any unearned premium is to be refunded to the insured. If a claim is pending at the time of cancelation, the claim cannot be affected by the cancelation. (See also "Renewability Provisions," page 249.)

#9: Conformity with State Statutes

Any policy provision that is in conflict with *state statutes* in the state where the insured lives at the time the policy is issued is automatically amended to conform with the minimum statutory requirements.

#10: Illegal Occupation

The *illegal occupation* provision specifies that the insurer is not liable for losses attributed to the insured's commission of, or being connected with, a felony or participation in any illegal occupation.

#11: Intoxicants and Narcotics

The insurer is not liable for any loss attributed to the insured while *intoxicated* or under the influence of *narcotics,* unless such drugs were administered on the advice of a physician.

Other Health Insurance Policy Provisions

The 12 mandatory provisions and 11 optional provisions just described comprise the substantive elements of individual health insurance policies. However, there are a number of other very important clauses and provisions that should be noted.

Insuring Clause

Generally, the *insuring clause* is a broad statement on the first page of the health policy, stipulating conditions under which benefits are to be paid. While these critical provisions vary considerably in health insurance contracts, they basically represent a company's "promise to pay" benefits for specific kinds of losses resulting from sickness or accidents. They usually specify that benefits are subject to all provisions and exclusions stated in the policy.

Consideration Clause

The *consideration clause* states the amount and frequency of premium payments. If the first premium has not been paid—even though the application

---

Ill. 20.1

NAIC Uniform Health Insurance Policy Provisions

Mandatory Provisions	Optional Provisions
1. Entire Contract	1. Change of Occupation
2. Time Limit on Certain Defenses	2. Misstatement of Age
3. Grace Period	3. Other Insurance in This Insurer
4. Reinstatement	4. Insurance with Other Insurer
5. Notice of Claims	5. Insurance with Other Insurers
6. Claims Forms	6. Relation of Earnings to Insurance
7. Proof of Loss	7. Unpaid Premiums
8. Time of Payment of Claims	8. Cancelation
9. Payment of Claims	9. Conformity with State Statutes
10. Physical Exam and Autopsy	10. Illegal Occupation
11. Legal Actions	11. Intoxicants and Narcotics
12. Change of Beneficiary	

has been completed and signed by the applicant—the necessary consideration is partially lacking. As is the case with life insurance, the legal consideration for a health policy consists of the application *and* payment of the initial premium. A copy of the application is attached to the policy.

Frequently, the consideration clause also lists the effective date of the contract and defines the initial term of the policy. In addition, it may specify the insured's right to renew the policy.

Conversion Privilege for Dependents

A single health policy may insure one person or more than one if the applicant is an adult family member and the others to be covered are members of his or her family. Thus, additional persons who may be insured include the husband, wife, dependent children or others dependent upon the adult applicant. To be eligible, children must meet certain age requirements. (See Ill. 20.2.)

If the insurance on a covered individual is terminated because he or she no longer fits the policy definition of "family member," that person has a right to take out a *conversion policy* without evidence of insurability. For example, if Faye divorces Stanley and thus no longer can be covered under his family policy, she has a right to obtain a conversion policy. When their children reach the limiting age for children's coverage, they also will be eligible for a conversion policy.

Free-Look Provision

Most states mandate that their health insurance policies contain a *free-look* provision permitting policyowners either 10 or 20 days in which to examine their new policies at no obligation. If they decide not to keep their policies, they may return them within the prescribed time limit and receive full refunds of premiums paid.

Ill. 20.2

Health Coverage for Dependent Children

Generally, children of the insured are eligible for coverage under a family policy until they attain a specified age, e.g., age 19, or age 23 if they remain in school. Adopted children, stepchildren and foster children usually are eligible for coverage. As long as a policy is in force, coverage for a child generally continues until the child marries or reaches the limiting age. However, a number of states have enacted special laws that require insurers to retain as insureds under the parent's individual health policy any child who reaches the limiting age, but is dependent on the insured and incapable of self-support because of mental or physical impairment.

Attaining a minimum age, such as 14 days, may be required for coverage; however, recent legislation in some states mandates that health policies insuring family members also provide coverage for newborn children from the date of birth. Typically, such legislation permits the insurer to require that notice of the birth of the child be given and an application and additional premium be submitted within a specified period.

Common Exclusions or Restrictions

Health insurance policies frequently cite a number of *exclusions* or conditions that are not covered. The common ones are injuries due to *war* or an act of war, *self-inflicted injuries* and those incurred while the insured is serving as a *pilot* or *crew member* of an aircraft.

Other exclusions are losses resulting from suicide, hernia (as an accidental injury), riots or the use of drugs or narcotics. Losses due to injuries sustained while committing a felony, or attempting to do so, also may be excluded. Foreign travel may not be excluded in every instance, but extended stays overseas or foreign residence may cause a loss of benefits.

Maternity Benefits

Maternity benefits generally are handled differently in individual health policies than in group health policies. When available for individual policies, a maternity provision may provide a fixed amount for childbirth or a benefit based upon a specified multiple of the daily hospital room benefit. Frequently, the maternity benefit is available only as an added benefit for an additional premium.

Maternity coverage in group health plans is discussed in Chapter 22.

Preexisting Conditions

As we have learned, medical expense and disability income policies usually exclude paying benefits for losses due to *preexisting conditions* pertaining to illness, disease or other physical impairments. For purposes of issuing individual health policies, insurers consider a preexisting condition to be one that the insured contracted (or one that was manifested) prior to the policy's effective date. Consequently, in the event the insured did not specifically cite the condition on the application and the insurer did not expressly exclude the condition from coverage, the preexisting condition provision would serve to exclude the condition nonetheless. However, such exclusions are subject to the "time limit on certain defenses" provision.

Any preexisting condition that the insured has disclosed clearly in the application usually is not excluded or, if it is, the condition is named specifically in an *excluding waiver* or *rider* (see below).

The treatment of preexisting conditions under group health plans is a little different and is discussed in Chapter 22.

Waivers for Impairments

The majority of health policies are standard and are issued as applied for. However, a few people have an existing impairment that increases the risk and so are required to pay an extra premium. A few people are uninsurable and must be declined. Others, however, fall in between and would not be able to obtain health insurance if *waivers* were not in use. Waivers usually are stated in simple language. For example: "This policy does not cover or extend to any disability resulting directly or indirectly from. . . ." A waiver is dated and bears the signature of an officer of the company and, in many cases, the applicant. This is usually called an "impairment rider."

If the insured's condition improves, the company may be willing to remove the waiver. Meanwhile, the person at least has health protection from other hazards that he or she otherwise could not obtain.

Renewability Provisions

One of the distinguishing features of health insurance policies is the provisions they contain that allow the insurer to continue or discontinue coverage. Known as *renewability provisions,* they vary from policy to policy. Generally speaking, the more favorable the renewability provision is to the insured policyholder, the higher the premium.

Cancelable Policies

The renewability provision in a *cancelable* policy allows the insurer to cancel or terminate the policy at any time, simply by providing written notification to the insured and refunding any advance premium that has been paid. Cancelable policies also allow the insurer to increase premiums.

Optionally Renewable Policies

The renewability provision in an *optionally renewable* policy gives the insurer the option to terminate the policy on a date specified in the contract. Furthermore, this provision allows the insurer to increase the premium for any *class* of optionally renewable insureds.* Usually termination or premium increases take place on policy anniversary dates or premium due dates.

Conditionally Renewable Policies

A *conditionally renewable* policy allows an insurer to terminate the coverage, but only in the event of one or more conditions stated in the contract. These conditions cannot apply to the insured's health; most frequently, they are related to the insured reaching a certain age or losing gainful employment. Usually, the premium for conditionally renewable policies may be increased, if such an increase applies to an entire class of policies.

Guaranteed Renewable Policies

The renewal provision in a *guaranteed renewable* policy specifies that the policy must be renewed, as long as premiums are paid, until the insured reaches a specified age, such as 60 or 65. Premium increases may be applied, but only for the entire class of insureds; they cannot be assessed to individual insureds.

Noncancelable Policies

A *noncancelable* or "noncan" policy cannot be canceled nor can its premium rates be increased under any circumstances; these rates are specified in the

---

*A "class" of insureds includes all insureds of policies of a particular kind or all insureds of a specific group. For example, a class of insureds may be those of a particular age or in a specific geographic region.

policy. The term of most noncancelable policies is to the insured's age 65. Noncan provisions are most commonly found in disability income policies; they are rarely used in medical expense policies.

Summary

To protect the rights of individual health insurance policyholders, the NAIC developed a set of *12 mandatory* and *11 optional policy provisions.* These provisions help assure consumers that the health policies they buy will meet at least a minimum level of standards. Other provisions, though not categorized as "required" or "optional," are equally important. Of special note are the *renewability provisions,* absent from life insurance policies, but an essential feature of health policies.

Key Concepts

In preparing for their licensing examination, students should be familiar with the following concepts:

entire contract	relation of earnings to insurance
time limit on certain defenses	unpaid premiums
grace period	cancelation
reinstatement	conformity with state statutes
notice of claims	illegal occupation
claims forms	intoxicants and narcotics
proof of loss	insuring clause
time of payment of claims	consideration clause
payment of claims	conversion privilege
physical examination and autopsy	free look
legal actions	exclusions and waivers
change of beneficiary	preexisting conditions
change of occupation	cancelable
misstatement of age	optionally renewable
other insurance in this insurer	conditionally renewable
insurance with other insurer	guaranteed renewable
insurance with other insurers	noncancelable

Chapter 20
Questions for Review   *(Answers are located at the end of the book.)*

1. A company may change the wording of a uniform policy provision in its health insurance policies only if

   a. the company's board of directors approves the change.
   b. the modified provision is not less favorable to the insurer.
   c. the applicant directs that it be changed.
   d. the modified provision is not less favorable to the insured.

2. Children of the insured are eligible for health insurance coverage until they attain age 19 or, if they remain in school full time, age

   a. 20.
   b. 21.
   c. 22.
   d. 23.

3. All of the following statements pertaining to the grace period and reinstatement provisions in health insurance policies are correct, EXCEPT:

   a. Craig's health policy has a grace period of 31 days. He had a premium due June 15 while he was on vacation. He returned home July 7, mailed his premium the next day and the insurer received it July 10. His policy would have remained in force.
   b. Warren's medical expense policy was reinstated on September 30 and he became ill and entered the hospital on October 5. His hospital expense will not be paid by the insurer.
   c. Under a health policy's reinstatement terms, insured losses from accidental injuries and sickness are covered immediately after reinstatement.
   d. States may require grace periods of 7, 10 or 31 days, depending on the mode of premium payment or term of insurance; however, many states require a 31-day grace period in any case.

4. Which of the following is the usual grace period for a semi-annual premium policy?

   a. 7 days
   b. 20 days
   c. 31 days
   d. 60 days

5. Diana, the beneficiary under her husband's AD&D policy, submits an accidental death claim on September 1, 1991, following his death; however, the company denies the claim on the basis that death was due to natural causes. She decides to talk to her attorney. When is the earliest she could bring legal action against the insurer?

   a. September 2, 1991
   b. October 1, 1991
   c. November 1, 1991
   d. September 1, 1992

6. All of the following are required uniform provisions in individual health insurance policies, EXCEPT:

   a. change of occupation.
   b. grace period.
   c. entire contract changes.
   d. reinstatement.

7. Under the misstatement of age provision in a health insurance policy, what can a company do if it discovers that an insured gave a wrong age at the time of application?

   a. Cancel the policy
   b. Increase the premium
   c. Adjust the benefits
   d. Assess a penalty

8. The conformity with state statutes provision in a health insurance policy stipulates that any policy provision that is in conflict with the statutes of the state where the insured resides is

   a. to be submitted to the insurance commissioner for approval.
   b. cause for the insured's policy to be voided.
   c. automatically amended to conform to the minimum requirements of the state's statutes.
   d. to be rewritten if the policy is returned to the company.

9. Which section of a health insurance policy specifies the conditions, times and circumstances under which the insured is NOT covered by the policy?

   a. Coinsurance provision   c. Insuring clause
   b. Coverages   d. Exclusions

10. Which kind of health insurance policy assures renewability up to a specific age of the insured, although the company reserves the right to change the premium rate on a class basis?

    a. Noncancelable   c. Optionally renewable
    b. Guaranteed renewable   d. Cancelable

11. According to the notice of claims provision in a health insurance policy, a claimant normally must notify the insurance company of loss within how many days after the loss occurs?

    a. 10 days   c. 30 days
    b. 20 days   d. 45 days

12. Which of the following types of health insurance policies prevents the company from changing the premium rate or modifying the coverage in any way?

    a. Optionally renewable   c. Guaranteed renewable
    b. Noncancelable   d. Cancelable

21 HEALTH INSURANCE UNDERWRITING AND PREMIUMS

Risk Factors • Premium Factors
• Tax Treatment • Cost Containment

Health insurers are increasingly finding themselves in a tough position. The high cost of medical care requires them to charge premiums that adequately cover the correspondingly high level of health insurance claims, and yet public sentiment and even competition from within the industry pressure companies to keep rates as low as possible. Health insurers are reacting to these conflicting forces by tightening their underwriting requirements—becoming more selective in the risks they will accept—and controlling claims through innovative measures. This chapter looks at the important topic of health insurance underwriting and covers the related subjects of health insurance premiums and tax treatment of premiums and benefits. Finally, we'll look at the emerging issues of cost control and case management.

Risk Factors in Health Insurance

While most of the underwriting factors that apply to life insurance are also applicable to health insurance, they take on greater significance in the context of health risks. With life insurance, there is but one death claim per insured. But with health insurance, multiple claims per insured is the rule rather than the exception. Thus, the classification of health insurance risks is critically important. Data accumulated over the years by insurance companies in underwriting health insurance serves as the primary basis for classifying risks.

Classifying risks for health insurance is more complex than simply deciding whether a risk is acceptable or not acceptable. The *degree of risk* is highly important when considering the probable future health of an individual applicant and the amount of premium to be charged. So home office underwriters are charged with the responsibility of scrutinizing health insurance applications with special care.

Many factors are reviewed in underwriting health insurance policies. Three of the most important factors are *physical condition, moral hazards* and *occupation*.

Physical Condition

An applicant's present *physical condition* is of primary importance when evaluating health risks. For example, the underwriter must know whether the individual has been treated for any chronic conditions, and any physical impairments of the applicant are checked out carefully. Hernias or ulcers, for example, may require surgical correction or treatment in the future and, thereby, represent an additional risk. Persons with an unusual body build, including extreme overweight or height, also represent higher risks to the insurer.

Moral Hazards

The *habits* or *lifestyles* of applicants also can flash warning signals that there may be additional risk for the insurer. Personalities and attitudes may draw attention in the underwriting process. Excessive drinking and the use of drugs represent serious moral hazards. Applicants who are seen as accident-prone or potential malingerers (feigning a continuing disability in order to collect benefits) likewise might be heavy risks, particularly those applying for disability income insurance. Other signals of high moral hazard can be a poor credit rating or dishonest business practices.

Occupation

A third significant factor involved with health insurance risks is the applicant's *occupation*. This is because occupation has a direct bearing on both the *probability of disability* and the *average severity of disability*.

Experience shows that disability benefit costs for insurers can vary considerably from occupation to occupation. There is little physical risk associated with professional persons, office managers or office workers, but occupations involving heavy machinery, strong chemicals or high electrical voltage, for example, represent a high degree of risk for the insurer.

Jobs requiring manual labor can also influence the length of recuperation periods for disabled workers and how soon they can return to work. Further, the sporadic nature of employment in certain occupations can have a bearing on claim costs because the number and size of such claims tend to rise when insureds are unemployed.

Some occupations involve irregular hours, uncertain earnings and, in some cases, not even a definite place of business—all of which contribute to higher risks for insurers. Examples are entertainers and authors, who generally do not have regular business hours. In addition, disability benefit costs to insurers also can be influenced by the social and economic character of persons in some occupational classifications.

For underwriting purposes, many insurers divide occupations into five classes: AAA, AA, A, B and C. The five classes range from the top classification (AAA), which includes professional and office workers, to more hazardous occupations in the lower (B and C) classes. Persons in a few occupations, such as steeplejacks, airplane test pilots or stunt flyers usually are uninsurable.

The applicant's occupation and the renewability factor of a policy also are connected from an underwriting standpoint. According to the change of occupation provision, if the insured changes to a less hazardous job, the insurer will return any excess unearned premium; however, if the change is to a more hazardous occupation, the benefits are reduced proportionately and the premium remains the same. The change of occupation clause generally is not included in guaranteed renewable policies, especially long-term disability income policies. Noncancelable policies are sold only to individuals in the higher occupational classes in which change of occupation is seldom a factor. Limited and industrial health policies usually are available at standard rates for all occupations, except those excluded by specific policy provisions.

Other Risk Factors

Additional health insurance risk factors include the applicant's *age, sex, medical* and *family history* and *avocations*.

1. *Age.* Generally, the older the applicant, the higher the risk he or she represents. Most individual health insurance policies limit the coverage to a specified age such as 60 or 65 (although some lifetime coverages are available).

2. *Sex.* An applicant's sex is also an underwriting consideration. Men show a lower rate of disability than women, except at the upper ages.

3. *History.* An applicant's medical history may point to the possibility of a recurrence of a certain health condition. Likewise, an applicant's *family history* may reflect a tendency he or she has toward certain medical conditions or health impairments.

4. *Avocations.* Certain hobbies an applicant may have—such as skydiving or mountain climbing—may increase his or her risk to the insurer. An applicant's avocations are carefully evaluated.

Insurable Interest

Finally, when evaluating health insurance risks, the underwriter must determine whether an *insurable interest* exists between the applicant and the individual to be insured. In health insurance, an insurable interest exists if the applicant is in a position to suffer a loss should the insured incur medical expenses or be unable to work due to a disability. As with life insurance, insurable interest is a prerequisite for issuing a health insurance policy.

Classification of Applicants

Once an underwriter has reviewed the various risk factors associated with an individual applicant and has measured them against the company's underwriting standards, there are four ways to classify the applicant and his or her request for health coverage: as a *standard risk,* a *preferred risk,* an *uninsurable risk* or a *substandard risk*.

Standard risk applicants are usually issued a policy at standard terms and rates. Preferred risks generally receive lower rates than standard risks, reflecting the fact that people in this class have a better-than-standard risk profile. Uninsurable applicants are usually rejected and denied coverage. Substandard risk applicants—those who pose a higher-than-average risk for one or more reasons—are treated differently. Substandard applicants may represent a very low risk on moral and occupational considerations and still pose a high risk because of their physical condition. Other substandard applicants may be in top physical condition, but work at a hazardous occupation. Besides outright rejection, there are three techniques commonly used by insurers in issuing health insurance policies to substandard risks:

1. attaching an *exclusion* (or *impairment*) rider or waiver to a policy;

2. charging an *extra premium;* or

3. *limiting the type* of policy.

Exclusion or impairment riders rule out coverage for losses resulting from chronic conditions or physical impairments. With the questionable risks excluded, policies then are issued at standard rates. When some occupational hazard exists, applicants may be charged an extra premium to compensate for the additional risk. The same may be true when applicants are overweight or show signs of high blood pressure, etc. Extra premiums may be charged only for a few years or on a permanent basis.

When applicants represent a substandard risk, the type of policy requested may be modified in some manner. For example, a policy may exclude all sickness or a specific kind of sickness, but cover all losses due to accidental injuries. In other cases, a policy may provide protection for a lower amount than requested or provide a shorter benefit period. Or a provision may be inserted calling for a longer waiting period than indicated in the application.

Only a small percentage of applicants are classified as substandard risks. And, with years of experience to guide them, insurers today reject a smaller percentage of applicants for health insurance than in the past.

Health Insurance Premium Factors

Rate-making for health insurance policies is more complex than for life insurance, primarily because it involves more than one type of benefit. The average frequency of covered health insurance losses further complicates premium computations. There are a number of variables—primary and secondary—all insurers take into account when determining the premium rate for a particular health insurance product.

Primary Premium Factors

At the base level, there are three primary factors that affect health insurance premiums: *morbidity, interest* and *expenses*. Note how closely these correspond to basic life insurance premium factors, except that morbidity is substituted for mortality.

Morbidity

Whereas mortality rates show the average number of persons within a larger group of people who can be expected to die within a given year at a given age, *morbidity* rates indicate the average number at various ages who can be expected to become *disabled* each year due to accident or sickness. Morbidity statistics also reveal the average duration of disability, so insurers can approximate not only how many in a large group will become disabled, but how long the disabilities can be expected to last.

Morbidity statistics, which are available to companies offering health insurance, have been collected over many, many years and reflect the disabilities of hundreds of thousands of people. They are compiled into morbidity tables.

Interest

Just as with life insurance, *interest* is a major element in establishing health insurance premiums. A large portion of every premium received is invested to earn interest. The interest earnings reduce the premium amount that otherwise would be required from policyowners.

Expenses

Every business has *expenses* that must be paid and the insurance business is no different. Each health insurance policy an insurer issues must carry its proportionate share of the costs for employees' salaries, agents' commissions, utilities, rent or mortgage payments, maintenance costs, supplies and other administrative expenses.

Secondary Premium Factors

In addition to these three primary factors, the actual rate assigned to a specific health policy by the underwriter depends on several other factors, including the *benefits* provided under the policy, past *claims experience,* the *age* and *sex* of the insured and the insured's *occupation* and *hobbies.*

Benefits

A health insurance policy may offer a specific type of benefit or a variety of benefits. For example, a hospital expense-only policy offers benefits to cover just hospitalization expenses while a comprehensive major medical policy covers a much broader range of medical expenses. The *number and kinds of benefits* provided by a policy affect the premium rate.

Another aspect is that, while two policies may provide identical types of benefits, the *amount of protection* or benefits in one policy may be higher than in another. So, the greater the benefits, the higher the premium, or, to state it another way, the greater the risk to the company, the higher the premium.

Claims Experience

Before realistic premium rates can be established for health insurance, the insurer must know what can be expected as to the dollar amount of the future claims. The most practical way to estimate the cost of future claims is to rely on claims tables based on *past claims experience.* For example, experience tables have been constructed for hospital expenses based on the amounts paid out in the past for the same types of expenses. Such tables, along with an added factor to account for rising hospital costs, enable companies to estimate the average amounts of future hospital expenses. Similarly, experience tables have been developed for surgical benefits, covering various kinds of surgery based on past experience. The same procedure is followed to estimate average claims expected in the future for other medical expenses. Such tables must be adjusted periodically, of course, to reflect more recent experience.

Age and Sex of the Insured

As discussed earlier, experience has shown that health insurance claims costs tend to increase as the age of the insured increases. For any given coverage, the older the insured, the higher the applicable premium rate.

Also, disabilities among women under age 55, on the average, have a greater frequency and longer duration than among men, so female premium rates for certain coverages are higher than the premium rates for males. At the older ages, however, that is generally not true.

Occupation and Hobbies

Because some types of work are more hazardous than others, the premium rates for a person's health insurance policy may be affected by his or her *occupation*. If an insured's occupation indicates a higher than normal risk to the company, the policy may carry an extra premium charge. (Insurers establish their own occupational classifications, which represent another element in the premium structure.) The same holds true for any dangerous *hobbies* in which the insured may participate.

Tax Treatment of Health Insurance Premiums and Benefits

The tax treatment of health insurance premiums and benefits depends, to a large degree, on the type of insurance in question.

Taxation of Disability Income Insurance

Premiums paid for personal disability income insurance are *not* deductible by the individual insured, but the disability benefits are *tax free* to the recipient.

When a group disability income insurance plan is paid for entirely by the employer and benefits are paid directly to individual employees who qualify, the premiums are *deductible* by the employer. The benefits, in turn, are *taxable* to the recipient. On the other hand, if an employee contributes to any portion of the premium, his or her benefit will be received tax free in proportion to the premium contributed. For example, if an employee pays 40 percent of the premium and the employer pays 60 percent, 40 percent of the benefit is tax free to the employee and 60 percent is taxable.

Also, a self-employed individual may deduct 25 percent of amounts paid for health insurance covering the individual, spouse and dependents.* The deduction cannot exceed self-employment net earnings and is not available where

---

*When this deduction was first introduced, it included an expiration date, after which the deduction would not be allowed. This expiration date has consistently been extended through various pieces of legislation, the latest being the Revenue Reconciliation Act of 1993.

the individual or spouse is eligible to participate on a subsidized basis in an employer-sponsored health plan.

Persons under age 65 who are retired on permanent and total disability may be eligible for a tax credit on their disability income. The credit is equal to 15 percent of an initial base amount ($5,000 if married with one spouse eligible or unmarried), less:

1. amounts received under pensions, annuities or Social Security disability benefits and

2. one-half the excess of the individual's adjusted gross income over specified amounts (e.g., $10,000 if married and filing a joint return or $7,500 if single).

Taxation of Medical Expense Insurance

Incurred medical expenses that are reimbursed by insurance may not be deducted from an individual's federal income tax. Furthermore, incurred medical expenses that are not reimbursed by insurance may only be deducted to the extent they exceed 7.5 percent of the insured's adjusted gross income. For example, an individual who has an adjusted gross income of $35,000 would be able to deduct only the amount of unreimbursed medical expenses over $2,625.

For purposes of figuring any deductible medical expenses, prescription drugs, insulin, hospital expenses, physician and surgeon fees, nursing care, dental care, rehabilitative treatments and medical insurance premiums can all be considered.

Benefits received by an insured under a medical expense policy are not included in his or her gross income, since they are paid to offset losses he or she incurred. However, medical expense insurance benefits must be included in gross income to the extent that reimbursement is received for medical expenses deducted in a prior year.

Cost Containment

Insurers face a complex dilemma: how to reduce health claims experience so that health insurance, especially medical expense insurance, remains affordable. Currently there is little direct influence insurers can exert over the medical profession to contain the cost of medical care; however, there are important actions insurers themselves can take toward the important goal of *cost containment*.

Policy Design

The *design* or *structure* of a policy and its provisions can have an impact on an insurer's cost containment efforts. A *higher deductible* will help limit claims, for example, and in fact the "average" deductible has increased in recent years. Whereas the typical deductible was $100 for an individual and $300 for a family just a few years ago, it is more common now to find deductibles in the $300 to $500 range for an individual and $900 or higher for a family. *Coinsurance* is another important means of sharing the cost of medical care between the insured and the insurer. *Shortened benefit periods* can also prove beneficial from a cost containment standpoint, in that they can reduce the tendency some people have to seek medical attention for a condition that has long since been resolved.

Medical Cost Management

Medical cost management is being widely recognized and applauded as the most promising means of controlling claims expenses. Basically, it is the process of controlling how policyowners utilize their policies. There are four general approaches insurers use for cost management: *mandatory second opinions, precertification review, ambulatory surgery* and *case management*.

Mandatory Second Opinions

In an effort to reduce unnecessary surgical operations, many health policies today contain a provision requiring the insured to obtain a *second opinion* before receiving non-life-threatening surgery. Benefits are often reduced if a second opinion is not obtained.

Precertification Review

To control hospital claims, many policies today require policyowners to *obtain approval* from the insurer before entering a hospital on a nonemergency basis. Even if the admission was on an emergency basis, most policies with this type of provision require the insured to notify the insurer within a short period of time (usually 24 hours) after being admitted. The insurer will then determine how much of the hospital stay it will cover, depending on the reason for the admission. If the insured wants to stay longer, the additional expense will be the responsibility of the insured, not the insurer.

Ambulatory Surgery

The advances in medicine now permit many surgical procedures to be performed on an *"outpatient"* basis where once an overnight hospital stay was required. To encourage insureds to utilize less expensive outpatient care, many policies offer some sort of inducement. For example, a policy may waive the deductible or coinsurance if the policyowner elects to be treated on an outpatient basis rather than as an admitted patient.

Case Management

Case management, as referred to here, involves a specialist within the insurance company, such as a registered nurse, who reviews a potentially large claim as it develops to discuss treatment alternatives with the insured. For example, the insured's policy might state that treatment for a kidney ailment can only be performed in a hospital or registered hemodialysis center. However, if it makes economic sense to the insurer—and practical sense to the insured—to have treatments conducted at the insured's home, the case manager might negotiate with the insured to allow treatment to be performed at home as long as certain conditions are met.

The purpose of case management is to let the insurer take an active role in the management of what could potentially become a very expensive claim.

Summary

The escalating cost of medical care makes it imperative that insurers exercise precaution in their *underwriting*. A number of important factors come together during the health underwriting process. Preexisting medical conditions as well as circumstances that may affect future medical losses are reviewed carefully by health underwriters. Health insurance premium rates are affected not only by the three primary factors of *morbidity, interest* and *expenses,* but by secondary factors as well, including the particular benefits provided by the policy and characteristics of the insured. As is true with all aspects of life and health insurance, the *tax treatment* of health insurance premiums and benefits is an important consideration from a personal financial standpoint. Typically, premiums paid for personal health insurance are not deductible and benefits received are not taxable.

In an effort to control health claims expenses, many insurers exercise some form of *cost containment,* from requiring second surgical opinions to instituting full case management.

Key Concepts

In preparing for their licensing examination, students should be familiar with the following concepts:

health insurance risk factors
substandard risks
health insurance premium factors

tax treatment of premiums and benefits
cost containment measures

Chapter 21
Questions for Review *(Answers are located at the end of the book.)*

1. Susan is covered under her employer-sponsored disability group plan. The premium is $50 a month: Susan pays $10 and the employer pays $40. Assuming Susan were to become disabled and receive monthly disability benefits of $700 from the plan, how much, if any, of the monthly benefit would be taxable income?

    a. $560
    b. $140
    c. $70
    d. $0

2. Assume the following individuals are issued health insurance policies with varying renewability provisions. All other factors being equal, who would pay the highest premium?

    a. Dan—cancelable
    b. Jim—optionally renewable
    c. Henry—conditionally renewable
    d. Jack—noncancelable

3. The purpose of medical cost management is to

    a. influence hospital charges and doctors' fees.
    b. discourage individuals from utilizing health care services.
    c. control health claims expenses.
    d. All of the above

4. All of the following are primary risk factors in underwriting individual health insurance policies, EXCEPT:

   a. geographical location.
   b. moral hazard.
   c. occupation.
   d. physical condition.

5. Which of the following statements most aptly describes health insurance benefits?

   a. Each policy offers a single type of benefit.
   b. Claims, not benefits, affect premium rates.
   c. Policyowners who have policies with identical benefits pay the same premiums.
   d. The greater the benefits, the higher the premium.

6. Which of the following would probably NOT be considered in underwriting a health insurance risk?

   a. An individual's personal habits
   b. An individual's credit rating
   c. An individual's medical history
   d. An individual's marital status

7. Which of the following factors would affect a health policy's premium rate?

   I. Age of the insured
   II. Occupation of the insured
   III. Type of benefit provided
   IV. The company's expense factor

   a. I and II only
   b. III only
   c. IV only
   d. All of the above

8. Rick, who has no health insurance, experienced $3,000 in medical expenses this year. Assuming his adjusted gross income was $29,000, how much of those medical expenses can he deduct from his income taxes, if any?

   a. $0
   b. $825
   c. $2,175
   d. $3,000

9. A table that reflects the average number of disabilities due to sickness or accidents at various ages is a/an

   a. mortality table.
   b. morbidity table.
   c. claims underwriting table.
   d. underwriting table.

10. The effect of an impairment rider attached to a health insurance policy is to

    a. increase the premium rate charged.
    b. decrease the amount of benefits provided.
    c. exclude from coverage losses resulting from specified conditions.
    d. All of the above

22 GROUP HEALTH INSURANCE

Nature of Group Health Insurance • Group Health Coverages
• Tax Treatment of Group Health Plans

Most of our discussion of health and accident insurance so far has focused on basic fundamentals and on individual policies. However, the majority of Americans obtain their health insurance coverage through a *group plan*. Every year employers contribute billions of dollars for health insurance benefits for their employees. Students of health insurance should be familiar with the unique characteristics of this type of insurance protection.

Nature of Group Health Insurance

In Chapter 9, we introduced the subject of group life insurance and discussed its basic principles. Like group life, group health is a plan of insurance that an employer (or other eligible group sponsor) provides for its employees. The contract for coverage is between the insurance company and the employer, and a *master policy* is issued to the employer. The individual insureds covered by the policy are not given separate policies; instead, they receive *certificates of insurance* and an outline or booklet that describes their benefits. Generally speaking, the benefits provided under a group health plan are more extensive than those provided under an individual health plan. Group health plans typically have higher benefit maximums and lower deductibles.

Characteristics of Group Health Insurance

The characteristics of group health insurance are similar to those of group life. These include eligibility standards for groups and for individuals within the groups, method of premium payments (contributory vs. noncontributory), lower cost, predetermined benefits, underwriting practices, conversion privileges and preexisting conditions provisions. Let's briefly review each.

Eligible Groups

To qualify for group health coverage, the group must be a *"natural group."* This means that it must have been formed for some reason other than to obtain insurance. Qualifying groups include employers, labor unions, trade associations, creditor-debtor groups, multiple employer trusts, lodges and the like.

State laws specify the minimum number of persons to be covered under a group policy. One state may stipulate 15 persons as a minimum number, while another state may require a minimum of ten. (Ten lives is the most typical minimum requirement.)

Individual Eligibility

Like group life, group health plans commonly impose a set of *eligibility requirements* that must be met before an individual member is eligible to participate in the group plan. It is common to find the following requirements:

- minimum of one to three months employment service and
- full-time employment status.

Contributory vs. Noncontributory

Group health plans may be *contributory* or *noncontributory*. If the employer pays the entire premium, the plan is noncontributory; if the employees share a portion of the premium, it is contributory. Almost universally, noncontributory group health plans require 100 percent participation by eligible members, whereas contributory group health plans require participation by 75 percent of eligible members. The reason for these minimum participation requirements is to protect the insurer against adverse selection and to keep administrative expenses in line with coverage units.

Lower Cost

Benefit for benefit, the cost of insuring an individual under a group health plan is *less* than the cost of insurance under an individual plan. This is because the administrative and selling expenses involved with group plans are far less.

Predetermined Benefits

Another characteristic of group health plans is that the benefits provided to individual insureds are *predetermined* by the employer in conjunction with the insurer's benefit schedules and coverage limits. For example, group disability benefits are tied to a position or earnings schedule, as are accidental death and dismemberment benefits.

Underwriting Practices

Generally speaking, the approach in underwriting group health plans is the same as underwriting group life plans: the insurer *evaluates the group as a whole,* rather than individuals within the group. Based on the group's risk profile, which is measured against the insurer's selection standards, the group is either accepted or rejected.

However, there are some changes taking place with regard to underwriting group medical expenses plans, especially for small groups. Whereas for large group medical plans it is common to accept all currently eligible members and new members coming into the group, this is not necessarily true any longer for smaller groups. In smaller groups the presence of even one "bad risk" can have a significant impact on the claims experience of the group. Consequently, most insurers today reserve the right to engage in *individual underwriting* to some degree with groups they insure.

As the term implies, individual underwriting is the process of reviewing a group member's individual risk profile. Most commonly this is done on two occasions: when a group is first taken on by an insurer and when a group member (e.g., an employee) tries to enter the plan after initially electing not to participate. In the latter case, the underwriter's objective is to reduce the risk of adverse selection. In the former case, individual underwriting is only done on members for whom the initial application indicates a potential risk problem (such as a preexisting condition). If the member is found to represent too great a risk, the insurer often retains the right to reject the member from participating in the plan, or at least charge an increased premium (or exclude coverage for the specified condition). It is important to note that if an insurer does reserve this right of individual underwriting, most states require the insurer to explain, in the policy, how it will exercise this right.

Rarely is an entire group rejected on the basis of one bad risk, unless the group is very small. The underwriter reviews a number of factors to determine whether or not the group should be accepted. (See Ill. 22.1.)

Conversion Privilege

Group health plans that provide medical expense coverage universally contain a *conversion privilege* for individual insureds, which allows them to convert their group certificate to an individual medical expense policy with the same insurer, if and when they leave their employment. Insurers are permitted to evaluate the individual and charge the appropriate premium, be it a standard rate or substandard rate; however, an individual cannot be denied coverage, even if he or she has become uninsurable.

The conversion must be exercised within a given period of time, usually 31 days. During this time, the individual remains insured under the group plan, whether or not a conversion ultimately takes place. Conversion privileges generally are reserved for those who were active in the group plan during the preceding three months.

Preexisting Conditions

Like individual health policies, group health insurance plans usually contain a provision that excludes preexisting conditions from coverage. However, whereas individual plans typically define "preexisting conditions" as those that first appeared before the policy was issued and were not cited on the application, a group plan typically defines a "preexisting condition" as one for which a participant received treatment during the three months prior to the effective date of the group coverage.

Group health plans that exclude preexisting conditions also usually specify when a condition will no longer be considered preexisting. For example, a plan may cover a preexisting condition once the group participant has gone without treatment for that condition for three months.

Ill. 22.1

General Group Underwriting Considerations

In spite of the many differences between types of groups, there are certain general underwriting considerations applicable to all or most types of groups.

- The reason for the group's existence (purchasing group insurance must be incidental to the group's formation, not the reason for it)

- The stability of the group (underwriters want to see a group of stable workers without an excessive amount of "turnover")

- The persistency of the group (groups that change insurers every year do not represent a good risk)

- The method of determining benefits (it must be by a schedule or method that prevents individual selection of benefits)

- How eligibility is determined (insurers want to see a sickness-related probationary period, for example, to reduce adverse selection)

- The source of premium payments, whether contributory or noncontributory (noncontributory plans are preferred since they require 100 percent participation, which helps spread the risk and reduces adverse selection)

- The prior claims experience of the group

- The size and composition of the group

- The industry or business with which the group is associated (hazardous industries are typified by higher-than-standard mortality and morbidity rates)

Group Health Insurance Coverages

All of the types of health insurance coverages discussed in this text—medical expense, disability income and accidental death and dismemberment—are available for group plans. Rather than repeat the discussion of these policies—their purpose and functions are the same whether it's a group product or an individual product—let's focus on the features of these coverages when they are part of a group plan.

Group Basic Medical Expense

The three standard forms of basic medical expense insurance—hospital, surgical and physicians' expenses—are available for group insurance. In addition, a number of newer coverages have been developed in recent years, including dental and vision care, prescription drugs, home health care, extended care facilities, diagnostic X rays and laboratory services. In fact, some of these specified coverages, such as vision and dental care, are available only on a group basis.

A group basic medical expense plan can combine two or more of these coverages or it may consist of only one type of coverage, such as hospital expense only.

III. 22.2

Dental and Vision Care—Popular Group Benefits

Relatively new to the array of health care benefits offered to groups are coverages for *dental care* and *vision care*.

Dental care coverage is designed to cover the costs associated with normal dental maintenance as well as oral surgery, root canal therapy and orthodontia. The coverage may be on a "reasonable and customary charge" basis or on a dollar-per-service schedule approach. Deductible and coinsurance features are typical (though some policies will cover routine cleaning and exams at 100 percent), as are maximum yearly benefit amounts, such as $1,000 or $2,000.

Vision care coverage usually pays for reasonable and customary charges incurred during eye exams by ophthalmologists and optometrists. Expenses for the fitting or cost of contact lenses or eyeglasses are often excluded.

Group Major Medical Plans

Like individual major medical plans, group major medical plans may be offered as a single, extensive plan (*comprehensive major medical*) or superimposed over a group basic plan (*supplemental major medical*). Participants are usually required to satisfy an initial deductible with comprehensive plans and either a corridor or an integrated deductible with supplemental plans.

Benefits provided by group major medical plans are usually more extensive than those of individual plans. For example, it is not uncommon to find group plans that offer individual benefit maximums of $1 million; still others do not set any maximum benefit limits. Too, deductibles are usually lower for group plans, typically ranging from $100 to $250, whereas deductibles for individual policies can be $500 or more.

There are two other characteristics of group medical expense plans that distinguish them from individual plans. These are the *coordination of benefits provision* and the treatment of *maternity benefits*.

Coordination of Benefits

The purpose of the *coordination of benefits* (COB) *provision,* found only in group health plans, is to avoid duplication of benefit payments and overinsurance when an individual is covered under more than one group health plan. The provision limits the total amount of claims paid from *all* insurers covering the patient to no more than the total allowable medical expenses. For example, an individual who incurs $700 in allowable medical expenses would not be able to collect any more than $700, no matter how many group plans he or she is covered by.

The COB provision establishes which plan is the *primary* plan, or the plan that is responsible for providing the full benefit amounts as it specifies. Once the primary plan has paid its full promised benefit, the insured may submit the claim to the secondary provider for any additional benefits payable. In no case, however, will the total amount the insured receives exceed the costs incurred, or the total maximum benefits available under all plans.

Coordinating benefits is appropriate for married couples, when each is covered by an employer group plan. For example, John and Cindy, a young married couple, each are participants in their own company's health plan and are also covered as dependents under their spouse's plan. John's plan would specify that it is the primary plan for John; Cindy's plan would be his secondary plan. Likewise, Cindy's plan would specify that it is the primary plan for Cindy; John's plan would be her secondary plan.

Maternity Benefits

Whereas it is common for individual health plans to exclude routine maternity care from coverage, group medical expense plans *must* provide *maternity benefits*. This is the result of a 1979 amendment to the Civil Rights Act, which requires plans covering 15 or more people to treat pregnancy-related claims no differently than any other allowable medical expense.

COBRA Continuation of Benefits

Participants in group medical expense plans are protected by a federal law that guarantees a continuation of their group coverage if their employment is terminated for reasons other than gross misconduct. Practically speaking, the law protects employees who are laid-off, but not those who are fired "for cause." (The circumstances that qualify for this continued coverage are noted in Ill. 22.3.)

This law, known as the *Consolidated Omnibus Budget Reconciliation Act of 1985* (or COBRA), requires employers with 20 or more employees to continue group medical expense coverage for terminated workers (as well as their spouses, divorced spouses and dependent children) for up to 18 months (or 36 months, in some situations) following termination.

Ill. 22.3

COBRA Continued Coverage for Former Employees

The following events would qualify for extended medical expense coverage under COBRA for a terminated employee:

- Employment is terminated (for other than gross misconduct): 18 months of continued coverage (or up to 29 months if disabled).

- Employee's hours are reduced (resulting in termination from the plan): 18 months of continued coverage (or up to 29 months if disabled).

- Employee dies: 36 months of continued coverage for dependents.

- Dependent child no longer qualifies as "dependent child" under the group plan: 36 months of continued coverage.

- Employee becomes eligible for Medicare: 36 months of continued coverage.

- Employee divorces or legally separates: 36 months of continued coverage for former spouse.

Some important points about this law should be noted. It is *not* the same as the policy conversion privilege by which an employee may convert a group certificate to an individual policy. COBRA permits the terminated employee to continue his or her group coverage.

The law does *not* require the employer to pay the cost of the continued group coverage; the terminated employee can be required to pay the premium, which may be up to 102 percent of the premium that would otherwise be charged. (The additional 2 percent is allowed to cover the insurer's administrative expenses.) The schedule of benefits will be the same during the continuation period as under the group plan.

Group Disability Income Plans

Group disability income plans differ from individual plans in a number of ways. Individual plans usually specify a flat income amount, based on the person's earnings, determined at the time the policy is purchased. In contrast, group plans usually specify benefits in terms of a percentage of the individual's earnings.

Like individual plans, group disability can include short-term plans or long-term plans. The definitions of "short term" and "long term," however, are different for group and individual.

Group short-term disability plans are characterized by maximum benefit periods of rather short duration, such as 13 or 26 weeks. Benefits are typically paid weekly and range from 50 percent to 100 percent of the individual's income.

Group long-term disability plans provide for maximum benefit periods of more than two years, occasionally extending to the insured's retirement age. Benefit amounts are usually limited to about 60 percent of the participant's income.

If an employer provides both a short-term plan and long-term plan, the long-term plan typically begins paying benefits only after the short-term benefits cease. Often, long-term plans use an "own occupation" definition of total disability for the first year or two of disability and then switch to an "any occupation" definition.

Most group disability plans require the employee to have a minimum period of service, such as 30 to 90 days, before he or she is eligible for coverage. In addition, most group plans include provisions making their benefits supplemental to workers' compensation benefits, so that total benefits received do not exceed a specified percentage of regular earnings. In some cases, group disability plans actually limit coverage to nonoccupational disabilities, since occupational disabilities normally qualify for workers' compensation benefits.

Group AD&D

Accidental death and dismemberment insurance is a very popular type of group coverage, frequently offered in conjunction with group life insurance plans. It may also be provided as a separate policy, in which case it is normally paid for entirely by the employee. Such employee-pay-all plans are called *voluntary group AD&D,* since plan participation is voluntary. Benefits may be provided for both occupational and nonoccupational losses, or for nonoccupational losses only. Voluntary group AD&D typically provides benefits for both types of losses.

Like individual AD&D, group AD&D pays a *principal sum* upon the insured's accidental death (or loss of any two body members). A *capital sum* is payable upon the accidental loss of one body member. Some group AD&D plans specify a higher death benefit if the insured dies while on company business.

Group AD&D, unlike group life and group medical, normally does not include a conversion privilege.

Other Types of Group Health Plans

In addition to the typical group health insurance plan—as would be utilized by an employer, for example—there are three additional types of plans worth noting: *blanket health insurance, franchise* (or *wholesale*) *health insurance* and *credit accident and health insurance.*

Blanket Health Plans

Blanket health insurance is issued to cover a group who may be exposed to the same risks, but the composition of the group—the individuals within the group—are constantly changing. A blanket health plan may be issued to an airline or a bus company to cover its passengers or to a school to cover its students.

Franchise Health Plans

Franchise health plans, sometimes called "wholesale plans," provide health insurance coverage to members of an association or professional society. Individual policies are issued to individual members; the association or society simply serves as the "sponsor" for the plan. Premium rates are usually discounted for franchise plans.

Credit Accident and Health Plans

Like credit life plans, *credit accident and health plans* are designed to help the insured pay off a loan in the event he or she is disabled due to an accident or sickness. If the insured becomes disabled, the policy provides for monthly benefit payments equal to the monthly loan payments due.

Tax Treatment of Group Health Plans

As an incentive for employers to provide health insurance benefits to their employees, the federal government grants favorable tax treatment to group plans. Let's briefly review this treatment.

Taxation of Group Health Premiums

Employers are entitled to take a tax deduction for premium contributions they make to a group health plan, as long as the contributions represent an "ordinary and necessary business expense." By the same token, individual participants do not include employer contributions made on their behalf as part of their taxable income.

As a general rule, individual premium contributions to a group health plan are not tax deductible. Only when unreimbursed medical expenses—expenses that can include any individual contributions to a group medical plan—exceed 7.5 percent of an individual's adjusted gross income can a tax deduction be taken. The deduction is limited to the amount exceeding 7.5 percent of adjusted gross income. Any premiums the individual contributes for group disability or group AD&D coverage are not considered qualifying medical expenses when determining this excess.

Taxation of Group Health Benefits

Any benefits an individual receives under a medical expense plan are not considered taxable income, since they are provided to cover losses the individual incurred. It is a somewhat different story with disability income plans, however. Disability benefit payments that are attributed to employee contributions are not taxable, but benefit payments that are attributed to employer contributions are taxable. Let's look at an example.

Anne is a participant in a contributory group disability income plan in which her employer pays two-thirds of the premium and Anne pays one-third. Her employer qualifies for a tax deduction for its share of the premium and, as is true with employer contributions to all group health plans, Anne is not taxed on those contributions. The premium portion that Anne pays does not qualify for a tax deduction for her.

Now assume Anne becomes disabled and receives disability income benefits of $900 a month. One-third of the monthly benefit—$300—would be tax-free, since it is attributed to the premium she paid; the remaining two-thirds of the payment—$600—would be taxable income, since it is attributed to the premium her employer paid.

Summary

Group health insurance—like group life insurance—is evidenced by one master contract that covers multiple lives. Virtually any health insurance product available as an individual contract is also available under the group umbrella. Thus, *medical expense insurance, disability income insurance* and *accidental death and dismemberment insurance* are all common group plans. In addition, there are a number of coverages, like vision and dental care, that are only available to groups.

Of utmost concern to insurance regulators is that employees be protected from loss of their insurance coverage if their job is terminated. Accordingly, nearly all states have provisions in their insurance laws that require group life and medical expense policies to provide a *conversion option* to terminating participants. The federal government has also exercised its regulatory prerogative by passing laws that protect terminated employees (COBRA) and that guarantee maternity cases will be treated the same as any other medical condition.

Key Concepts

In preparing for their licensing examination, students should be familiar with the following concepts:

master policy	group AD&D
certificate of insurance	group health underwriting
contributory vs. noncontributory plans	conversion privilege
	preexisting conditions
group basic medical expense	COBRA
group major medical expense	taxation of group health insurance
group disability income	

Chapter 22
Questions for Review *(Answers are located at the end of the book.)*

1. Which of the following statements regarding group health insurance is/are correct?

   I. The insurer, not the employer, stipulates the minimum number of persons that must be covered under a group plan.
   II. Group health plans provide more extensive benefits than individual health plans.
   III. If a group plan provides medical expense benefits, it must be with a comprehensive policy.
   IV. COBRA requirements are directed at employers with 20 or fewer employees.

   a. I and II only
   b. II, III and IV only
   c. II only
   d. I, III and IV only

2. Which type of group health coverage typically does NOT contain a conversion privilege?

   a. Basic medical expense
   b. Comprehensive medical expense
   c. Disability income
   d. Accidental death and dismemberment

3. Which of the following can an individual include as "qualifying expenses" for purposes of determining a medical tax deduction?

   I. Premium contributions paid by the employer to a group medical expense plan
   II. Premium contributions paid by the employer to a group disability plan
   III. Premium contributions paid by the individual to a group medical expense plan
   IV. Premium contributions paid by the individual to a group disability plan

   a. I and II only
   b. III and IV only
   c. III only
   d. IV only

4. Dan is a participant in his company's group health plan. One of the plan's provisions specifies that, in the event he is eligible for benefits under another policy, his group plan will serve as the primary plan. What is this provision called?

   a. Excess coverage provision
   b. Coordination of benefits provision
   c. Other insurance with this insurer provision
   d. Double indemnity provision

5. A vacation cruise line that wants group health coverage for its passengers would purchase

   a. franchise health insurance.
   b. wholesale health insurance.
   c. blanket health insurance.
   d. credit health insurance.

6. The purpose of the COBRA requirements concerns

   a. coordination of health benefits.
   b. continuation of health insurance.
   c. Medicare supplement coverage.
   d. nondiscrimination in group health plans.

7. Gerald's group health plan provides basic hospital expense coverage and supplemental major medical coverage. What type of deductible would Gerald have, if any?

   a. Flat
   b. Dual
   c. Corridor
   d. No deductible

8. Sally is covered by her employer's noncontributory group disability income plan, the premium for which is $50 a month. If she were to become disabled and receive $1,000 a month, how much of each benefit payment would be taxable income to her?

   a. $1,000
   b. $950
   c. $50
   d. $0

9. All of the following statements regarding group disability income plans are true, EXCEPT:

   a. Benefits are specified in terms of a percentage of the participant's earnings.
   b. Benefits paid under the group plan are supplemental to workers' compensation benefits.
   c. Employees covered under both a short-term and long-term plan collect benefits from each simultaneously.
   d. A minimum length of service may be required before an employee is eligible to participate in the plan.

10. An individual purchased group credit accident and sickness insurance to cover his car loan. Following an accident, the individual was disabled for eight months. Which of the following benefits were paid under the policy?

   I. The insured received monthly income benefits.
   II. The insured's creditor received an amount equal to eight months of the loan payment.

   a. I only
   b. II only
   c. Both I and II
   d. Neither I nor II

23 Uses of Health Insurance

Proper Health Program • Individual Needs • Business Needs

It may at first seem that the uses of health insurance are self-explanatory: one purchases health insurance to protect against the cost of health care—or, more accurately, health insurance provides protection against the costs associated with the loss of one's health. However, just as life insurance can be used creatively to meet a variety of needs, so too can the different types of health insurance plans be used in various ways to meet an individual's or business's unique needs. This chapter looks at the question, "What are the uses of health insurance?"

A Proper Health Insurance Program

What is a "proper" health insurance program? That question cannot be answered without first addressing several preliminary issues. Is the insurance for an individual only, a family or a business? Is coverage currently available from a group plan or social insurance program? How willing is the policyowner to assume some responsibility for medical care expenses (through policy deductibles and coinsurance) in exchange for reduced premiums? These and other questions must first be answered before reaching a conclusion as to the "right" health insurance program.

Individual Needs for Health Insurance

At one time it was acceptable to expect one's family to provide support when illness or disability struck. Those days are now long past; today, we all must prepare for and assume the responsibility of covering the cost of medical care. However, unless one is independently wealthy, the prospect of covering costs out-of-pocket is not an attractive one; indeed, it can be downright terrifying.

The loss of one's health can have wide-ranging consequences. Not only does the cost of medical care come with a high price tag, but the loss of income that often accompanies a disabling illness or injury can compound the devastating effects of the health loss. Current demographics, which show that most families have both parents working, emphasize the need to consider both parents' income needs when designing a complete health insurance program.

Medical Expense Insurance Needs

While it is difficult to measure the importance of one type of insurance over another, it is fair to presume that a health insurance program must begin with an adequate amount of *medical expense insurance.* Without proper protection devoted to these potential costs, even the most basic medical care can quickly exhaust an individual's savings; a catastrophic claim can spell financial disaster.

At one time, most medical policies were the basic medical expense type. However, today it is more common to find most Americans covered under some form of a major medical policy or a service plan such as Blue Cross/Blue Shield or an HMO. If the policyowner can afford the cost, an ideal policy is a combination plan in which a basic plan is enhanced by a supplementary major medical plan. Under this approach, the insured obtains the "first dollar" benefits of the basic plan and also has the expansive protection offered by the major medical plan.

Most policyowners, of course, are concerned with the cost of their health insurance and find that some financial sacrifice may be required. For example, an individual major medical plan with a $100 individual deductible is going to cost more than a comparable plan with a $500 deductible. A plan with an 80/20 coinsurance provision will cost more than a comparable plan with a 75/25 coinsurance provision. The question the policyowner must answer is, "Am I willing to assume more of the cost risk of *possible* future claims in exchange for the *definite* cost savings offered by a plan with a higher deductible or coinsurance limit?"

Group vs. Individual Coverage

More Americans are protected under a group medical expense policy than an individual policy. The benefit to the group member, even assuming the plan is contributory, is the significantly less out-of-pocket cost than a comparable individual plan. The group plan participant can take comfort in knowing that even if he or she should terminate employment, continued coverage is guaranteed through the *conversion privilege* built into every group health policy.

Disability Income Insurance Needs

The importance of protecting one's earnings is sometimes overlooked in the insurance needs analysis process—a regrettable fact for the many people who become disabled every year. Americans too often assume that Social Security will provide the income necessary to survive if disability strikes. This is an unfortunate assumption; not only is the definition of "disabled" to qualify for Social Security benefits extremely narrow, but there is no assurance that the benefits will meet the disabled person's needs.

Social Security disability income should be viewed as a possible source of income to augment a personal plan. Whether the personal plan is based on a group policy or an individual policy, it should be regarded as the primary source of income if earnings are lost due to disability.

Policyowners can control the premium cost of a disability income plan by electing a longer elimination period than might otherwise be desired. The length of the benefit period also has a direct impact on the premium.

Because of the favorable tax treatment given to individually funded disability income policies, a plan that provides about 60 percent of predisability gross earnings can be considered sufficient. This is because disability income benefits are income tax free if the individual insured paid the premiums. An individual who earns $3,000 a month may only take home $2,000 after taxes. Consequently, a disability plan that provides a monthly tax-free benefit of $1,800 would likely be sufficient.

In the case of group disability income plans, the group member has little choice as to the level of benefits provided; the plan document must have a schedule of benefits that identifies what the participant will receive if disabled. On the other hand, the group member benefits to the extent the employer contributes to the disability income premiums.

If both parents in a family are actively employed, then disability income must be considered for each. If each parent's income is indispensable for the financial support of the family, then it is safe to assume that the loss of *either* income would present a financial problem.

Business Needs for Health Insurance

Many health insurance producers have found a niche servicing the business market. There is a good, practical reason for this—the health insurance needs of the business market are as great as the needs of individuals.

Business uses of health insurance can be broadly divided into two categories: *employee benefit plans* and *business continuation plans.*

Employee Benefit Plans

While the term *"employee benefit plan"* can encompass a wide variety of benefit offerings—life insurance, a pension or profit-sharing plan, vacation pay, deferred compensation arrangements, funeral leave, sick time—it is rare when it does not include some kind of provision for health insurance or health benefits. The large and rapid increases in the cost of health care are likely the primary reasons for the popularity of employer-sponsored health plans, and many people rely on these plans as their sole source of health insurance.

Group Health Insurance

As we have learned, a *group health plan* can consist of medical insurance, disability income insurance, accidental death and dismemberment insurance —alone or in any combination. In fact, it is not uncommon to find all of these coverages included in a single group insurance plan.

By providing its employees with a plan for health insurance, an employer derives a number of benefits.

- The plan contributes to employee morale and productivity.

- The plan enables the employer to provide a needed benefit that employees would otherwise have to pay for with personal after-tax dollars (this helps hold down demands for wage increases).

- The plan places the employer in a competitive position for hiring and retaining employees.

- The employer can obtain a tax deduction for the cost of contributing to the plan.

- The plan enhances the employer's image in both public and employee relations.

Cafeteria Plans

Many times, employer-provided health insurance benefits are part of a *cafeteria plan*. As its name implies, cafeteria plans (also known as Section 125 plans) are benefit arrangements in which employees can pick and choose from a menu of benefits, thus tailoring their benefits package to their specific needs. Employees can select the benefits they value or need and forgo those of lesser importance to them. The employer allocates a certain amount of money to each employee to "buy" the benefits he or she desires; if the cost of the benefits exceeds the allocation, the employee may contribute the balance.

The types of flexible benefits usually available under a cafeteria plan include medical coverage, accidental death and dismemberment insurance, short-term and long-term disability, life insurance and dependent care. Some plans provide for "choices within the choices": an employee may have the option of selecting from various levels of medical plans or choosing from among a variety of HMOs, for example.

Business Continuation Plans

Just as life insurance provides a way to help a business continue in the event an owner or key employee dies, health insurance also serves continuation purposes in the event of a disabling sickness or injury. It does so through the following plans.

Business Overhead Expense Insurance

Business overhead expense insurance is designed to reimburse a business for overhead expenses in the event a business owner becomes disabled. It is sold on an individual basis to professionals in private practice, self-employed business owners, partners and occasionally close corporations.

Overhead expenses include such things as rent or mortgage payments, utilities, telephones, leased equipment, employees' salaries and the like—all the expenses that would continue and must be paid, regardless of the owner's disability. Business overhead expense policies do not include any compensation for the disabled owner; they are designed to help the day-to-day operation of his or her business continue during the period of disability.

The benefits payable under these kinds of policies are limited to the covered expenses incurred or the maximum that is stated in the policy. For example, assume Dr. Miller is the insured under a business overhead expense policy that pays maximum monthly benefits of $4,500. If Dr. Miller became disabled and actual monthly expenses were $3,950, the monthly benefits paid would be $3,950. If Dr. Miller's actual expenses were $4,700, the benefits payable would be $4,500.

The premium for business overhead insurance is a legitimate, tax-deductible business expense. The benefits when paid, however, are treated as taxable income.

Business Health Insurance

Business health insurance is available to indemnify a business for the loss of the services of a key employee, a partner or an owner should disability strike. In the event of a disability, this insurance provides the business with funds to bridge the period necessary to secure and train a worthy successor.

Determining the precise economic loss a business will face if a key individual becomes disabled is somewhat difficult to measure; the cost of securing an experienced, competent replacement or the income the employee or owner currently earns are two common approaches.

Disability Buy-Outs

A *disability buy-sell agreement* operates in much the same way as a life insurance buy-sell agreement; however, in this case, the plan sets forth the terms for selling and buying a partner's or stock owner's share of a business in the event he or she becomes disabled and no longer able to participate in the business. It is a legal, binding arrangement, funded with a disability income policy.

Unlike typical disability income insurance plans that pay benefits in the form of periodic payments, the buy-out plan usually contains a provision allowing for a lump-sum payment of the benefit, thereby facilitating the buy-out of the disabled's interest. However, if the owners desire, the plan often permits the buy-out to occur through the use of periodic income payments.

Disability buy-out plans are characterized by lengthy elimination periods, often as long as two years. The reason for this is simple: since the plan involves the sale of a disabled partner's or owner's interest in the business, it is important to be quite sure that the disabled person will not be able to return to the business.

Considering the fact that a disabled partner can represent a double liability—the remaining partners must not only make up the slack left by the disabled partner's absence but usually must pay him or her an income as well—it is understandable why the disability buy-out plan is popular with business owners.

Summary

The uses of health insurance—notably medical expense and disability income—are as varied as the need for it is vital. Both the personal market and the business market have many uses for these important insurance products. Often the insured's concern is not "Should I have it?" but "How can I afford it?" Fortunately, every type of health insurance plan offers some way for the owner to reduce premium costs, including increasing the deductible or lengthening the elimination period.

Key Concepts

In preparing for their licensing examination, students should be familiar with the following concepts:

- individual vs. group health insurance
- employee benefit plans
- business overhead expense insurance
- business health insurance
- disability buy-out insurance

Chapter 23
Questions for Review *(Answers are located at the end of the book.)*

1. Methods of keeping premium costs to a minimum in a health policy include all of the following, EXCEPT:

    a. modifying benefit amounts.
    b. increasing the deductible.
    c. waiving the right to receive benefit payments when due.
    d. extending the elimination period.

2. Fred owns a small hardware store and is covered under a business overhead expense policy. If he becomes disabled, he can expect all the following expenses to be covered, EXCEPT:

    a. his employees' salaries.
    b. his salary.
    c. utility bills.
    d. property and liability insurance premiums.

3. Which of the following characteristics is associated with disability buy-out plans?

    a. A short elimination period
    b. The option to elect a lump-sum payment
    c. Provisions to cover the business's overhead expenses
    d. All of the above

4. What is the income tax consequence to Marie if her employer pays for her group disability income coverage?

    I. The premium payments are taxable income to her.
    II. The premium payments are tax deductible by her.

    a. I only
    b. II only
    c. Both I and II
    d. Neither I nor II

5. With regard to health insurance policies, which of the following statements is true?

   a. A major medical plan with a $100 deductible is less expensive than one with a $500 deductible.
   b. More Americans are covered by an individual medical expense policy than a group policy.
   c. The appropriate benefit payable under a disability income policy should equal the insured's monthly gross income.
   d. A disability policy with a six-month elimination period is less expensive than one with a 60-day elimination period, all other factors being equal.

APPENDIX

This appendix contains both a sample whole life participating life insurance policy and sample application, as well as a sample health insurance policy and application. They are both representative of typical policies and applications issued by insurance companies in the United States and contain the standard language and provisions found in actual forms.

SUPERIOR MUTUAL LIFE INSURANCE COMPANY OF AMERICA

Superior Mutual agrees, in accordance with the provisions of this policy, to pay to the beneficiary the death proceeds upon receipt at the Home Office of due proof of the insured's death.

Ten-Day Right To Examine Policy You may return this policy by delivering it to the Home Office or to an agent of the Company within 10 days after receiving it. Immediately on such delivery, the policy will be void as of the date of issue and any premium paid will be refunded.

Jacob Carson
President

Richard Clitt
Secretary

Insured: Daniel K. Williams
Policy Number: 0000-0000-00
Policy Date: November 5, 1994

CONTENTS

Face Page	1	Reinstatement	7
Policy Specifications	3	Change of Plan	7
Table of Guaranteed Values	4	Cash Values	8
General Provisions	5	Policy Loans	8
Owner and Beneficiary	5	Dividends	9
Premiums	6	Payment of Proceeds	10
Surrender of the Policy	7	Payment Options Tables	12

INDEX

Applicable Benefit	6	Net Cash Value	8
Assignment	5	Nonpayment of Premium	6
Automatic Premium Loan Option	6	Owner	5
Basis of Values	4	Paid-Up Insurance Option	6
Beneficiary	5	Payment Options	10
Cash Values	8	Payment Options Tables	12
Change of Plan	7	Policy Loans	8
Death Proceeds	10	Premiums	6
Dividends	9	Protection of Proceeds	5
Entire Contract	5	Reinstatement	7
Extended Term Insurance Option	6	Schedule of Benefits and Premiums	3
General Provisions	5	Suicide Exclusion	5
Grace Period	6	Surrender of the Policy	7
Incontestability	5	Table of Guaranteed Values	4
Lapse	6	Ten-Day Right to Examine Policy	1
Misstatement of Age or Sex	5		

Insured: Daniel K. Williams
Policy Number: 0000-0000-00
Date of Issue: November 5, 1994
Sum Insured: $50,000

Age: 39 Male
Risk: Standard

SCHEDULE OF BENEFITS AND PREMIUMS

Benefit	Amount of Benefit	Annual Premium Amount Payable
Whole Life	$50,000	$809.00 for life

Total initial annual premium—nonsmoker basis $809.00

Whole life insurance policy. Death proceeds payable at death of insured. Premiums payable during insured's lifetime. Annual dividends.

Male Insured: Daniel K. Williams
Policy Number: 0000-0000-00

Age at Issue: 39

TABLE OF GUARANTEED VALUES

End of Policy Year	Cash Value	Amount of Paid-Up Insurance	Extended Term Insurance Years	Days
1	$ 0.00	*	0	0
2	0.00	*	0	0
3	365.50	*	1	120
4	981.00	*	3	67
5	1,616.50	*	4	260
6	2,537.50	*	6	252
7	3,486.50	11,450	8	128
8	4,464.00	13,950	9	265
9	5,471.50	16,350	10	320
10	6,511.50	18,550	11	304
11	7,584.50	20,650	12	217
12	8,690.50	22,550	13	68
13	9,832.00	24,400	13	230
14	11,008.00	26,100	13	345
15	12,219.50	27,650	14	59
16	13,258.50	28,700	14	32
17	14,316.00	29,600	13	349
18	15,393.00	30,450	13	283
19	16,489.00	31,150	13	198
20	17,607.00	31,800	13	94
AGE 55	14,316.00	29,600	13	349
AGE 60	19,537.50	33,650	12	340
AGE 65	24,341.50	37,650	11	285

*Not available; benefit less than $10,000

Basis of Values: All cash values and net single premiums, except as otherwise provided under dividends, are based on:

The Commissioner's 1980 Standard Ordinary Mortality Table, smoker and nonsmoker, male and female, except that values for extended term insurance are based on the Commissioner's 1980 Extended Term Insurance Table, smoker and nonsmoker, male and female.

GENERAL PROVISIONS

Entire Contract—This policy is a contract between the owner and Superior Mutual. This policy, with a copy of the application attached to it, is the entire contract. Agents are not permitted to change this contract or extend the time for paying premiums.

All statements in the application are considered representations and not warranties. Superior Mutual will not use any statement to contest this policy or defend a claim unless the statement is in the application.

Incontestability—Except for failure to pay premiums, this policy cannot be contested after it has been in force during the insured's lifetime for two years from its date of issue. This time limit does not apply to any waiver of premium rider that may be a part of this policy.

Suicide Exclusion—The risk of suicide of the insured, while sane or insane, within two years of the date of issue of this policy is not assumed. The beneficiary will receive the sum of the premiums paid, less debt.

Misstatement of Age or Sex—If the insured's age or sex is misstated, the amount payable under this policy will be that which the premiums paid would have purchased at the correct age and sex. This provision as it relates to a misstatement of sex does not apply if this policy is issued in a unisex premium class as shown on page 3.

Protection of Proceeds—To the extent allowed by law, the proceeds of this policy and any payments made under it will be exempt from attachment by the claims of creditors of the payee. No beneficiary can assign, transfer, anticipate or encumber the proceeds or payments unless you give them this right.

OWNER AND BENEFICIARY

Owner—The insured is the owner of this policy unless another is named as owner in the application. The owner may exercise the following rights without the consent of any beneficiary:

- obtain a loan to pay the premiums on this policy;
- elect a different dividend option;
- withdraw dividend accumulations;
- surrender dividend additions;
- change the method of premium payment with the consent of the Company; and
- change the ownership of this policy.

You may exercise all other rights and options granted by this policy, subject to the consent of any irrevocable beneficiary. The consent of any revocable beneficiary is not required.

Assignment—This policy may be assigned by written request. An absolute assignment will transfer ownership of the policy from you to the assignee. The policy may also be collaterally assigned as security. The limitations on your ownership rights while a collateral assignment is in force are set forth in the assignment. An assignment will take place only when recorded at the Home Office. When recorded, the assignment will take effect as of the date the written request was signed. Any rights created by the assignment will be subject to any payments made or actions taken by Superior Mutual before the change is recorded.

Superior Mutual will not be responsible for the validity of any assignment. If you assign this policy as collateral, any excess of the amount due the assignee will accrue to those otherwise entitled to it.

Beneficiary—The beneficiary is named by you in the application to receive the death proceeds. The interest of any beneficiary will be subject to any assignment. You may declare your choice of any beneficiary to be revocable or irrevocable. A revocable beneficiary may be changed by you at a later time. An irrevocable beneficiary must consent in writing to any change. Unless otherwise indicated, the beneficiary will be revocable.

A change of beneficiary may be made by written request while the insured is living. The change will take place as of the date the request is signed even if the insured is not living on the day the request is received. Any rights created by the change will be subject to any payments made or actions taken by Superior Mutual before the written request is received.

The interest of a beneficiary who dies before the insured will pass to the surviving beneficiaries in proportion to their share in the proceeds unless otherwise provided. If all beneficiaries die before the insured, the death proceeds will pass to the owner.

PREMIUMS

Premiums—The payments to Superior Mutual to keep this policy in force are the premiums. This policy will not be in force until the first premium is paid.

Premium due dates are computed from the date of issue. Premiums are payable in advance either at the Home Office or to the agent. The annual premium amounts are shown on page 3. A receipt signed by a Company officer will be given on request after payment.

Premiums may be paid annually, semi-annually, quarterly or by any other method allowed by Superior Mutual. You may change the method of premium payments only with the prior consent of the Company.

Grace Period—A premium may be paid during a period of 31 days beginning on the premium due date. The policy will remain in force during this grace period.

Nonpayment of Premium—Any premium that is not paid by its due date, either directly or by an automatic premium loan, is in default. A lapse occurs if the premium remains unpaid at the end of the 31-day grace period. After lapse, the policy will be continued in force under one of the following guaranteed insurance benefit options if there is a net cash value available.

Paid-Up Insurance Option—This is insurance for the insured's lifetime with no further premiums due. The amount of paid-up insurance is that amount that can be purchased for a net single premium at the insured's age on the date of default by the total of the cash value of the policy plus any dividend accumulations less any debt.

Paid-up insurance shares in dividends. Any dividend additions not subject to debt will continue in force.

If the paid-up insurance benefit is less than $10,000, this option will not be available. In such event, the net cash value will be used to purchase extended term insurance.

Extended Term Insurance Option—This is insurance for a limited period of time with no further premiums due. The amount of extended term insurance will equal the sum insured, plus any dividend additions or dividend accumulations, less any debt. The length of time the insured will be covered will be that which the net cash value will buy as a net single premium at the insured's age on the date of default. Extended term insurance does not share in dividends.

Applicable Benefit—Paid-up insurance will apply in the following situations if the amount of paid-up insurance is $10,000 or more:

- the amount of paid-up insurance equals or exceeds the amount of extended term insurance; or
- the policy is not in a standard premium class; or
- by written request, you elect paid-up insurance. This request may be made at any time, but not later than 62 days after the due date of the unpaid premium.

Extended term insurance will be the automatic benefit if the paid-up insurance benefit does not apply.

Automatic Premium Loan Option—This option will be in effect if elected in the application or by written request before the premium due date. You may withdraw this election at any time by written request.

While this option is in effect and the policy has a loan value, a loan will automatically be made on the premium due date to pay the unpaid premium. Interest will be waived if the automatic premium loan is repaid within 31 days of the date it is made.

The automatic premium loan option is subject to the following conditions:

- Any dividend accumulations will first be used to pay the unpaid premium unless you request otherwise. The balance of the unpaid premium will be paid by a policy loan.
- If the loan value of this policy is insufficient to pay the premium due, a loan will be made to pay the premium due for a shorter period of time.
- Regardless of the method of premium payment, if the loan value of this policy is not sufficient to pay the premium for a three-month period, no loan will be made. In that case, no premium will be paid and there will be a lapse.

SURRENDER OF THE POLICY

Surrender—Upon written request while the insured is living you may surrender this policy for its net cash value. The policy will terminate on the date of the request. You may receive the net cash value in a lump sum or you may apply it under a payment option.

Superior Mutual may postpone payment of the net cash value for up to 6 months from the date you apply for it. If payment is postponed for 30 days or more, the proceeds will earn interest during the period of postponement at a rate not less than 3½% per year.

REINSTATEMENT

Reinstatement Following Lapse—You may reinstate this policy during the lifetime of the insured if the policy has lapsed and has not been surrendered. If you reinstate the policy within 62 days following the date of default, you must pay the premium that was due. You may reinstate more than 62 days after the date of default, but not more than five years after that date, by providing Superior Mutual with the following:

- evidence of insurability;
- payment of all past due premiums plus interest compounded annually at the rate of 6% from the date of default; and
- payment or reinstatement of any debt outstanding on the date of default. Interest is payable on this debt from the date of default to the date of reinstatement at the loan interest rates that would have been applicable during said period in the absence of default.

The Company will waive evidence of insurability for reinstatement of the policy (but not any riders attached to it) if:

- the insured is in a standard premium class;
- the policy is in force as extended term insurance; and
- the period of time remaining for such extended term insurance coverage on the date of reinstatement is at least five years.

CHANGE OF PLAN

Exchange of Policy—If no premium is in default, you may exchange this policy for a new policy on another plan of insurance. Superior Mutual will not require evidence of insurability. The cash value of the new policy must exceed the cash value of this policy.

The new policy will be issued by Superior Mutual:

- on any whole life policy being issued on the date of issue;
- on the life of the insured only;
- with the same age, date of issue, sum insured and risk class as this policy; and
- at premium rates in use on the date of issue.

Riders will be available subject to evidence of insurability and consent of the Company.

The new policy will be subject to any debt and assignments outstanding on this policy.

Exchange Cost—If you exchange this policy within one year of the date of issue, you must pay any increase in the total premiums. Superior Mutual will not give credit for any premium paid for riders issued with this policy unless such riders are issued with the new policy.

If you exchange this policy one year or more after the date of issue, you must pay an amount equal to the increase in cash values on the date of exchange.

Any dividend additions that exist on the date of the exchange will be surrendered and their cash value applied to the payment. However, if the exchange is to a limited payment whole life plan, you may transfer dividend additions to the new policy.

CASH VALUES

Cash Value—The policy's guaranteed cash values are shown in the Table of Values. These values assume that all premiums have been paid. They do not include dividends or debt.

The values during a policy year will make allowance for full policy months elapsed and any premiums paid for that year. Values for policy years not shown are calculated on the same basis as those in the Table of Values. These values will be furnished on request.

Within 62 days from the due date of any unpaid premium, the policy's net cash value will be its net cash value on that premium due date.

The cash value for any paid-up insurance (including dividend additions) or extended term insurance will be the net single premium for that insurance at the insured's attained age. For 31 days after each policy anniversary, the cash value will not be less than the cash value on that anniversary.

Benefits provided by any rider attached to this policy will be excluded in determining policy values, unless stated otherwise in the rider.

Net Cash Value—The net cash value of this policy is the cash value, plus the value of any dividend additions and dividend accumulations, less any debt.

POLICY LOANS

Policy Loan—Loans may be obtained by request to the Home Office on the sole security of this policy.

When Available—Loans are available while this policy is in force other than as extended term insurance. For up to six months from the date of the request, Superior Mutual may delay granting a loan, other than to pay premiums on policies it has issued.

Amount Available—A loan may be for any amount up to the loan value less existing debt. The loan value is the amount that, with interest at the applicable loan rates then in effect equals the cash value of the policy and the cash value of any dividend additions as of the next policy anniversary or premium due date, whichever is earlier. Any unpaid premium will be deducted from the amount loaned.

Loan Interest Rate—The loan interest rate is adjustable each year. On each January 1, Superior Mutual will establish an interest rate applicable to new and existing policy loans for that calendar year commencing on said date. You will be notified of the policy loan interest rate:

- when a policy loan is requested;
- not later than 60 days after an automatic premium loan has been made; and
- not less than 30 days in advance if a loan exists on the policy and the interest rate is changed.

The annual loan interest rate will not exceed the maximum rate allowable which is the higher of:

- the Published Monthly Average for October of the prior year; or
- the rate used by the Company to compute the cash surrender values under the policy during the applicable period plus 1% per year.

Published Monthly Average means:

- Moody's Corporate Bond Yield Average—Monthly Average Corporates as published by Moody's Investors Services, Inc. or any successor to it; or
- a substantially similiar average set by regulation issued by the Department of Insurance if Moody's Corporate Bond Yield Average—Monthly Average Corporates is no longer published.

The Company may raise the annual loan interest rate on January 1 if that rate is ½% or more below the maximum rate allowable. The Company shall lower the annual loan interest rate on January 1 if it is ½% or more above the maximum rate allowable.

In no event will the loan interest rate exceed the maximum rate allowed by law of the state in which this policy is delivered.

POLICY LOANS (continued)

Loan Interest Payments—Interest on a loan is payable at the end of each policy year at the rates in effect for such policy year or on a pro rata basis for such shorter period as the loan may exist. Interest not paid when due will be added to the loan principal and bear interest at the loan rates established by Superior Mutual.

Repayment—Loans made prior to lapse may only be repaid prior to lapse of this policy. Loans made after lapse on paid-up insurance may be repaid while this policy is in force as paid-up insurance.

Foreclosure—If the debt exceeds the cash value of this policy and the cash value of any dividend additions, the policy will terminate. If debt exceeds cash value during a policy year solely because of a change in interest rate made during the policy, the policy will not terminate during that policy year prior to the date it would have terminated if the interest rate had not changed. A notice of pending termination will be mailed to you at your last known address and to the last known address of any assignee. If the excess debt is not paid within 31 days after the notice is mailed, the policy will terminate with no value.

DIVIDENDS

Annual Dividends—This policy is entitled to share in the divisible surplus as determined each year by Superior Mutual. The Company will distribute this share as a dividend beginning at the end of the first policy year. Dividends are payable only while the policy is in force other than as extended term insurance. Each dividend may be applied in one of the following ways:

- paid in cash; or
- used to reduce premium; or
- used to buy participating paid-up insurance (called dividend additions); or
- left with Superior Mutual as a fund (called dividend accumulations) to earn interest at a rate set by the Company. The annual interest rate will not be less than 3½%.

If you make no election, the dividend will be used to buy dividend additions.

Purchase Price of Dividend Additions—The purchase price of dividend additions will be set by Superior Mutual. The purchase price will be the net single premium for the benefit provided at the insured's attained age. Superior Mutual may change the purchase price for dividend additions but any change will apply only to dividend additions purchased after the date of change.

Cash Value of Dividend Additions—The cash value of dividend additions equals the net single premium for the paid-up insurance at the insured's attained age. This net single premium was determined on the same basis as was used for the purchase price of those dividend additions.

Basis of Net Single Premiums for Dividend Additions—All net single premiums are based on the Commissioner's 1980 Standard Ordinary Mortality Table, Smoker or Nonsmoker, male, female or Table B for unisex (or appropriate increases in such tables for non-standard risks). Interest will not be less than the rate used to calculate cash values.

Dividend at Death—A pro rata share of any dividend apportioned by the Company for the year of death will be added to the death proceeds if:

- the insured dies after the first policy year; and
- the policy is in force on the date of death.

Withdrawal of Dividend Accumulations—You may withdraw all or a part of the dividend accumulations at any time. If the automatic premium loan option has been elected, dividend accumulations will be used to pay unpaid premiums before a loan is made. You may request that dividend accumulations not be used to pay premiums.

Surrender of Dividend Additions—You may surrender dividend additions for their net cash value at any time if their value has not been otherwise used under the terms of this policy.

Paid-Up Privilege—You may exercise this privilege when the sum of the cash value of the policy, the cash value of any dividend additions and any dividend accumulations equals or exceeds the net single premium at the insured's age for the sum insured. At such time, on written request, this policy may be endorsed as fully paid-up. The dividend additions and dividend accumulations will be surrendered and their value applied to the cost of the paid-up policy. Any debt will continue in force. The net single premium and the basis of values for the paid-up insurance policy will be the same as that in use for dividend additions at the time the policy becomes fully paid-up.

PAYMENT OF PROCEEDS

Death Proceeds—The amount payable upon the death of the insured will be the sum insured plus any dividend, dividend accumulations, dividend additions and any one year term insurance in force on the date of death. Any premium paid for the period beyond the end of the policy month of the insured's death will be added to the death proceeds. Premiums that were waived will not be added to the death proceeds. Any debt and any premium due for the policy month in which the insured dies will be deducted from the death proceeds.

If a payment option is selected, the beneficiary, when filing proof of claim, may pay to the Company any amount that would otherwise be deducted from the proceeds.

Interest will be paid on lump-sum death proceeds at a rate not less than 3½% per year or the minimum rate set by law, if greater. Interest will be paid from the date of death to the payment date.

Payment Options—Upon written request, all or part of the death proceeds may be placed under one or more of the payment options below or any other option offered by the Company. Also, on surrender of this policy the net cash value may be placed under one or more of the options instead of being paid in one sum.

The amounts payable under a payment option for each $1,000 of value applied will be the greater of:

(a) the rate per $1,000 of value applied based on the Company's non-guaranteed current payment option rates for this class of policies; or
(b) the rate in this policy for the applicable payment option.

Option A: Payments for a Specified Number of Years. (Table A) The Company will make equal payments for any selected number of years (not greater than 30). Payments may be made annually, semi-annually, quarterly or monthly.

Option B: Lifetime Monthly Payments. (Table B) Payments are based on the payee's age on the date the first payment will be made. One of three variations may be chosen. Depending upon this choice, payments will end:

(1) upon the death of the payee, with no further payments due (Life Annuity), or
(2) upon the death of the payee, but not before the sum of the payments equals or exceeds the amount applied under this option (Life Annuity with Installment Refund), or
(3) upon the death of the payee, but not before a selected period (5, 10 or 20 years) has elapsed (Life Annuity with Period Certain).

Option C: Interest Payments. The rate of interest will be determined by the Company each year but will not be less than 3½%. Payments may be made annually, semi-annually, quarterly or monthly. Payments will end when the amount left with the Company has been withdrawn. However, payments will not continue after the death of the payee. Any unpaid balance plus accrued interest will be paid in a lump sum.

Option D: Payments for a Specified Amount. Payments will be made until the unpaid balance is exhausted. Interest will be credited to the unpaid balance. The rate of interest will be determined by the Company each year but will not be less than 3½%. Payments may be made annually, semi-annually, quarterly or monthly. The payment level selected must provide for the payment each year of at least 8% of the amount applied.

Option E: Lifetime Monthly Payments for Two Payees. (Table E) One of three variations may be chosen. After the death of one payee, payments will continue to the survivor:

(1) in the same amount as the original amount;
(2) in an amount equal to ⅔ of the original amount; or
(3) in an amount equal to ½ of the original amount.

Payments are based on the payees' ages on the date the first payment is due. Payments will end upon the death of the surviving payee.

Selection of Payment Options—The amount applied under any one option for any one payee must be at least $5,000. The periodic payment for any one payee must be at least $50.

Subject to the owner and beneficiary provisions, you may change any option selection before the

PAYMENT OF PROCEEDS (continued)

proceeds become payable. If you make no selection, the beneficiary may select an option when the proceeds become payable.

You may give the beneficiary the right to change from Option C or D to any other option at any time. If the payee selects Option C or D when this policy becomes a claim, the right may be reserved to change to any other option. The payee who elects to change options must be a payee under the option selected.

Additional Deposits—An additional deposit may be added to any proceeds when they are applied under Option B or E. A charge not to exceed 3% will be made. The Company may limit the amount of this deposit.

Rights and Limitations—A payee does not have the right to assign any amount payable under any option. A payee does not have the right to commute any amount payable under Option B or E. A payee will have the right to commute any amount payable under Option A only if the right is reserved in the written request selecting the option. If the right to commute is exercised, the commuted values will be computed at the interest rates used to calculate the benefits. The amount left under Option C, and any unpaid balance under Option D, may be withdrawn by the payee only as set forth in the written request selecting the option.

A corporate or fiduciary payee may select only Option A, C or D. Such selection will be subject to the consent of the Company.

Payment Dates—The first payment under any option, except Option C, will be due on the date this policy matures by death or otherwise, unless another date is designated. Payments under Option C begin at the end of the payment period selected, measured from policy maturity.

The last payment under any option will be made as stated in the description of that option. However, should a payee under Option B or E die prior to the due date of the second monthly payment, the amount applied less the first monthly payment will be paid in a lump sum or under any option other than Option E. Such payment will be made to the surviving payee under Option E or the succeeding payee under Option B.

Payment Rates—The Payment Option Tables show payment rates for Options A, B and E. For policy proceeds placed under these options within five years of the date of surrender or the date the proceeds are otherwise payable, the more favorable of the rates contained in this policy or the rates in use by the Company as of the date the proceeds are applied will be the basis for the periodic payments. Payments that commence more than five years after such date or as a result of additional deposits will be based on the rates in use by the Company as of the date the first payment is due.

PAGE 11

PAYMENT OPTIONS

TABLE A

Payments for Specified Number of Years
Payments Per $1,000 Applied
Based on Interest at 3½% Per Year

YEARS	ANNUAL	SEMI-ANNUAL	QUARTERLY	MONTHLY
1	1000.00	504.30	253.23	84.65
2	508.60	256.49	128.79	43.05
3	344.86	173.91	87.33	29.19
4	263.04	132.65	66.61	22.27
5	213.99	107.92	54.19	18.12
6	181.32	91.44	45.92	15.35
7	158.01	79.69	40.01	13.38
8	140.56	70.88	35.59	11.90
9	127.00	64.05	32.16	10.75
10	116.18	58.59	29.42	9.83
11	107.34	54.13	27.18	9.09
12	99.98	50.42	25.32	8.46
13	93.78	47.29	23.75	7.94
14	88.47	44.62	22.40	7.49
15	83.89	42.31	21.24	7.10
16	79.89	40.29	20.23	6.76
17	76.37	38.51	19.34	6.47
18	73.25	36.94	18.55	6.20
19	70.47	35.54	17.85	5.97
20	67.98	34.28	17.22	5.75
21	65.74	33.15	16.65	5.56
22	63.70	32.13	16.13	5.39
23	61.85	31.19	15.66	5.24
24	60.17	30.34	15.24	5.09
25	58.62	29.56	14.85	4.96
26	57.20	28.85	14.49	4.84
27	55.90	28.19	14.15	4.73
28	54.69	27.58	13.85	4.63
29	53.57	27.02	13.57	4.53
30	52.53	26.49	13.30	4.45

PAGE 12

PAYMENT OPTIONS (continued)

TABLE B

**Monthly Payments Per $1,000 Applied
Based on Interest at 3½% Per Year**

Age	OPTION B (1) Life Annuity	OPTION B (2) Instal. Refund Annuity	OPTION B (3) Life Annuity With			Age	OPTION B (1) Life Annuity	OPTION B (2) Instal. Refund Annuity	OPTION B (3) Life Annuity With		
			5 Years Certain	10 Years Certain	20 Years Certain				5 Years Certain	10 Years Certain	20 Years Certain
0-5	3.09	3.09	3.09	3.09	3.09						
6	3.10	3.10	3.10	3.10	3.10	46	3.98	3.91	3.98	3.97	3.92
7	3.11	3.11	3.11	3.11	3.11	47	4.03	3.95	4.03	4.01	3.96
8	3.12	3.11	3.12	3.12	3.12	48	4.08	4.00	4.08	4.06	4.00
9	3.13	3.12	3.13	3.13	3.13	49	4.14	4.05	4.13	4.11	4.05
10	3.14	3.13	3.14	3.14	3.14	50	4.19	4.10	4.19	4.17	4.10
11	3.15	3.14	3.15	3.15	3.15	51	4.25	4.15	4.25	4.23	4.14
12	3.16	3.15	3.16	3.16	3.16	52	4.32	4.20	4.31	4.29	4.20
13	3.17	3.16	3.17	3.17	3.17	53	4.38	4.26	4.38	4.35	4.25
14	3.18	3.17	3.18	3.18	3.18	54	4.46	4.32	4.45	4.42	4.30
15	3.19	3.19	3.19	3.19	3.19	55	4.53	4.38	4.52	4.49	4.36
16	3.21	3.20	3.21	3.20	3.20	56	4.61	4.45	4.60	4.56	4.42
17	3.22	3.21	3.22	3.22	3.21	57	4.69	4.52	4.68	4.64	4.48
18	3.23	3.22	3.23	3.23	3.23	58	4.78	4.59	4.77	4.72	4.54
19	3.25	3.24	3.25	3.24	3.24	59	4.88	4.67	4.86	4.81	4.60
20	3.26	3.25	3.26	3.26	3.25	60	4.98	4.75	4.96	4.90	4.66
21	3.27	3.26	3.27	3.27	3.27	61	5.09	4.83	5.07	5.00	4.73
22	3.29	3.28	3.29	3.29	3.28	62	5.20	4.92	5.18	5.10	4.79
23	3.31	3.29	3.31	3.30	3.30	63	5.32	5.02	5.30	5.21	4.86
24	3.32	3.31	3.32	3.32	3.32	64	5.46	5.12	5.42	5.33	4.93
25	3.34	3.33	3.34	3.34	3.33	65	5.60	5.22	5.56	5.44	4.99
26	3.36	3.35	3.36	3.36	3.35	66	5.74	5.33	5.70	5.57	5.06
27	3.38	3.36	3.38	3.38	3.37	67	5.90	5.45	5.85	5.70	5.12
28	3.40	3.38	3.40	3.40	3.39	68	6.07	5.57	6.02	5.84	5.18
29	3.42	3.40	3.42	3.42	3.41	69	6.26	5.70	6.19	5.98	5.24
30	3.44	3.42	3.44	3.44	3.43	70	6.45	5.84	6.37	6.13	5.30
31	3.46	3.44	3.46	3.46	3.45	71	6.66	5.98	6.57	6.29	5.35
32	3.49	3.47	3.49	3.48	3.47	72	6.89	6.14	6.78	6.45	5.41
33	3.51	3.49	3.51	3.51	3.50	73	7.13	6.30	7.00	6.62	5.45
34	3.54	3.52	3.54	3.54	3.52	74	7.39	6.47	7.23	6.79	5.49
35	3.57	3.54	3.57	3.56	3.55	75	7.68	6.65	7.48	6.97	5.53
36	3.60	3.57	3.59	3.59	3.58	76	7.98	6.84	7.75	7.14	5.57
37	3.63	3.60	3.63	3.62	3.60	77	8.30	7.04	8.03	7.33	5.60
38	3.66	3.62	3.66	3.65	3.63	78	8.65	7.25	8.32	7.51	5.62
39	3.69	3.65	3.69	3.69	3.66	79	9.02	7.47	8.64	7.69	5.65
40	3.73	3.69	3.73	3.72	3.70	80	9.43	7.71	8.96	7.87	5.67
41	3.76	3.72	3.76	3.76	3.73						
42	3.80	3.75	3.80	3.79	3.76						
43	3.84	3.79	3.84	3.83	3.80						
44	3.89	3.83	3.88	3.88	3.84						
45	3.93	3.87	3.93	3.92	3.88						

Rates for ages 81 and over are the same as those for age 80

PAGE 13

PAYMENT OPTIONS (continued)

TABLE E(1)

**Monthly Payments Per $1,000 Applied
Joint & Survivor
Based on Interest at 3½% Per Year**

OLDER AGE

YOUNGER AGE	50	55	60	65	70	75	80
50	3.70	3.77	3.82	3.86	3.89	3.91	3.93
55		3.92	4.01	4.08	4.14	4.17	4.20
60			4.22	4.34	4.43	4.50	4.54
65				4.61	4.77	4.90	4.98
70					5.16	5.38	5.54
75						5.92	6.23
80							7.00

TABLE E(2)

**Initial Monthly Payments Per $1,000 Applied
Joint & ⅔ Survivor
Based on Interest at 3½% Per Year**

OLDER AGE

YOUNGER AGE	50	55	60	65	70	75	80
50	4.03	4.16	4.31	4.47	4.65	4.83	5.02
55		4.33	4.50	4.69	4.89	5.10	5.32
60			4.72	4.95	5.19	5.44	5.69
65				5.25	5.55	5.87	6.18
70					5.99	6.39	6.79
75						7.03	7.57
80							8.50

TABLE E(3)

**Initial Monthly Payments Per $1,000 Applied
Joint & ½ Survivor
Based on Interest at 3½% Per Year**

OLDER AGE

YOUNGER AGE	50	55	60	65	70	75	80
50	4.22	4.39	4.60	4.85	5.14	5.47	5.83
55		4.56	4.79	5.06	5.38	5.74	6.13
60			5.02	5.32	5.68	6.08	6.52
65				5.65	6.05	6.51	7.02
70					6.52	7.05	7.65
75						7.75	8.48
80							9.52

Payment rates for combinations of ages not shown may be obtained from the Company upon request.

NOTICE

The insured, by virtue of this policy, is a member of the SUPERIOR MUTUAL LIFE INSURANCE COMPANY OF AMERICA, and is entitled to vote, either in person or by proxy, at any and all meetings of the Company. The Annual Meetings are held at the Company's Home Office on the third Wednesday of June in each year, at ten o'clock A.M.

Whole Life Insurance Policy. Death proceeds payable at death of insured. Premiums payable for the period shown on page 3. Annual dividends.

PAGE 15

LIFE INSURANCE APPLICATION
Superior Mutual Life Insurance Company

PART 1 The following questions relate to the person proposed for insurance

1. Proposed insured - First name, middle initial, last name ☐ Male ☐ Female

2. Date of birth (month / day / year)
3. Age nearest birthday
4. Place of birth

5. Telephone numbers
   Day: Night:
6. Address for premium notices (bills will be sent to owner at this address)

7. Residence of insured (if different)

8. Social Security number of the insured
9. Amount of existing SMLI Insurance $

10. Any other name now or previously known by (incl. maiden name, if applicable)

11. Within the last 12 months has the insured smoked: Cigarettes? ☐ Yes ☐ No   (a urine test may be required)   Cigars or a pipe? ☐ Yes ☐ No

12. Insurance Amount & Plan
    Basic Policy $ _____ Plan _____
    Insured Rider $ _____ Plan _____
    Children Rider $ _____ Term to age 22 Insurance (complete Child Rider questionnaire)
    Waiver of Premium ☐ Yes ☐ No (issue ages 15-55 only)

13. Dividends (if selection is missing or not available, #4 will be effective)
    1 ☐ Pay in Cash
    2 ☐ Reduce amount due - any excess dividend as ☐ #4 ☐ #3 ☐ #1
    3 ☐ Purchase paid-up life additions (not available on term insurance)
    4 ☐ Accumulate at interest
    5 ☐ Purchase one-year term additions (not available on term insurance)

14. Premium payment frequency   ☐ Annual ☐ Semi-annual ☐ Quarterly
    Automatic Premium Loan Provision to be effective on permanent insurance unless requested otherwise.

15. Owner (if no owner is shown, the applicant will be the owner.)
    Class   Name (please print clearly)   Age   Relationship to insured
    1
    2
    3

16. Beneficiary
    Class   Name(s) (please print clearly)   Relationship to insured

    If two or more beneficiaries are named state the class: 1, 2, 3, etc. Surviving beneficiaries in the lowest class share equally. All decisions made by SMLI in good faith as to the identity of beneficiaries not designated by name shall be conclusive as to SMLI's liability and any payment made in accordance therewith shall, to the extent thereof, discharge SMLI of it's obligation for such payment.

17. Will coverage applied for replace or change any existing life insurance or annuity (other than SBLI)? If "Yes" submit form A-52. ☐ Yes ☐ No

18. If group insurance conversion:
    Group name _____
    Date group insurance terminated _____
    ☐ Policy terminated
    ☐ Employment terminated
    Note: Part 2 on the reverse side should be completed only if Waiver of Premium is requested in question 12 or #5 in question 13.

19. Conversion or exchange of existing SMLI insurance (other than group):
    Total Face Amount _____ Plan _____
    Policy numbers:

    The above policies are hereby tendered (1) for endorsement, if a rider insurance conversion, or (2) for surrender, if basic policy conversion or exchange; in consideration for and effective as of the date of issue of the insurance herein applied for. If a surrender, pay any cash or dividend values to me. (The above policies must accompany this application.)
    For Term Conversions, Part 2 on the reverse side should be completed only if #5 is selected in question 13 or if Waiver of Premium is requested in question 12.
    For Exchanges, Part 2 on the reverse side must be completed in all cases unless notified otherwise.

20. Special Requests

21. How did you hear about SMLI
    ☐ Family member has SMLI ☐ Newspaper ☐ Radio ☐ TV ☐ Mail insert
    ☐ Bank lobby sign ☐ Friend or relative ☐ Other:

22. Changes made by SMLI

23. Issuing bank:
    No.   Name:

1. Under penalty of perjury, I certify that the Social Security Number(s) is/are correct and that I am not subject to backup withholding.
2. I hereby certify that the statements above are correct and agree that SMLI, believing them to be correct, shall rely and act on them.
3. If SBLI makes a change in space 22, it will be approved by my acceptance of the policy.
4. I agree that the insurance applied for shall not take effect until the first full premium is paid and the policy delivered while each person to be insured is in good health. Once submitted, this application will remain the property of SMLI

_____ X_____ X_____
Date   Signature of Insured (if age 15 or over)   Signature of First Owner in question 15, if any

             X_____
             Signature of Applicant (if other than Insured)   Social Security No. of Owner, if any, otherwise Applicant _____
             If Insured is under 15 check if: ☐ Mother ☐ Father ☐ Guardian

Action	Date	By	Agent No.	Agent Signature		
R/R			Agency	Source, if diff.	Initial Premium Rec'd. $	Date Received

Name of Proposed Insured (print)

PART 2 — To be completed by the SMLI agent if non-medical. (If this is to be a medical application, the examiner will complete this section.)

1. (a) Employer's name and address

   (b) Job title and exact duties

   (c) Years so employed
   (d) Change in occupation contemplated? ☐ Yes ☐ No
       Other occupations last 2 years? ☐ Yes ☐ No

Details of "YES" answers. Identify the question number. Include diagnosis, dates, duration, names and addresses of all attending physicians and medical facilities. Give reason for checkup, treatment, and medication.

2. (a) Do you intend to reside or travel outside the United States and Canada except for vacations? ☐ Yes ☐ No
   (b) Have you ever made claim for or received any pension or disability benefits? ☐ ☐
   (c) Have you ever had an application for life or health insurance declined, postponed, modified or offered at other than regular premiums for your age? ☐ ☐

3. (a) Do you participate in parachuting, motor racing or any other hazardous avocations? ☐ ☐
   (b) Do you own, operate or are you licensed to operate an airplane? ☐ ☐
   (c) How many flights have you made in the past twelve months in other than commercial airlines/airplanes? #If any _____ ☐ None

4. Have you ever consulted any doctor or practitioner for, or suffered from any illness or disease of: Yes No
   (a) The brain or nervous system? ☐ ☐
   (b) The heart, blood vessels, or lungs? ☐ ☐
   (c) The stomach or intestines? ☐ ☐
   (d) The skin, glands, middle ear, hearing, eyes, or vision? ☐ ☐

5. Have you ever had or been advised to have an electrocardiogram, X-ray, or other diagnostic test? ☐ ☐

6. Have you ever had or been treated for rheumatism, bone disease, cancer, syphilis or other venereal disease, or any disorder of the muscles or bones, including the spine, back, or joints? ☐ ☐

7. Have you ever had or been treated for: chest pain, dizziness, fainting, convulsions, allergies, asthma, shortness of breath, persistent cough, repeated headache, paralysis, stroke, or diabetes? ☐ ☐

8. Have you ever been treated for or had any known indication of:
   (a) Alcoholism? ☐ ☐
   (b) Mental or nervous disorder? ☐ ☐
   (c) Any deformity or congenital disorder? ☐ ☐

9. Have you ever used or dealt in barbiturates, excitants or hallucinogens, narcotics or other habit forming drugs? ☐ ☐

10. Are you now being treated or taking medicine for any condition or disease? ☐ ☐

11. Have you ever consulted a doctor or practitioner for, or had any known indication of, any illness, disease, or physical defect or disorder not included in the above questions? ☐ ☐

12. Other than above, within the past 3 years, have you had a checkup, consultation, illness, injury, surgery, or been a patient in a hospital, clinic, sanitarium or other medical facility? ☐ ☐

13. Females age 15 and over only:
    (a) Ever had any disorder of menstruation, pregnancy, or of the female organs or breasts? ☐ ☐
    (b) Are you now pregnant? ☐ ☐
    (c) Ever had a caesarean section? ☐ ☐
    (d) Are uterine functions now irregular? ☐ ☐
    (e) Number of children _____

14. Height (in shoes) ___ft. ___in. Weight (clothed) _____lbs.
    Has weight changed in the past two years? ☐ Yes ☐ No
    If "Yes": Gain _____lbs., Loss _____lbs. How long at present weight? _____

15. Family History - Indicate below any diabetes, cancer, high blood pressure, heart or kidney disease, mental illness or suicide.

Family Member	Age if Living	State of Health (If not good, give details or cause of death.)	Age at Death
Father			
Mother			
Brothers & Sisters No. Living ___ No. Dead ___			

_____   X _____
Date   Signature of Examiner (Agent if non-medical)

I hereby certify that the above answers and statements are correct and I agree that SMLI believing them to be correct shall rely and act on them. I agree that they shall be a part of my application for insurance or policy change request. I acknowledge receipt of the attached **Disclosure Notice and MIB Notification.**

I HEREBY AUTHORIZE any licensed physician, medical practitioner, hospital, clinic or other medical or medically related facility, insurance company, the Medical Information Bureau or other organization, institution or person, that has any records or knowledge of the Proposed Insured or his/her health to give to the Medical Director, Superior Mutual Life, any such information.

A photographic copy of this authorization shall be as valid as the original.

_____   _____   X _____
Name of Proposed Insured (please print)   Date   Signature of Proposed Insured (Parent or Guardian if insured under age 15)

PART 3 — To be completed by an Examiner authorized by SMLI. Omit if Non-Medical.			
16. Males only Chest (inspiration) _____ in. Chest (expiration) _____ in. Waist _____ in.	17. Blood Pressure Systolic Diastolic (All sound ceases) If over 138/88, repeat twice 3 minutes apart	18. Pulse Rate _____ Quality _____ Irregularities per minute _____	19. Urinalysis Albumin _____ Sugar _____
20. For question 14 answers Did you measure? ☐ Yes ☐ No Did you weigh? ☐ Yes ☐ No	21. Did you observe any indication of physical or mental impairment or abnormality not indicated in Part 2? ☐ Yes ☐ No If "Yes" explain:		

I have personally seen the person whose name appears in part 2. I am satisfied as to the identity of that person. I certify that the answers in Part 2 were correctly recorded by me.

_____   X _____   Paramed Stamp:
Date   Examiner

A consumer inspection report, if we request one, may include information obtained through personal interviews with your neighbors, friends or others with whom you are acquainted. This inquiry includes information as to your character, general reputation, personal characteristics and mode of living. You have the right to make a written request within a reasonable period of time to receive additional, detailed information about the nature and scope of this investigation. Please direct any such request to Medical Director, Superior Mutual Life.

Information regarding your insurability will be treated as confidential. We may, however, make a brief report thereon to the Medical Information Bureau (MIB), a nonprofit membership organization of insurance companies, which operates an information exchange on behalf of its members. If you apply to another MIB member company for life or health insurance coveage, or a claim for benefits is submitted to such a company, MIB, upon request, will supply such company with the information in its files.

We will not reject your application because of data furnished by MIB; it may simply alert us to the possible need for further information. MIB files do not contain medical reports from doctors or hospitals, nor do they indicate whether any insurance applications have been accepted or rejected.

Upon receipt of a request from you, MIB will arrange disclosure of any information it may have in your file. (Medical information will be disclosed only to your attending physician.) If you question the accuracy of the information in the MIB file, you may contact MIB and seek a correction in accordance with the procedures set forth in the Federal Fair Credit Reporting Act. The address of the MIB office is P.O. Box 105, Essex Station, Boston MA 02112, telephone (617) 426-3660. We may also release information in our file to other life insurance companies to whom you apply for life or health insurance, or to whom a claim for benefits may be submitted.

Individual Health Policy

Contents

Definitions	2	Exclusions and Limitations	9
Coverage Description	4	Claims	9
Authorization Provision	8	Contract	10

Index

Carry-Over Deductible	4	Medicare	3
Claim Forms	10	Mental Illness	3
Conformity with State Statutes	11	Misstatement of Age/Sex	11
Congenital Illness or Defect of a Newborn Child	8	Non-Renewal	10
		Notice of Claim	9
Consideration	10	Other Health Insurance Plan	3
Conversion	11	Part A	3
Covered Complications of Pregnancy	7	Part B	3
Covered Expenses	5	Payment of Benefits	4
Covered Person	2	Payment of Benefits When Eligible for Medicare	5
Custodial Care	2		
Deductible Amount	4	Payment of Claims	10
Dental Service	2	Physical Examination	10
Disabled Dependents	2	Physical Medicine	3
Effective Date of Coverage	2	Physician	3
Eligible Dependents	2	Policy Owner	3
Eligible for Medicare	2	Preexisting Condition	3
Entire Contract; Changes	10	Proofs of Loss	10
Expenses not Covered by this Policy	9	Reasonable and Customary Charge	3
Family Cap Maximum	4	Reduction of Payment Reinstatement	11
Grace Period	10	Right to Change Deductible	4
Hospice Program	2	Sickness	4
Hospital	2	Skilled Nursing Facility	4
Human Organ/Tissue Transplant or Replacement	7	Termination of Dependent Coverage	11
		Termination of Insured's Coverage	11
Immediate Family	3	Time Limit on Certain Defenses	10
Injury	3	Time of Payment of Claims	10
Legal Action	10	Unauthorized Admission, Confinement, or Surgery	8
Maximum Family Deductible	4		
Medically Necessary Care	3		

DEFINITIONS

"You," "Your" and "Yours" means the Insured named on the Policy Schedule. "Time," "Us" and "Ours" means the Company.

COVERED PERSON: Covered person means the insured and all eligible dependents shown on the policy schedule, or added by endorsement.

CUSTODIAL CARE means care given to a covered person if the person:

1. is mentally or physically disabled and such disability is expected to last for an indefinite time;
2. needs a protected, monitored and/or controlled environment;
3. needs help to support the essentials of daily living; and
4. is not under active and specific medical, surgical and/or psychiatric treatment, which will reduce the disability to the extent necessary for the person to function outside a protected, monitored and/or controlled environment.

DENTAL SERVICE means any medical or surgical procedure that involves the hard or soft tissue of the mouth that requires treatment as a result of a disease or condition of the teeth or gums. Treatment for neoplasms is not considered a dental service.

DISABLED DEPENDENTS: This section amends the Eligible Dependents section. An unmarried child who cannot support himself due to mental incapacity or physical handicap may continue to be insured. This child must be fully dependent upon you for support. The Company may inquire of you two months prior to attainment by a dependent of the limiting age set forth in this policy, or at any reasonable time thereafter, whether such dependent is in fact a disabled and dependent person. In the absence of proof submitted within 60 days of such inquiry that such dependent is a disabled and dependent person, the Company may terminate coverage of such person at or after attainment of the limiting age. In the absence of such inquiry, coverage of any disabled and dependent person shall continue through the term of such policy or any extension or renewal thereof.

EFFECTIVE DATE OF COVERAGE: A covered person's effective date of coverage is: (1) the policy date, if the covered person is listed on the application and the policy schedule; or (2) the date of policy endorsement, if the covered person is added to the policy after it is issued.

ELIGIBLE DEPENDENTS: Eligible dependents are those dependents shown on the policy schedule or added by endorsement. This may include: (1) Your lawful spouse; and (2) Unmarried dependent children, including step-children and adopted children (or children who are in your custody pursuant to an interim court order of adoption), if they are legally dependent on you for their support and under 21 years of age.

Your newborn children, born while the policy is in force, will be covered for 60 days after birth. For coverage beyond 60 days after birth, written application must be made to the Company within that 60-day period. An additional premium will be required retroactive to date of birth. Other eligible dependents may be added by you upon evidence of insurability satisfactory to the Company. Additional premium will be required.

ELIGIBLE FOR MEDICARE means that the covered person is either:

1. covered by both Part A and Part B of Medicare; or
2. not covered for both Part A and Part B of Medicare because of:
   a. a failure to enroll when required;
   b. a failure to pay any premium that may be required for full coverage of the person under Medicare; or
   c. a failure to file any written request, claim or document required for payment of Medicare benefits.

HOSPICE PROGRAM means a coordinated interdisciplinary program for meeting the special physical, psychological, spiritual and social needs of dying covered persons and their immediate families. The covered person must be enrolled in the program by a physician.

HOSPITAL means a place other than a convalescent, nursing or rest home, that:

- provides facilities for medical, diagnostic and acute care on an inpatient basis. If these services are not on its own premises, they must be available through a prearranged contract;
- provides 24-hour nursing care supervised by registered nurses;
- has X ray and lab facilities either on its premises or available through a prearranged contract;
- charges for these services.

A special ward, floor or other accommodation for convalescent, nursing or rehabilitation purposes is not considered a hospital.

IMMEDIATE FAMILY means you, your spouse, and the children, brothers, sisters and parents of either you or your spouse.

INJURY: Injury means accidental bodily injury sustained by a covered person while covered under this policy.

MEDICALLY NECESSARY CARE means confinement, treatment or service that is rendered to diagnose or treat a sickness or injury. Such care must be (1) prescribed by a physician; (2) considered to be necessary and appropriate for the diagnosis and treatment of the sickness or injury; and (3) commonly accepted as proper care or treatment of the condition by the U.S. medical community. Medically necessary care does not include care considered to be: (1) experimental or investigative in nature by any appropriate technological assessment body established by any state or federal government; (2) provided only as a convenience to the covered person or provider; and (3) in excess (in scope, duration or intensity) of that level of care which is needed to provide safe, adequate and appropriate diagnosis and treatment. The fact that a physician may prescribe, order, recommend or approve a service or supply does not, of itself, make the service or supply medically necessary.

MEDICARE: Medicare means the Health Insurance for the Aged Act, Title XVIII of the Social Security Act as amended.

MENTAL ILLNESS: Mental illness means a mental or nervous disorder, including neuroses, psychoneurosis, psychopathy, psychosis and other emotional disorders. Affective disorders (including bipolar disorders and major depression), alcoholism, drug addiction and chemical dependency are also included in this definition.

OTHER HEALTH INSURANCE PLAN: This means any plan that provides insurance, reimbursement or service benefits for hospital, surgical or other medical expenses. This includes: (1) individual or group health insurance policies; (2) nonprofit health service plans, including Blue Cross and Blue Shield; (3) health maintenance organization subscriber contracts; (4) self-insured group plans; (5) welfare plans; (6) medical coverage under homeowners or automobile insurance; and (7) service provided or payment received under laws of any national, state or local government. This does not include Medicaid.

If coverage is provided on a service basis, the amount of benefits under such coverage will be taken as the cost of the service in the absence of such coverage.

PART A means the Hospital Insurance Benefits for the Aged portion of Medicare.

PART B means the Supplementary Medical Insurance for the Aged portion of Medicare.

PHYSICAL MEDICINE means the diagnosis and treatment of physical conditions relating to bone, muscle or neuromuscular pathology.

PHYSICIAN: A person licensed by the state to treat the kind of injury or sickness for which a claim is made. The physician must be practicing within the limits of his or her license.

POLICY OWNER: The insured shown on the policy schedule unless someone else is designated the owner on the application.

PREEXISTING CONDITIONS: A preexisting condition is a condition not fully disclosed on the application for insurance:

1. for which the covered person received medical treatment or advice from a physician within the six-month period immediately preceding that covered person's effective date of coverage; or
2. which produced signs or symptoms within the six-month period immediately preceding that covered person's effective date of coverage.

The signs or symptoms must have been significant enough to establish manifestation or onset by one of the following tests:
a. The signs or symptoms would have allowed one learned in medicine to make a diagnosis of the disorder; or
b. The signs or symptoms should have caused an ordinarily prudent person to seek diagnosis or treatment.

Preexisting conditions will be covered after the covered person has been insured for two years, if the condition is not specifically excluded from coverage.

REASONABLE AND CUSTOMARY CHARGE means the lesser of:

1. The actual charge;
2. What the provider would accept for the same service or supply in the absence of insurance; or

3. The reasonable charge as determined by the Company, based on factors such as:
   a. the most common charge for the same or comparable service or supply in a community similar to where the service or supply is furnished;
   b. the amount of resources expended to deliver the treatment and the complexity of the treatment rendered; and
   c. charging protocols and billing practices generally accepted by the medical community or specialty groups; or
   d. inflation trends by geographic region.

SICKNESS: Sickness means an illness, disease or condition of a covered person that manifests itself after the covered person's effective date of coverage. For sickness that manifests itself during the first 15 days following the effective date, coverage is provided only for covered expense incurred after that 15-day period.

SKILLED NURSING FACILITY means a nursing home, licensed as a skilled nursing facility, operating in accordance with the laws of the state in which it is located and meeting the following requirements:

1. Is primarily engaged in providing room, board and skilled nursing care for persons recovering from sickness or injury;
2. Provides 24-hour-a-day skilled nursing service under the full-time supervision of a physician or graduate registered nurse;
3. Maintains daily clinical records;
4. Has transfer arrangements with a hospital;
5. Has a utilization review plan in effect;
6. Is not a place for rest, the aged, drug addicts, alcoholics or the mentally ill; and
7. May be a part of a hospital.

COVERAGE DESCRIPTION

DEDUCTIBLE AMOUNT: The deductible amount for each covered person during each calendar year is the larger of:

- the basic deductible amount shown in the policy schedule; or
- the amount of benefits paid for covered expenses by any other health insurance plan as defined in the policy.

The deductible amount must be:

- incurred each calendar year; and
- deducted from covered expenses.

A calendar year begins on January 1 and ends December 31.

MAXIMUM FAMILY DEDUCTIBLE AMOUNT: A maximum family deductible amount equal to three times the basic deductible amount will satisfy the deductible requirements for all covered persons in a family during a calendar year.

FAMILY CAP MAXIMUM: The maximum expense amount incurred per family for covered expense will not exceed the family cap maximum shown in the policy schedule for any calendar year.

CARRY-OVER DEDUCTIBLE: Any covered expense incurred and applied to a covered person's basic deductible amount during the last three months of a calendar year may also be used to reduce that person's basic deductible amount for the next calendar year.

The maximum family deductible and the carry-over deductible provisions will not apply if the benefits paid by other health insurance are used as the deductible.

RIGHT TO CHANGE DEDUCTIBLE AMOUNT: You may apply for an increase or decrease in the basic deductible amount within a 60-day period after a premium rate change, or during the first 30 days of a calendar year, provided that: (1) the new basic deductible amount is one that is available on this form, (2) a request for the change is made in writing to the Company, and (3) no claims have been incurred during that calendar year.

If you request a decrease in the deductible amount, the Company will require proof of continued insurability of all covered persons.

PAYMENT OF BENEFITS: Benefits for covered expense incurred will be paid in accordance with sections A and B of the covered expense provision.

If benefits paid by other health insurance are used as the deductible amount, all covered expense will be paid at 100 percent, but payment will not exceed the amount that would have been paid in the absence of other health insurance.

PAGE 4

Where applicable, the rate of payment starts again for each covered person each new calendar year after the deductible amount has been met. The Company will pay up to the lifetime maximum benefit shown in the policy schedule for each covered person.

If the payment by other health insurance is used as the deductible amount, the lifetime maximum benefit will be increased. The maximum benefit will be increased by $3 for each $1 paid by other coverage over the basic deductible.

PAYMENT OF BENEFITS WHEN ELIGIBLE FOR MEDICARE: When any covered person is eligible for Medicare, he or she will be deemed to have Part A and Part B Medicare coverage that is primary to the coverage under this policy. Services covered by Medicare will not be covered by this policy to the extent that benefits are payable by Medicare. If there is remaining covered expense after Medicare pays for assigned services, benefits will be paid at 100 percent up to the amount approved by Medicare; for unassigned services, benefits will be paid at 100 percent up to our reasonable and customary charge limit. Payment of benefits for services not covered by Medicare will be determined by the terms and limits of this policy.

COVERED EXPENSE: Covered expense means expense that is (a) incurred for services, treatment or supplies prescribed by a physician and described in Section A or B below; (b) incurred by a covered person as the result of sickness or injury as defined; (c) incurred for medically necessary care; and (d) incurred while the covered person's coverage is in force. Covered expense does not include any charge in excess of the reasonable and customary charge.

A. The following items of covered expense are subject to the deductible and rate of payment as described in this policy and shown in the policy schedule.

1. Room, board and general nursing care while confined in a semi-private room, ward, coronary care or other intensive care unit in a hospital. For confinement in a private room, the covered expense is limited to the hospital's most common daily charge for a semi-private room.
2. Other hospital services including services performed in a hospital outpatient department or in a free-standing surgical facility.
3. Physician services and surgical services, including second surgical opinions by board-certified specialists. This does not include services rendered by members of your immediate family.
4. Reconstructive surgery to restore function for conditions resulting from accidental injury provided the injury occurred while the covered person is insured under this plan. Reconstructive surgery that is incidental to or follows covered surgery performed as the result of trauma, infection or other diseases of the involved part.

   Reconstructive surgery for congenital defects provided the covered person has been insured continuously under this plan since the time of birth.
5. Hospice programs when (a) the physician projects a life expectancy of six months or less; and (b) the physician enrolls a covered person in the program. Notification is to be made in writing to the Company within seven days of admission to a licensed hospice facility. Covered expense includes up to 30 days of inpatient treatment at a hospice facility. Hospice home care is covered in addition to benefits provided under item 6. Benefits for services that include inpatient hospice services, hospice home care and counselling under the authorized hospice program are limited to $15,000 during the covered person's lifetime.
6. Up to 40 home health care visits in any 12-month period. One visit consists of up to four hours of home health aide service within a 24-hour period by anyone providing services or evaluating the need for home health care.

For home health care to be a covered expense, the physician must certify that:
a. hospitalization or confinement in a skilled nursing facility would otherwise be required;
b. medically necessary care is not available from members of the covered person's immediate family or persons living with the covered person without causing undue hardship; and
c. the home health care will be provided by a state-licensed or Medicare-certified home health agency.

Home health care does not include:
a. services not included in the home health care plan established for the covered person by the physician;

b. services provided by the covered person's immediate family or anyone residing with the covered person;
c. homemaker services; or
d. custodial care.
7. Professional ambulance service to the nearest hospital that is able to handle the sickness or injury. One trip to a hospital for a covered person for each sickness or injury is covered.
8. X ray, radioactive treatment, laboratory tests and anesthesia services.
9. Outpatient physical medicine benefits to a maximum of $500 for each covered person per calendar year. Physical medicine benefits include but are not limited to: rehabilitative speech, physical, occupational and cognitive therapies; biofeedback; sports medicine; cardiac exercise programs; adjustments and manipulations. The limitation does not apply to the treatment of burns, fractures, complete dislocations, joint replacements or related conditions for which a covered person is hospitalized for surgery and physical medicine that immediately follows hospitalization.
10. Rental, up to the purchase price, or purchase, when approved in advance by the Company of (a) a basic wheelchair, basic hospital bed or basic crutches; (b) the initial permanent basic artificial limb, eye or external breast prosthesis; and (c) oxygen and the equipment needed to administer oxygen.

Casts, orthopedic braces, splints, dressings and sutures.

Dental braces, dental appliances, corrective shoes, orthotics or repairs to or replacement of prosthetic devices are not covered expenses.
11. Drugs that require the written prescription of a licensed physician. However, if a prescription drug benefit rider is attached to this policy, covered drugs will be paid under that rider (to age 65 or prior Medicare eligibility), instead of under this policy.
12. Whole blood, blood plasma and blood products, if not replaced.
13. Dental service for an injury to a sound natural tooth when the expense is incurred within six months following the injury.

"Sound" is defined as:
a. organic and formed by nature;
b. not extensively restored or endodontically treated; and
c. not extensively decayed or involved in peridontal disease.
14. Treatment of mental illness. Expense incurred by a covered person while confined as an inpatient to a hospital or psychiatric hospital for mental illness as defined in the policy. Coverage is limited to a maximum benefit of $2500 for a covered person during a calendar year. Outpatient treatment, drugs or medications are not covered.
15. Sterilization, if the covered person has been insured on this policy for at least two years.
16. Treatment of temporomandibular joint dysfunction except for: crowns that correct vertical dimension; splints, orthopedic repositioning appliances, biteplates and equilibration treatments (including splint equilibration and adjustments); bite functional or occlusal registration, with or without splints, and kinesiographic analysis; any orthodontic treatment, including extraction of teeth; study models, except for the complete model made necessary when surgical intervention is completed. Surgical charges for correction of orthognathic conditions are covered.

B. The following items 1, 2 and 3 of covered expense will not be subject to the basic deductible amount or the 80 percent rate of payment. Covered expense will be considered for payment under this section before it is considered under any other section of the policy. Covered expense for which a benefit is payable under this section will not be considered for payment under any other section of the policy.

1. Skilled nursing care: Medically necessary care in a skilled nursing facility for up to 30 days provided (a) the covered person enters the skilled nursing facility within 14 days after discharge from an authorized hospital confinement; (b) the skilled nursing facility confinement is for the same condition that required the hospital confinement; and (c) such care is authorized by the Company within seven days following admission to the skilled nursing facility. The daily benefit for confinement in a skilled nursing facility will not exceed one-half of the semi-private hospital room rate for the area.
2. Second and third opinions required by the Company's authorization service. Only an exam, X ray and lab work, and a written report by the physician rendering the opinion

are included. You will be supplied with a list of three recommended physicians from whom the second or third opinion may be sought. The service may allow another physician to be consulted if the physician is (a) a board-certified specialist in the field of the proposed treatment; (b) is not financially associated with the first physician; and (c) does not perform the treatment.

3. Pre-admission testing. X rays and lab work performed on an outpatient basis before an authorized hospital admission provided (a) the tests are related to a scheduled admission; (b) the charges for the tests would have been covered expense if the individual was confined as an inpatient in a hospital; and (c) the tests were not repeated in or by the hospital, or elsewhere.

HUMAN ORGAN/TISSUE TRANSPLANT OR REPLACEMENT: Covered expense incurred by a covered person for the following human organ or tissue transplants or replacements if the procedure is authorized as indicated below, to a maximum lifetime benefit of $250,000 for each covered person.

Human organ transplant. The following procedures are covered if the procedure is authorized in writing by the Company prior to the beginning of the donor search and selection:

a. Bone marrow transplant
b. Heart transplant
c. Liver transplant

No benefits will be paid if the procedure has not been authorized by the Company prior to the beginning of the donor search and selection. To begin the authorization process, the physician or the physician's assistant must contact the Company's authorization service.

Tissue transplant or replacement. The following procedures are covered if authorized according to the procedures outlined in the authorization provision:

a. Cornea transplant
b. Prosthetic tissue replacement, including joint replacement
c. Vein or artery graft
d. Heart valve replacement
e. Implantable prosthetic lens in connection with cataracts

Donor Expenses. Expense incurred for surgery, storage and/or transportation service related to donor organ acquisition is also covered, up to a maximum benefit of $10,000 per covered procedure.

If the transplanted organ is from a live donor, expense incurred by the donor that is not paid by any other plan of insurance will be covered as though the donor's expense were the expense of the covered person.

No benefits will be paid for any transplant not authorized in writing by the Company prior to the beginning of donor search and selection or any transplant or replacement procedure not specifically listed above.

Kidney Disease or End Stage Renal Disease. Expense incurred for dialysis, transplantation and donor-related services to a maximum of $30,000 for each covered person during a calendar year. The transplant must be authorized in writing by the Company prior to the beginning of the donor search and selection. No benefits will be paid if the procedure has not been authorized by the Company prior to the beginning of such search.

Together with expense for dialysis and/or transplantation, expense incurred for surgery, storage and/or transportation service related to donor organ acquisition is limited to the $30,000 annual maximum. If the transplanted organ is from a live donor, expense incurred by the donor that is not paid by any other plan of insurance will be covered as though the donor's expense were the expense of the covered person, and included in the $30,000 annual maximum.

The limits in this provision for kidney disease or end stage renal disease provide for coordination with the governmental coverage for end stage renal disease.

COVERED COMPLICATIONS OF PREGNANCY: You, your spouse or a dependent child are covered for complications of pregnancy as defined below. Benefits are provided on the same basis as any covered sickness. Covered complications of pregnancy are limited to:

1. Conditions (when pregnancy is not ended) whose diagnoses are distinct from pregnancy, but are caused or adversely affected by pregnancy. Some examples: acute nephritis, nephrosis and cardiac decompensation.
2. Non-elective caesarean section
3. Ectopic pregnancy that is terminated

4. Spontaneous termination of pregnancy (miscarriage) that occurs before the 26th week of gestation; or missed abortion

Covered complications of pregnancy do not include: high-risk pregnancy or delivery, false labor, premature labor, occasional spotting, physician prescribed rest, morning sickness, pre-eclampsia or placenta previa.

CONGENITAL ILLNESS OR DEFECT OF A NEWBORN CHILD: Congenital illness or defect of a child of the insured born while this policy is in force will not be considered a preexisting condition. Benefits will be provided on the same basis as any other sickness.

AUTHORIZATION PROVISION

This plan requires pre-authorization of all hospital admissions, inpatient surgeries, outpatient surgeries and transplants. The payment of benefits for covered expense described under the "Coverage Description" section of this policy may be reduced if the authorization procedure described below is not followed.

AN AUTHORIZATION DOES NOT GUARANTEE THAT BENEFITS WILL BE PAID. PAYMENT OF BENEFITS WILL BE DETERMINED BY THE TERMS AND LIMITS OF THE POLICY.

ELECTIVE ADMISSION OR SURGERY: For non-emergency hospital confinement, inpatient surgery, outpatient surgery or day surgery performed in a hospital, you must have the physician ordering the confinement or surgery obtain authorization before the patient is admitted to the hospital or has surgery performed. The authorization is obtained by the physician or physician's assistant from the Company's authorization service. The service can be reached by telephone during normal business hours, each Monday through Friday. A toll-free number and the name of the Company's authorization service is provided on the ID card given to you by the Company. You must instruct the physician to obtain the authorization by using the authorization form provided by the Company.

The service may require a second opinion prior to granting authorization. In such case, you will be supplied with a list of three recommended physicians from whom the second opinion may be sought. However, the service may allow another physician to be consulted who (a) is a board-certified specialist in the field of the proposed treatment or surgery; (b) is not financially affiliated with the first physician; and (c) does not perform the surgery or provide the treatment. If the second opinion confirms the need for admission, then the admission will be considered AUTHORIZED. If the second opinion does not confirm the need for surgery or treatment, the service may allow a third opinion to be sought from a physician meeting the qualifications described for second opinions.

The physician may proceed with treatment on the basis of verbal authorization from the service. This will be followed by a written authorization sent to you, the hospital and the physician. The authorization remains valid for 60 days from the date of the written authorization. For treatment beginning after the 60-day period, a new authorization must be obtained.

EMERGENCY ADMISSIONS: Emergency admissions are admissions for life-threatening conditions or for a condition for which the absence of immediate treatment would cause permanent disability. An emergency admission must also be authorized in the same manner as an elective admission or surgery, as soon as it is reasonably possible to give notice of such confinement. Otherwise that portion of an emergency confinement occurring beyond 48 hours after admission (excluding Saturdays, Sundays and legal holidays) is considered UNAUTHORIZED.

UNAUTHORIZED ADMISSION, CONFINEMENT, OR SURGERY: If authorization is obtained in accordance with the above procedures, the hospital admission or surgery will be considered authorized; otherwise, it will be considered UNAUTHORIZED. An admission, confinement or surgery for which authorization was obtained shall be considered UNAUTHORIZED if (a) the authorization is no longer valid when confinement begins or surgery is performed; or (b) the type of treatment, admitting physician or hospital differs from the authorized treatment, physician or hospital.

Also, that portion of a hospital confinement, whether non-emergency or emergency, that exceeds the number of authorized days will be considered UNAUTHORIZED, unless an extension is granted. To receive an extension, the physician must call the Company's authorization service at least 24 hours prior to the originally scheduled discharge date and request an extension. The authorization service may or may not authorize an extension. Unauthorized extensions will be considered on the same basis as an unauthorized admission.

REDUCTION OF PAYMENT: The first $500 of covered expense incurred for unauthorized hospital admissions, confinements (or the unauthorized portion thereof) or any surgery shall not be paid by the Company; nor will that $500, or any portion thereof, be applied to the basic deductible amount requirement or rate of payment determination. As described under the Coverage Description section, to be a covered expense, the services, treatment and supplies must be medically necessary and the resulting charges reasonable and customary.

EXCLUSIONS AND LIMITATIONS

EXPENSES NOT COVERED BY THIS POLICY:
This policy does not provide benefits for the following:

1. preexisting conditions during the first two years coverage is in force; except as provided by the policy;
2. expense incurred for a sickness during the first 15 days after a covered person's effective date of coverage;
3. intentionally self-inflicted injury, suicide or suicide attempt, whether sane or insane;
4. care, treatment or services while in a government hospital, unless the covered person is legally required to pay for such services in the absence of insurance;
5. injury or sickness to the extent that benefits are paid by Medicare or any other government law or program (except Medicaid); or any Motor Vehicle No-Fault Law;
6. injury or sickness covered by any Worker's Compensation Act or Occupational Disease Law;
7. war or any act of war; injury or sickness while in the military service of any country (any premium paid for a time not covered will be returned pro-rata);
8. treatment of Temporomandibular Joint Dysfunction except as provided in item 16 of the covered expense provision;
9. dental service including X rays, care or treatment except as provided under item 13 of the covered expense provision;
10. treatment for infertility; confinement, treatment or services related to artificial insemination; restoration of fertility, reversal of sterilization or promotion of conception; or expense incurred for genetic counselling, testing or treatment;
11. eyeglasses, contact lenses, hearing aids, eye exams, eye refraction or eye surgery for correction of refraction error;
12. normal pregnancy or childbirth (except as may be provided by rider), routine well-baby care including hospital nursery charges at birth; abortion or caesarean section except as provided in the Covered Complications of Pregnancy provision;
13. expense incurred for weight reduction or weight-control programs, including surgery; treatment, medication or hormones to stimulate growth;
14. reconstructive or plastic surgery that is primarily a cosmetic procedure, including medical or surgical complications therefrom; except as provided in item 4 of the covered expense provision;
15. the first $500 of otherwise covered expense incurred during any unauthorized hospital confinement or the unauthorized portion of a confinement or unauthorized surgery (see Reduction of Payment provision);
16. treatment, removal or repair of tonsils or adenoids during the first six months of coverage, except on an emergency basis;
17. expense incurred due to injury or sickness due to committing a felony or while under the influence of illegal narcotics;
18. sales tax or gross receipt tax;
19. custodial care.

CLAIMS

NOTICE OF CLAIM: If a covered person incurs covered expense, you must give the Company written notice of claim. The notice must be given within 60 days after the claim begins, or as soon as is reasonably possible. The notice must be given to the Company or its agent, and must include your name and policy number.

CLAIM FORMS: When notice of claim is received, the Company will send you claim forms. If you do not receive the forms within 15 days after the giving of such notice, you shall be deemed to have complied with the proof of loss requirements if: (1) you give the Company a written statement of the nature and the extent of the loss for which claim is made; and (2) such statement is given within the time limit stated in the Proofs of Loss provision.

PROOFS OF LOSS: You must give the Company written proof of loss within 90 days after the covered expense is incurred. If written proof is not given in the time required, this will not make the claim invalid as long as the proof is given as soon as reasonably possible. In no event, except in the absence of legal capacity, may proof be given later than one year from the time otherwise required.

PAYMENT OF CLAIMS: Benefits will be paid to you unless you have assigned them to a doctor, hospital or other provider. Any benefits unpaid and unassigned at your death, will be paid to the designated beneficiary or your estate.

TIME OF PAYMENT OF CLAIMS: Benefits for covered expense will be paid promptly upon receipt of written proof of loss. If not paid within 30 days of receipt of proof of loss, interest at the rate of 8 percent per annum will be paid, in addition, after the 30th day.

PHYSICAL EXAMINATION: While a claim is pending, the Company has the right to have a covered person examined as often as reasonably necessary. This will be at the Company's expense.

CONTRACT

CONSIDERATION: This policy is issued on the basis of the statements and agreements in the application and payment of the required premium. Premium payment in advance on or before the policy date, will keep this policy in force from the policy date until the first renewal date. The premium is set out in the policy schedule. Each renewal premium is due on its due date subject to the grace period. All periods of insurance will begin and end at 12:01 A.M., standard time, at your residence.

ENTIRE CONTRACT; CHANGES: This policy, your attached application and any endorsements constitute the entire contract. No change in this policy is valid unless approved by an executive officer of the Company. The approval must be endorsed by the officer and attached to the policy. No agent can change this policy or waive any of its provisions.

TIME LIMIT ON CERTAIN DEFENSES: After two years from the effective date of coverage, no misstatement made in the application (unless fraudulent) will be used to void the policy or deny any claim beginning after the two year period.

No claim for expense incurred by a covered person that begins more than two years from that person's effective date of coverage will be reduced or denied on the grounds that a disease or physical condition (not excluded from coverage by name or specific description) had existed prior to the covered person's effective date.

GRACE PERIOD: There is a grace period of 31 days for the payment of each premium due after the first premium. The policy will stay in force during this grace period. If the premium is not paid by the end of the grace period, this policy will lapse. No coverage will be provided during the grace period if the covered person has similar coverage available through another carrier and does not pay premium to the Company.

NON-RENEWAL: The grace period does not apply if the Company has given you written notice that it will not renew the policy. This notice must be sent to you at least 30 days before the premium is due. Notice will be mailed to your last known address on the Company's records. Coverage will continue for any period for which premium has been accepted.

The Company can only decline to renew the policy on the renewal date occurring on, or after and nearest, each anniversary. The anniversary will be based on the policy date or last reinstatement date. This does not apply if premiums are not paid. Non-renewal will not prejudice any expense incurred while the policy was in force.

LEGAL ACTION: You cannot bring legal action to recover on this policy before at least 60 days have passed from the time written proof has been given to the Company. No action can be brought after three years from the time written proof has been given to the Company. The time limit is five years in Kansas; six years in South Carolina.

TERMINATION OF INSURED'S COVERAGE: Your coverage will end on the date the policy lapses or is non-renewed.

TERMINATION OF DEPENDENT COVERAGE: Coverage will end for your dependent children on the date the policy lapses or is non-renewed, or on the premium due date following the earliest to occur of (a) the date of their marriage, (b) the date they reach age 21 (or age 25 if the dependent is enrolled in and actively pursuing a full-time course of study at an accredited institution of higher learning), or (c) the date they are no longer dependent on you. Coverage will end on your spouse: (a) on the date the policy lapses or is non-renewed; or (b) on the premium due date following the date of a divorce. Benefits will still be paid to the end of the time for which premiums were accepted.

CONVERSION: A spouse or a dependent child who is no longer eligible for coverage on this policy can obtain a similar policy. No proof of good health will be required, but written application must be made within 60 days after that person's coverage terminates.

MISSTATEMENT OF AGE OR SEX: If any age or sex has been misstated, an adjustment in the benefits payable will be made to recover any past premiums due.

REINSTATEMENT: If you do not pay a renewal premium within the time granted, your policy will lapse. It will be reinstated if the Company or its agent accepts the premium without requiring an application.

If the Company or its agent requires an application for reinstatement, and the application and one modal premium are received within six months of the lapse date, the policy will be reinstated when approved by the Company. The Company has 45 days to act on your application. Your policy will be reinstated unless the Company notifies you in writing of its disapproval.

You will be covered for an injury sustained on or after the reinstatement date. You will be covered for a sickness that begins more than ten days after the reinstatement date.

After the policy is reinstated, you and the Company will have the same rights as existed just before the due date. These rights are subject to any provisions endorsed or attached to the policy. Premium cannot be required for more than 60 days before the date.

CONFORMITY WITH STATE STATUTES: If this policy, on its effective date, is in conflict with any laws in your state of residence, it is changed to meet the minimum requirements of such laws.

MAJOR MEDICAL INSURANCE APPLICATION

Name _____ Occupation _____ Sex _____
     Last   First   Middle   M/F

Billing Address _____ Height _____ Weight _____
               Street   City   State   Zip Code   Ft. In.   Lbs.

Date of Birth _____ Place of Birth _____ Phone (_____) _____
            Mo./Day/Yr.   City/State   Area Code   Number

Social Security # _____ Business Phone (_____) _____
                                                                 Area Code   Number

1) I am a member actively at work at least 30 hours a week ☐ Yes ☐ No

YOUR CHOICE OF DEDUCTIBLE: ☐ PLAN A—$250 ☐ PLAN B—$500 ☐ PLAN C—$1,000
HOW WOULD YOU LIKE YOUR PREMIUM BILLED: ☐ Monthly ☐ Quarterly
WHICH PLAN ARE YOU APPLYING FOR: ☐ Comprehensive ☐ Basic

If you wish to include your spouse and/or eligible dependent children, complete this section:

NAME (First, Middle, Last)	SEX	DATE OF BIRTH	HEIGHT	WEIGHT
Your Spouse				
Your Children				

THE FOLLOWING QUESTIONS ARE TO BE ANSWERED FOR EACH PERSON APPLYING FOR COVERAGE. ANY MISSTATEMENTS MAY AFFECT YOUR COVERAGE—GIVE FULL DETAILS TO ALL "YES" ANSWERS IN THE SPACE PROVIDED.

In the last 10 years, has any person proposed for insurance been diagnosed, treated by or consulted a licensed physician or practitioner for any of the following:

                                                                    Yes No   Yes No

a. Abnormal blood pressure, chest pain, stroke, heart attack or murmur or any other heart, blood or circulatory disorder .... ☐ ☐
f. Ulcer, colitis, rectal disorder or any disorder of the digestive system, liver or gallbladder .... ☐ ☐

b. Cancer, tumor, growth, enlarged lymph nodes, skin disorder or discolored areas or lesions of the skin or mouth .... ☐ ☐
g. Diabetes, thyroid disorder, speech impairment or disorder of the eyes, ears, nose or throat .... ☐ ☐

c. Emphysema, lung or respiratory disorder .... ☐ ☐
h. Seizures or neurological disorder, mental, nervous or emotional disorder, psychiatric or psychological counseling or treatment .... ☐ ☐

d. Arthritis, or any disorder of the back or neck, muscles, bones or joints .... ☐ ☐
i. Alcoholism, drug or chemical dependency or substance abuse .... ☐ ☐

e. Kidney or urinary system disorder, disorder of the prostate or reproductive system, or breast disorder .... ☐ ☐
j. Acquired Immune Deficiency Syndrome or AIDS Related Complex (ARC) .... ☐ ☐

Continued

For Office Use Only	Eff. _____	Ren. Date _____	Paid _____
	CC _____	Cert. No. _____	

NOTICE OF INSURANCE INFORMATION PRACTICES

TO PROPERLY UNDERWRITE AND ADMINISTER YOUR INSURANCE COVERAGE A CERTAIN AMOUNT OF INFORMATION MUST BE COLLECTED. THE APPLICATION FOR INSURANCE CONTAINS INFORMATION OBTAINED FROM YOU NECESSARY FOR THIS PURPOSE. IN ADDITION, AS PART OF OUR REGULAR UNDERWRITING PROCEDURE, OTHER INFORMATION MAY BE COLLECTED FROM OTHER SOURCES ABOUT YOU OR YOUR ELIGIBLE DEPENDENTS WHO MAY BE PROPOSED FOR INSURANCE.

GENERALLY, DISCLOSURE OF PERSONAL INFORMATION WILL NOT BE MADE TO THIRD PARTIES. HOWEVER, IN SOME CIRCUMSTANCES THE INSURANCE COMPANY OR YOUR AGENT WILL MAKE DISCLOSURE OF PERSONAL INFORMATION WITHOUT YOUR AUTHORIZATION TO THIRD PARTIES. THIS MIGHT INCLUDE THE DISCLOSURE OF PERSONAL INFORMATION TO PERSONS OR ORGANIZATIONS WHO MAY WISH TO MARKET PRODUCTS OR SERVICES, INCLUDING AFFILIATES OF THE INSURANCE COMPANY, BUT ONLY IF YOU HAVE NOT INDICATED TO US IN WRITING THAT YOU OBJECT TO OUR DOING SO.

YOU HAVE THE RIGHT TO OBTAIN ACCESS TO PERSONAL INFORMATION ABOUT YOU OR YOUR ELIGIBLE DEPENDENTS, IF PROPOSED FOR INSURANCE, COLLECTED BY THE COMPANY OR YOUR AGENT, EXCEPT INFORMATION RELATING TO A CLAIM, CIVIL OR CRIMINAL PROCEEDING. MEDICAL INFORMATION WILL ONLY BE RELEASED THROUGH A DOCTOR, PRACTITIONER, OR OTHER MEDICAL PROFESSIONAL SELECTED BY YOU WHO IS LICENSED TO PROVIDE PROFESSIONAL CARE RELEVANT TO THE NATURE OF THE INFORMATION. YOU ALSO HAVE THE RIGHT TO SEEK CORRECTION OF INFORMATION YOU BELIEVE TO BE INACCURATE.

Yes No

2) Are you or any of your dependents currently pregnant? **If yes, list name and due date.** ☐ ☐

_____

3) In the last 2 years, has any person proposed for insurance taken prescription medication for more than 30 days? **If yes, state condition, name of medication, dosage and frequency in space provided below.** ☐ ☐

4) In the last 5 years, have you or any of your dependents to be insured had any physical disorder, illness, injury, surgery, or check-up, or consultation other than admitted above? ☐ ☐

Complete the following for each "YES" answer to questions 1 through 4:

Ques. No.	Name of Person	Date of Treatment From To	Reason for Checkup, Diagnosis, Illness or Condition Frequency of Attacks	Treatment or Findings, Medication, Recommendations, Hospitalization and/or Surgery Degree of Recovery	Name and Address of Each Physician, Practitioner and Medical Facility

If additional space is needed use a separate sheet. Sign, date and return it with this form.

Yes No

5) Has any person proposed for insurance had health insurance declined, postponed, ridered, rated, cancelled or had reinstatement or renewal refused? **If yes, state the name of company, action, reason and date in the space below.** ☐ ☐

6) Does any person proposed for insurance now carry health insurance or have an application pending with another company? **If yes, state name of applicant, company, type and amount of coverage and requested effective date in the space below.** ☐ ☐

7) Will the coverage you are applying for replace any coverage listed above? **If yes, give details below.** ☐ ☐

_____
_____
_____
_____

I understand and agree that the statements and answers in this application are complete and true to the best of my knowledge and belief and shall form a part of the contract of insurance. I also understand and agree that the insurance applied for, if issued, shall be subject to such statements and answers and will take effect on the effective date stated on the schedule provided the applicable first premium has been paid.

I AUTHORIZE any physician, medical practitioner, hospital, clinic, other medical or medically related facility, insurance or reinsuring company, Medical Information Bureau, consumer reporting agency, employer, or the Veterans Administration, having information available as to advice, diagnosis, treatment, or care of any physical or mental condition concerning me, my spouse, or my minor children, including information about drugs, alcoholism, or mental illness, and any other non-medical information concerning me, my spouse, or my minor children to give to the Company, its affiliates, its legal representative, or its reinsurers any and all such information.

I UNDERSTAND the information obtained by use of the Authorization will be used by the Company or its affiliates to determine eligibility for insurance.

I KNOW that I may request to receive a copy of this Authorization.

I ACKNOWLEDGE having received and read the Notice Regarding Medical Information Bureau and the Notice of Insurance Information Practices (where applicable).

I AGREE that a copy of this Authorization shall be as valid as the original.

I AGREE that this Authorization shall remain valid for two years from the date shown below.

_____ X_____ X_____
DATE   SIGNATURE OF PROPOSED INSURED   SIGNATURE OF SPOUSE (IF APPLYING)

Appendix

The National Association of Life Underwriters

Code of Ethics

PREAMBLE: Those engaged in life underwriting occupy the unique position of liaison between the purchasers and the suppliers of life and health insurance and closely related financial products. Inherent in this role is the combination of professional duty to the client and to the company, as well. Ethical balance is required to avoid any conflict between these two obligations. Therefore,

I Believe It To Be My Responsibility

To hold my profession in high esteem and strive to enhance its prestige.

To fulfill the needs of my clients to the best of my ability.

To maintain my clients' confidences.

To render exemplary service to my clients and their beneficiaries.

To adhere to professional standards of conduct in helping my clients to protect insurable obligations and attain their financial security objectives.

To present accurately and honestly all facts essential to my clients' decisions.

To perfect my skills and increase my knowledge through continuing education.

To conduct my business in such a way that my example might help raise the professional standards of life underwriting.

To keep informed with respect to applicable laws and regulations and to observe them in the practice of my profession.

To cooperate with others whose services are constructively related to meeting the needs of my clients.

Adopted April, 1986
NALU Board of Trustees

Reprinted with permission from the National Association of Life Underwriters

The National Association of Health Underwriters

Code of Ethics

To hold the selling, servicing, and distribution of Disability Income and Health Insurance Plans as a professional and a public trust and do all in my power to maintain its prestige.

To keep the needs of those whom I serve paramount.

To respect my client's trust in me, and never do anything which would betray that trust or confidence.

To give all service possible when service is needed.

To present policies factually and accurately—providing all information necessary for the issuance of sound insurance coverage to the public I serve.

To use no advertising which may be false or misleading.

To consider the sale of Disability Income and Health Insurance Plans as a career, know and abide by the insurance laws of my state, and seek constantly through study to increase my knowledge and improve my ability to meet the needs of my client.

To be fair and just to my competitors, and engage in no practice which might reflect unfavorably on myself or my industry.

To treat prospects, clients, and companies fairly by submitting applications which reveal all available information pertinent to the underwriting of a policy.

To be loyal to my clients, associates, fellow agents and brokers, and the company or companies whose products I represent.

Reprinted with permission from the National Association of Health Underwriters.

GLOSSARY

This glossary of life and health insurance words and phrases will serve as a handy reference. Because the explanations are concise and the statements general, they should not be regarded or used as technically complete statements.

A

absolute assignment Policy assignment under which the assignee (person to whom the policy is assigned) receives full control over the policy and also full rights to its benefits. Generally, when a policy is assigned to secure a debt, the owner retains all rights in the policy in excess of the debt, even though the assignment is absolute in form. (66) (See **assignment**)

accelerated benefits rider A life insurance rider that allows for the early payment of some portion of the policy's face amount should the insured suffer from a terminal illness or injury. (77)

acceptance (See **offer and acceptance**)

accidental bodily injury provision Disability income or accident policy provision that requires that the injury be accidental in order for benefits to be payable. (218, 226)

accidental death and dismemberment (AD&D) Insurance providing payment if the insured's death results from an accident or if the insured accidentally severs a limb above the wrist or ankle joints or totally and irreversibly loses his or her eyesight. (190, 225)

accidental death benefit rider A life insurance policy rider providing for payment of an additional benefit related to the face amount of the base policy when death occurs by accidental means. (75)

accidental dismemberment Often defined as "the severance of limbs at or above the wrists or ankle joints, or the entire irrevocable loss of sight." Loss of use in itself may or may not be considered dismemberment. (225)

accidental means provision Unforeseen, unexpected, unintended cause of an accident. Requirement of an accident-based policy that the cause of the mishap must be accidental for any claim to be payable. (218, 226)

accident and health insurance Insurance under which benefits are payable in case of disease, accidental injury or accidental death. Also called *health insurance, personal health insurance* and *sickness and accident insurance.* (189)

accumulation unit Premiums an annuitant pays into a variable annuity are credited as accumulation units. At the end of the accumulation period, accumulation units are converted to annuity units. (141)

acute illness A serious condition, such as pneumonia, from which the body can fully recover with proper medical attention. (235)

adhesion A life insurance policy is a "contract of adhesion" because buyers must "adhere" to the terms of the contract already in existence. They have no opportunity to negotiate for terms, rates, values, etc. (26)

adjustable life insurance Combines features of both term and whole life coverage with the length of coverage and amount of accumulated cash values as the adjustable factors. Premiums may be increased or decreased to fit the specific needs. Such adjustments are not retroactive and apply only to the future. (53)

administrative-services-only (ASO) plan Arrangement under which an insurance company or an independent organization, for a fee, handles the administration of claims, benefits and other administrative functions for a self-insured group. (199)

adverse selection Selection "against the company." Tendency of less favorable insurance risks to seek or continue insurance to a greater extent than others. Also, tendency of policyowners to take advantage of favorable options in insurance contracts. (126, 265)

Advertising Code Rules established by the National Association of Insurance Commissioners (NAIC) to regulate insurance advertising. (20)

agency Situation wherein one party (an agent) has the power to act for another (the principal) in dealing with third parties. (29)

agent Anyone not a duly licensed broker, who solicits insurance or aids in placing risks, delivering policies or collecting premiums on behalf of an insurance company. (29)

agent's report The section of an insurance application where the agent reports his or her personal observations about the applicant. (110)

aleatory Feature of insurance contracts in that there is an element of chance for both parties and that the dollar value given by the policyowner (premiums) and the insurer (benefits) may not be equal. (26)

alien insurer Company incorporated or organized under the laws of any foreign nation, province or territory. (18)

ambulatory surgery Surgery performed on an outpatient basis. (260)

amount at risk Difference between the face amount of the policy and the reserve or policy value at a given time. In other words, the dollar amount over what the policyowner has contributed of cash value toward payment of his or her own claim. Because the cash value increases every year, the net amount at risk naturally decreases until it finally reaches zero when the cash value or reserve becomes the face amount. (97)

annually renewable term (ART) A form of renewable term insurance that provides coverage for one year and allows the policyowner to renew his or her coverage each year, without evidence of insurability. Also called *yearly renewable term (YRT)*. (40)

annuitant One to whom an annuity is payable, or a person upon the continuance of whose life further payment depends. (133)

annuity A contract that provides a stipulated sum payable at certain regular intervals during the lifetime of one or more persons, or payable for a specified period only. (133)

annuity unit The number of annuity units denotes the share of the funds an annuitant will receive from a variable annuity account after the accumulation period ends and benefits begin. A formula is used to convert accumulation units to annuity units. (141)

any occupation A definition of total disability that requires that for disability income benefits to be payable, the insured must be unable to perform *any* job for which he or she is "reasonably suited by reason of education, training or experience." (222)

apparent authority The authority an agent appears to have, based on the principal's (the insurer's) actions, words, deeds or because of circumstances the principal (the insurer) created. (30)

application Form supplied by the insurance company, usually filled in by the agent and medical examiner (if applicable) on the basis of information received from the applicant. It is signed by the applicant and is part of the insurance policy if it is issued. It gives information to the home office underwriting department so it may consider whether an insurance policy will be issued and, if so, in what classification and at what premium rate. (109)

approval receipt Rarely used today, a type of conditional receipt that provides that coverage is effective as of the date the application is approved (before the policy is delivered). (116)

Armstrong Investigation Investigation of a large number of insurance companies in the United States in 1905 that led to the enactment of stricter state supervision and insurance requirements. (16)

assessment insurance Plan by which either the amount of insurance is variable or the number and amount of the assessments are variable. It is offered by assessment associations, either pure or advance. (12)

assessment mutual insurer An insurance company characterized by member-insureds who are assessed an individual portion of each loss that occurs. No premium payment is payable in advance. (12)

assignee Person (including corporation, partnership or other organization) to whom a right or rights under a policy are transferred by means of an assignment. (66)

assignment Signed transfer of benefits of a policy by an insured to another party. The company does not guarantee the validity of an assignment. (66)

assignment provision (health contracts) Commercial health policy provision that allows the policyowner to assign benefit payments from the insurer directly to the health care provider. (195)

assignor Person (including corporation, partnership or other organization or entity) who transfers a right or rights under an insurance policy to another by means of an assignment. (66)

assurance; insurance Terms are synonymous. "Assurance" is used more commonly in England than in the United States. (3)

attained age With reference to an insured, the current insurance age. (40)

authority The actions and deeds an agent is authorized to conduct on behalf of an insurance company, as specified in the agent's contract. (29)

authorized company Company duly authorized by the insurance department to operate in the state. (18)

automatic premium loan provision Authorizes insurer to automatically pay any premium in default at the end of the grace period and charge the amount so paid against the life insurance policy as a policy loan. (68, 75)

average indexed monthly earnings (AIME) The basis used for calculating the primary insurance amount (PIA) for Social Security benefits. (150)

average monthly wage (AMW) The average wage base for computing virtually all Social Security benefits prior to 1979. (149)

aviation exclusion Either attached by rider or included in standard policy language, excepting from coverage certain deaths or disabilities due to aviation, such as "other than a fare-paying passenger." (68)

B

back dating The practice of making a policy effective at an earlier date than the present. (118)

basic medical expense policy Health insurance policy that provides "first dollar" benefits for specified (and limited) health care, such as hospitalization, surgery or physician services. Characterized by limited benefit periods and relatively low coverage limits. (204)

beneficiary Person to whom the proceeds of a life or accident policy are payable when the insured dies. The various types of beneficiaries are: primary beneficiaries (those first entitled to proceeds); secondary beneficiaries (those entitled to proceeds if no primary beneficiary is living when the insured dies); and tertiary beneficiaries (those entitled to proceeds if no primary or secondary beneficiaries are alive when the insured dies). (81)

benefit May be either money or a right to the policyowner upon the happening of the conditions set out in the policy. (5)

benefit period Maximum length of time that insurance benefits will be paid for any one accident, illness or hospital stay. (204, 220)

Best's Insurance Report A guide, published by A.M. Best, Inc., that rates insurers' financial integrity and managerial and operational strengths. (20)

binding receipt Given by a company upon an applicant's first premium payment. The policy, if approved, becomes effective from the date of the receipt. (116)

blackout period Period following the death of a family breadwinner during which no Social Security benefits are available to the surviving spouse. (175)

blanket policy Covers a number of individuals who are exposed to the same hazards, such as members of an athletic team, company officials who are passengers in the same company plane, etc. (270)

Blue Cross Independent, nonprofit membership organization providing protection against the costs of hospital care in a limited geographical area. Benefit payments are made directly to the hospital; benefits vary among Blue Cross organizations. (13, 196)

Blue Shield Independent, nonprofit membership organization providing protection against the costs of surgery and other items of medical care in a limited geographical area. Benefit payments are made directly to the doctor. (13, 196)

broker Licensed insurance representative who does not represent a specific company, but places business among various companies. Legally, the broker is usually regarded as a representative of the insured rather than the company. (14, 28)

business continuation plans Arrangements between business owners that provide that the shares owned by any one of them who dies or becomes disabled shall be sold to and purchased by the other co-owners or by the business. (176, 278)

business health insurance Issued primarily to indemnify a business for the loss of services of a key employee, partner or active close corporation stockholder. (279)

business overhead expense insurance A form of disability income coverage designed to pay necessary business overhead expenses, such as rent, should the insured business owner become disabled. (278)

buy-sell agreement Agreement that a deceased business owner's interest will be sold and purchased at a predetermined price or at a price according to a predetermined formula. (176, 177, 178, 279)

C

cafeteria plan Employee benefit arrangements in which employees can select from a range of benefits. (278)

cancelable contract Health insurance contract that may be terminated by the company or that is renewable at its option. (249)

capital sum Amount provided for accidental dismemberment or loss of eyesight. Indemnities for loss of one member or sight of one eye are percentages of the capital sum. (226)

career agency system A method of marketing, selling and distributing insurance, it is represented by agencies or branch offices committed to the ongoing recruitment and development of career agents. (15)

case management The professional arrangement and coordination of health services through assessment, service plan development and monitoring. (260)

cash or deferred arrangements A qualified employer retirement plan under which employees can defer amounts of their salaries into a retirement plan. These amounts are not included in the employee's gross income and so are tax deferred. Also called *401(K) plans*. (162)

cash refund annuity Provides that, upon the death of the annuitant before payments totaling the purchase price have been made, the excess of the amount paid by the purchaser over the total annuity payments received will be paid in one sum to designated beneficiaries. (138)

cash surrender option A nonforfeiture option that allows whole life insurance policyowners to receive a payout of their policy's cash values. (70)

cash surrender value Amount available to the owner when a life insurance policy is surrendered to the company. During the early policy years, the cash value is the reserve less a "surrender charge"; in later policy years, it usually equals or closely approximates the reserve value at time of surrender. (42, 70)

cash value The equity amount or "savings" accumulation in a whole life policy. (40, 93)

chronic condition A treatable but not curable illness, such as arthritis or hypertension. (235)

class designation A beneficiary designation. Rather than specifying one or more beneficiaries by name, the policyowner designates a class or group of beneficiaries. For example, "my children." (83)

classification Occupational category of a risk. (255)

cleanup fund Basic use for life insurance; reserve to cover costs of last illness, burial, legal and administrative expenses, miscellaneous outstanding bills, etc. Also called *final expense fund*. (174)

close corporation A corporation owned by a small group of stockholders, each of whom usually has a voice in operating the business. (179)

closed-panel HMO A group of physicians who are salaried employees of an HMO and who work in facilities provided by the HMO. (197)

COBRA "Consolidated Omnibus Budget Reconciliation Act of 1985," extending group health coverage to terminated employees and their families for up to 18 or 36 months. (268)

coinsurance (percentage participation) Principle under which the company insures only part of the potential loss, the policyowners paying the other part. For instance, in a major medical policy, the company may agree to pay 75 percent of the insured's expenses, with the insured to pay the other 25 percent. (209)

collateral assignment Assignment of a policy to a creditor as security for a debt. The creditor is entitled to be reimbursed out of policy proceeds for the amount owed. The beneficiary is entitled to any excess of policy proceeds over the amount due the creditor in the event of the insured's death. (67)

combination company Company whose agents sell both weekly premium life and health insurance and ordinary life insurance. (11)

commercial health insurers Insurance companies that function on the reimbursement approach, which allows policyowners to seek medical treatment then submit the charges to the insurer for reimbursement. (195)

commissioner Head of a state insurance department; public officer charged with supervising the insurance business in a state and administering insurance laws. Called "superintendent" in some states, "director" in others. (17)

Commissioner's Standard Ordinary (CSO) Table Table of mortality based on intercompany experience over a period of time, which is legally recognized as the mortality basis for computing maximum reserves on policies issued within past years. The 1980 CSO Table replaced the 1958 CSO Table. (91)

common disaster provision Sometimes added to a policy and designed to provide an alternate beneficiary in the event that the insured as well as the original beneficiary die as the result of a common accident. (88)

competent parties To be enforceable, a contract must be entered into by competent parties. A competent party is one who is capable of understanding the contract being agreed to. (25)

comprehensive major medical insurance Designed to give the protection offered by both a basic medical expense and major medical policy. It is characterized by a low deductible amount, coinsurance clause and high maximum benefits. (207)

concealment Failure of the insured to disclose to the company a fact material to the acceptance of the risk at the time application is made. (27)

conditional contract Characteristic of an insurance contract in that the payment of benefits is dependent on or a condition of the occurrence of the risk insured against. (26)

conditionally renewable contract Health insurance policy providing that the insured may renew the contract from period to period, or continue it to a stated date or an advanced age, subject to the right of the insurer to decline renewal only under conditions defined in the contract. (249)

conditional receipt Given to policyowners when they pay a premium at time of application. Such receipts bind the insurance company if the risk is approved as applied for, subject to any other conditions stated on the receipt. (115)

consideration Element of a binding contract; acceptance by the company of payment of the premium and statements made by the prospective insured in the application. (25)

consideration clause That part of an insurance contract setting forth the amount of initial and renewal premiums and frequency of future payments. (64, 246)

contestable period Period during which the company may contest a claim on a policy because of misleading or incomplete information furnished in the application. (65, 242) (See **incontestable clause**)

contingent beneficiary Person or persons named to receive proceeds in case the original beneficiary is not alive. Also referred to as *secondary* or *tertiary beneficiary*. (83, 84)

contract An agreement enforceable by law whereby one party binds itself to certain promises or deeds. (24)

contract of agency A legal document containing the terms of the contract between the agent and company, signed by both parties. Also called *agency agreement*. (28)

contributory plan Group insurance plan issued to an employer under which both the employer and employees contribute to the cost of the plan. Generally, 75 percent of the eligible employees must be insured. (See **noncontributory plan**) (125, 264)

conversion privilege Allows the policyowner, before an original insurance policy expires, to elect to have a new policy issued that will continue the insurance coverage. Conversion may be effected at attained age (premiums based on the age attained at time of conversion) or at original age (premiums based on age at time of original issue). (40, 129, 247, 265)

convertible term Contract that may be converted to a permanent form of insurance without medical examination. (42)

coordination of benefits (COB) provision Designed to prevent duplication of group health insurance benefits. Limits benefits from multiple group health insurance policies in a particular case to 100 percent of the expenses covered and designates the order in which the multiple carriers are to pay benefits. (267)

corridor deductible In superimposed major medical plans, a deductible amount between the benefits paid by the basic plan and the beginning of the major medical benefits. (208)

cost of living (COL) rider A rider available with some policies that provides for an automatic increase in benefits (typically tied to the Consumer Price Index), offsetting the effects of inflation. (76, 221)

coverage requirements Standards of coverage that prevent retirement plans from discriminating in favor of highly compensated employees. A plan must pass an IRS coverage test to be considered qualified. (160)

credit accident and health insurance If the insured debtor becomes totally disabled due to an accident or sickness, the policy premiums are paid during the period of disability or the loan is paid off. May be individual or group policy. (270)

credit life insurance Usually written as decreasing term on a relatively small decreasing balance installment loan that may reflect direct borrowing or a balance due for merchandise purchased. If borrower dies, benefits pay balance due. May be individual or group policy. (53, 130)

credit report A summary of an insurance applicant's credit history, made by an independent organization that has investigated the applicant's credit standing. (112)

cross-purchase plan An agreement that provides that upon a business owner's death, surviving owners will purchase the deceased's interest, often with funds from life insurance policies owned by each principal on the lives of all other principals. (178, 180)

currently insured Under Social Security, a status of limited eligibility that provides only death benefits. (148)

D

death rate Proportion of persons in each age group who die within a year; usually expressed as so many deaths per thousand persons. (91) (See **expected mortality**)

debit insurer (See **home service insurer**)

decreasing term insurance Term life insurance on which the face value slowly decreases in scheduled steps from the date the policy comes into force to the date the policy expires, while the premium remains level. The intervals between decreases are usually monthly or annually. (39)

deductible Amount of expense or loss to be paid by the insured before a health insurance policy starts paying benefits. (208)

deferred annuity Provides for postponement of the commencement of an annuity until after a specified period or until the annuitant attains a specified age. May be purchased either on single-premium or flexible premium basis. (137)

deferred compensation plan The deferral of an employee's compensation to some future age or date. These plans are frequently used to provide fringe benefits, such as retirement income, to selected personnel. (182)

defined benefit plan A pension plan under which benefits are determined by a specific benefit formula. (162)

defined contribution plan A tax-qualified retirement plan in which annual contributions are determined by a formula set forth in the plan. Benefits paid to a participant vary with the amount of contributions made on his or her behalf and the length of service under the plan. (161)

delayed disability provision A disability income policy provision that allows a certain amount of time after an accident for a disability to result, and the insured remains eligible for benefits. (220)

dependency period Period following the death of the breadwinner up until the youngest child reaches maturity. (175)

deposit term Has modest endowment feature. Normally is sold for ten-year terms with a higher first-year premium than for subsequent years. If policy lapses, insured forfeits his or her "deposit" and receives no refund. (41)

disability Physical or mental impairment making a person incapable of performing one or more duties of his or her occupation. (216)

disability buy-sell agreement An arrangement between business co-owners that provides that shares owned by any one of them who becomes disabled shall be sold to and purchased by the other co-owners or by the business using funds from disability income insurance. (279)

disability income insurance A type of health insurance coverage, it provides for the payment of regular, periodic income should the insured become disabled from illness or injury. (190, 215)

dividend Policyowner's share in the divisible surplus of a company issuing insurance on the participating plan. (12, 71)

dividend options The different ways in which the insured under a participating life insurance policy may elect to receive surplus earnings: in cash; as a reduction of premium; as additional paid-up insurance; left on deposit at interest; or as additional term insurance. (72)

domestic insurer Company within the state in which it is chartered and in which its home office is located. (18)

dread disease policy (See **limited risk policy**)

E

elimination period Duration of time between the beginning of an insured's disability and the commencement of the period for which benefits are payable. (219)

employee benefit plans Plans through which employers offer employees benefits such as coverage for medical expenses, disability, retirement and death. (181, 277)

endowment Contract providing for payment of the face amount at the end of a fixed period, at a specified age of the insured, or at the insured's death before the end of the stated period. (48)

endowment period Period specified in an endowment policy during which, if the insured dies, the beneficiary receives a death benefit. If the insured is still living at the end of the endowment period, he or she receives the endowment as a living benefit. (48)

enhanced whole life A whole life insurance policy issued by a mutual insurer, in which policy dividends are used to provide extra death benefits or to reduce future premiums. (49)

enrollment period Period during which new employees can sign up for coverage under a group insurance plan. (126)

entire contract provision An insurance policy provision stating that the application and policy contain all provisions and constitute the entire contact. (63, 242)

entity plan An agreement in which a business assumes the obligation of purchasing a deceased owner's interest in the business, thereby proportionately increasing the interests of surviving owners. (178, 179)

errors and omissions insurance Professional liability insurance that protects an insurance producer against claims arising from service he or she rendered or failed to render. (31)

estoppel Legal impediment to denying the consequences of one's actions or deeds if they lead to detrimental actions by another. (31)

evidence of insurability Any statement or proof of a person's physical condition, occupation, etc., affecting acceptance of the applicant for insurance. (40)

examiner Physician authorized by the medical director of an insurance company to make medical examinations. Also, person assigned by a state insurance commissioner to audit the affairs of an insurance company. (110)

excess interest Difference between the rate of interest the company guarantees to pay on proceeds left under settlement options and the interest actually paid on such funds by the company. (100)

exclusion ratio A fraction used to determine the amount of annual annuity income exempt from federal income tax. The exclusion ratio is the total contributions or investment in the annuity divided by the expected ratio. (143)

exclusion rider A health insurance policy rider that waives the insurer's liability for all future claims on a preexisting condition. (248)

exclusions Specified hazards listed in a policy for which benefits will not be paid. (68)

expected mortality Number of deaths that theoretically should occur among a group of insured persons during a given period, according to the mortality table in use. Normally, a lower mortality rate is anticipated and generally experienced.

experience rating Review of the previous year's claims experience for a group insurance contract in order to establish premiums for the next period. (125)

express authority The specific authority given in writing to the agent in the contract of agency. (30)

extended term insurance Nonforfeiture option providing for the cash surrender value of a policy to be used as a net single premium at the insured's attained age to purchase term insurance for the face amount of the policy, less indebtedness, for as long a period as possible, but no longer than the term of the original policy. (71)

extra percentage tables Mortality or morbidity tables indicating the percentage amount increase of premium for certain impaired health conditions. (94)

F

face amount Commonly used to refer to the principal sum involved in the contract. The actual amount payable may be decreased by loans or increased by additional benefits payable under specified conditions or stated in a rider. (98)

facility of payment provision Clause permitted under a uniform health insurance policy provision allowing the company to pay up to $1,000 of benefits or proceeds to any relative appearing entitled to it if there is no beneficiary or if the insured or beneficiary is a minor or legally incompetent. (87)

Fair Credit Reporting Act Federal law requiring an individual to be informed if he or she is being investigated by an inspection company. (17, 112)

family income policy Combination of ordinary life and decreasing term insurance covering a period of 5, 10, 15 or 20 years. The term insurance is sufficient to provide (often when supplemented by interest on the ordinary life insurance) a specified monthly income from the date of death until the end of the specified income period. The principal sum of the ordinary insurance is payable when monthly income from the term insurance ceases or upon subsequent death. (50)

family maintenance (family protection) policy Similar to the family income policy. Combines ordinary and term insurance, but without the decreasing insurance feature. Beginning at the insured's death, provides for payment of an income for a fixed period of 10, 15 or 20 years, as selected, from the date of death (not from the date of issue, as in the family income policy), with payment of the principal sum of the ordinary insurance at the end of the fixed period. (51)

family plan policy All-family plan of protection, usually with permanent insurance on the primary wage earner's life and with spouse and children automatically covered for lesser amounts of protection, usually term, all included for one premium. (52)

FICA Contributions made by employees and employers to fund Social Security benefits (OASDHI). (146)

fiduciary Person occupying a position of special trust and confidence, e.g., in handling or supervising affairs or funds of another. (30)

final expense fund Basic use for life insurance; reserve to cover costs of last illness, burial, legal and administrative expenses, miscellaneous outstanding bills, etc. Also called *cleanup fund*. (174)

fixed-amount settlement option A life insurance settlement option whereby the beneficiary instructs that proceeds be paid in regular installments of a fixed dollar amount. The number of payment periods is determined by the policy's face amount, the amount of each payment and the interest earned. (100)

fixed annuity A type of annuity that provides a guaranteed fixed benefit amount, payable for the life of the annuitant. (140)

fixed-period settlement option A life insurance settlement option in which the number of payments is fixed by the payee, with the amount of each payment determined by the amount of proceeds. (100)

flat deductible Amount of covered expenses payable by the insured before major medical benefits are payable. (208)

foreign insurer Company operating in a state in which it is not chartered and in which its home office is not located. (18)

franchise insurance Life or health insurance plan for covering groups of persons with individual policies uniform in provisions, although perhaps different in benefits. Solicitation usually takes place in an employer's business with the employer's consent. Generally written for groups too small to qualify for regular group coverage. May be called *wholesale insurance* when the policy is life insurance. (129, 270)

fraternal benefit insurer Nonprofit benevolent organization that provides insurance to its members. (13)

fraud An act of deceit; misrepresentation of a material fact made knowingly, with the intention of having another person rely on that fact and consequently suffer a financial hardship. (32)

free look Provision required in most states whereby policyowners have either 10 or 20 days to examine their new policies at no obligation. (64, 247)

fully insured A status of complete eligibility for the full range of Social Security benefits: death benefits, retirement benefits, disability benefits and Medicare benefits. (148)

funding In a retirement plan, the setting aside of funds for the payment of benefits. (161)

G

general agent Independent agent with authority, under contract with the company, to appoint soliciting agents within a designated territory and fix their compensation. (15)

government insurer An organization that, as an extension of the federal or state government, provides a program of social insurance. (14)

grace period Period of time after the due date of a premium during which the policy remains in force without penalty. (64, 242)

graded premium whole life Variation of a traditional whole life contract providing for lower than normal premium rates during the first few policy years, with premiums increasing gradually each year. After the preliminary period, premiums level off and remain constant. (47)

gross premium The total premium paid by the policyowner, it generally consists of the net premium plus the expense of operating minus interest. (93)

group credit insurance A form of group insurance issued by insurance companies to creditors to cover the lives of debtors for the amounts of their loans. (130, 270)

group insurance Insurance that provides coverage for a group of persons, usually employees of a company, under one master contract. (38, 124, 276)

guaranteed insurability (guaranteed issue) Arrangement, usually provided by rider, whereby additional insurance may be purchased at various times without evidence of insurability. (74, 222)

guaranteed renewable contract Health insurance contract that the insured has the right to continue in force by payment of premiums for a substantial period of time during which the insurer has no right to make unilaterally any change in any provision, other than a change in premium rate for classes of insureds. (249)

guaranty association Established by each state to support insurers and protect consumers in the case of insurer insolvency, guaranty associations are funded by insurers through assessments. (20)

H

hazard Any factor that gives rise to a peril. (7)

health insurance Insurance against loss through sickness or accidental bodily injury. Also called *accident and health, accident and sickness, sickness and accident* or *disability insurance.* (189)

health maintenance organization (HMO) Health care arrangement stressing preventive health care, early diagnosis and treatment on an outpatient basis. Persons generally enroll voluntarily by paying a fixed fee periodically. (13, 196)

home service insurer Insurer that offers relatively small policies with premiums payable on a weekly basis, collected by agents at the policyowner's home. (14, 41)

hospital benefits Payable for charges incurred while the insured is confined to, or treated in, a hospital, as defined in a health insurance policy. (204)

hospital expense insurance Health insurance benefits subject to a specified daily maximum for a specified period of time while the insured is confined to a hospital, plus a limited allowance up to a specified amount for miscellaneous hospital expenses, such as operating room, anesthesia, laboratory fees, etc. Also called *hospitalization insurance*. (204) (See **medical expense insurance**)

hospital indemnity Form of health insurance providing a stipulated daily, weekly or monthly indemnity during hospital confinement; payable on an unallocated basis without regard to actual hospital expense. (211)

human life value An individual's economic worth, measured by the sum of his or her future earnings that is devoted to his or her family. (9, 172)

I

immediate annuity Provides for payment of annuity benefit at one payment interval from date of purchase. Can only be purchased with a single payment. (137)

implied authority Authority not specifically granted to the agent in the contract of agency, but which common sense dictates the agent has. It enables the agent to carry out routine responsibilities. (30)

incontestable clause Provides that, for certain reasons such as misstatements on the application, the company may void a life policy after it has been in force during the insured's lifetime, usually one or two years after issue. (65)

increasing term insurance Term life insurance in which the death benefit increases periodically over the policy's term. Usually purchased as a cost of living rider to a whole life policy. (39) (See **cost of living rider**)

indemnity approach A method of paying health policy benefits to insureds based on a predetermined, fixed rate set for the medical services provided, regardless of the actual expenses incurred. (203)

independent agency system A system for marketing, selling and distributing insurance in which independent brokers are not affiliated with any one insurer but represent any number of insurers. (15)

indexed whole life A whole life insurance policy whose death benefit increases according to the rate of inflation. Such policies are usually tied to the Consumer Price Index (CPI). (47)

individual insurance Policies providing protection to the policyowner, as distinct from group and blanket insurance. Also called *personal insurance*.

individual retirement account (IRA) A personal qualified retirement account through which eligible individuals accumulate tax-deferred income up to a certain amount each year, depending on the person's tax bracket. (165)

industrial insurance Life insurance policy providing modest benefits and a relatively short benefit period. Premiums are collected on a weekly or monthly basis by an agent calling at insureds' homes. (14, 37) (See **home service insurer**)

inspection receipt A receipt obtained from an insurance applicant when a policy (upon which the first premium has not been paid) is left with him or her for further inspection. It states that the insurance is not in effect and that the policy has been delivered for inspection only. (115)

inspection report Report of an investigator providing facts required for a proper underwriting decision on applications for new insurance and reinstatements. (111)

installment refund annuity An annuity income option that provides for the funds remaining at the annuitant's death to be paid to the beneficiary in the form of continued annuity payments. (138)

insurability All conditions pertaining to individuals that affect their health, susceptibility to injury, or life expectancy; an individual's risk profile. (108)

insurability receipt A type of conditional receipt that makes coverage effective on the date the application was signed or the date of the medical exam (whichever is later), provided the applicant proves to be insurable. (116)

insurable interest Requirement of insurance contracts that loss must be sustained by the applicant upon the death or disability of another and loss must be sufficient to warrant compensation. (28, 108, 255)

insurance Social device for minimizing risk of uncertainty regarding loss by spreading the risk over a large enough number of similar exposures to predict the individual chance of loss. (1, 3)

insurer Party that provides insurance coverage, typically through a contract of insurance. (5)

insuring clause Defines and describes the scope of the coverage provided and limits of indemnification. (63, 246)

integrated deductible In superimposed major medical plans, a deductible amount between the benefits paid by the basic plan and those benefits paid by major medical. All or part of the integrated deductible may be absorbed by the basic plan. (208)

interest adjusted net cost method A method of comparing costs of similar policies by using an index that takes into account the time value of money (117)

interest-only option (interest option) Mode of settlement under which all or part of the proceeds of a policy are left with the company for a definite period at a guaranteed minimum interest rate. Interest may either be added to the proceeds or paid annually, semiannually, quarterly or monthly. (99)

interest-sensitive whole life Whole life policy whose premiums vary depending upon the insurer's underlying death, investment and expense assumptions. (53)

interim term insurance Term insurance for a period of 12 months or less by special agreement of the company; it permits a permanent policy to become effective at a selected future date. (118)

irrevocable beneficiary Beneficiary whose interest cannot be revoked without his or her written consent, usually because the policyowner has made the beneficiary designation without retaining the right to revoke or change it. (85)

J

joint and last survivor policy A variation of the joint life policy that covers two lives but pays the benefit upon the death of the second insured. (52)

joint and survivor annuity Covers two or more lives and continues in force so long as any one of them survives. (139)

joint life policy Covers two or more lives and provides for the payment of the proceeds at the death of the first among those insured, at which time the policy automatically terminates. (52)

juvenile insurance Written on the lives of children who are within specified age limits and generally under parental control. (52)

K

Keogh plans Designed to fund the retirement of self-employed individuals; name derived from the author of the Keogh Act (HR-10), under which contributions to such plans are given favorable tax treatment. (164)

key-person insurance Protection of a business against financial loss caused by the death or disablement of a vital member of the company, usually individuals possessing special managerial or technical skill or expertise. (180, 278)

L

lapse Termination of a policy upon the policyowner's failure to pay the premium within the grace period. (64)

law of large numbers Basic principle of insurance in that the larger the number of individual risks combined into a group, the more certainty there is in predicting the degree or amount of loss that will be incurred in any given period. (6)

legal purpose In contract law, the requirement that the object of, or reason for, the contract must be legal. (25)

legal reserve Policy reserves maintained according to the standard levels established through the insurance laws of the various states. (96)

level premium funding method The insurance plan (used by all regular life insurance companies) under which, instead of an annually increasing premium that reflects the increasing chance of death, an equivalent level premium is paid. Reserves that accumulate from more than adequate premiums paid in the early years supplement inadequate premiums in the later years. (41, 44, 95)

level term insurance Term coverage on which the face value remains unchanged from the date the policy comes into force to the date the policy expires. (39)

license Certification issued by a state insurance department that an individual is qualified to solicit insurance applications for the period covered; usually issued for one year, renewable on application without need for repeating the original qualifying requirements. (18)

lien system Plan for issuing coverage for substandard risks. A standard premium is paid but there is a lien against the policy to reduce the amount of insurance if the insured dies from a cause that resulted in the substandard rating. (95)

life annuity Payable during the continued life of the annuitant. No provision is made for the guaranteed return of the unused portion of the premium. (137)

life expectancy Average duration of the life remaining to a number of persons of a given age, according to a given mortality table. Not to be confused with "probable lifetime," which refers to the difference between a person's present age and the age at which death is most probable, i.e., the age at which most deaths occur. (92)

life income settlement option A settlement option providing for life insurance or annuity proceeds to be used to buy an annuity payable to the beneficiary for life—often with a specified number of payments certain or a refund if payments don't equal or exceed premiums paid. (101, 137)

life insurance Insurance against loss due to the death of a particular person (the insured) upon whose death the insurance company agrees to pay a stated sum or income to the beneficiary. (3)

limited pay life insurance A form of whole life insurance characterized by premium payments only being made for a specified or limited number of years. (45)

limited policies Restrict benefits to specified accidents or diseases, such as travel policies, dread disease policies, ticket policies, etc. (211, 227)

limited risk policy Provides coverage for specific kinds of accidents or illnesses, such as injuries received as a result of travel accidents or medical expenses stemming from a specified disease. (211) (See **special risk policy**)

Lloyd's of London An association of individuals and companies that underwrite insurance on their own accounts and provide specialized coverages. (12)

loading Amount added to net premiums to cover the company's operating expenses and contingencies; includes the cost of securing new business, collection expenses and general management expenses. Precisely: excess of gross premiums over net premiums. (93)

loan value Determinable amount that can be borrowed from the issuing company by the policyowner using the value of the life insurance policy as collateral. (68)

long-term care policy Health insurance policies that provide daily indemnity benefits for extended care confinement. (211)

loss sharing A basic principle of insurance whereby a large number contribute to cover the losses of a few. (5)

lump sum Payment of entire proceeds of an insurance policy in one sum. The method of settlement provided by most policies unless an alternate settlement is elected by the policyowner or beneficiary. (99)

M

major medical expense policy Health insurance policy that provides broad coverage and high benefits for hospitalization, surgery and physician services. Characterized by deductibles and coinsurance cost-sharing. (207)

mandatory second opinion To control costs, many health policies provide that, in order to be eligible for benefits, insureds must get a second opinion before receiving non-life-threatening surgery. (260)

master policy Issued to the employer under a group plan; contains all the insuring clauses defining employee benefits. Individual employees participating in the group plan receive individual certificates that outline highlights of the coverage. Also called *master contract*. (125, 263)

maturity value Proceeds payable on an endowment contract at the end of the specified endowment period, or payable on an ordinary life contract at the last age of the mortality table if the insured is still living at that age. Maturity value of a policy is the same as the face amount of the policy and is equal to the reserve value of the contract on its maturity date. Actual amount payable by the company may be increased by dividend additions or accumulated dividend deposits, or decreased by outstanding loans. (43, 49)

McCarran-Ferguson Act Also known as Public Law 15, the 1945 act exempting insurance from federal antitrust laws to the extent insurance is regulated by the states. (16)

Medicaid Provides medical care for the needy under joint federal-state participation (Kerr-Mills Act). (198)

medical cost management The process of controlling how policyowners utilize their policies. (260) (See **mandatory second opinion, precertification, ambulatory surgery** and **case management**)

medical examination Usually conducted by a licensed physician; the medical report is part of the application, becomes part of the policy contract, and is attached to the policy. A "nonmedical" is a short-form medical report filled out by the agent. Various company rules, such as amount of insurance applied for or already in force, applicant's age, sex, past physical history and data revealed by inspection report, etc., determine whether the examination will be "medical" or "nonmedical." (110)

medical expense insurance Pays benefits for nonsurgical doctors' fees commonly rendered in a hospital; sometimes pays for home and office calls. (189, 203)

Medical Information Bureau (MIB) A service organization that collects medical data on life and health insurance applicants for member insurance companies. (110)

medical report A document completed by a physician or other approved examiner and submitted to an insurer to supply medical evidence of insurability (or lack of insurability) or in relation to a claim. (110)

Medicare Federally sponsored health insurance and medical care program for persons age 65 and older; administered under provisions of the Social Security Act. (198)

Medicare Part A Compulsory hospitalization insurance that provides specified inhospital and related benefits. All workers covered by Social Security finance its operation through a portion of their FICA tax. (230)

Medicare Part B Voluntary program designed to provide supplementary medical insurance to cover physician services, medical services and supplies not covered under Medicare Part A. (230)

Medicare supplement policy Health insurance that provides coverage to fill the gaps in Medicare coverage. (198, 211)

minimum deposit insurance A cash value life insurance policy having a first-year loan value that is available for borrowing immediately upon payment of the first-year premium. (47)

minimum premium plan (MMP) Designed to support a self-insured plan, a minimum premium plan helps insure against large, unpredictable losses that exceed the self-insured level. (199)

miscellaneous expenses Hospital charges, other than for room and board, e.g., X rays, drugs, laboratory fees, etc., in connection with health insurance. (204)

misrepresentation Act of making, issuing, circulating or causing to be issued or circulated, an estimate, illustration, circular or statement of any kind that does not represent the correct policy terms, dividends or share of surplus or the name or title for any policy or class of policies that does not in fact reflect its true nature. (18)

misstatement of age or sex provision If the insured's age or sex is misstated in an application for insurance, the benefit payable usually is adjusted to what the premiums paid should have purchased. (67, 244)

misuse of premium Improper use of premiums collected by an insurance producer. (18)

modified endowment contract (MEC) A life insurance policy under which the amount a policyowner pays in during the first years exceeds the sum of net level premiums that would have been payable to provide paid-up future benefits in seven years. (49)

modified whole life Whole life insurance with premium payable during the first few years, usually five years, only slightly larger than the rate for term insurance. Afterwards, the premium is higher for the remainder of life than the premium for ordinary life at the original age of issue, but lower than the rate at the attained age at the time of change. (46)

money-purchase plan A type of qualified plan under which contributions are fixed amounts or fixed percentages of the employee's salary. An employee's benefits are provided in whatever amount the accumulated or current contributions will produce for him or her. (162)

moral hazard Effect of personal reputation, character, associates, personal living habits, financial responsibility and environment, as distinguished from physical health, upon an individual's general insurability. (7, 254)

morale hazard Hazard arising from indifference to loss because of the existence of insurance. (7)

morbidity The relative incidence of disability due to sickness or accident within a given group. (256)

morbidity table Shows the incidence and extent of disability that may be expected from a given large group of persons; used in computing health insurance rates. (257)

mortality The relative incidence of death within a given group. (91)

mortality table Listing of the mortality experience of individuals by age; permits an actuary to calculate, on the average, how long a male or female of a given age may be expected to live. (91)

mortgage insurance A basic use for life insurance, so-called because many family heads leave insurance for specifically paying off any mortgage balance outstanding at their death. The insurance generally is made payable to a family beneficiary instead of to the mortgage holder. (174)

multiple employer group Plan where the employees of two or more employers not financially related are covered under one master policy. (131)

multiple employer trust (MET) Several small groups of individuals that need life and health insurance but do not qualify for true group insurance band together under state trust laws to purchase insurance at a more favorable rate. (131)

multiple employer welfare arrangement (MEWA) Similar to a multiple employer trust (MET) with the exception that in a MEWA, a number of employers pool their risks and self-insure. (131)

multiple protection policy A combination of term and whole life coverage that pays some multiple of the face amount of the basic whole life portion (such as $10 per month per $1,000) throughout the multiple protection period (such as to age 65). (52)

mutual insurer An insurance company characterized by having no capital stock, it is owned by its policyowners and usually issues participating insurance. (12)

N

National Association of Insurance Commissioners (NAIC) Association of state insurance commissioners active in insurance regulatory problems and in forming and recommending model legislation and requirements. (19)

National Association of Health Underwriters (NAHU) NAHU is an organization of health insurance agents that is dedicated to supporting the health insurance industry and to advancing the quality of service provided by insurance professionals. (20)

National Association of Life Underwriters (NALU) NALU is an organization of life insurance agents that is dedicated to supporting the life insurance industry and to advancing the quality of service provided by insurance professionals. (20)

National Service Life Insurance (NSLI) Created by Congress in 1940 for providing policies for individuals on active duty in military service. Persons entering military service after December 31, 1956 cannot purchase this insurance. However, persons discharged with a service-connected disability may purchase it within a certain time limit. (154)

natural group A group formed for a reason other than to obtain insurance. (125, 263)

needs approach A method for determining how much insurance protection a person should have by analyzing a family's or business's needs and objectives should the insured die, become disabled or retire. (173)

net premium Calculated on the basis of a given mortality table and a given interest rate, without any allowance for loading. (93)

noncancelable and guaranteed renewable contract Health insurance contract that the insured has the right to continue in force by payment of premiums set forth in the contract for a substantial period of time, during which the insurer has no right to make unilaterally any change in any contract provision. (249)

noncontributory plan Employee benefit plan under which the employer bears the full cost of the employees' benefits; must insure 100 percent of eligible employees. (126, 264)

nondisabling injury Requires medical care, but does not result in loss of time from work. (220)

nonduplication provision Stipulates that insureds shall be ineligible to collect for charges under a group health plan if the charges are reimbursed under their own or their spouse's group plan. (269)

nonforfeiture options Privileges allowed under terms of a life insurance contract after cash values have been created. (70)

nonforfeiture values Those benefits in a life insurance policy that by law, the policyowner does not forfeit even if he or she discontinues premium payments; usually cash value, loan value, paid-up insurance value and extended term insurance value. (69)

nonmedical insurance Issued on a regular basis without requiring a regular medical examination. In passing on the risk, the company relies on the applicant's answers to questions regarding his or her physical condition and on personal references or inspection reports. (109)

nonparticipating Insurance under which the insured is not entitled to share in the divisible surplus of the company. (75)

nonqualified plan A retirement plan that does not meet federal government requirements and is not eligible for favorable tax treatment. (157)

notice of claims provision Policy provision that describes the policyowner's obligation to provide notification of loss to the insurer within a reasonable period of time. (243)

offer and acceptance The offer may be made by the applicant by signing the application, paying the first premium and, if necessary, submitting to a physical examination. Policy issuance, as applied for, constitutes acceptance by the company. Or, the offer may be made by the company when no premium payment is submitted with application. Premium payment on the offered policy then constitutes acceptance by the applicant. (24)

Old-Age, Survivors, Disability and Hospital Insurance (OASDHI) Retirement, death, disability income and hospital insurance benefits provided under the Social Security system. (146)

open certificate Rates and policy provisions may be changed. Fraternal benefit societies are required by law to issue this type of certificate. Also called *open policy*. (13)

open-panel HMO A network of physicians who work out of their own offices and participate in the HMO on a part-time basis. (197)

optionally renewable contract Health insurance policy in which the insurer reserves the right to terminate the coverage at any anniversary or, in some cases, at any premium due date, but does not have the right to terminate coverage between such dates. (249)

ordinary insurance Life insurance of commercial companies not issued on the weekly premium basis; amount of protection usually is $1,000 or more. (37)

other insureds rider A term rider, covering a family member other than the insured, that is attached to the base policy covering the insured. (77)

overhead insurance Type of short-term disability insurance reimbursing the insured for specified, fixed, monthly expenses, normal and customary in operating the insured's business. (278)

overinsurance Excessive amount of insurance carried by an insured that might create a temptation to cause an insured loss deliberately or to prolong an insured disability or hospital stay longer than necessary, etc. (216)

own occupation A definition of total disability that requires that in order to receive disability income benefits the insured must be unable to work at his or her *own* occupation. (217)

P

paid-up additions Additional life insurance purchased by policy dividends on a net single premium basis at the insured's attained insurance age at the time additions are purchased. (73)

paid-up policy No further premiums are to be paid and the company is held liable for the benefits provided by the contract. (45)

parole evidence rule Rule of contract law that brings all verbal statements into the written contract and disallows any changes or modifications to the contract by oral evidence. (32)

partial disability Illness or injury preventing insureds from performing at least one or more, but not all, of their occupational duties. (217)

participating Plan of insurance under which the policyowner receives shares (commonly called dividends) of the divisible surplus of the company. (71)

participation standards Rules that must be followed for determining employee eligibility for a qualified retirement plan. (158)

partnership A business entity that allows two or more people to strengthen their effectiveness by working together as co-owners. (178)

payor rider Available under certain juvenile life insurance policies, upon payment of an extra premium. Provides for the waiver of future premiums if the person responsible for paying them dies or is disabled before the policy becomes fully paid or matures as a death claim, or as an endowment, or the child reaches a specified age. (75)

per capita rule Death proceeds from an insurance policy are divided equally among the living primary beneficiaries. (85)

peril The immediate specific event causing loss and giving rise to risk. (7)

period certain annuity An annuity income option that guarantees a definite minimum period of payments. (139)

permanent flat extra premium A fixed charge added per $1,000 of insurance for substandard risks. (94)

personal producing general agency system (PPGA) A method of marketing, selling and distributing insurance in which personal producing general agents (PPGAs) are compensated for business they personally sell and business sold by agents with whom they subcontract. Subcontracted agents are considered employees of the PPGA, not the insurer. (15)

per stirpes rule Death proceeds from an insurance policy are divided equally among the named beneficiaries. If a named beneficiary is deceased, his or her share then goes to the living descendants of that individual. (84)

policy loan In life insurance, a loan made by the insurance company to the policyowner, with the policy's cash value assigned as security. One of the standard nonforfeiture options. (65)

policy provisions The terms or conditions of an insurance policy as contained in the policy clauses. (62, 242)

precertification The insurer's approval of an insured's entering a hospital. Many health policies require precertification as part of an effort to control costs. (263)

preexisting condition An illness or medical condition that existed before a policy's effective date; usually excluded from coverage, through the policy's standard provisions or by waiver. (210, 248, 265)

preferred provider organization (PPO) An association of health care providers, such as doctors and hospitals, that agree to provide health care services to members of a particular group, at fees negotiated in advance. (13, 196)

preferred risk A risk whose physical condition, occupation, mode of living and other characteristics indicate a prospect for longevity for unimpaired lives of the same age. (113)

preliminary term insurance Term insurance attached to a newly issued permanent life insurance policy extending term coverage of a preliminary period of 1 to 11 months, until the permanent insurance becomes effective. The purpose is to provide full life insurance protection immediately, but to delay the start of the larger permanent insurance premium and the anniversary to a later date. (118)

premium The periodic payment required to keep an insurance policy in force. (90, 253)

premium factors The three primary factors considered when computing the basic premium for insurance: mortality, expense and interest. (90)

presumptive disability benefit A disability income policy benefit that provides that if an insured experiences a specified disability, such as blindness, he or she is presumed to be totally disabled and entitled to the full amount payable under the policy, whether or not he or she is able to work. (217)

primary beneficiary In life insurance, the beneficiary designated by the insured as the first to receive policy benefits. (83)

primary insurance amount (PIA) Amount equal to a covered worker's full Social Security retirement benefit at age 65 or disability benefit. (150)

principal An insurance company that, having appointed someone as its agent, is bound to the contracts the agent completes on its behalf. (29)

principal sum The amount under an AD&D policy that is payable as a death benefit if death is due to an accident. (225)

private insurer An insurer that is not associated with federal or state government. (11)

probationary period Specified number of days after an insurance policy's issue date during which coverage is not afforded for sickness. Standard practice for group coverages. (126, 219)

proceeds Net amount of money payable by the company at the insured's death or at policy maturity. (99)

producer A general term applied to an agent, broker, personal producing general agent, solicitor or other person who sells insurance. (18)

professional liability insurance (See **errors and omissions insurance**)

profit-sharing plan Any plan whereby a portion of a company's profits is set aside for distribution to employees who qualify under the plan. (161)

proof of loss A mandatory health insurance provision stating that the insured must provide a completed claim form to the insurer within 90 days of the date of loss. (243)

proper solicitation High professional standards that require an agent to identify himself or herself properly, that is, as an agent soliciting insurance on behalf of an insurance company. (114)

pure endowment Contract providing for payment only upon survival of a certain person to a certain date and not in event of that person's prior death. This type of contract is just the opposite of a term contract, which provides for payment only in event the insured person dies within the term period specified. (47)

pure risk Type of risk that involves the chance of loss only; there is no opportunity for gain; insurable. (7)

qualified plan A retirement or employee compensation plan established and maintained by an employer that meets specific guidelines spelled out by the IRS and consequently receives favorable tax treatment. (157)

rate-up in age System of rating substandard risks that involves assuming the insured to be older than he or she really is and charging a correspondingly higher premium. (95)

rating The making of insurance rates. Also the premium classification given an applicant for life or health insurance. (94)

reasonable and customary charge Charge for a health care service consistent with the going rate or charge in a given geographical area for an identical or similar service. (205)

rebating Returning part of the commission or giving anything else of value to the insured as an inducement to buy the policy. It is illegal and cause for license revocation in most states. In some states, it is an offense by both the agent and the person receiving the rebate. (19)

reciprocal insurer Insurance company characterized by the fact its policyholders insure the risks of other policyholders. (12)

recurrent disability provision A disability income policy provision that specifies the period of time during which the recurrence of a disability is considered a continuation of a prior disability. (220)

reduced paid-up insurance A nonforfeiture option contained in most life insurance policies providing for the insured to elect to have the cash surrender value of the policy used to purchase a paid-up policy for a reduced amount of insurance. (70)

re-entry option An option in a renewable term life policy under which the policyowner is guaranteed, at the end of the term, to be able to renew his or her coverage without evidence of insurability, at a premium rate specified in the policy. (40)

refund annuity Provides for the continuance of the annuity during the annuitant's lifetime and, in any event, until total payments equal to the purchase price have been made by the company. (138)

reimbursement approach Payment of health policy benefits to insureds based on actual medical expenses incurred. (203)

reinstatement Putting a lapsed policy back in force by producing satisfactory evidence of insurability and paying any past-due premiums required. (64, 242)

reinsurance Acceptance by one or more insurers, called reinsurers, of a portion of the risk underwritten by another insurer who has contracted for the entire coverage. (12)

relative value scale Method for determining benefits payable under a basic surgical expense policy. Points are assigned to each surgical procedure and a dollar per point amount, or conversion factor, is used to determine the benefit. (205)

renewable term Some term policies provide that they may be renewed on the same plan for one or more years without medical examination, but with rates based on the insured's advanced age. (40)

renewal option An option that allows the policyowner to renew a term policy before its termination date without having to provide evidence of insurability. (40)

replacement Act of replacing one life insurance policy with another; may be done legally under certain conditions. (19) (See **twisting**)

representation Statements made by applicants on their applications for insurance that they represent as being substantially true to the best of their knowledge and belief, but that are not warranted as exact in every detail. (27) (See **warranties**)

reserve Fund held by the company to help fulfill future claims. (96)

reserve basis Refers to mortality table and assumed interest rate used in computing rates. (96)

residual disability benefit A disability income payment based on the proportion of income the insured has actually lost, taking into account the fact that he or she is able to earn some income. (218)

results provision (See **accidental bodily injury provision**)

revocable beneficiary Beneficiary whose rights in a policy are subject to the policyowner's reserved right to revoke or change the beneficiary designation and the right to surrender or make a loan on the policy without the beneficiary's consent. (85)

rider Strictly speaking, a rider adds something to a policy. However, the term is used loosely to refer to any supplemental agreement attached to and made a part of the policy, whether the policy's conditions are expanded and additional coverages added, or a coverage or condition is waived. (73, 221)

risk Uncertainty regarding loss; the probability of loss occuring for an insured or prospect. (6)

risk pooling (See **loss sharing**)

risk selection The method a home office underwriter uses to choose applicants that the insurance company will accept. The underwriter must determine whether risks are standard, substandard or preferred and set the premium rates accordingly. (107)

rollover IRA An individual retirement account established with funds transferred from another IRA or qualified retirement plan that the owner has terminated. (168)

S

salary continuation plan An arrangement whereby an income, usually related to an employee's salary, is continued upon an employee's retirement, death or disability. (183)

salary reduction SEP A qualified retirement plan limited to companies with 25 or fewer employees. It allows employees to defer part of their pretax income to the plan, lowering their taxable income. (164) (See **Simplified Employee Pension Plan**)

schedule List of specified amounts payable, usually for surgical operations, dismemberment, fractures, etc. (205)

secondary beneficiary An alternate beneficiary designated to receive payment, usually in the event the original beneficiary predeceases the insured. (83)

Section 457 plans Deferred compensation plans for employees of state and local governments in which amounts deferred will not be included in gross income until they are actually received or made available. (163)

Self-Employed Individuals Retirement Act Passed by Congress in 1962, this Act enables self-employed persons to establish qualified retirement plans similar to those available to corporations. (164)

self-insurance Program for providing insurance financed entirely through the means of the policyowner, in place of purchasing coverage from commercial carriers. (14, 199)

self-insured plan A health insurance plan characterized by an employer (usually a large one), labor union, fraternal organization or other group retaining the risk of covering its employees' medical expenses. (199)

service insurers Companies that offer prepayment plans for medical or hospital services; well-known examples are Blue Cross/Blue Shield plans and health maintenance organizations. (13, 196)

Servicemembers' Group Life Insurance (SGLI) All servicemembers on active duty are automatically covered for a specified amount of this group term life insurance, unless they elect no coverage or lesser amounts. The insurance is written by commercial companies and premiums are shared by insured and federal government. (14, 153)

service provider An organization that provides health coverage by contracting with service providers, to provide medical services to subscribers, who pay in advance through premiums. Examples of such coverages are HMOs and the Blue Cross/Blue Shield plans. (13, 196)

settlement options Optional modes of settlement provided by most life insurance policies in lieu of lump-sum payment. Usual options are: lump-sum cash; interest-only; fixed-period; fixed-amount; and life income. (99)

simplified employee pension plan (SEP) A type of qualified retirement plan under which the employer contributes to an individual retirement account set up and maintained by the employee. (164)

single dismemberment Loss of one hand or one foot, or the sight of one eye. (226)

single-premium whole life insurance Whole life insurance for which the entire premium is paid in one sum at the beginning of the contract period. (45)

Social Security Programs first created by Congress in 1935 and now composed of Old-Age, Survivors and Disability Insurance (OASDI), Medicare, Medicaid and various grants-in-aid, which provide economic security to nearly all employed people. (146, 198)

sole proprietorship The simplest form of business organization whereby one individual owns and controls the entire company. (177)

special agent An agent representing an insurance company in a given territory. (15)

special class Applicants who cannot qualify for standard insurance, but may secure policies with riders waiving payment for losses involving certain existing health impairments. (256)

special questionnaires Forms used when, for underwriting purposes, the insurer needs more detailed information from an applicant regarding aviation or avocation, foreign residence, finances, military service or occupation. (111)

special risk policy Provides coverage for unusual hazards normally not covered under accident and health insurance, such as a concert pianist insuring his or her hands for a million dollars. (227) (See **limited risk policy**)

specified disease insurance (See **limited risk policy**)

speculative risk A type of risk that involves the chance of both loss and gain; not insurable. (7)

spendthrift provision Stipulates that, to the extent permitted by law, policy proceeds shall not be subject to the claims of creditors of the beneficiary or policyowner. (87)

split-dollar life insurance An arrangement between two parties where life insurance is written on the life of one, who names the beneficiary of the net death benefits (death benefits less cash value), and the other is assigned the cash value, with both sharing premium payments. (181)

spousal IRA An individual retirement account that persons eligible to set up IRAs for themselves may set up jointly with a nonworking spouse. (168)

standard provisions Forerunners of the Uniform Policy Provisions in health insurance policies today. (241)

standard risk Person who, according to a company's underwriting standards, is entitled to insurance protection without extra rating or special restrictions. (94, 255)

stock bonus plan A plan under which bonuses are paid to employees in shares of stock. (161)

stock insurer An insurance company owned and controlled by a group of stockholders whose investment in the company provides the safety margin necessary in issuance of guaranteed, fixed premium, nonparticipating policies. (11)

stock redemption plan An agreement under which a close corporation purchases a deceased stockholder's interest. (180)

stop-loss provision Designed to stop the company's loss at a given point, as an aggregate payable under a policy, a maximum payable for any one disability or the like; also applies to individuals, placing a limit on the maximum out-of-pocket expenses an insured must pay for health care, after which the health policy covers all expenses. (210)

straight life income annuity (straight life annuity, life annuity) An annuity income option that pays a guaranteed income for the annuitant's lifetime, after which time payments stop. (137)

straight whole life insurance (See **whole life insurance**)

subscriber Policyowner of a health care plan underwritten by a service insurer, such as Blue Cross/Blue Shield. (195)

substandard risk Person who is considered an under-average or impaired insurance risk because of physical condition, family or personal history of disease, occupation, residence in unhealthy climate or dangerous habits. (94, 255) (See **special class**)

successor beneficiary (See **secondary beneficiary**)

suicide provision Most life insurance policies provide that if the insured commits suicide within a specified period, usually two years after the issue date, the company's liability will be limited to a return of premiums paid. (68)

supplementary major medical policy A medical expense health plan that covers expenses not included under a basic policy and expenses that exceed the limits of a basic policy. (207)

surgical expense insurance Provides benefits to pay for the cost of surgical operations. (205)

surgical schedule List of cash allowances payable for various types of surgery, with the respective maximum amounts payable based upon severity of the operations; stipulated maximum usually covers all professional fees involved, e.g., surgeon, anesthesiologist. (205)

surrender value (See **cash surrender value**)

T

taxable wage base The maximum amount of earnings upon which FICA taxes must be paid. (149)

tax-sheltered annuity An annuity plan reserved for nonprofit organizations and their employees. Funds contributed to the annuity are excluded from current taxable income and are only taxed later, when benefits begin to be paid. Also called *tax-deferred annuity* and *403(b) plan.* (143, 163)

temporary flat extra premium A fixed charge per $1,000 of insurance added to substandard risks for a specified period of years. (95)

temporary insurance agreement (See **binding receipt**)

term insurance Protection during limited number of years; expiring without value if the insured survives the stated period, which may be one or more years, but usually is 5 to 20 years, because such periods generally cover the needs for temporary protection. (38)

term of policy Period for which the policy runs. In life insurance, this is to the end of the term period for term insurance, to the maturity date for endowments and to the insured's death (or age 100) for permanent insurance. In most other kinds of insurance, it is usually the period for which a premium has been paid in advance; however, it may be for a year or more, even though the premium is paid on a semiannual or other basis.

tertiary beneficiary In life insurance, a beneficiary designated as third in line to receive the proceeds or benefits if the primary and secondary beneficiaries do not survive the insured. (84)

third-party administrator (TPA) An organization outside the members of a self-insurance group which, for a fee, processes claims, completes benefits paperwork and often analyzes claims information. (199)

third-party applicant A policy applicant who is not the prospective insured. (108)

time limit on certain defenses A provision stating that an insurance policy is incontestable after it has been in force a certain period of time. It also limits the period during which an insurer can deny a claim on the basis of a preexisting condition. (242)

total disability Disability preventing insureds from performing any duty of their usual occupations or any occupation for remuneration; actual definition depends on policy wording. (216)

traditional net cost method A method of comparing costs of similar policies that does not take into account the time value of money. (117)

travel-accident policies Limited to indemnities for accidents while traveling, usually by common carrier. (227)

trust Arrangement in which property is held by a person or corporation (trustee) for the benefit of others (beneficiaries). The grantor (person transferring the property to the trustee) gives legal title to the trustee, subject to terms set forth in a trust agreement. Beneficiaries have equitable title to the trust property. (82)

trustee One holding legal title to property for the benefit of another; may be either an individual or a company, such as a bank and trust company. (82)

twisting Practice of inducing a policyowner with one company to lapse, forfeit or surrender a life insurance policy for the purpose of taking out a policy in another company. Generally classified as a misdemeanor, subject to fine, revocation of license and sometimes imprisonment. (18) (See **misrepresentation**)

U

unallocated benefit Reimbursement provision, usually for miscellaneous hospital and medical expenses, that does not specify how much will be paid for each type of treatment, examination, dressing, etc., but only sets a maximum that will be paid for all such treatments. (204)

underwriter Company receiving premiums and accepting responsibility for fulfilling the policy contract. Company employee who decides whether or not the company should assume a particular risk. The agent who sells the policy. (107)

underwriting Process through which an insurer determines whether, and on what basis, an insurance application will be accepted. (107, 113, 253)

Unfair Trade Practices Act A model act written by the National Association of Insurance Commissioners (NAIC) and adopted by most states empowering state insurance commissioners to investigate and issue cease and desist orders and penalties to insurers for engaging in unfair or deceptive practices, such as misrepresentation or coercion. (20)

Uniform Individual Accident and Sickness Policy Provisions Law NAIC model law that established uniform terms, provisions and standards for health insurance policies covering loss "resulting from sickness or from bodily injury or death by accident or both." (241)

Uniform Simultaneous Death Act Model law that states when an insured and beneficiary die at the same time, it is presumed that the insured survived the beneficiary. (86)

unilateral Distinguishing characteristic of an insurance contract in that it is only the insurance company that pledges anything. (26)

uninsurable risk One not acceptable for insurance due to excessive risk. (94, 108)

universal life Flexible premium, two-part contract containing renewable term insurance and a cash value account that generally earns interest at a higher rate than a traditional policy. The interest rate varies. Premiums are deposited in the cash value account after the company deducts its fee and a monthly cost for the term coverage. (54)

valued contract A contract of insurance that pays a stated amount in the event of a loss. (26)

variable annuity Similar to a traditional, fixed annuity in that retirement payments will be made periodically to the annuitants, usually over the remaining years of their lives. Under the variable annuity, there is no guarantee of the dollar amount of the payments; they fluctuate according to the value of an account invested primarily in common stocks. (141)

variable life insurance Provides a guaranteed minimum death benefit. Actual benefits paid may be more, however, depending on the fluctuating market value of investments behind the contract at the insured's death. The cash surrender value also generally fluctuates with the market value of the investment portfolio. (55)

variable universal life insurance A life insurance policy combining characteristics of universal and variable life policies. A VUL policy contains unscheduled premium payments and death benefits and a cash value that vary according to the underlying funds whose investment portfolio is managed by the policyowner. (56)

vesting Right of employees under a retirement plan to retain part or all of the annuities purchased by the employer's contributions on their behalf or, in some plans, to receive cash payments or equivalent value, on termination of their employment, after certain qualifying conditions have been met. (160)

Veterans' Group Life Insurance (VGLI) Low-cost nonrenewable, but convertible, five-year term insurance to which Servicemembers' Group Life Insurance (SGLI) is converted automatically at the time an insured servicemember is discharged, separated or released from active duty. At the end of the five-year period, the veteran may convert his or her VGLI to an individual policy with any company participating in the program. (14, 153)

void contract An agreement without legal effect; an invalid contract. (32)

voidable contract A contract that can be made void at the option of one or more parties to the agreement. (32)

voluntary group AD&D A group accidental death and dismemberment policy paid for entirely by employees, rather than an employer. (270)

waiver Agreement waiving the company's liability for a certain type or types of risk ordinarily covered in the policy; a voluntary giving up of a legal, given right. (31, 248)

waiver of premium Rider or provision included in most life insurance policies and some health insurance policies exempting the insured from paying premiums after he or she has been disabled for a specified period of time, usually six months in life policies and 90 days or six months in health policies. (74, 221)

war clause Relieves the insurer of liability, or reduces its liability, for specified loss caused by war. (68)

warranties Statements made on an application for insurance that are warranted to be true; that is, they are exact in every detail as opposed to representations. Statements on applications for insurance are rarely warranties, unless fraud is involved. (27) (See **representation**)

whole life insurance Permanent level insurance protection for the "whole of life," from policy issue to the death of the insured. Characterized by level premiums level benefits and cash values. (42)

wholesale insurance (See **franchise insurance**)

workers' compensation Benefits paid workers for injury, disability or disease contracted in the course of their employment. Benefits and conditions are set by law, although in most states the insurance to provide the benefits may be purchased from regular insurance companies. A few states have monopolistic state compensation funds. (200)

yearly renewable term insurance (YRT) (See **annually renewable term**)

QUESTIONS FOR REVIEW ANSWER KEY

Chapter 1
1. d
2. d
3. c
4. b
5. a

Chapter 2
1. c
2. d
3. a
4. c
5. a

Chapter 3
1. b
2. c
3. b
4. b
5. d

Chapter 4
1. d
2. c
3. b
4. c
5. c
6. a
7. c
8. c
9. c
10. c
11. b
12. a
13. a
14. c
15. c

Chapter 5
1. d
2. c
3. a
4. d
5. a
6. b
7. c
8. c
9. d
10. b
11. d
12. d

Chapter 6
1. d
2. b
3. c
4. c
5. d

Chapter 7
1. c
2. c
3. b
4. c
5. d
6. a
7. d
8. a
9. b
10. d
11. b

Chapter 8
1. d
2. a
3. b
4. c
5. a
6. a
7. b
8. b
9. b
10. b

Chapter 9
1. c
2. b
3. b
4. b
5. a

Chapter 10
1. a
2. b
3. b
4. b
5. a
6. b
7. b

Chapter 11
1. c
2. b
3. b
4. c
5. c
6. c
7. a

Chapter 12
1. c
2. b
3. d
4. c
5. a
6. d
7. c
8. d
9. c
10. d

Chapter 13
1. d
2. a
3. c
4. d
5. c
6. b
7. c
8. b

Chapter 14
1. d
2. b
3. c
4. c
5. b

Chapter 15
1. a
2. c
3. b
4. c
5. c
6. b
7. c
8. d

Chapter 16
1. c
2. b
3. c
4. d
5. c
6. c
7. c
8. b
9. d
10. d

Chapter 17
1. b
2. d
3. b
4. b
5. c
6. d
7. c
8. b
9. c
10. b

Chapter 18
1. d
2. c
3. b
4. a

Chapter 19
1. d
2. c
3. d
4. a
5. c
6. b
7. c

Chapter 20
1. d
2. d
3. c
4. c
5. c
6. a
7. c
8. c
9. d
10. b
11. b
12. b

Chapter 21
1. a
2. d
3. c
4. a
5. d
6. d
7. d
8. b
9. b
10. c

Chapter 22
1. c
2. d
3. c
4. b
5. c
6. b
7. c
8. a
9. c
10. b

Chapter 23
1. c
2. b
3. b
4. d
5. d